Classics of International Relations

Classics of International Relations introduces, contextualizes and assesses 24 of the most important works on international relations of the last 100 years. Providing an indispensable guide for all students of IR theory, from advanced undergraduates to academic specialists, it asks why are these works considered classics? Is their status deserved? Will it endure? It takes as its starting point Norman Angell's best-selling *The Great Illusion* (1910) and concludes with Daniel Deudney's award-winning *Bounding Power* (2007). The volume does not ignore established classics such as Hans J. Morgenthau's *Politics Among Nations* and Kenneth Waltz's *Theory of International Politics*, but seeks to expand the 'IR canon' beyond its core realist and liberal texts. It thus considers emerging classics such as Andrew Linklater's critical sociology of moral boundaries, *Men and Citizens in the Theory of International Relations*, and Cynthia Enloe's pioneering gender analysis, *Bananas, Beaches and Bases*. It also innovatively considers certain 'alternative format' classics such as Stanley Kubrick's satire on the nuclear arms race, *Dr. Strangelove*, and Errol Morris's powerful documentary on war and US foreign policy, *The Fog of War*. With an international cast of contributors, many of them leading authorities on their subject, *Classics of International Relations* will become a standard reference for all those wishing to make sense of a rapidly developing and diversifying field.

Classics of International Relations is designed to become a standard reference text for advanced undergraduates, postgraduates and lecturers in the field of IR.

Henrik Bliddal is Director of the Science and Technology Committee at the NATO Parliamentary Assembly in Brussels, Belgium.

Casper Sylvest is Associate Professor of International Relations at the Department of Political Science, University of Southern Denmark.

Peter Wilson is Senior Lecturer in International Relations at the London School of Economics and Political Science, UK.

Classics of International Relations

Essays in Criticism and Appreciation

Edited by
Henrik Bliddal, Casper Sylvest and Peter Wilson

Routledge
Taylor & Francis Group

LONDON AND NEW YORK

First published 2013
by Routledge
2 Park Square, Milton Park, Abingdon, Oxon OX14 4RN

Simultaneously published in the USA and Canada
by Routledge
711 Third Avenue, New York, NY 10017

Routledge is an imprint of the Taylor & Francis Group, an informa business

British Library Cataloguing in Publication Data
A catalogue record for this book is available from the British Library

Library of Congress Cataloging in Publication Data
Classics of international relations : essays in criticism and appreciation / edited by Henrik Bliddal, Casper Sylvest and Peter Wilson.
 pages cm
 Includes bibliographical references and index.
1. International relations. I. Bliddal, Henrik.
 JZ1242.C54 2013
 327–dc23
   2012050841

ISBN: 978-0-415-69980-8 (hbk)
ISBN: 978-0-415-69981-5 (pbk)
ISBN: 978-0-203-76147-2 (ebk)

Typeset in Times New Roman
by Taylor & Francis Books

MIX
Paper from
responsible sources
FSC
www.fsc.org FSC® C013056

Printed and bound in Great Britain by
TJ International Ltd, Padstow, Cornwall

Contents

List of contributors

Lucian M. Ashworth is Professor and Head of the Political Science Department at Memorial University of Newfoundland, Canada. He writes on the history of international thought, with a particular interest in the interwar period. He is the author of *Creating International Studies: Angell, Mitrany and the Liberal Tradition* (Ashgate, 1999) and *International Relations and the Labour Party: Intellectuals and Policy Making from 1918-1945* (I. B. Tauris, 2007). He is currently working on a book project for Pearson entitled *A History of International Thought*.

J. Samuel Barkin is Professor of Global Governance in the McCormack Graduate School of Policy and Global Studies at the University of Massachusetts Boston. His work focuses on international relations theory and international environmental politics. His recent publications include *Realist Constructivism: Rethinking International Relations Theory* (Cambridge University Press, 2010) and *Saving Global Fisheries* (MIT Press, 2013).

Henrik Bliddal is Director of the Science and Technology Committee at the NATO Parliamentary Assembly. He holds an MSc in Political Science from the University of Copenhagen, Denmark. Henrik is a former editor of the Danish journal *Politik* and the author of *Reforming Military Command Arrangements* (Strategic Studies Institute, 2011).

Alan Chong is Associate Professor at the S. Rajaratnam School of International Studies, Singapore. He has published widely on the notion of soft power and the role of ideas in constructing the international relations of Singapore and Asia. His publications have appeared in *The Pacific Review*, the *Review of International Studies*, and *Alternatives: Global, Local, Political*.

Richard Devetak is Associate Professor and Head of the School of Political Science and International Studies at the University of Queensland, Australia. He is co-editor of *The Globalization of Political Violence* (Routledge, 2008) and co-author of *Theories of International Relations*, 5th edition (Palgrave Macmillan, 2013).

Bryan-Paul Frost is James A. and Kaye L. Crocker Endowed Professor of Political Science and adjunct professor in the Philosophy program at the University of Louisiana at Lafayette, USA. He is contributor, translator and co-editor (with Daniel J. Mahoney) of *Political Reason in the Age of Ideology: Essays in Honor of Raymond Aron* (Transaction, 2007). He has also published widely on Alexandre Kojève, US political thought and Greek and Roman political philosophy.

Randall Germain is Professor of Political Science at Carleton University, Canada. His research examines the political economy of global finance and theoretical developments in IPE. Among his publications are *The International Organization of Credit* (Cambridge University Press, 1997) and *Global Politics and Financial Governance* (Palgrave Macmillan, 2010). From 2009 until 2012 he was Chair of the Department of Political Science at Carleton University.

Juliette Gout is a doctoral student in the School of Political Science and International Studies at the University of Queensland, Australia. Her research is focused on the Kantian public sphere and the legacy of the Enlightenment for international political theory.

Nicolas Guilhot is senior researcher at the Centre National de la Recherche Scientifique–New York University joint research centre. He has previous taught at the London School of Economics and Political Science and Columbia University, New York, USA. His work focuses on the history of international relations theory. He is the author of *The Democracy Makers: Human Rights and the Politics of Global Order* (Columbia University Press, 2005) and editor of *The Invention of International Relations Theory* (Columbia University Press, 2011).

Marsha Henry is Lecturer in Gender, Development and Globalisation in the Gender Institute, London School of Economics and Political Science. Her research has looked at various aspects of gender and development, and gender, peacekeeping and militarization. Her publications have appeared in *International Peacekeeping, Globalizations, Security Dialogue,* and *Conflict, Security and Development.*

Andrew Hurrell is Montague Burton Professor of International Relations at Oxford University, UK, and a Fellow of Balliol College. His research interests cover theories of international relations, emerging powers and global order, the history of thought on international relations, comparative regionalism, and the international relations of the Americas. His most recent book is *On Global Order: Power, Values and the Constitution of International Society* (Oxford University Press, 2007).

Alexandra Hyde is a doctoral student at the Gender Institute, London School of Economics and Political Science, UK. She is writing an ethnography of a British Army base overseas from the perspective of civilian women married to servicemen.

Torbjørn L. Knutsen is Professor of International Relations at the University of Trondheim, Norway (NTNU). His books include *A History of International Relations Theory*, 2nd edition (Manchester University Press, 1997), *The Rise and Fall of World Orders* (Manchester University Press, 1999), *Ways of Knowing: Competing Methodologies in Social and Political Research* (Palgrave Macmillan, 2007, with Jonathon Moses), and *Exit Afghanistan* (Universitetsforlaget, 2012, with Gjert Lage Dyndal). He is currently working on issues concerning democracy, peace, terrorism and foreign policy.

Tom Lundborg is research fellow at the Swedish Institute of International Affairs. He is the author of *Politics of the Event: Time, Movement, Becoming* (Routledge, 2012).

Jeanne Morefield is Associate Professor of Politics at Whitman College, Washington, DC, USA. She is the author of *Covenants Without Swords: Idealist Liberalism and the Spirit of Empire* (Princeton University Press, 2005), and is currently working on

Empires of Forgetting for Oxford University Press which explores themes of nostalgia and amnesia in Anglo-US imperial thought.

Brian C. Schmidt is Associate Professor of Political Science at Carleton University, Canada. He is the author of *The Political Discourse of Anarchy: A Disciplinary History of International Relations* (SUNY Press, 1998), co-editor of *Imperialism and Internationalism in the Discipline of International Relations* (SUNY Press, 2005), and editor of *International Relations and the First Great Debate* (Routledge, 2012). He has published widely on the history of International Relations.

William Smith is Assistant Professor in the Department of Government and Public Administration at the Chinese University of Hong Kong. His research is in the field of contemporary political theory, with particular focus on the issues of deliberative democracy, civil disobedience, and international political thought. His work has appeared in a wide range of journals, including *The Journal of Political Philosophy*, *Ethics & International Affairs*, and *Review of International Studies*.

Brent J. Steele is Associate Professor of Political Science and International Relations and Director of Faculty Programs for the Office of International Programs at the University of Kansas, USA. His research has focused on a variety of issues, and specifically dealing with US foreign policy, just war theory, torture and accountability in global politics. He is the author of *Ontological Security in International Relations* (Routledge, 2008) and most recently *Alternative Accountabilities in Global Politics* (Routledge, 2012).

Casper Sylvest is Associate Professor of International Relations at the University of Southern Denmark. He is the author of *British Liberal Internationalism, 1880-1930: Making Progress?* (Manchester University Press, 2009) and a series of articles on liberal and realist visions of world politics during the nineteenth and twentieth centuries. He has published widely, combining his interests in the study of politics, history, law and technology. He is currently writing a book with Rens van Munster on social and political thought after the thermonuclear revolution.

Shiping Tang is Professor at the School of International Relations and Public Affairs (SIRPA), Fudan Univeristy, Shanghai, China. He is the author of *A Theory of Security Strategy for Our Time: Defensive Realism* (Palgrave Macmillan, 2010), *A General Theory of Institutional Change* (Routledge, 2011), and many articles. His book, *Social Evolution of International Politics*, is forthcoming from Oxford University Press.

Nick Vaughan-Williams is Reader in International Security at the University of Warwick, UK. His monograph *Border Politics: The Limits of Sovereign Power* (Edinburgh University Press, 2009) was Gold Winner of the 2011 Association for Borderlands Studies Book Award.

Thomas C. Walker currently teaches International Relations at the Grand Valley State University in West Michigan, USA. His research interests include philosophy of science, the history of international thought, and international conflict and peace. Before returning home to Michigan, he taught at SUNY-Albany and Dartmouth College. His work has appeared in *International Studies Quarterly*, *Perspectives on Politics*, and *International Studies Review*.

Peter Wilson is Senior Lecturer in International Relations at the London School of Economics and Political Science, UK, and Secretary of the International Studies Committee of the Gilbert Murray Trust. He is the author of *The International Theory of Leonard Woolf* (Palgrave Macmillan, 2003), co-author of *The Economic Factor in International Relations* (I. B. Tauris, 2001), and co-editor of *Thinkers of the Twenty Years' Crisis* (Clarendon Press, 1995). He has published papers on the English school, regime theory, grounded theory, international law, E. H. Carr, Leonard Woolf, Gilbert Murray, and C. A. W. Manning. He is currently working on a book on Manning with David Long.

Anders Wivel is Associate Professor at the University of Copenhagen's Department of Political Science, Denmark. He has published widely on realism, European security, and small state foreign policy. His most recent book is *Explaining Foreign Policy: International Diplomacy and the Russo-Georgian War* (Lynne Rienner, 2012, co-authored with Hans Mouritzen).

1 Introduction

Henrik Bliddal, Casper Sylvest and Peter Wilson[1]

For better or worse, International Relations (IR), like all fields of academic enquiry, gains its identity and establishes a degree of coherence by reference to tradition: its core concerns, staple approaches, and landmark or 'classic' contributions. This book provides introductions to and critical engagements with classical works of IR since *c.* 1900; i.e. the point when IR began to emerge as a recognizable socio-intellectual space, with its own concerns, debates and literature, if not yet its own professional space within the academy. At a time when the research agenda of the field is expanding and fragmenting, there is a growing trend to introduce IR through a combination of theory exegesis and a return to the discipline's founding fathers and classic books. At the same time, the changing nature of academic learning in conjunction with the proliferation of scholarly books and articles means that students and even some faculty rarely have the time or the opportunity to engage properly with more than a handful of these books. *Classics of International Relations* speaks to this predicament. It provides coherence by introducing the intellectual landmarks and core concerns of the field and gives students and scholars authoritative treatments of a considered selection of classics. *Classics of International Relations* aims to contribute to the ongoing debate about the identity of the discipline. Not shying away from the politics involved in establishing a canon, the book's broad and inclusive understanding of 'the classic' – covering inter alia the acknowledged classic, the classic in-the-making, and the 'alternative format' classic – is intended to facilitate such debate.

This Introduction has four aims. First, to provide a brief history of the idea of a classic text. Second, to set out the broad concept of classics around which the volume is organized. Third, to justify the purposes of the book and discuss some of the pitfalls involved in bringing it together. The volume is inescapably involved in the process of canonizing, engaging as it does in potentially powerful practices of inclusion and exclusion. Fourth, to provide a brief overview of the organization of the volume and set out the principles that have informed our selection of classics.

What is a classic?

The notion of a classic work of IR, history, sociology, politics or indeed any field of scholarly and scientific endeavour derives from literature. It is a notion tied to the process of secular canon-formation from the beginning. The Romans used the term *classici* to distinguish citizens of the pre-eminent class, those enjoying a certain fixed income, from the poorer citizenry beneath them, *infra classem*. The first writer to employ the term *classicus* figuratively was Aulus Gellius in the second century AD.[2] He used it to distinguish superior, authoritative texts, i.e. texts that could constitute a model for future writers, from those less worthy. Since that time, the term has been used repeatedly to distinguish the finest literary products of Western civilization from the mass. A classic work goes beyond the merely useful, noteworthy and valuable. It is a work that is considered in some important respects seminal or exemplary. A classic work is required reading for a person of culture. It is a work that all such persons ought to read or at least 'ought to have on their bookshelves'.[3] Yet it cannot be assumed that there was ever a time when a consensus prevailed, on anything more than a very general level, on the qualities and characteristics that define a classic. A classic work is certainly one that to some degree has stood the test of time. It is a work that continues to be read across the generations and in this sense is said to have 'endured'. But how many generations does a 'classic' need to cross? How long does it need to endure? What is it, most importantly, about this classic that has enabled it to cross the generations and endure? In addition to crossing generations, a classic is often deemed to be a work that crosses frontiers. Its appeal goes beyond the country and perhaps even the culture of its birth, often in time being translated into many different languages. But how many frontiers does it need to cross?

To these questions many answers have been given, with the outer boundaries of a centuries-old debate being defined by two broad positions. The first position, which held sway until the twentieth century, and could still be heard in the strong voices of T. S. Eliot and Q. D. Leavis well into that century, might be termed the essentialist. The second position, which holds sway today, though containing many disparate evocations, might be termed the sociological. The essentialist position finds one of its strongest statements in a celebrated essay by the nineteenth-century French literary critic, Charles Augustin Sainte-Beuve. He acknowledged at the outset that the question 'What is a classic?' is delicate and different answers could be proposed 'according to times and seasons'. He went on to present, however, his own unequivocally essentialist account of what a classic work entails. 'The idea of a classic implies something that has continuance and consistence, and which produces unity and tradition, fashions and transmits itself, and endures.' It is a work that enriches the human mind, increases its treasure, and causes it 'to advance a step'. It discovers some 'moral and not equivocal truth' and reveals 'some eternal passion in that heart where all seemed known and discovered'. It expresses itself in a form 'broad and great, refined and sensible, sane and beautiful'; and in a style peculiar to itself yet which is 'found to be also that of the whole world, a style new without neologism, new and old, easily contemporary with all time'.[4] The idea that a classic expresses certain timeless verities and speaks not to this or that culture but to the whole world goes to the heart of the essentialist position. However, the conceptual vessels 'timeless verities' and 'speaking to the whole world' are in themselves quite empty and have been filled in a variety of ways. Eliot, for example, contended in 1944 that the classic must display inter alia wit, magniloquence, maturity and urbanity. The one work that Eliot considered to be a true classic, Virgil's *Aeneid* (according to him, Dante, Shakespeare, Racine and Milton wrote, at best, 'relative classics'), moreover exhibited comprehensiveness, centrality, a sense of destiny and the gift of prophecy. But it also possessed a certain universality: 'The classic must ... express the maximum possible of the whole range of feeling which represents the character of the people who speak that language'. Universality for Eliot unlike Sainte-Beuve was paradoxical; it resided in this 'comprehensiveness in particularity'.[5]

Such nuances in Eliot's essay anticipate the sociological position which received its best-known expression in Frank Kermode's *The Classic,* published some three decades later. According to Kermode, classics are 'old books which people still read'.[6] An important factor in the making of a classic is 'a more or less continuous chorus of voices asserting the value of a classic'. This contrasts with what Kermode calls Eliot's 'imperial' model which expresses the timeless verities of a culture or civilization.[7] Rather than containing anything timeless, classic works possess 'an openness to accommodation which keeps them alive under endlessly varying dispositions'.[8] Here, Kermode echoes Ezra Pound's contention of the 1930s that '[a] classic is a classic not because it conforms to certain structural rules, or fits certain definitions (of which its author had quite probably never heard). It is a classic because of a certain eternal and irrepressible freshness'.[9] He also anticipates Calvino's contention that '[a] classic is a book that has never finished saying what it has to say' and '[t]he classics are books that we find all the more new, fresh, and unexpected upon reading'.[10] For the essentialists, a classic is by and large a closed book which specialized study and learning can partly open. As late as 1969, Leavis maintained that many peripheral readings of a classic were possible but only one central reading.[11] In Kermode's view, however, the classic is an open text capable of generating new meanings and understandings, ideas and interpretations. The classic signifies different things to different generations and different people within those generations. Classic works endure not because they lack substance and are open to infinite interpretation, but because they possess substance that is 'patient of interpretation'. Rather than express timeless verities, a work becomes a classic because it is sufficiently complex and open-ended to enable different cultures, generations and societies to find in it new meaning.[12]

From this brief exegesis one conclusion can be drawn: classic is a status we give to a work that separates it from often worthy but professedly inferior peers. It says this is a book one should read. It says this is a book one should prioritize over others because of its timeless qualities or because of the high value a given society, community or culture attaches to it. It is a term inextricably linked to the notion of a secular canon, a body of works if not sacred and eternal then in some important respects superior and deemed to be of continuing value and importance.

What is an IR classic?

There has been no comparable debate about what makes a classic of IR. The field has a number of texts that are routinely referred to as classics, a number of others to which classic status is occasionally attributed. All too often, however, the label is employed as a loose synonym for 'landmark' or 'groundbreaking'. This reflects an unsatisfactory degree of critical self-awareness in applying the concept and an underdeveloped appreciation of its discursive functions and possibilities. Before suggesting a typology that will help us to heighten our consciousness and sharpen our appreciation of the IR classic, it is important to make some preliminary distinctions regarding the use of the prefix 'classic' in IR discourse.

First, it is important to distinguish a classic work, in the sense understood in this volume, from a work of the classical tradition. The term classical tradition (also sometimes termed 'international theory')[13] is usually used to refer to that broad body of thought that predates IR as a specialized and professional field of study, and to which the IR community continuously adds by the 'discovery' of old works. Its originators are philosophers, political theorists, lawyers or publicists who have written significant, perhaps profound, things about the international system or society, who have influenced later thought, and whose works are deemed to be worthy of serious study. Among them can be counted such illustrious names as Vitoria, Hobbes, Grotius, Vattel, Rousseau, Smith, Burke, Kant, Hegel and Gentz – to cite the subjects of one well-known collection of essays[14] – though the extent to which such disparate figures may be said to constitute in any meaningful sense a 'tradition' can be, and indeed has been, questioned.[15]

Second, it is important to distinguish a classic work from a work that employs the classical approach. The classical approach is a term originating from and still mainly used by those associated with the English school of IR.[16] The classical approach, in Bull's words, signifies 'that approach to theorizing that derives from philosophy, history, and law, and that is characterized above all by explicit reliance on the exercise of judgment' and 'the scientifically imperfect process of perception or intuition'.[17] Bull derived this understanding of the approach from what he took to be the analytical methods of classical, i.e. pre-twentieth century, thinkers, thus closely linking the classical tradition and the classical approach. He held these methods to be superior, or at least more honest and realistic, than the behavioural, scientific or quantitative methods that were at the time taking hold in the social sciences. Bull's definition and his subsequent argument are concerned with methodology and epistemology, not with the status of any body of work or particular work. While he certainly used the word 'classical' to lend gravitas to an approach he personally favoured, he was not using it to suggest that by the very fact of being 'classical' it was superior to others.

The classic work as understood in this volume, therefore, has no logical connection to the classical tradition or to the classical approach. These refer to particular types, bodies and methods of work, not a work's status. It is perfectly possible for classic works to hail from the 'scientific' as from the 'classical' camp (to use Bull's imperfect categories). The fact that the majority of IR classics as specified here come from the classical camp says perhaps more about the age of this camp than its intellectual superiority. It also, however, reflects the non-positivist inclinations of the editors, our understanding of the discipline as a conversation between competing theoretical standpoints rather than a quest from a single standpoint for a single, universally valid, truth – the goal of much 'scientific' theory.

There are, we contend, five types of classic work in the field of IR. We have arrived at three of these types by reflecting on the works that are generally or increasingly deemed to be classics, not through the application of any a priori conceptions or understandings. Our approach here is therefore 'sociological', not 'essentialist', though the possibility of arriving at some essentialist conclusions have not been ruled out. Yet to this fairly conventional understanding of classic must be added, if we are to capture the current IR field in all its diversity, two further types. The five types are:

(i) The acknowledged or undisputed classic. These are works such as *The Twenty Years' Crisis* and *Theory of International Politics* whose status as classics few in IR would deny.
(ii) The archetypal classic. These are works seen as the best expressions of an important school of thought, paradigm or approach. They are widely deemed and utilized as exemplars of that approach. Examples include *The Anarchical Society* (English school) and *Political Theory and International Relations* (cosmopolitanism).

(iii) The classic in the making. These are works published relatively recently such as *Social Theory of International Politics* and *Bounding Power*, which show signs in terms of their disciplinary impact of becoming classics in the future.

(iv) The overlooked classic. These are works such as *Three Guineas* and *Bananas, Beaches and Bases*, which have a small but intense following within certain disciplinary sub-groups but which have yet to be more broadly acknowledged. A parallel in the world of film would be the cult classic.

(v) Alternative format classic. Types (i) to (iv) generally betray a conventional understanding of 'text': a published, academic book; the academic monograph. A broader notion of text would embrace film, literature, art, music. The alternative format classic is a cultural reference point. While not emanating from the discipline, it is a work that has had such an impact on the way international relations are conceived within broader society that it has come to assume a prominent place in teaching and in scholarly debates.

These types are not mutually exclusive. *The Anarchical Society*, for example, is an acknowledged classic and an archetypal classic. *Inside/outside* is an archetypal classic and a classic in the making. The types are sufficiently clear and coherent, however, to enable us to sharpen our thinking on the IR classic and, more broadly, the canon-forming process in IR.

Purposes and pitfalls of the volume

From the outset, this book has been conceived as a 'crossover' volume which will appeal to both scholars and students, engaging as it does in the ongoing and necessary conversation about the nature and identity of IR. In this section we set out the intellectual and pedagogic justifications for the volume and outline some of the pitfalls in constructing it.

There are a good number of reasons why it is intellectually fruitful to study and reflect on academic disciplines and their constitutive and regulative practices.[18] Such practices are powerful. They structure not only the professional life of academics and the development of academic institutions but also what students learn and take away from their university experiences. Particularly in the social sciences, disciplines engage in various kinds of soul-searching often with the explicit aim of finding a core concern, devising a better approach, developing more effective theories or providing a historical justification for respecting or celebrating diversity. IR is no exception. Indeed, post-Cold War IR can be seen as the reflexive discipline par excellence. Debates between gatekeepers and disciplinary anarchists, the development of the historiography of the discipline into a serious scholarly concern, as well as a now long-standing debate on the philosophy of science have all contributed to this state of affairs.

Yet there is little agreement on the health and vitality of the discipline. For some observers, it is significant and beneficial that recent decades have witnessed a rapid increase and expansion of approaches, theories, and thematic foci. These developments are often described in a language of turns. These are turns away from something well known or established. They disperse IR scholarship, encroach upon neighbouring fields, and expand our intellectual horizon. In short, IR is witnessing increasing diversity with ample room for further exploration and innovation. To some, however, the downside of diversity is fragmentation. In this assessment, the overall effect is negative, not only because specialization leads to intellectual isolation and tribalism but also because fragmentation is often accompanied by the rise of 'methodologism', defined as 'an overdone focus on methodological techniques, especially techniques for measuring causal relationships'.[19] The result is not a diversification and enrichment of intellectual stimuli but a descent into ever narrower, more technical and (for some) tedious debates. Recently, Benjamin Cohen has even argued that International Political Economy journals are 'full of articles that are thoroughly peer-reviewed and edited with care. With rare exceptions, research meets the highest standards of scholarship. It's just not very interesting.'[20] Some of these different experiences of the state of IR might have their roots in transatlantic differences over what counts as worthwhile knowledge and what are the most appropriate means of acquiring it. Nevertheless, a good deal of scholarship on both sides of the Atlantic contradicts and complicates the picture.[21]

Given this predicament, casting a critical eye over the intellectual structure of the discipline, its past and present achievements, is likely to be a productive endeavour.[22] Obviously, we do this all the time, for example in the predominant way of organizing the textbook: through stylized 'isms' that are set against a range of similarly stylized 'isms'. This practice clearly has drawbacks. '"Isms" are evil', David Lake has recently argued, because among other things they reify existing traditions, reward extremism and encourage tribalism. On the other hand, Henry Nau retorts that 'isms' are inevitable and to some extent useful, even if potentially dangerous.[23] It is probable that most scholars and teachers of IR appreciate the merit of both positions.

A partly overlapping alternative to the textbook presentation of the field, as being populated by different (sometimes warring) 'isms', is the historical construction of the discipline as a series of great debates. Particularly during the last couple of decades, this strategy has met with resistance, not least because the historical accuracy of this trope has been strongly challenged.[24] Other scholars are more sanguine, however, arguing that historically 'the debate' is an important organizing device of the field and that telling the story of 'great debates' helps to provide coherence in an otherwise fragmenting field.[25]

A third strategy is to 'introduce persons instead of paradigms', to identify the masters of the discipline.[26] This has been done with some success in the past, but it is a line of attack that is perhaps particularly predisposed to hagiography. Few masters are flawless, after all. Moreover, as Ken Booth has forcefully argued, trying to identify masters 'in the making' is fraught with dilemmas of power, bias, selection.[27]

In contrast to these strategies, we focus on *classics*. In this respect, our trail has partly been blazed by the German volume *Schlüsselwerke der Politikwissenschaft*, which similarly appraises and critiques classics in order to create a debate about the body of classic works, in this case those of Political Science, including IR.[28] For its editor, Steffen Kailitz, a classic of Political Science needs: a) to have an original argument that advances our knowledge about politics in a significant way; and b) to be received as a fundamental text by a significant share of the members of the discipline across frontiers. Weakness in one area can be compensated for by strength in the other. Unfortunately, he does not engage in deeper reflections on the term classic, and appears to mix elements of what we have termed the essentialist and sociological positions. In addition, he restricts himself to the first three of our types of classics, without distinguishing between different types and does not reflect on the process of 'classicization'. In practical terms, however, he has taken a similar approach to ours.

We use the strategy of focusing on classics of IR in a way that deliberately tries to avoid *some* of the risks associated with alternative strategies. Focusing on individual works (mainly but not exclusively the academic monograph) and basing our selection on a combination of established views and a concern to include more recent works from a variety of theoretical perspectives go some way towards overcoming self-indulgence and hagiography. Moreover, expanding the concept of classics (some would say, to its limit and beyond) is in itself a way of interrogating the process through which classics become classics and a way of making us alert to the process by which knowledge is produced and disseminated. Our broad concept of classics is similarly intended to raise critical awareness and to make readers interrogate the kind(s) of knowledge a discipline like IR needs, rewards and excludes. Finally, our strategy allows for a more detailed and contextual engagement with classic works. Reading a classic in its context – as a product of its time, place and intellectual milieu – provides an opportunity for more rounded and nuanced interpretations of the figures behind these works; figures whose thinking, style, approaches and foci naturally changed over their (often long) careers and in ways that conventional strategies are often unable to grasp.[29]

Still, 'classicization' is no innocent business and we certainly do not want to discount any remaining problems, not least the potentially powerful practices of inclusion and exclusion mentioned above or the risk that we unthinkingly enforce the status quo. One such point of contention is likely to be our predominant focus on what is sometimes called general IR, i.e. studies that attempt to grasp the totality of relations at the international or global level, and/or seek to draw general conclusions about the nature, determinants and health of international relationships and the institutions and practices they generate. Here our navigating tools have been a range of central concepts (or narratives that animate these concepts): war, peace, power, the state, law, order, justice, diplomacy, anarchy and sovereignty. This is not meant to be a denigration of important sub-fields such as Foreign Policy Analysis and International Political Economy, and indeed we do recognize that works from such sub-fields can and sometimes do have a wider impact. Some works of that nature have been included in this volume.

In sum, while as editors we acknowledge from the outset the disciplinary politics involved and the dilemmas and questions raised in the production of a volume such as this, we do not consider them to be compelling reasons for not undertaking the project. After all, one of the main aims of the book is to spur debate. We fully expect that some will disagree with the approach and that only a few, if any, will agree with our selections *tout court*. However, as we shall specify in more detail below, the classics covered are indeed highly valued and are seen as exemplary or as having made a seminal contribution to knowledge, consciousness and/or debates about international/global politics. In short, they have acquired, to a greater or lesser degree, an elevated status. We ask how they got there, if they are likely to stay there, what they provide for us (as scholars and students of the subject) and what we do to them when we read, appraise, critique or use them in research and teaching. In this sense, the volume is an intervention in an ongoing dialogue, and we find consolation in the view that debates of this nature are periodically necessary and can be fruitful even if, or perhaps because, the only certain thing that can be said about them is that they will not provide consensus.

This brings us to the pedagogic reasons for producing this volume. While there is, then, a continuing interest in the legacy of the field, a sustained engagement with theories or studies from the past is often stymied by the short format of textbook chapters where classic works, authors or arguments are encapsulated in a few paragraphs or sentences, or relegated to the odd fact box. Moreover, there is a case to be made that the nature of higher education, the development of information technology, the explosion in research output and wider societal changes relating to the distribution, circulation and consumption of knowledge, work against the solitary study of classics. When Ole Wæver and Iver Neumann published *The Future of International Relations: Masters in the Making* in 1997, they hinted in this direction by warning that the book could have been called '[h]ow to save 500 hours of IR reading: books you always pretend to have read but actually never did'. In a biting review, Ken Booth foresaw that the book would become 'a substitute for the real thing', and a poor one at that.[30]

There seems to be a fair amount of romanticizing going on here. Was extensive reading of big and/or difficult books ever the dominant practice for more than a minority of students? Moreover, the argument that broad-theme crossover volumes like the present book make a virtue of a necessity is too one-sided. Some students of IR will never turn to the classics themselves, a fact that this book is unlikely to change. Others, however, will use the chapters in this volume as a companion to their own critical, independent engagement with the classics. Moreover, it is possible that some students after reading this volume will be encouraged to engage with one or more classics directly, and henceforth will take a more informed, critical stance towards existing interpretations. Finally, the volume also serves a pedagogic function in providing an *aide memoire* and useful contextual information for teachers and lecturers whose knowledge of the IR classics may date back some years, who have not had time to keep up with the secondary literature on them, and whose familiarity with classical works will inevitably be greater in some cases than in others. In this regard we hope to provide teachers of and lecturers on the subject with a bigger picture wherein they can better situate their specialist knowledge for their students.

Selection and organization

It would be remiss if we did not mention the origins of this volume. Of the 24 contributions, earlier versions of four chapters were published in late 2009 in a special issue of the Danish journal *Politik*.[31] The issue 'International Relations Classics Reappraised: The Nines' examined 10 IR books that coincidentally celebrated 'big anniversaries' in 2009. The core idea was to invite the reader 'to either revisit these standards of IR or to go out and pick them up for the first time'.[32] Encouraged by the success of this issue, two of the contributors and the editor of *Politik* at the time decided to take this idea one step further. With *Classics of International Relations* you hold the result of this decision in your hands.

Since we were fully aware of the pitfalls that compiling a list of classics of IR contains, we did not rely solely on our own intellectual judgements. The continuous reflection among the editors on which works to include benefited enormously from discussions with and reactions from colleagues at a number of academic institutions, as well as from the detailed comments made by three anonymous reviewers of the book proposal. The feedback we received made us confident that the book and the list of 24 classics covered would inspire debate in the discipline, but also justify the substantial scholarly effort and time put into the chapters by our contributors.

This process did not include the use of citation counts, which might intuitively make sense. While they are generally useful, they would have provided a skewed picture. For instance, citation counts are biased towards the present and would have been of little help in capturing the status of early twentieth-century works. Also, they would have been of little help in identifying our 'overlooked' classics – a controversial notion for sure but one we wished to give a dry run in this volume.

In order to narrow down an initial list of over 30 potential classics, but also to generate discussions among the editors about potential blind spots, we sent out a survey to IR faculty members at eight leading universities in Europe, the USA, and Australia.[33] We posed three sets of questions: one concerning the wisdom of our initial list of classics; and two open-ended questions about other candidates for inclusion, including non-book formats. The responses we received, as one might expect in a heterogeneous field such as IR, were diverse, some of them conventional, others highly surprising. However, the data we gathered from the survey was extremely helpful in refining our judgement. Also helpful were the comments and criticisms received from three anonymous reviewers. A major point of criticism was that our initial selection of works was too conventional. The reviewers challenged the occlusion of works from various alternative traditions and schools of thought, e.g. anarchism, environmentalism, Marxism, critical theory, globalization, systems theory and world order modelling. While undoubtedly important and influential in varying degrees, however, we did not merely want to include 'token works' representing all the traditions and schools in IR. Instead, all works covered in this volume had to stand on their own, among other things by having had a substantial impact on wider IR debates, or having accumulated such prestige within a disciplinary sub-group that to occlude them would be perverse. Nevertheless, this criticism was one that required careful consideration. Ultimately, we decided to include chapters on Charles R. Beitz's *Political Theory and International Relations*, a foundational book of international political theory; Andrew Linklater's *Men and Citizens in the Theory of International Relations*, which also emerged from political theory, but also from Marxist sociology and Frankfurt School critical theory; and Robert W. Cox's *Production, Power and World Order*, another critical approach to IR, but one with roots in Gramscian thought and International Political Economy. We felt uneasy about leaving out a number of other strong contenders, but lines need to be drawn, however temporary, and distinctions made, however uncertain. We are nonetheless confident that the 24 volumes finally selected stand up to scrutiny in terms of their historiographical and broader discursive importance, and their collective ability to speak to the concerns at the heart of IR.

While different organizing principles were discussed, the principle finally selected was chronological. The key reason is that chronology, combined with our broad concept of classic, breaks up some of the conventionalism that follows from focusing on classics. In particular, it averts the reification of traditional narratives of the discipline which revolve around a select list of works containing timeless truths or wisdoms that all students must learn. Presenting overlooked and alternative classics alongside acknowledged and archetypal classics lessens the danger that the book conveys a narrow view of the discipline. In many ways, chronology is an old-fashioned tool. Yet it is very effective to have a chapter on *Dr. Strangelove*, for example, follow a conventional work such as Claude's *Power and International Relations*, and to have Beitz's (re)introduction of political theory into IR debates track the ultimate manifesto of neorealist orthodoxy, Waltz's *Theory of International Politics*. It highlights the dynamic, partly dialectical, but deeply unpredictable nature of academic production and avoids the strong tendency in conventional accounts of seeing past ideas merely in terms of what they contributed to some landmark discovery. By labelling a text an 'IR classic' we are of course providing a strong signpost to those studying the subject. However, we are not suggesting that IR classics present timeless truths, that they are necessarily the best works in the field, or that their status is permanent and brooks no doubt. Rather they are important in some way that strongly commands our attention and respect, even if we may have profound reservations about their contents.

It is also important to stress that in using chronology as our organizing principle, we do not want to imply that there is 'progression' in IR over time. We do not want to suggest that newer books are more 'advanced' and 'better' at explaining international relations than older ones. Clearly, our volume is premised on the fact that there may be some wisdom (and sometimes a great deal) contained in books that are 50 or even 100 years old. It is a traditional work of scholarship in its desire to preserve and reflect on 'old' knowledge at a time when there is heavy institutional pressure to concentrate on what is 'cutting edge' and 'new'. Still, we also do not seek comfort in nostalgia for the past. Clearly times change, and perspectives on international politics change as well. In fact, the last classic discussed in this volume, Deudney's *Bounding Power*, shows that continuity and change in international politics often go hand-in-hand. Genuinely new problems arise that require new answers, but the past can also hold the keys to unlock at least some of these answers. That, in the end, is a central message of *Classics of International Relations*. The most fruitful debates about our subject take place not when contemporary scholars simply meet to discuss contemporary problems but when they meet to discuss them with knowledge and understanding of past ideas – ideas that were themselves once new. Only with knowledge of the past, including past ideas and their evolution, can we escape enslavement by the *zeitgeist* and obtain that most liberating of intellectual commodities – perspective.[34]

Notes

1 We would like to thank Lucian M. Ashworth, Duncan Bell and Peter Marcus Kristensen for comments on an earlier draft and Stefan Kristiansen for extensive help with a survey (see Note 33).
2 Charles Augustin Sainte-Beuve, *What Is a Classic?* Available at: http://classiclit.about.com/library/bl-etexts/csaintebeuve/bl-csaintebeuve-classic.htm (accessed 12 September 2012), first published as 'Qu-est-ce qu'un classique?', *Le Constitutionnel*, 21 October 1850; Frank Kermode, *The Classic: Literary Images of Permanence and Change*, Cambridge, MA: Harvard University Press, [1975] 1983, p. 15.
3 Fay Weldon, 'Today', *BBC Radio 4*, 8 August 2012.
4 Sainte-Beuve, *What Is a Classic?*, pp. 1–4.
5 T. S. Eliot, *What Is a Classic?*, London: Faber & Faber, 1944, pp. 7–32; Kermode, *The Classic*, pp. 37–38.
6 Kermode, *The Classic*, p. 43.
7 Kermode, *The Classic*, p. 117. Eliot contended that a classic is a work that becomes the voice of something lasting, of lasting importance – as Virgil became 'the voice of timeless Empire'. Eliot's understanding of Empire defies easy comprehension. It is a religio-cultural as much as a political expression.
8 Kermode, *The Classic*, p. 44.
9 Ezra Pound, *ABC of Reading*, New York: New Directions Publishing, [1934] 2011, pp. 13–14.
10 Italo Calvino, *Why Read the Classics?*, London: Penguin Classics, [1980] 2009, pp. 3–10.
11 See Kermode, *The Classic*, pp. 133–34.
12 Kermode, *The Classic*, pp. 75, 121 and 134.
13 See e.g. Martin Wight, *International Theory: The Three Traditions* (ed. Gabriele Wight and Brian Porter), London: Leicester University Press, 1991.
14 Ian Clark and Iver B. Neumann (eds), *Classical Theories of International Relations*, Basingstoke: Palgrave Macmillan, 1996.
15 See e.g. Tim Dunne, 'Mythology or Methodology? Traditions in International Theory', *Review of International Studies*, 1993, vol. 19, 305–18; Ian Clark, 'Traditions of Thought and Classical Theories of International Relations', in Clark and Neumann, *Classical Theories*, pp. 1–19.

16 See Barry Buzan, *From International to World Society? English School Theory and the Social Structure of Globalisation*, Cambridge: Cambridge University Press, 2004; Andrew Linklater and Hidemi Suganami, *The English School of International Relations: A Contemporary Reassessment*, Cambridge: Cambridge University Press, 2006.

17 Hedley Bull, 'International Theory: The Case for a Classical Approach', *World Politics*, 1966, vol. 18, p. 361.

18 Constitutive practices include the kind of questions that get asked, the kind of answers considered legitimate, the range of methods deemed appropriate, and the types of sources considered valid. Regulative practices include the methods by which work gets selected for publication, the means by which publication status is determined, the channels through which knowledge is disseminated and reproduced, and the processes by which appointments to professional bodies and editorships are made and research grants awarded.

19 Stephen van Evera, 'Director's Statement: Trends in Political Science and the Future of Security Studies', *MIT Security Studies Program: Annual Report 2009–2010* (2010), p. 4. A similar critique has also, of course, been levelled against various types of post-positivist scholarship.

20 Benjamin Cohen, 'Are IPE Journals Becoming Boring?', *International Studies Quarterly*, 2010, vol. 54, 887–91, at p. 887.

21 Ole Wæver, 'The Sociology of a Not so International Discipline', *International Organization*, 1998, vol. 52, 687–727, esp. Figure 3; Ole Wæver and Barry Buzan, 'After the Return to Theory: The Past, Present, and Future of Security Studies', in Alan Collins (ed.), *Contemporary Security Studies*, 2nd edn, Oxford: Oxford University Press, 2010, pp. 463–83.

22 See also Duncan Bell, 'Writing the World: Disciplinary History and Beyond', *International Affairs*, 2009, vol. 85, 3–22. We return to question of the state of IR in the Conclusion to this volume.

23 David A. Lake, 'Why "Isms" Are Evil: Theory, Epistemology, and Academic Sects as Impediments to Understanding and Progress', *International Studies Quarterly*, 2010, vol. 55, 465–80; Henry R. Nau, 'No Alternative to "Isms"', *International Studies Quarterly*, 2010, vol. 55, 487–91. See also Lucian M. Ashworth, 'The Poverty of Paradigms: Subcultures, Trading Zones and the Case of Liberal Socialism in Interwar International Relations', *International Relations*, 2012, vol. 26, 35–59; Duncan Bell, 'Introduction: Under an Empty Sky – Realism and Political Theory', in Bell (ed.), *Political Thought and International Relations: Variations on a Realist Theme*, Oxford: Oxford University Press, 2008, pp. 1–25.

24 Peter Wilson, 'The Myth of the First Great Debate', *Review of International Studies*, 1998, vol. 24, 1–16; Casper Sylvest, 'Interwar Internationalism, the British Labour Party and the Historiography of International Relations', *International Studies Quarterly*, 2004, vol. 48, 409–32; Brian Schmidt (ed.), *International Relations and the First Great Debate*, London and New York: Routledge, 2012.

25 Ole Wæver, 'Still a Discipline after all these Debates?', in Tim Dunne, Milja Kurki and Steve Smith (eds), *International Relations Theories*, 2nd edn, Oxford: Oxford University Press, 2010, pp. 297–318. See also Ole Wæver, 'The Speech Act of Realism: The Move That Made IR' in Nicolas Guilhot (ed.), *The Invention of International Relations Theory*, New York: Columbia University Press, 2011, pp. 97–127.

26 K. W. Thompson, *Masters of International Thought*, Baton Rouge, LA: Louisiana State University Press, 1980; Iver Neumann and Ole Wæver (eds), *The Future of International Relations: Masters in the Making*, London: Routledge, 1997; Filippo Andreatta (ed.), *Le Grandi Opere delle Relazioni Internazionali*, Bologna: Il Mulino, 2011.

27 Ken Booth, 'Masterdebating in International Relations', *Millennium: Journal of International Studies*, 1998, vol. 27, 141–44.

28 Steffen Kailitz (ed.), *Schlüsselwerke der Politikwissenschaft*, Wiesbaden: Verlag für Sozialwissenschaften, 2007. Kailitz uses the terms 'key works' (*Schlüsselwerke*) and 'classics' (*Klassiker*) interchangeably.

29 The case for reading works in their context has been forcefully made by the Cambridge School of Political Thought. See primarily Quentin Skinner, *Visions of Politics, Vol. I: On Method*, Cambridge: Cambridge University Press, 2002. This and other approaches emphasising the importance of context for meaning and understanding have made some impact in studies of international thought during the last decade.

30 Neumann and Wæver pointed out that they did not choose this title, since their aim was not to 'replace the reading of primary texts by secondary ones'. Neumann and Wæver, *The Future of International Relations*, p. 6; Ken Booth, 'Master-Debating International Relations', p. 142.

31 We thank *Politik* and its publisher DJØF Forlag for permission to draw on the articles on *The Great Illusion* (an earlier version, *Europe's Great Illusion* from 1909, was reappraised), *International Politics in the Atomic Age*, *Man, the State, and War* and *Theory of International Politics*. The special issue also contained a chapter on *The Twenty Years' Crisis* but the chapter in this volume does not draw on it.

32 Henrik Bliddal, 'International Relations Classics Reappraised: The Nines', *Politik*, 2009, vol. 12, p. 2.

33 Specifically, we sent them to all scholars in the following institutions: the Department of International Relations, London School of Economics and Political Science (LSE); the Department of International Politics, Aberystwyth University, UK; the Department of Political Science, University of Copenhagen, Denmark; the Freie Universität Berlin (various departments and centres), Germany; the Center for International Studies and Research at the Institut d'études politiques in Paris, France; the Department of Political Science, University of Chicago, USA; the Woodrow Wilson School of Public and International Affairs and Department of Politics, Princeton University, USA; and the School of Politics and International Relations at the Australian National University.

34 As brilliantly argued in Wight, *International Theory*, p. 6.

2 A pillar of air? Norman Angell and *The Great Illusion*

Torbjørn L. Knutsen

Few books on international relations can beat the best-selling record of Norman Angell's *The Great Illusion* (*TGI*).[1] It was published in London, UK in 1910 and sold around two million copies prior to World War I. It then faded from view. Why? A common explanation is that its thesis was mistaken. Angell's critics commonly claim that the book's main message, that war was now impossible, was disproved by the outbreak of World War I in 1914. This is a deeply unfair criticism. *TGI* never claimed that war was impossible. The book was, in fact, a passionate warning of the dangers of imminent war. If the statesmen of the West did not change their ways – if they did not come round to a more sensible view of international affairs – costly wars would erupt. The argument that supported this message has been part and parcel of the professional study of International Relations (IR) ever since: in an interdependent world, large-scale war will bring economic disaster for everybody.

Angell strongly believed that war did not pay. Yet why did so many readers misunderstand this simple message? Why has the book largely been forgotten today, rather than hailed as a classic in interdependence theory? In order to answer these questions, it is useful to begin with the book's early reception. Its first reviews show that academic commentators did not misunderstand the book's basic message. But others did. One reviewer, T. G. Martin, noted that the book's most eager fans also appeared to be the greatest distorters of its message.[2] This observation, that the most committed peace activists tended to read the book the most selectively, suggests one reason why *TGI* has been so misunderstood: it is a book of many messages. Different readers have found different points and meanings in it.

The first chapter of the book introduces the reader to the core idea around which its argument is built: that during the second half of the nineteenth century, the industrial states of the world went through an evolution that made them dependent on each other for trade and finance. War among the great powers would cause this network of interdependence to unravel, and bring the entire economic system down. Subsequent chapters introduce other ideas that add greater complexity to the thesis. One such addition is that language shapes our perception of the world. Upon this argument hinges the very concept of 'illusion' in the book's title. Through it Angell infers that if people were provided with a new vocabulary better able to capture the realities of an interdependent world, then they would also more easily understand and adapt to the political realities of that world. This notion of 'adaptation' – a notion which is grafted onto a social-evolutionary outlook – plays a crucial role in the book. Ideas such as these – interdependence, adaptation and the effects of language on politics – are all central to *TGI*. They are also an integral part of twentieth-century IR. In this sense, a study of *TGI* is also an exercise in disciplinary history, as it involves the early use of some of the key terms and theories in IR.

This chapter will first draw a quick sketch of the book's author. It will then present the structure and the argument in this important but much-misunderstood and over-looked IR classic. The chapter will close with an examination of the three concepts that carry the book's argument – interdependence, adaptation and the formative effects of language.

The author

Ralph Norman Angell Lane was born in 1872. He was an inquisitive and precocious child and rebelled against the inhibitive conventions of Victorian society. Upon com-pleting elementary school in England he travelled abroad. He went to secondary school in France, returned to London to attend business school, and then spent a year in Geneva. During his formative years he read works that exposed 'the world's injustices, miseries, and follies'[3] – Voltaire, Thomas Paine, J. S. Mill, Charles Kingsley, William Morris and Herbert Spencer foremost among them.

At the age of 18 he decided that Europe was spent, so he emigrated to the New World. In 1891 he travelled to the USA and set himself up as a homesteader in the Wild West to lead a 'simple life'.[4] He worked at different jobs to make ends meet, among them prospecting, cattle-herding, vine-planting, well-digging, mail-carrying and book-keeping. He ended up as a newspaper reporter on the *San Francisco Chronicle* and, later, the *St. Louis Globe-Democrat*.

Mr Lane, the journalist

When the Spanish-American War broke out in 1898, Ralph Norman Lane was sur-prised to note that so many Americans were pleased by the prospect of a scrap with colonial Spain. This surprise planted in his mind a question that he would wrestle with in several subsequent books, including *TGI*. Where did this popular belligerence come from? He bore the question in mind when he returned to Europe later that year.

Disappointed with the 'simple life' and with the belligerent attitude of the USA, Lane became the editor of an English-language newspaper in Paris. He wrote for the French *Éclair* about US attitudes towards the war with Spain. He filed articles for US newspapers about French attitudes towards Captain Dreyfus. When armed conflict erupted in South Africa, he wrote for French newspapers about the escalating Boer War, and the way in which it fanned British sentiments of patriotism. In 1901 he began to address more systematically the common theme that he observed in these various conflicts: how patriotisms, passions and myths undermine people's common sense. Drawing on his triangular travels, he wrote a comparative study of popular reactions to the Boer War, the Dreyfus affair and to the Spanish-American War. This book, *Patriotism under Three Flags*,[5] explored the irrational forces which undermined people's common sense and rational judgement. Thus, he identified a phenomenon which would con-stitute a recurring theme through his writings for the next 50 years. *Patriotism under Three Flags* maintained that most people are not guided through life by facts and rational analysis but by interpretations and opinions that surround the facts. Most people do not really follow the reasoning of a carefully argued analysis; they are caught up in the language that encases it.

The young author was so excited by this insight that he toyed with the thought of dropping journalism to become a freelance philosopher. He changed his mind when his publisher informed him of his book's disappointing sales. Instead of writing books on philosophy, he accepted an offer from Alfred Harmsworth to manage the Paris-based edition of the British newspaper, the *Daily Mail*. This job gave Lane a stellar location from which he could observe modern journalism and its relations with the modern public. He pondered his central question about widespread belligerence, wrestled with the interrelationship between the popular press and its mass audience, and developed insights into the forces that shaped (and twisted) people's perceptions of the world.

He pursued the issue in a second book, *Europe's Optical Illusion.*[6] It continued the discussion of how myths and emotions undermined people's rational analysis. But the author cast his net more broadly now: ordinary people are not the only ones who are swayed by irrational forces in politics, he argued, the governing elites are equally affected. Also, he added an economic aspect to the argument: great changes had recently taken place in trade, and Western international statesmen did not seem to be aware of the immensity of these changes. They were still prisoners of an old language and old, obsolete ways of thought.

Mr Angell, the activist

Europe's Optical Illusion was not published under the name of Ralph Lane. To distance himself from Harmsworth and the paper for which he worked, he published it under his less frequently used middle names: Norman Angell. The book sold well, but received a curious reception. Its simple argument was often misconstrued. Its message was twisted and bent out of shape and the public seemed to infer from the book that war had now become impossible. Angell was puzzled by this widespread misunderstanding. Although he knew that people are set in their ways and that it is difficult to convert them to a new and more accurate view of the world, he was determined to try.

So he dipped his quill anew and began to revise his book. His aim was to provide the public as well as the politicians with concepts and terms that captured world affairs better than did the old ones. He sought to introduce a new vocabulary that was better adapted to the realities of an interdependent world. The result was a new and greatly expanded text with a new title *The Great Illusion: A Study of the Relation of Military Power in Nations to their Economic and Social Advantage*. The book was published in the autumn of 1910. Translations quickly appeared and the book soon sold well in other countries – especially in France, Germany, the Netherlands and in Scandinavia. The book proved so great a success that it induced Angell to quit journalism and launch a new career.

The book

One reason for the success of the book was that it rode the wave of a burgeoning peace movement. It greatly stimulated discussions on the causes of war and the preconditions for peace. Another reason was Angell himself. His books may have catapulted him to fame, but his charm, sharp wit and boundless energy sustained it. He quickly became a peace activist of note and a public intellectual known for his lecture tours and pronouncements on contemporary affairs. He lent his name to peace clubs and anti-war organizations. Although he rode the wave of the peace movement, he also exerted a formative force on it.

A third reason for the book's success was that its author was backed by powerful sponsors. One of them was Viscount Esher, the chairman of the British Committee of Imperial Defence. He was impressed by *Europe's Optical Illusion* and sent copies to many of his influential friends. He wrote to Angell and intimated that the book might be as important for the field of Political Science as Darwin's *Origin of Species* had been for biology.[7] If Angell was willing to expand on his analysis, Esher continued, it might be possible to provide him with financial support and some secretarial assistance. When Angell expressed interest in the proposal, Esher asked some of England's wealthy industrialists to sponsor him. A fund was established in the name of one of them, Sir Richard Garton. Backed by the Garton Foundation for Encouraging the Study of International Policy Angell could afford to devote himself to the study of international affairs and to write *TGI*.

Esher, Garton and other industrialists agreed that war was bad for business. They were attracted to Angell's argument because it distanced itself from the religious reasoning and pacifism that had traditionally dominated the anti-war movement. *TGI* was not a moralist tract, but an appeal to common sense and scientific argument. It drew on economic theories of trade and finance to procure the key concept of interdependence, and it invoked current theories of social evolution to develop an argument of adaptation. Such arguments dovetailed nicely with the orientation of the British business community. In 1913 the Garton Foundation sponsored the establishment of *War and Peace: A Norman Angell Monthly* – one of the world's first journals of international affairs.

The economics of the case

TGI consists of three parts – two aspects of 'the case' (as Angell calls it) and a conclusion. The first part, called 'The Economics of the Case', explains why war no longer pays. In the wake of the Industrial Revolution, the states of the world have expanded trade and financial dealings with each other and developed an intricate international division of labour. As a consequence of this development, industrial states have become 'interdependent'. If war were to break out among such states, it would cause the network of interdependence to unravel. Since all states rely on this network for their wealth and welfare, such a war would not only result in the usual battlefield destruction, it would bring in its wake unprecedented economic disaster as well.

The book's first chapter opens with a discussion of how the British fear Germany's naval build-up. Angell does not deny that the British fear is real. Yet, he argues that the Germans have nothing to gain from an attack on England. In fact, he continues, the Germans have everything to lose. Germany's miraculous growth during the final decade of the nineteenth century was fuelled by British investments. If the Germans were to attack the UK, they would not only injure the British investors and harm the British economy, they would unleash a deep economic crisis in both countries and undermine Germany's as well as UK's prosperity and power.

The main message of the first part is that the industrial countries of the world have been joined together by new bonds, in particular by financial interaction that has produced a 'delicate interdependence of our credit-built finance' (p. 32). This is a novel phenomenon in world politics. It is an outcome partly of the evolution of technologies and production, and partly of increased trade. It has two primary effects. First, productive capital has become international. Second, there is no longer an obvious connection between a country's power and its wealth. One industrial state can no longer attack another and be enriched by the conquest. Angell's message, then, is not that interdependence makes war impossible, but that it makes war a losing and irrational proposition for everybody. It is not the likelihood of war which is the illusion, but the benefits of war. In an interdependent world, where even a small crisis will cause economic havoc, an all-out attack would be economic suicide.

The Human Nature of the Case

The second part of *TGI* is entitled 'The Human Nature of the Case'. It argues that neither statesmen nor scholars have understood the full importance of interdependence and the way it affects world affairs. The leaders of the great powers cling to an obsolete view of power politics, even though it endangers them all. This view is sustained by three key ideas: (i) that human beings are not fully rational; (ii) that human nature is constant; and (iii) that human existence is a struggle in which only the fittest survive.

   Angell agrees with the first of these ideas. Indeed, the claim that people's perceptions of world affairs are distorted by emotions and undermined by myths and sheer pigheadedness, runs as a red thread through his writings. Angell acknowledges that humans are endowed with reason and equipped with a capacity to learn. The problem is that they do not always apply their reason well. However, history shows that mankind learns over time. Societies reject their erroneous conceptions and replace them with more sensible views. Human societies evolve and adapt to changing circumstances, but only in the long run.

   In spite of a pessimistic view of human nature, Angell maintains an optimistic view of human evolution. Thus, he relies on social-evolutionary theories just as much as the adherents of *realpolitik*. However, Angell charges realists with being woefully ignorant of the most basic principles of these theories. They have, for example, totally misunderstood the concept of the 'survival of the fittest', because they think that 'fitness' refers to strength whereas it really refers to plasticity. The species that are the 'fittest' are those most able to adapt, not those which are physically strongest, argues Angell.[8] The Tyrannosaurus rex did not die out because it was weak; it died out because it could not adapt to changing circumstances. Adaptation, not strength, is the key concept in evolutionary theories. And if organisms are going to adapt to their environment, they must have a plastic quality to them. Anyone who invokes social-evolutionary theories to analyse human affairs must necessarily attribute plastic qualities to human nature. They cannot use evolutionary arguments and at the same time claim that human nature is constant.

   This is an elegant critique, and it demolishes the second key idea that sustains power politics: that human nature is constant. Angell then elaborates on this critique to attack the third key idea of power politics: that the best guarantee for the survival of a state is military strength. In an interdependent world, Angell argues, strength and military power give a nation no commercial advantage. 'The wealth, prosperity, and well-being of a nation depend in no way upon its political power' (p. 34). Rather, prosperity and well-being depend on the nation's ability to adapt to changing circumstances. He shows that the most rapidly growing economies in the early twentieth century did not, in fact, belong to the most powerful states but to smaller industrial countries that had neither colonies nor significant military power. The source of their welfare and their safety was not military might but their adaptability. These states had, in contrast to the Tyrannosaurus rex, successfully adapted to the changing nature of world affairs.

The conclusion

Part One of *TGI* argues that war is an irrational act in an interdependent world. War is futile. It no longer pays. Part Two adds that world's leaders do not seem to understand this. Instead, they persist in viewing world affairs in the obsolete and illusive terms of power politics. They have failed to adapt to the changing realities of world affairs. Part Three of the book assesses the political implications of these arguments and affords a piece of good advice for the statesmen of the world – especially for British leaders, to whom Angell proposes a more updated and sensible foreign policy agenda. The UK may well build battleships and introduce conscription. However, this must not be presented as preparation for war, but rather as preparation to prevent war. There is always a danger that such preparations may be misperceived and thus increase political tension. Therefore this agenda must be accompanied by a campaign to combat the 'great illusion' of the age and alter the knowledge of politicians and the popular opinion.

The eponymous great 'illusion' is, then, a collectively held, cognitive perspective sustained by an obsolete terminology that prevents statesmen and scholars from seeing the world as it really is. British, French, German and US statesmen recreate or reconstitute this dangerous 'great illusion' whenever they think and talk about world affairs. Whenever they discuss order and security in their old and obsolete terms, they reconfirm their erroneous ideas of interstate struggles and military fitness. As a consequence, they actually make the world less safe. This 'illusion' can only be dispelled by education. Since human nature is plastic and malleable, humans can learn and develop new knowledge that will change their ways and help them adapt to new realities. If collective superstitions and falsehoods have been dispelled in the past, then systematic education can purge present illusions and replace them with accurate, fact-based knowledge.

Theories and logic of persuasion

There is no denying that Angell presented a simple and forceful argument. However, it was not entirely original. Frederic Seebohm and James Lorimer had employed the term 'interdependence' a generation earlier. Ivan Bloch and William T. Stead had gauged the implications of interdependence on military affairs.[9] Angell, however, wrote more persuasively than most of them. His *TGI* sketched the outline of the trade relations of the industrial world. It showed in simple terms how the Americas, the Indies and Asia supplied raw materials to the great powers of Europe. It explained how powers like the UK and France supplied capital to Russia and Germany, investments which provided rich returns to British and French rentiers (p. 129).

However, Angell did not rely on the interdependence argument alone. *TGI*'s first three chapters present 'seven facts' about the contemporary world. The first two rely on the concept of interdependence and support the book's core argument: (i) an industrial nation can no longer conquer another because that nation would quickly find such a conquest to be commercially suicidal; (ii) the great powers of the world are joined together in a web of 'delicate interdependence of credit-built finance'. The remaining five 'facts' do not fit the overall argument as well. Two of them touch on the concepts of conquest and interdependence. The rest point to broad themes like colonialism, empire, self-determination, economic development and growth. Critics took issue with these 'facts'.[10] Angell, in turn, wrote revised editions of *TGI* in 1911 and 1912, in which he tried to answer his critics. However, he succeeded only in making his argument more complex. The effect of it all was to kick up a good deal of dust that clouded his simple main point. His central theory of interdependence was shrouded by petty controversies.

Angell on adaptation

Angell's argument of interdependence has attracted much attention. His elegant skewering of social Darwinism, however, has been largely forgotten. Yet, Angell's argument of adaptation, more affected by Spencer than by Darwin, may be both the more original and the more elegant part of his book. The way Angell invoked the concept of adaptation to demonstrate the logical inconsistency of power politics is polemically brilliant. First, he identified the basic assumptions of traditional *realpolitik* – a constant view of human nature and a view of politics as a power struggle. Then he demonstrated their flaws. Finally, he presented an alternative and progressive view of human history. His argument was simple: 'Man's irresistible drift away from conflict and towards co-operation is but the complete adaptation of the organism (man) to its environment (the planet, nature)' (p. 163). In the distant past, war might have served some purpose of group cohesion or the acquisition of land and loot. But no more. In the age of industrialism and interdependence conquest and war are destructive activities for the human species. The establishment of organizations and institutions for solidarity and cooperation, by contrast, are constructive. They increase humanity's chance of survival and further the evolution of the human species. Solidarity and cooperation fuel the evolution of industry, of productive economies and of rising wealth and prosperity. They make relations among states steadily more peaceful and orderly.[11]

   This was a seductive view for progressives. However, it ran into difficulties early in the twentieth century. The outbreak of World War I showed that Angell's view relied on an excessively optimistic notion of unilinear progress. For although the industrial states clearly grew more interdependent during the final quarter of the nineteenth century, this growth did not continue into the twentieth. It unravelled during World War I. Angell was quick to spot this flaw when war erupted in 1914 and he promptly amended his views. Before the war, he had argued that 'when nations realised the futility of conquest, they would just drop the effort'.[12] After the war he adopted a more practical view. In the 1933 edition of *TGI* he advocated an international arrangement of collective security – a 'conscious international organization of power'. Angell repeated the claim in his interwar essay 'The International Anarchy' – where the title as well as the text is rife with realist allusions.[13]

Angell and political language

It is largely overlooked that *TGI* hinged not only on the principles of interdependence and adaptation, but also on an argument about the formative effect of language on human society. Angell had long wrestled with the question of how people can cling to absurd political beliefs, even when these beliefs run counter to their own interests. This was the central question in *Patriotism under Three Flags* and *Europe's Optical Illusion*. Both books provided the same basic answer: people maintain obsolete views because 'our vocabulary is a survival of conditions no longer existing, and our mental conceptions follow at the tail of our vocabulary. International politics are still dominated by terms applicable to conditions which the process of modern life has altogether abolished'.[14] In the concluding part of *TGI*, Angell outlines the political implications of this argument. If conflict was an outcome of obsolete language, then peace could be established by replacing the old mental conceptions of that language with new ones, and ensure that they are collectively held. This was the task of education. Traditional ways of grasping the world in terms of rivalry and power must be un-learned. New concepts – like 'interdependence' and 'adaptation' – must be introduced to the discussion of world affairs to drive out the old, illusory approaches.

This discussion about the role of language in politics was, perhaps, Angell's boldest and most original contribution to the discussion of war and peace. It was, however, hazily formulated and unkindly received. E. H. Carr saw Angell as the last surviving exponent of the utopian view that the war was simply a 'failure of understanding' and that education would lead to peace.[15] Angell thinks that by changing some words in our language, we can change the world, Carr claimed.

Carr was only half right. For Angell does not really fit Carr's image of the utopian as naïve liberal, deriving doctrines of harmony from the utilitarian philosophy of Jeremy Bentham. For example, Angell did not share the Benthamite assumption of humans as fully rational creatures; he argued instead that irrational forces undermine people's common sense and rational judgement. Angell cites classic liberals like Adam Smith and J. S. Mill although none of them tally well with his argument about the nature of language. Liberals tended to quietly assume that language was a neutral tool for thought and communication. Angell entertained different views – views that were closer to Kant, Herder, Marx and others who believed language to be both a result of socialization and a socializing mechanism in its own right.

An assessment

TGI marked the beginning of Angell's extraordinary and prolific writing career. During the next four decades he published over 40 books on international affairs. He addressed a variety of themes but tended to orbit the key themes of interdependence, adaptation and the formative effect of language on politics and society. These themes provided the core of an approach which was popularly referred to as 'Norman Angellism'. Prior to World War I this approach stirred debates about the causes of war and the preconditions for peace. It inspired a great number of clubs and organizations. More than 100 peace groups, International Politics clubs, Norman Angell leagues and war and peace societies sprang up in Great Britain during the years leading up to World War I. *TGI* thrust Angell into the spotlight. The book was translated into at least 25 languages over the years. It comprehensively addressed the problems of its age. It offered a new perspective on the strife and the mounting tensions in an interdependent world. It sustained Angell's fame for years – it was instrumental in earning him a knighthood in 1931 and the Nobel Peace Prize in 1933. Yet, although it was republished in new editions after World War I, it steadily faded from view.

Why has this book largely been forgotten rather than hailed as a classic? It is tempting to borrow a line from Alan Ginsburg who explained the sudden rise and popularity of Bob Dylan in the early 1960s, by referring to him as 'a pillar of air'; as an artist of striking originality, great talent and passion but with a message so general, vague and plastic that it appealed to the tastes of many audiences and suited many political purposes. Angell, like Dylan, produced striking and passionate work. Both delivered many messages – some of them vague, some of them working at cross-purposes, yet connected to the main issues of the age. Thus, one important reason why *TGI* has been forgotten is that although the book is striking and insightful, it suffers from prolixity. It purports to address the problem of war, but its initial analysis of the Anglo-German arms race quickly fractures into colourful discussions of free trade, property rights, colonialism, conquests and confiscations. It is not a laser but a prism.

The book is a veritable *tour d'horizon* of the international scene of its times. This was undoubtedly part of its success. However, it was also its biggest problem. For as Angell spun out his argument, his simple, initial notion of interdependence was pulled in many directions.[16] This made its core argument hard to pin down. Different readers came away with different views about the prospects for war and the preconditions for peace. Thus, the book lent itself to various interpretations.

Another reason for the book's fading from memory is that it was quickly eclipsed by a wave of more scholarly competitors. Following the outbreak of war in 1914, a torrent of books was published that addressed the causes of war and preconditions for peace. Compared to these new, more academic discussions, *TGI* appeared more like a pamphlet than a sustained, scholarly analysis. Angell, like Thomas Paine, was sharp, engaging and persuasive. However, he lacked the time, the patience and the scholarly tools to develop careful theoretical arguments. In 1910 *TGI* was a fresh approach that appealed to common sense, economic theories of trade and finance and Spencer's sociology of development. However, the book was written by a skilled journalist and was hardly a work of academic scholarship. It refers to old authors like Smith and Mill often enough, but the references are sweeping and they support the argument of interdependence only in the most general of terms.[17] It omits contemporary economists and lawyers who also discuss interdependence. When Angell needed support for his arguments, he invariably drew on newspapers rather than academic books and scholarly journals. Thus, he refers to the famous journalist and editor William T. Stead who had gauged the implications of interdependence on military affairs, but he omits any mention of Ivan Bloch, upon whose original work Stead relied.[18] By 1920 Angell's lustre faded as other authors emerged – academicians who drew on history, law and the new social sciences and whose investigations contributed to the founding of IR as a scholarly discipline.[19]

TGI played a role in this founding of IR, but it was indirect. When the book was published in 1910, it greatly excited the international peace movement, and fuelled a popular debate about the causes of war and the preconditions for peace. It contributed massively to a debate that provided wide interest in and a boost to the scholarly study of international affairs. However, Angell was a journalist and a peace activist who worked the public sphere. He read and wrote for newspapers and popular journals and did not really connect with the growing academic IR community. Once the new scholarly field was established, Angell remained outside of it.

A final reason for the fading of *TGI* is that its argument was superseded by events. World War I severed the trade networks that Angell relied on for his economic argument. The Great War was succeeded by the Great Depression, which unravelled the webs of trade and finance even further. Then came World War II. In the wake of such events the concept of interdependence lost its purchase on world affairs and much of its appeal. Following World War II it took a generation to rebuild the global webs of interaction. Only during the 1970s did the world regain an international transaction density that approached pre-World War I levels. When it did, the interdependence argument resurfaced in IR scholarship. By then, however, its long history – and Angell's formative role in it – was largely forgotten.

There are many reasons why *TGI* was shifted onto a track towards oblivion rather than towards the IR Hall of Fame. Some will argue that the main responsibility for this lies with Angell, who struggled in vain to formulate a clear and parsimonious argument. Others will argue that the responsibility lies with an audience who misinterpreted the book and misunderstood its message. That it was particularly misunderstood by its most eager fans, may seem to give an ironic touch to the book's impact history. In fact, it rather confirms Angell's central thesis – namely, that most people are set in their ways and selective in their perceptions and would rather cleave to habit and old outlooks than change their views.

Notes

1 Norman Angell, *The Great Illusion: A Study of The Relation of Military Power in Nations to their Economic and Social Advantage,* London: William Heinemann, 1910. Page numbers placed in parentheses in the text refer to this edition.
2 T. G. Martin, 'The Illusions of Norman Angell', *War and Peace*, 1913, vol. 1, p. 22.
3 Norman Angell, *After All*, New York: Farrar, Straus and Young, 1951, p. 8.
4 Angell, *After All*, pp. 24ff. The story of Angell's extraordinary life is more reliably told in Martin Ceadel, *Living the Great Illusion*, Oxford: Oxford University Press, 2009.
5 Ralph Lane, *Patriotism under Three Flags*, London: T. Fisher Unwin, 1903.
6 Norman Angell, *Europe's Optical Illusion*, London: Simpkin, Marshall, Hamilton, Kent, 1909. See Torbjørn L. Knutsen, 'Norman Angell and *Europe's Optical Illusion*', *Tidsskriftet Politik*, vol. 12, 5–10.
7 Angell, *After All*, p. 163.
8 It was Herbert Spencer who coined the famous quip about 'the survival of the fittest' (see e.g. Herbert Spencer, *Principles of Biology. Vol. I*, New York: D. Appleton & Co, [1864] 1871, pp. 444ff.). Spencer, like Angell, did not equate 'fitness' with 'strength'. Angell writes mockingly that the advocates of *realpolitik* use a language that may be suitable for discussions of training studios, but not to debates on evolution.
9 Torbjørn L. Knutsen, 'A Lost Generation? IR Scholarship before World War I', *International Politics*, 2008, vol. 45, 650–74.
10 In his *The Struggle for Bread* (London: Bodley Head, 1912) Victor W. Germains protested Angell's claim that conquest never pays. William Fullerton argued that Angell entertained the simplistic notion that war was triggered by greed and misperception (William Morton Fullerton, *The Problem of Power*, New York: Charles Scribners' Sons, 1913).
11 Angell relies on examples from Charles Darwin (*Descent of Man*, New York: Barnes & Noble, [1871] 2001, p. 112) to prove his point. However, it is Spencer's sociology that provides the logic of his argument, and it is Spencer who is quoted to account for the transition from militant to industrial stages of social evolution when war no longer pays (cf. Herbert Spencer, *Political Institutions*, London: Williams and Norgate, pp. 208ff., 253ff.). See also Casper Sylvest, *British Liberal Internationalism, 1880–1930*, Manchester: Manchester University Press, 2009, pp. 106ff., 214ff.
12 Norman Angell, *TGI*, London: William Heinemann, 1933, pp. 369ff.
13 Norman Angell, 'The International Anarchy', in Leonard Woolf (ed.), *The Intelligent Man's Way to Prevent War*, London: Victor Gollancz, 1933, pp. 19–67.

14 Angell, *Europe's Optical illusion*, p. 41.

15 E. H. Carr, *The Twenty Years' Crisis,* New York: Palgrave Macmillan, [1939] 2001, p. 28.

16 This problem increased with time, as Angell tried to clarify his arguments in a steady stream of new editions of the book, but with little success. He had a tendency, as he recognized later in life, to delve into 'side issues and incidental matters arising in the course of the discussion' and to leave the main claims either buried or underdeveloped (quoted in Ceadel, *Living The Great Illusion*, p. 103).

17 *TGI* invoked several 'classical' thinkers – Aristotle, Grotius, Nietzsche and Renan to name a few. Their names, however, are merely noted in passing. They add little to the argument of the book and largely serve as academic décor. Angell cites Adam Smith and J. S. Mill and other liberal classics to substantiate his theory of interdependence, but he does not cite Seebohm or Lorimer or others who had in fact employed the term 'interdependence' to discuss changes in world trade and international law a generation earlier.

18 Alfred Fried, the founder of the German Peace Society, noticed Angell's lack of academic rigour and scholarly connections at once. He wrote to Angell and pointed out that *TGI* overlooked the works of Bloch, Novicow and other scholars whose arguments would support Angell's larger point. Angell was grateful for the tip, and added brief references to these authors in later editions of his book (Ceadel, *Living The Great Illusion*, p. 111).

19 Among these authors were John Hobson, Leonard Woolf, G. Lowes Dickinson, Alfred Zimmern, David P. Heatley, S. H. Allen and James Bryce (see Knutsen, 'A Lost Generation?').

3 A democratic critique of the state: G. Lowes Dickinson's *The European Anarchy*

Jeanne Morefield

In a 1934 biography of friend and mentor Goldsworthy Lowes Dickinson, E. M. Forster noted that 'with the possible exception of *The Choice Before Us*', all that Dickinson wrote 'between 1914 and 1918 is likely to be forgotten'.[1] Forster could not have been more wrong. Dickinson's 1916 book *The European Anarchy* (hereafter *EA*), which Forster described as a 'short, historical survey', would have enduring impact on the discipline of International Relations (IR) by first popularizing the term 'international anarchy'.[2] Generations of IR scholars have embraced the fundamentally anarchic nature of the international realm as their stock-in-trade, and critics of the idea have been forced to respond to the central role it has played in the discursive terrain of the discipline.[3] Ironically, however, since World War II, the majority of IR scholars writing about the concept have tended to draw very different moral, political and conceptual lessons from the idea of international anarchy than those drawn by Dickinson. When read closely for its content rather than just its title, *EA* calls both the anarchic state system and the state form itself into question in ways that continue to challenge some of the discipline's fundamental assumptions.

This chapter explores Dickinson's challenge to contemporary IR scholarship by looking more closely at *EA* in its historical context. After briefly examining Dickinson's life and career it moves on to discuss how the term 'international anarchy' has been absorbed into contemporary IR discourse. It then looks more closely at the text itself, paying particular attention to Dickinson's intellectual influences and his critique of sovereignty. It concludes by arguing that, although Dickinson's critique of sovereignty was not conceptually well developed, it did suggest an expanded form of global democratic accountability that made *EA* both ahead of its time and a text of enduring interest for international thought.

Historical background and reception

Born in 1862, Dickinson attended King's College, Cambridge, UK, and in 1887 was elected to a fellowship at King's where he stayed (aside from brief periods of travelling) until his death in 1935. Dickinson had an enormous influence on what Roger Fry described as 'generation after generation of undergraduates' including Forster and Keynes.[4] In addition to *EA*, Dickinson published a wide range of books, plays and dialogues throughout his career, including *Revolution and Reaction in Modern France* (1892), *Letters from a Chinese Official* (1901), *Goethe and Faust* (1928), and *Plato and His Dialogues* (1932). As the breadth of these texts suggests, Dickinson's career stands as testament to an intellectual life led before the concretion of academic specialization.

He has been variously described as a classicist, a historian and a political scientist, and his work on international relations was deeply influenced by an overall critical humanist perspective on intellectual inquiry that embraced a variety of historical, philosophical, literary and political perspectives.

EA occupies a somewhat unique status in the IR canon. The concept it inaugurated has had a considerable impact on the shape of the discipline, but few scholars have dwelt for any length of time on the text itself or the political theory of the author. Hedley Bull, for instance, argued in 1966 that international anarchy was 'the central fact of international life and the starting point of theorizing about it', and later, in *The Anarchical Society,* that the phrase itself was 'made famous by Goldsworthy Lowes Dickinson'.[5] However, Bull never examined Dickinson's work in any detail and never mentioned *EA* again. Likewise, Martin Wight's *International Theory* identified international anarchy as one of the 'three traditions' of international political thought and yet not once evoked Dickinson's name.[6]

Perhaps because international anarchy is a fundamentally structuring principle of their theories, neo-realists will occasionally discuss Dickinson but always, like Bull, in a fleeting, gestural manner. In *Man, the State, and War*, Kenneth Waltz referred briefly to Dickinson's reversal 'of the dominant inside-out' explanation of world politics but gave no details of Dickinson's thought.[7] More recently, John Mearsheimer has argued that '[p]robably the best brief for offensive realism is a short, obscure book written during World War I by G. Lowes Dickinson, a British academic who was an early advocate of the League of Nations'.[8] But while Mearsheimer quotes briefly from *EA* in *The Tragedy of Great Power Politics*, he makes no inquiry into the book's argument, noting merely that his own book will develop the fully fledged account of 'offensive' realism that Dickinson evidently failed to theorize adequately in 1916.

For neo-realist theorists like Mearsheimer who assume anarchy to be a permanent and 'tragic' fact of international life, the biggest problem is that Dickinson did not make this assumption. Rather, he was a firm believer in what Bull describes as the 'second doctrine' of international anarchy, which 'accepts the description' but then 'combines it with the demand that the international anarchy be brought to an end'.[9] In this respect, international anarchy was not the only IR term Dickinson invented; he is also widely credited with coining the term 'league of nations'. During World War I, Dickinson set aside his usual academic life to devote himself 'as far as there was any opportunity for such work, to propaganda for a league of nations'.[10] In September 1914, shortly after the onset of the war, Dickinson wrote a pamphlet entitled *The War and the Way Out* in which he articulated the first, systematic plan for a 'permanent league' of European nations capable of both adjudicating and enforcing international law.[11] This pamphlet provided the first blueprint for a post-war league and pro-league working groups in the UK and the USA quickly seized upon it as a model for their own proposals.[12]

In contrast to post-war IR theorists like Mearsheimer, scholars of the history of international thought in the twentieth century do not ignore this part of Dickinson's life but often they tend to go to the other extreme by reducing his writings on international politics to simple reflections on his activism. Both Michael Joseph Smith and Andreas Osiander, for instance, argue that Dickinson's understanding of international anarchy was conditioned almost exclusively by this moral commitment to the league of nations idea. For Smith, Dickinson's insistence that war was 'not a fatal product of human nature' situated him firmly within the camp of 'idealist provocateurs' against whom interwar realists like Carr would eventually position themselves.[13] Osiander goes further, arguing that Dickinson's commitment to the league of nations idea infected his work with a tone of moralism that kept it from rising to a level of focused paradigmatic rigour. Rather, according to Osiander, Dickinson's work ought to be considered a reflection of his 'cast of mind or political creed'.[14]

However, to reduce Dickinson's theory of international anarchy to a mere reflection of his political sympathies does as much of a disservice to his broader vision as does the neo-realist refusal to engage his politics. Both approaches fail to take the actual content of Dickinson's critique seriously and thus, both fail to capture the essence of that which makes *EA* such a radically suggestive text to this day: the critical analysis of state sovereignty that is its *raison d'être*.

Intellectual influences and Dickinson's critique of sovereignty

The fact that Dickinson was interested in the question of sovereignty prior to and during World War I is hardly surprising given the number of pluralist scholars mounting forceful critiques of the modern state during this period. 'Pluralism' in this context does not refer to the school of IR thought later articulated by Hedley Bull and others. In his work, Bull distinguished between 'solidarist' approaches to international thought based on theorizing universal norms of political order and 'pluralist' notions grounded in the primacy of the sovereign state as the key actor in international relations.[15] By contrast, the central aim of the English pluralists was to call the very necessity of the sovereign state into question. From the late nineteenth century through the first decade of the twentieth century, Neville Figgis developed a critique of the late medieval state through a reading of Otto von Gierke that was then adapted and expanded by English pluralists such as G. D. H. Cole and Harold Laski as well as the French legal theorist Leon Duguit. Central to Cole, Laski and Duguit's understanding of contemporary politics was an excoriating account of the modern, juridical view of sovereignty that privileged a centralizing state over already existing, imbricated and endangered forms of political authority.[16]

One can see a similar, if nascent, critique of sovereignty developing throughout Dickinson's pre-war writings. As a humanist with a pressing interest in the ability of human beings to challenge entrenched cultural, moral and political world views, Dickinson's diverse reflections on social issues, literature and philosophy frequently pushed up against the borders of the modern idea of statehood. In *Letters from a Chinese Official*, for instance, Dickinson's fictitious Chinese observer complained that Europeans 'have dissolved all human and personal ties', and then endeavoured to replace these social networks with 'the impersonal activity of the State'.[17] In 1908 Dickinson expanded upon this idea in *Justice and Liberty: A Political Dialogue* by having the protagonist develop an impassioned critique of the relationship between 'individualist' accounts of accumulation and a form statehood ruled by the interests of the 'governing class'.[18] Just prior to the war, Dickinson wrote a play entitled 'War and Peace: A Dramatic Fantasia'. This never-performed play contained a veritable mayhem of unruly characters meant to represent not only countries (the UK, Germany, the USA, China) but also political ideologies (socialists, suffragettes, futurists), human emotions, political parties and the occasional archangel (one of whom is named Norman).[19] The end of the play leaves the reader with the distinct impression that sovereign states are simply incapable of containing the raucous, heterogeneous shenanigans of the world's people.

   Thus, while Brian Schmidt has argued that the outbreak of the war prompted
Dickinson to 'completely change' intellectual directions, away from a study of classics
and literature towards an analysis of international relations, Dickinson's earlier writings
suggest that he was interested in at least one of its aspects, sovereignty, well before the
war.[20] For Forster, the onset of hostilities in 1914 simply intensified what he describes
as Dickinson's already established 'holy war' against 'the anthropomorphic State'.[21]
However, the real war did prompt Dickinson to reconfigure the aim of his own 'holy war'.
While other pluralists like Laski and Cole also wrote about the relationship between
the state and international politics during this period, their primary goal was not to
develop a theory of international relations but, rather, to formulate an 'anti-statist
group socialism'.[22] Dickinson, by contrast, shifted his emphasis towards analysis of the
relationship between the state's internal and external dimensions. Sylvest has argued
that while many British internationalists during World War I and the interwar period
were influenced by pluralist critiques of the state, 'no leading internationalists pro-
fessed to be a pluralist', particularly once they became involved with the pragmatic
politics of the League of Nations and its 'state centered internationalism'.[23] Dickinson,
however, was somewhat of an exception to this rule. For all that he supported the
League, Dickinson's evolving theory of international politics, as articulated first in *EA*
and then in *The International Anarchy*[24] (hereafter *IA*), was premised on a pluralist
inflected critique of the state itself, and on a belief that any analysis of global politics
capable of imagining peace must assume a 'complete and radical change of policy, not
in this or that State, but in all States'.[25]
   The first inklings of Dickinson's approach to international politics were apparent
from the very inception of the war when he baulked at the enthusiasm with which most
English historians threw their scholarly authority behind the claim that Germany was
solely responsible for the conflict because of a flaw in its national culture.[26] By contrast,
Dickinson insisted that the war was caused not by the actions or dispositions of any
one state but by a problem inherent in the nature of modern sovereignty itself, a critique evident in his 1914 pamphlet, *The War and the Way Out.* While this text has
been cited by historians largely for the fact that it contained the first references to the
league of nations idea in the UK, it also entailed a vigorous critique of what
Dickinson referred to as the 'governmental theory' of international politics. Dickinson
described the 'governmental theory' through an ironic parody of a realist jeremiad
against pacifism:

> The world is divided politically into States. These States are a kind of abstract
> being, distinct from the men, women, and children who inhabit them. They are in
> perpetual and inevitable antagonism to one another … That being so, war is an
> eternal necessity.[27]

Dickinson's parody here suggested there was nothing 'factually' true about the state
form. In the spirit of early twentieth-century pluralism, he both acknowledged that
states were powerful political organizations but also insisted that they were abstrac-
tions, legal fictions, real but also 'distinct' from the human beings that comprised
them.[28] Speaking in the voice of an impatient realist, tut-tutting at the pacifist's
inability to grasp the imperilled heart of the situation, Dickinson suggests that this
fictive form of international political organization had become so naturalized that
alternatives to its logic looked like an affront to the 'facts' of the world.

Dickinson's argument in *The War and the Way Out* spoke volumes about the pluralist direction of his international thought at the very beginning of the war. However, the argument itself was based largely on Dickinson's intuitions about the international climate. Dickinson himself later admitted that he had 'made, at the time, no special study of international relations' and to the reader it is clear that the argument itself falls flat in a number of places.[29] This lack of rigour was a problem that Dickinson himself clearly understood and which he spent the next two years addressing by engaging in a careful study of the 'circumstances and events' that led up to the war. In the process, he took his largely unformed 'governmental theory' and translated it into a more nuanced analysis of the relationship between sovereignty and what he now termed the international anarchy.

The result was *EA*, which can be understood as Dickinson's test drive of the historical methodology and conceptual apparatus he later used to write *IA*, a work he described to a friend as 'a more serious and laboured book'.[30] Dickinson clearly saw *EA* as his first foray into the study of international politics and as an attempt to fuse the core intuition of his anti-war writings (that 'Europe had long been a powder magazine') with a historical inquiry that focused on the events leading up to the war.[31] In this spirit, Dickinson mined sources as diverse as diplomatic cables and the private letters of foreign correspondents, from both combatants and neutral states alike, for insight into the way domestic populations, diplomats, the press and statesmen understood the build-up to the conflict.[32] The goal of this inquiry was, first, to refute the predominant nationalist interpretation that blamed the war entirely on German aggression. More importantly, however, the book aimed to demonstrate that leaders in the UK, France and Germany alike all believed, in the years leading up to the war, that the intentions of other states were aggressive and that their own state's protection required military and territorial expansion. Dickinson's historical dissection of available materials suggested, in contrast, that the war was a by-product of sovereign state aggression combined with an international system constructed around sovereign states. War emerged from the 'normal working of the European anarchy,' where everything jingoistic, aggressive and violent about states went unconstrained by any higher power or law (p. 105).

The notion of international anarchy that Dickinson developed in this text was explicitly indebted to Hobbes. As Hobbes noted in *The Leviathan*, in 'the condition of mere nature', self-interested and pugnacious individuals will fall into a state of 'anarchy' characterized by a perpetual 'war of all against all', a condition that only ends with the creation of the forceful sovereign state.[33] However, in the international realm, anarchy never ends. 'Persons Artificial' remained in a state of perfect liberty in relationship to each other and therefore in a state of constant war or the threat of war 'with their frontiers armed, and canons planted against their neighbours round about'.[34] Dickinson argued similarly that where there was an 'aggregation of states' relating to each other in the absence of common law and common force, then 'there will be what Hobbes truly asserted to be the essence of such a situation, a chronic state of war, open or veiled' (p. 14). For Dickinson, because the motivation behind the ideology of statehood was the aggrandizement of the state itself, because there were no ethical and legal limits on this aggrandizement, and because nothing succeeds like success, all states could and eventually would fall before the logic of expansion and jingoism. 'It is not only the jingoism of Germany that Europe has to fear', he argued, 'it is the jingoism that success may make supreme in any country that may be victorious' (p. 132). Under conditions where states have no incentive but to behave aggressively, peace itself was merely 'latent war', during which time states armed themselves in a manner they might argue was intended to be defensive but which was always motivated by the underlying aggression of *raison d'état*. When overt war broke out 'some one state' might be the 'immediate offender', argued Dickinson, but the 'main and permanent offence is common to all states. It is the anarchy which they are all responsible for perpetuating' (ibid.).

Dickinson's use of Hobbes here is interesting and slightly counterintuitive. He was not a Hobbes scholar and it is clear from both his published writings and his papers that he never wrote about Hobbes outside of *EA* and *IA*. More importantly, as a humanist with a deep and abiding faith in people's capacity for critical reason, Dickinson's notion of human nature could not have been more different from that of Hobbes who believed that individuals themselves were always motivated by the self-oriented, expansive desires identical to those that Dickinson ascribes to states. By contrast, Dickinson's patent refusal to theorize about human nature beyond what he saw as the basic desire of human beings to seek the good was one of the most outstanding features of his personality and his scholarship, and perhaps what most differentiated his ontological impulses from both Hobbes and those of later human nature realists such as Morgenthau. In the words of George Santayana, Dickinson 'prayed, watched, and labored to redeem human life, and began by refusing to understand what human life is'.[35] In effect, this refusal to 'understand' human life meant that Dickinson never believed war to be the inevitable result of something inherently violent or self-absorbed in human nature.[36] The question for Dickinson was not 'why do people fight?' in a general sense but, rather, 'how do organized political communities enable fighting?' We could be 'social animals', we could even be driven by a 'herd' instinct arising from some residual, primitive sense of family. That, however, was a question 'for biologists to settle'. All we know about people, Dickinson argued, is that they are creators of institutions and communities that sometimes 'shape' individuals into forms that can become dangerous.[37] War, argued Dickinson, 'is not a fatal product of human nature. It is an effect of that nature when put under certain conditions', namely, the conditions of sovereign statehood.[38]

It is equally curious that Dickinson was writing about Hobbes's understanding of anarchy well before Hobbes had become an iconic figure of twentieth-century IR.[39] So, whence came Dickinson's reading of Hobbes? While it is possible that he might have been imitating a language already brought into limited circulation in the USA during this time by scholars of international law, Dickinson did not mention such influences.[40] Rather, it is more likely, given his intellectual inclinations and circles, that his reading of Hobbes was influenced by the historical sensibilities of the English pluralists such as Laski who identified Hobbes with the historical emergence of a particularly modern theory of the monistic, juridical state.[41]

Dickinson's use of Hobbes in *EA* was similarly historical and similarly critical. He evoked Hobbes in the earliest pages of the book in the same paragraph in which he located the origins of modern international conflict in a particular historical moment. In a manner as grave and rhetorically bombastic as Rousseau's claim that the origins of inequality could be found in the actions of the first man to enclose a plot of land and then 'take it into his head to say *this is mine*', Dickinson identified the 'turning point' in the 'great and tragic history of Europe' with 'the emergence of the sovereign State at the end of the fifteenth century' (p. 13). Dickinson labelled the theory behind this emergence 'Machiavellianism' because it took the state as both the end and means of politics. The combination of this state-oriented theory, Dickinson argued, with the deepening historical involvement of European nations in expansive colonial projects during the sixteenth century produced an international political environment characterized primarily by the 'mutual aggression and defense of beings living in a "state of nature"'(p. 16).

There is, then, nothing transcendental or ahistorical about Dickinson's use of Hobbes in *EA*. Unlike later IR theorists, Dickinson turned to Hobbes' description of the 'chronic state of war' not to provide him with an essentialized account of the state as it naturally is but, rather, to understand better why states – and the populations they contain – behave the way they do under modern historical conditions. For Dickinson, Hobbes' observations on the anarchic nature of international politics were descriptively correct while his ontological assumptions about human nature were wrong. Thus, the international anarchy was never, for Dickinson, a *fait accompli*. Rather, it was always potentially subject to the transformative interventions of human beings themselves.

Dickinson's challenge to contemporary IR

Like Dickinson, many IR scholars today accept anarchy as the basic state of affairs in international politics. They differ, of course, in their understandings of how far it is possible, within such a system, to sustain peaceful relations between states. Offensive realists such as Mearsheimer have argued that the 'tragedy' of great power politics arises from the fact that, under conditions of anarchy, states have no option but to look for opportunities to maximize power. Others, like Waltz, Keohane and Nye argue that the features of anarchy actually do not rule out cooperation between states pursuing, in Waltz's words, an 'appropriate amount of power', while constructivists such as Wendt theorize 'cultures' of anarchy.[42] For Dickinson, however, the process of identifying sources of international conflict went beyond merely grappling with the relationships *between* states. Rather, as noted above, Dickinson was also concerned with the form of the modern state itself. In other words, most contemporary adherents to the notion of international anarchy accept the sovereign state as the fundamental, constitutive unit of analysis, the past and future existence of which is rarely called into question. Realists, neo-realists, and constructivists may disagree about the reasons *why* states want power or even *if* they want power, but they rarely historicize the state form itself, nor do they imagine that this form might be sufficiently altered so as to fundamentally change the nature of international politics. By neither historicizing nor problematizing the state, these thinkers reiterate a distinction between the discrete realms of domestic and international politics that obscures the connection between what happens within states and international politics.[43]

By contrast, *EA* and *IA* were concerned with the way that the modern state form itself engendered violent international conflict. In this sense, Mearsheimer is right to notice a certain similarity between his own account of 'offensive' realism and Dickinson's approach. In both theories, states are driven towards aggression. For Mearsheimer this aggression takes the form of great power competition for global hegemony, while Dickinson understood it as a 'rivalry for empire between all the Great Powers', but in both cases, the tendency remains the same (p. 130). However, for Mearsheimer, this 'offensive' behaviour is generated by the anarchic system itself. By contrast, for Dickinson, the fact that the international system was anarchic served to exacerbate the fundamental problems inherent in the modern state form. *EA* and *IA* thus both read, to a large extent, like extended litanies of examples where states reconfigured basic human impulses or compelled national populations to behave badly. For instance, during the Great War, all governments on either side of the conflict appealed to the holistic, self-justifying rhetoric of statehood, Dickinson argued, to convince their populations of the malevolence of other states such that 'to each set of belligerents the war appears as one forced upon them by sheer wickedness' (p. 130). Rampant nationalism, for Dickinson, was not a unique cultural flaw of the Germans but, rather, intrinsic to the very process by which all states obscured internal diversity of opinions, transforming complicated societies into seamless projections of wholes. It is 'misleading', Dickinson argued, 'to talk of "Germany" and the "German" attitude. There is every kind of German attitude' (p. 84). Dickinson also argued that this same logic could compel not just groups but also individuals to engage in behaviour they ordinarily would understand as wrong. He illustrated this phenomenon with a striking example drawn from an incident in the *Life of Salisbury*, where the Russian ambassador, Ignatieff, attempted to redraw the frontier lines on a contested map during the 1877 Constantinople Conference and then, when caught in the act, blithely admitted to cheating without a trace of guilt.[44] For Dickinson, this example highlighted precisely how the logic of *raison d'état* could turn perfectly moral individuals into liars.

By emphasizing Dickinson's critique of the state here I do not mean to suggest that his account of international anarchy was in some way secondary or incidental to his analysis of international politics. Rather, I wish to emphasize the extent to which Dickinson believed these two problems – the problem of sovereignty and the problem of anarchy – to be intimately connected. Preventing violence on a global scale, for Dickinson, required severing the connection between an international 'state of nature' and the splenetic, self-absorbed, obfuscating impulses of the modern state form in two ways. First, in *EA,* Dickinson called again (as he had in *The War and the Way Out*) for the creation of an international organization capable of checking state power and enforcing international law. Dickinson's second claim was far bolder, however, in its suggestion that transforming the condition of 'latent war' into long-term peace required not just the creation of international institutions but the fostering of a new culture of international democratic accountability which entailed a widespread rejection by the world's people of the self-contained notion of statehood with its 'complex of feeling, prejudice, tradition, and false theory' (p. 141). Dickinson, thus, proposed to break the back of *raison d'état* by exposing it to the democratic sanction of the very people in whose name politicians and diplomats claimed to act, arguing that 'nations, called democratic, should really become so in their foreign policy as well as in their domestic affairs' (p. 139). In other words, given that sovereign states corrupted even the best of their representatives (e.g. Ignatieff) Dickinson proposed a transparent, democratic approach wherein states were prevented from engaging in militarist expansion, annexation, or imperial overreach 'behind the back of the public for reasons which cannot be avowed' (p. 140). In this way, Dickinson's solution to the problem of anarchy by necessity entailed a marked re-imagining of contemporary sovereignty with its bounded, inward-looking scope for democratic politics.

It is this conceptual move in *EA* – the move which requires anyone concerned with international politics to rethink the relationship between sovereignty and democracy – that has driven so many contemporary readers of Dickinson either to ignore his politics altogether (e.g. Mearsheimer) or to dismiss him as a moralizer (e.g. Smith and Osiander.) For the majority of contemporary realists nothing could be more idealistic than suggesting that states cede power in international affairs, the very thing that makes them sovereign, to the direct will of their people. Dickinson, by contrast, argued that this attitude was self-fulfilling, that when enough 'soldiers, sailors, politicians, journalists, and plain men' believed both Machiavellianism and the international anarchy to be 'unalterable' they also contributed to making it so. Those, he maintained, 'who hold this philosophy also devote their lives to making sure that it shall come true; for it is impossible to hold any view about life without thereby contributing to its realization'.[45] Dickinson never entertained the possibility that an anarchic world of power-driven, unaccountable states was a permanent condition, and would be appalled by the way many contemporary IR scholars theorize around and about it as if the object itself – international anarchy – was an immutable fact. Writing from both the middle and in the immediate wake of the most devastating war anyone had ever imagined, Dickinson simply refused to accept this.

Conclusion

While Dickinson's critique of sovereignty and its relationship to international anarchy in *EA* is highly suggestive, it should be noted that in some ways it is not entirely coherent. For instance, Dickinson argued throughout *EA* that modern states were moved by a basic 'will to power' and that, in the context of an international system unable to check that power, war was inevitable. However, it is never entirely clear from Dickinson's writings *why* modern states behaved this way. For Hobbes and Morgenthau, states reflected the self-oriented nature of human beings, a conclusion that Dickinson, as a humanist, rejected. By contrast, Dickinson's analysis reversed this causation, casting modern states as the reason why human beings acted aggressively rather than imagining states as mirror images of human nature. Dickinson's critique located the aggressive tendencies of states in a particularly modern historical moment and thus resisted attempts to naturalize either the state or human nature. However, he never fully explained why it is that, since Machiavelli, the ideology of *raison d'état* has reigned supreme. It is also not clear from his analysis how a people, thoroughly conditioned by the jingoism and violence of state ideology, could purge themselves of their 'prejudices and preconceptions' (p. 17) and transform their politics. Thus, it is not entirely surprising that, during the last century, IR scholars have tended to use the term 'international anarchy' as a place-holder for their own interpretations of the international system rather than wrestle with Dickinson's more internally complicated and often conceptually messy critique of the state.

In addition, the actual policy details of Dickinson's first solution for solving the problems of international anarchy (the creation of international institutions) were both far milder than, and strangely out of sync with, the audacity of his call for 'a radical change' in the spirit of international politics that would broaden the ambit of democratic accountability (p. 136). Dickinson thus argued, for instance, that states must relinquish some of their sovereignty in order to create a 'kind of machinery for settling their disputes and organizing their common purposes' (p. 152), but the shape of that machinery remained remarkably vague in *EA*. Indeed, this language of 'machinery' itself resonated squarely with the way that mainstream, liberal members of the League of Nations Union (none of whom were interested in a radical transformation of sovereignty) also talked about the post-war world.[46] However, even the least mainstream aspect of Dickinson's institutional proposals – his suggestion that this international body serve as 'a real and effective counterpoise to aggression from any Power in the future' by maintaining international peace 'by force' (p. 152) – seems, oddly, to reproduce the very problem of sovereignty on a global level. In other words, it is not clear from Dickinson's analysis why an interstate body with the capacity to 'overawe' its members in a Hobbesian sense would behave any less aggressively or would warp human nature any less than a body aimed at 'overawing' its citizens on a domestic level.

In the final analysis, then, it is not Dickinson's specific ideas about international institutions but, rather, his more general call for a disruption of the theory of democracy that situated accountability within the inward looking purview of the sovereign state, which makes *EA* both a prescient and enduringly suggestive text for our time. Since sovereign states tended to rationalize power in their own interest and condition their citizens to do likewise, the only real 'guarantee of peace' Dickinson argued, lay in the democratization of foreign policy. Together with a few other radicals at the time associated with the Union of Democratic Control, Dickinson argued in *EA* that the sheath of sovereign authority (adumbrated by the power of secret diplomacy), which surrounded the modern state must become more porous to the democratic will of its citizens thus empowering these citizens to not only guide foreign policy but to hold their own states accountable for violations of international law. Only this, he argued, would render international law itself more than 'a cobweb stretched before the mouth of a cannon' (p. 142). In this sense, Dickinson's work prefigured that of contemporary cosmopolitan theorists such as David Held who similarly push the notion of democratic accountability beyond the state, as well as that of pluralists like William Connolly who strive to decentralize our democratic imaginary in a globalized world by insisting upon a 'compromise of sovereignty in both its "internal" and "external" manifestations'.[47] While, disappointingly, *EA* never theorized what such a 'compromise' might look like, Dickinson's work stands as an early gesture towards the possibility of an international politics in which global citizens are able to hold individual states to account for their actions in the world. And, in an era of WikiLeaks, when the aggressive, non-democratic, violent practices of states are increasingly visible to all, Dickinson's challenge to 'secret diplomacy' and his push for democratic control of international politics seems both more necessary and possible than ever. If we understand a classic to be a work of enduring interest and relevance for our times, few texts in the history of contemporary IR match *EA*.

Notes

1 E. M. Forster, *Goldsworthy Lowes Dickinson*, New York: Harcourt Brace, 1934, p. 173.
2 Goldsworthy Lowes Dickinson, *The European Anarchy,* London: Macmillan, 1916. Page numbers placed in parentheses in the text refer to this edition.
3 See Ian Hall, 'World Government as Empire: The International Historian as Theorist', *International Affairs*, 2006, vol. 82, p. 1161.
4 Memoir of Goldsworthy Lowes Dickinson published by King's College, January 1933. See The Papers of Goldsworthy Lowes Dickinson, King's College, Cambridge, hereafter King's/ PP/GLD/6/10/Bibliographia/fol.17. Thanks to King's for allowing me access to the papers.
5 Hedley Bull, 'Sovereignty and Anarchy in International Relations', in Herbert Butterfield and Martin Wight (eds), *Diplomatic Investigations: Essays in the Theory of International Politics,* London: Allen and Unwin, 1966, p. 35; Hedley Bull, *The Anarchical Society*, New York: Columbia University Press, 1977, p. 47.
6 Martin Wight, *International Theory: Three Traditions*, New York: Holmes and Meier, 1991, p. 7.
7 Kenneth Waltz, *Man the State and War*, New York: Columbia University Press, 1959, p. 10.

8 John Mearsheimer, *The Tragedy of Great Power Politics*, Chicago, IL: University of Chicago Press, 2001, p. 21. See also B. I. Plank, 'Goldsworthy Lowes Dickinson and the Causes of War: A Theoretical and Historical Analysis', PhD, LSE, 2011.
9 Bull, 'Society and Anarchy', p. 38.
10 G. Lowes Dickinson, *The Autobiography of G. Lowes Dickinson*, ed. Dennis Proctor, London: Duckworth, 1973, p. 190.
11 G. Lowes Dickinson, *The War and the Way Out*, London: The Chancery Lane Press, 1914, p. 39.
12 See Henry Winkler, *The League of Nations Movement in Great Britain*, New Brumswich, NJ: Rutgers University Press, 1952, pp. 16–18; George Egerton, *Great Britain and the Creation of the League of Nations*, Chapel Hill, NC: University of North Carolina Press, 1978, p. 8.
13 Michael Smith, *Realist Thought From Weber to Kissinger*, Baton Rouge, LA: Louisiana State Press, 1986, pp. 55–56.
14 Andreas Osiander, 'Re-reading Early Twentieth Century IR Theory: Idealism Revisited', *International Studies Quarterly,* 1998, vol. 42, p. 413.
15 See Hedley Bull, 'The Grotian Conception of International Society', in Kai Alderson and Andrew Hurrell (eds), *Hedley Bull on International Society*, New York: Macmillan, 2000.
16 See G. D. H. Cole, 'The Nature of the State and Its External Relations', *Proceedings of the Aristotelian Society*, 1915–16, vol. 16; Harold Laski, 'The Pluralist State', *The Philosophical Review*, 1919, vol. 28; Leon Duguit, *Les Transformations du Droit Public*, Paris: Armand Colin, 1913.
17 G. Lowes Dickinson, *Letters from a Chinese Official,* New York: McClure and Phillips, 1903, p. 15.
18 G. Lowes Dickinson, *Justice and Liberty; A Political Dialogue*, New York: Doubleday, 1920, p. 132.
19 G. Lowes Dickinson, 'War and Peace: A Dramatic Fantasia,' King's/PP/GLD/4/3/Plays.
20 Brian Schmidt, *The Political Discourse of Anarchy*, New York: SUNY Albany Press, 1998, p. 160.
21 Forster, *Dickinson*, p. 159.
22 See Isaac Kramnick and Barry Sheerman's analysis of Cole and Laski, in *Harold Laski: A Life on the Left*, New York: Penguin Press, 1993, p. 251,
23 Casper Sylvest, 'Beyond the State? Pluralism and Internationalism in Early Twentieth-Century Britain', *International Relations*, 2007, vol. 21, p. 80.
24 Dickinson, *The International Anarchy*, London: Century, 1926.
25 Dickinson, *Autobiography*, p. 144.
26 See Catherine Cline 'British Historians and the Treaty of Versailles', *Albion: A Quarterly Journal Concerned with British Studies*, 1988, vol. 20, p. 46.
27 Dickinson, *War and the Way Out*, p. 9.
28 The notion of the unified state as a fiction had already been well developed at this time by Duguit.
29 Dickinson, *Autobiography*, p. 194.
30 Letter to A. J. Grant, 1926, King's/PP/GLD/5/11/5/Correspondence/fol.8.
31 Dickinson, *Autobiography*, p. 194.
32 Dickinson later described his approach to writing *EA* in characteristically humble terms as 'right enough, as anyone could easily be right (if that were any good) by merely standing aloof' (letter to A. J. Grant, 1926, King's/PP/GLD/5/11/5/Correspondence/fol.8).
33 Thomas Hobbes, *The Leviathan*, Harmondsworth: Penguin Classics, 1985, p. 395.
34 Hobbes, *Leviathan,* p. 266.
35 George Santayana, *My Host the World*, London: Cresset Press, 1953, p. 31.
36 Dickinson, *Causes of International War*, New York: Harcourt Brace and Howe, 1920, p. 9.
37 Dickinson, *Causes of International War*, p. 10.
38 Dickinson, *Causes of International War*, p. 16
39 On the discovery of Hobbes as an IR thinker see David Armitage, 'Hobbes and the Foundations of Modern International Thought', in James Tully and Annabel Brett (eds), *Rethinking the Foundations of Modern Political Thought*, Cambridge: Cambridge University Press, 2006.
40 See Schmidt, *Political Discourse of Anarchy*, pp. 151–88.
41 Laski, *Pluralist State*, p. 568.
42 See the chapters by Schmidt, Wivel, and Chong in this volume.
43 For an account of this distinction see Helen Milner, 'The Assumption of Anarchy in International Relations Theory: A Critique', *Review of International Studies*, 1991, vol. 17, 67–85.

Milner does not mention Dickinson in this article and understands the idea of international anarchy as a strictly post-war phenomenon.

44 *IA*, p. 27.

45 *IA*, p. 47.

46 Such as Gilbert Murray, Lionel Curtis, and Alfred Zimmern. For an example of the language of 'machinery' see Zimmern, *The League of Nations and the Rule of Law*, London: Macmillan, 1936.

47 In particular, see Held's notion of the 'most affected' in his introduction to *Global Governance and Public Accountability*, New York: Wiley-Blackwell, 2005. See also William Connolly, 'Democracy and Territoriality', in Frederick Dolan and Thomas Dumm (eds), *Rhetorical Republic: Governing Representations in American Politics*, Amherst, MA: University of Massachusetts Press, 1993, p. 250.

4 Attacking Hitler in England: patriarchy, class and war in Virginia Woolf's *Three Guineas*

Peter Wilson[1]

'Scarcely a human being in the course of history has fallen to a woman's rifle'.[2]

One of the most original essays on international politics written during the first half of the twentieth century is not obviously about international politics. Its title, echoing with a class twist Brecht's *Threepenny Opera*,[3] gives no clue to its contents. Staple issues such as diplomacy, the League, sanctions, foreign policy and collective security are not covered. Its starting point is a simple question: how can we go about preventing war? The answer it gives is anything but simple: we can only begin to think about this question once we have reflected on the society and the civilization (hierarchical, patriarchal, acquisitive and pugnacious) we (or rather men) have constructed. As a mode of writing the essay defies easy categorization. It is more than a polemical essay but less than a social or political treatise. As one would expect from one of the most important novelists of the twentieth century, it is a piece of imaginative writing. Yet it brims with facts, footnotes and references. Froula describes it as 'an epistolary essay, a compound public letter'.[4]

Themes

The subtitle of *Three Guineas* could be 'Preventing War from the Woman's Angle'.[5] Interestingly, Virginia Woolf had considered 'Men Are Like That' as a possible title, and the book was serialized in *Atlantic Monthly* under the Euripidean 'Women Must Weep, or Unite Against War'.[6] It takes its cue from a letter from a certain gentleman representing a certain political society asking its recipient (i.e. Woolf) to join that society, subscribe to its funds and sign a certain manifesto. The letter contains the question (p. 153): 'How in your opinion are we to prevent war?' This is the stimulus for what follows: a series of ratiocinations on how a woman of a certain class might go about answering that letter, 'a letter ... perhaps unique in the history of human correspondence, since when before has an educated man asked a woman how in her opinion war can be prevented?' (ibid.). Woolf's correspondent is middle-aged, educated, comfortable, but still socially engaged having not yet settled for the 'contended apathy of middle life' (p. 154). We later learn that he is a lawyer (p. 167), a member of the English Bar (p. 173), and an Oxford graduate (p. 189). In the process of composing her reply, the author feels compelled to respond first to two further letters that have been lying unanswered for some time on her desk. The first is from an honorary treasurer appealing for money to help rebuild a ladies' college. The second is from an honorary secretary requesting a subscription to a society dedicated to helping young women find positions in the professions.[7] What on the surface appear to be separate requests are shown to be highly interdependent. The guinea symbolizes the sum of earned income the author is eventually prepared to conditionally grant to each.

It is impossible to do justice in a summary to the many layers of meaning and the complex arguments within *Three Guineas*. It is undoubtedly the product of a highly original mind, and part of that originality resides in Woolf's rejection of the conventional language of politics and her desire to speak 'not in any language known to men'.[8] For the student of International Relations (IR) the argument can be presented in terms of a number of themes. Not all of them pertain to the subject conventionally understood, but they are all integral to Woolf's conviction that war begins at home, in the social and cultural fabric of society.

1. Experience and perception

Owing to their radically different experiences in the private and public realms men and women, while looking at the same things, perceive them differently: 'Though we see the same world we see it through different eyes' (p. 175). This presents difficulties in cross-sex communication even between those inhabiting the same 'educated' class. Until the late nineteenth century, the daughters of educated men received little 'paid for' education, whereas vast sums were expended on the sons of educated men. When men looked at the great quadrangles, halls, and playing fields of Harrow, Eton, Oxford and Cambridge, they recalled innumerable memories and the discovery and enjoyment of traditions. When women looked at them they saw their sacrifices and their hardships, all the things foregone to provide for the education of their brothers.

2. Gendered character of war

Fighting is a male not a female habit. The question 'Why do men fight?' is difficult for women to answer. Some knowledge of politics, international relations and economics is necessary. However, having 'untrained minds', having received no 'paid-for' education, women had no access to this knowledge. The only knowledge they had access to was biography and autobiography, and from these sources it can be gleaned that men fight because fighting is a noble and worthwhile profession, a source of excitement, and an outlet for 'manly qualities' (pp. 157–60). But then we have the view of Wilfred Owen and the poets that war is inhumane, beastly, and foolish. No same-sex consensus prevails on the meaning and value of war. Yet the British parliament had just voted to spend £300 million per annum on arms. Was the public presumption that Owen was wrong and war is valuable? Perhaps it was valuable for patriotic reasons, a product of love of country, of England, the home of democracy and the castle of liberty? This is what patriotism meant to the educated man. But to his sister? Her position in the home of democracy was different. She enjoyed none of the wealth, status and privileges of her brother. Indeed, they had been bought at her expense (pp. 158–64).

3. Power

Women had no power to prevent war. They could not join the armed forces and 'fight for peace'. They were not eligible to become members of the stock exchange. They were barred from the diplomatic service and the higher reaches of the Church. They could submit articles and send letters to the newspapers. However, the press was controlled by men. Since 1919 women could enter the UK civil service and join the Bar. However, the position of women in these professions was weak and insecure. The daughters of educated men therefore had no power. Even refusing to work would make no difference. If men in the legal profession downed tools the country would grind to a halt. If their female colleagues were to do so the impact would be negligible. Women were thus weaker than men of their own class. However, they were weaker than working-class women. At least working-class women could refuse to make shells and bombs in the munitions factories. The daughters of educated men were the weakest of all classes: they had no weapons available to them to enforce their will (pp. 165–68).

4. Independent influence

Only with an independent income comes independent influence. From the guinea earned by educated men sprung all they most valued: wife, children, home and influence. With the passing in 1870 of the Married Women's Property Act, allowing married women to keep their own earnings and accrue capital, the 1918 extension of the franchise to women over 30, and the Sexual Disqualification Removal Act of 1919, women now had if not a guinea then a sixpence of their own – and the true influence that went with it (pp. 172–74).

5. Persistence of sexual inequality

While in many areas of life women had won formal equality with men, real equality lagged stubbornly behind. Men owned practically all the property; they occupied practically all the public offices; they held nearly all the professorships and lectureships; they occupied all the high positions in the Church, the law and medicine. There remained many 'inner and secret chambers' which women could not enter (p. 181).

6. Education and war

Women could use their newfound independent influence, their 'guinea', to build a college that would teach students to hate war. There was no doubt that this thing called 'university education' was of supreme value. Nearly all the men who had ruled England during the last 500 years had received a university education. Vast sums of money, and all the toil and privation this entailed, were involved in providing it. Perhaps the greatest testimony to its value was the desire of women, during the last 200 years, and against all impediments and prejudices, to filch some for themselves. The strength of this desire led in the late nineteenth century to the creation of 'colleges for the sisters'.[9] However, these colleges were 'unbelievably and shamefully poor' (p. 194). The male colleges, despite having been founded in various cases by benefactresses, were incredibly mean when it came to supporting them. They refused to recognize their degrees. They refused to allow their graduates to attach letters after their names. All this demonstrated that university education on the old plan trained people not to despise fighting but to fight tenaciously to retain their privileges and possessions. And was not fighting and possessiveness closely connected with war?

Therefore, if any guinea was to be given to build a new college it must be on the condition that 'it will use it to produce the kind of society, the kind of people that will help to prevent war' (pp. 198–99). Ideally the college would have no chapels, museums and libraries with old books. It would permit no teaching of the arts of dominating, ruling, killing and money-making. It would allow no lectures, examinations, distinctions, parades and symbols which breed competition and jealousy. It would award no degrees. Yet the prospect of such a college was frustrated by reality. To get appointments and earn their guineas the women of Girton and Newnham would need their degrees and their letters. Therefore no guinea of earned money could go to building a college on the new plan, just as no guinea of earned money should go to building a college on the old plan (p. 202).

7. *The professions and war*

The only weapon women had available to them against war was the new weapon of independent opinion based on independent income. Women who worked in the professions, therefore, had to be called upon to use their influence to prevent war. However, recruitment of women into the professions was slow, and the income earned by professional women was much lower than that earned by men. Prejudice against women was a fundamental fact of professional life. Women, it was claimed, were unsuited to professional work. Their entry into the workforce merely took jobs away from suitably qualified men. It also deprived the labour market of much-needed domestic workers. The home was the natural place for women, and the migration of women away from the home upset the natural economic order. The Government should intervene and insist on employers giving more work to men.

Was this not, in embryo, the voice of the dictator, and an expression of the same obliteration of freedom for which we condemned the Nazis and the fascists? For Hitler had declared: 'There are two worlds in the life of the nation, the world of men and the world of women. Nature has done well to entrust the man with the care of his family and the nation. The woman's world is her family, her husband, her children, and her home' (p. 229). The seeds of fascism and dictatorship were, thus, alive and well in the heart of England. Those women who daily encountered this prejudice in the office without arms were fighting the Nazis and fascists as surely 'as those who fight him with arms in the limelight of publicity' (p. 229). While these attitudes existed we had no right to trumpet the cause of freedom and justice in other countries. The dictator needed to be crushed at home before we could set about crushing him abroad (p. 230).[10]

Overcoming this prejudice was vital if women's position in the professions and if the independence of women's voices were to be strengthened. Yet, there was another danger. In joining the procession of professional life might not the daughter of educated men acquire the very qualities – possessiveness, pugnacity, competitiveness, pride, 'unreal loyalties'[11] – that she wished to eliminate? Combative psychology was deeply embedded in the mindset of professional men. During the nineteenth century they fought numerous battles: the Battle of Westminster; the Battle of Whitehall; the Battle of the Universities; the Battle of Harley Street; the Battle of the Royal Academy. All of these battles were about the same things and involved the same waste of time, strength, temper and money: 'Almost the same daughters ask almost the same brothers for almost the same privileges. Almost the same gentlemen intone the same refusals for the same reasons' (p. 248). God, nature, law and property were invoked to defend their privileges against the women who would usurp them. This showed that 'the professions have a certain undeniable effect on the professors' (p. 249); they instil the very values and qualities that lead to war.

Thus, if women were to join the procession on the same terms was there any guarantee that they would not become as possessive, jealous and pugnacious, as sure of the verdict of God, nature, law and property, and as ready to tolerate war, as men? Furthermore, if women acquired the same positions as men and earned the same incomes, would they not have to make the same sacrifices – of time for family, friendship, travel, art, music, culture? The moral, spiritual and intellectual value of professional life was not commensurate with its cash value. And was not the degradation of moral, spiritual, and intellectual life connected with the degradation of political life and war?

Women were, thus, caught between the patriarchy, servility, nullity and hypocrisy of the private house and the possessiveness, jealousy, pugnacity and acquisitiveness of the professions (p. 261). If they were to enter the professions, therefore, they must seek to change them and not slavishly imitate existing (male) ways and means. They should not sell their brains merely for money. They should avoid accumulation and possessiveness. They should rid themselves of unreal loyalties. They should resist the seduction of honour and fame. Only by maintaining a mind of one's own and a will of one's own will the daughters of educated men be able to use them to 'abolish the inhumanity, the beastliness, the horror, the folly of war' (pp. 274–75).

8. Peace begins at home

The word 'feminist' implied a sectarian struggle for women's rights only. However, the real struggle was for the rights of all persons and respect for the principles of justice, liberty and equality. The suffragettes were the advance guard of today's movement for peace. They were fighting the tyranny of the patriarchal state as the peace movement fights the tyranny of the Fascist state. Both were now fighting to destroy the words tyrant and dictator. But at home and abroad these words were far from obsolete. At home they still had meaning in Whitehall and Westminster, in Oxford and Cambridge. Abroad their meaning was wide and resounding. Across Europe, democrats and Jews and many other groups now experienced the discrimination, the oppression and the deprivation of liberty felt by their mothers and grandmothers in their struggle for freedom and equality (pp. 301–05).

9. The Outsiders' Society

Patriotism was a problematic word for women. What did women own of England? Women had little to thank England for in the past, and not much to thank it for in the present. The only rational stance towards the state and its call to duty was indifference. England had for the greater part of her history treated her like a slave, deprived her of education, denied her a share in its possessions, denied her a means of protecting herself, and forced her to pay large sums every year for others to 'protect' her. The 'outsider' would therefore say:

> [I]f you insist upon fighting to protect me, or 'our' country, let it be understood, soberly and rationally between us, that you are fighting to gratify a sex instinct which I cannot share; to procure benefits which I have not shared and probably will not share; but not to gratify my instincts, or to protect either myself or my country. For ... in fact as a woman, I have no country. As a woman I want no country. As a woman my country is the whole world (p. 313).

Daughters of educated men could best serve the cause of peace and civilization not by joining men's society, in which all that is distinctive about women's experience and identity would be lost, but by forming their own Outsiders' Society. This society would have no funds, offices, committees, or secretary. It would hold no meetings or conferences. It would require no oaths, but members would bind themselves not to fight with arms, to refuse to make munitions, to refuse to nurse the wounded, and not to incite their brothers to fight (pp. 309–10). Outsiders would also commit themselves to earn their own living, and press for the state to provide a living wage to those whose profession is marriage and motherhood. This, among other things, would enable the half-man to become whole – there would be no need for him to grind out his round, week in week out, to maintain his family. Outsiders would bind themselves to expose all tyranny, cease all competition, eschew all capital accumulation, and refuse to join any profession hostile to freedom. Through these means they would help to create a civilized society that protects cultural and intellectual liberty and teaches its citizens to hate war (pp. 316–20).

Reception

Three Guineas was published at the height of Woolf's lifetime fame and it received glowing reviews. Agnes Allen described it as a logically remorseless and formidable critique of 'male civilization in England'.[12] In the view of K. John it was 'artful, witty and entertaining'. There was 'no questioning the justice of Mrs Woolf's demands, or the beauty of her gospel'.[13] The *Times Literary Supplement* described it as a 'penetrating discourse upon women's position in society' which 'challenges every thinking mind today'. It was a 'brilliant and searching pamphlet' and its author 'the most brilliant pamphleteer in England'.[14] For Theordora Bosanquet, *Three Guineas* was a 'revolutionary bomb of a book', 'provocative', 'controversial', 'visionary' and 'prophetic'.[15]

The praise, however, was not unalloyed. John contended that most women are not and do not wish to be 'outsiders'. They do not mind official dress, they 'glow with pride in their country', they 'love all the red on the map', and they 'understand the pleasure of dominating, and the pleasure of fighting'.[16] Woolf too eagerly assumed that on becoming independent women would want the same things as she wanted. The fact that among women could be counted anti-suffragists as well as suffragists, fascists as well as pacifists, was conveniently overlooked. Woolf, in sum, imputed too much emotional, intellectual and political unity to women, even those from the same educated class.[17] Future Poet Laureate, Cecil Day-Lewis, sensed in Woolf's refusal to join a predominantly male peace society, and her call for educated women to remain 'outsiders', a 'strong whiff of intransigent feminism mingled with the laughing gas of liberal anarchism'. He found Woolf's 'feminine isolationism' illogical. If her class was the weakest of all classes with no weapon to enforce its will, surely it made sense for it to join forces with working women who did possess a weapon? Moreover, if class society and war had an economic basis, as she tacitly acknowledged, surely it made sense for all those, men and women, who were oppressed to join forces in an anti-capitalist, anti-fascist, and anti-war front?[18] Indeed, more than a few eyebrows were raised at Woolf's remedy for war, her non-cooperating and self-abnegating Outsiders' Society. One correspondent called it a 'counsel of perfection'.[19] The most damning verdict, however, came from literary critic Q. D. Leavis. 'Mrs Woolf is not living in the contemporary world', she declared. Woolf's knowledge of the universities was out of date. Her understanding of the 'modern woman/daughter' no less the 'Victorian man/father' was based on hearsay not research. As well as being ill-informed her argument was self-indulgent, bad-tempered and 'peevishly sarcastic'. Indeed, it was not an argument at all but 'a sort of chatty restatement of the rights and wrongs of women of Mrs Woolf's class'. Any unity it possessed was emotional not rational. Her examples were selective. Her proposals were nebulous. In sum, *Three Guineas* was an incoherent and irresponsible work not worthy of serious critical attention.[20]

Critical legacy

Yet serious critical attention *Three Guineas* has received in abundance, particularly with the (re)emergence of the feminist movement in the 1960s, 'Woolf Studies' in the 1970s, and Gender Studies in the 1990s. If anything, the controversy surrounding the book has intensified, with feminist and gender scholars seeing it as profound, insightful, path-breaking, prescient, even realistic,[21] and more conservative commentators seeing it as incoherent, contradictory, self-indulgent, naïve and utopian.[22] However, such a binary does not do justice to the vast range of comment and criticism that *Three Guineas* continues to provoke within these camps as well as between them. It is hard to think of a volume in the history of social and political studies that has inspired such a diverse range of critical engagements.

To illustrate this point, there is, in the first place, some debate over the extent to which Woolf should be considered a political writer. According to her husband, 'Virginia was the least political animal that has lived since Aristotle invented the definition'.[23] He did not think highly of *Three Guineas*. In contrast to the vision and intensity of her novels it was marked by 'a certain laboriousness and deadness' and was 'oppressed by the weight of its facts and arguments'.[24] Virginia Woolf's nephew-biographer considered *Three Guineas* an aberration and a failure – the former because of her general indifference to politics, the latter because of her tenuous attempt to connect the struggle for women's rights with fascism and war.[25] Against this Carroll has argued that Woolf was an intensely political writer, even (indeed especially) in terms of Aristotle's definition.[26] Her indifference was not to politics but 'politics as usual': party politics, 'speechifying', and the world of the professional politician. She cultivated indifference to 'politics as usual' as a deliberate policy. Contrary to the view that held sway until the 1970s, Carroll contends that there is a political philosophy at work, though often in the form of 'serpentine insinuations',[27] in all of Woolf's writing. It is a political philosophy of struggle – against an oppressive patriarchal social system. Bell's assertion of a tenuous connection between the struggle for women's rights and fascism and war, betrays a deep misunderstanding of Woolf's outlook on politics. In Carroll's view the contention that dictatorship, war and sex domination share the same ultimate source in 'the force of the fathers' should not to be so complacently dismissed.[28]

A second engagement concerns the form of *Three Guineas*. There is general agreement that it is a polemic, an attack on patriarchy conducted in words. However, some contend that from Woolf's pen the words form pictures. The impact of her book is visual as much as intellectual. Amy Lilly argues, for example, that *Three Guineas* should be seen as an exhibition of carefully constructed and arranged images. Woolf is as much curator as author. She guides the reader/viewer through a series of everyday objects – newspaper cuttings, letters, biographies, photographs – and invites her/him to scrutinize them from a different/woman's angle. In doing so she demonstrates the ubiquity and pervasiveness of patriarchal attitudes and practices, which usually tend to be 'seen' only in their most extreme form, and more 'abroad' than 'at home'. Woolf, thus, employs the method of the exhibition to get her readers/viewers to see more acutely. *Three Guineas* is a book about making hitherto invisible relations between patriarchy, fascism and war 'visible to all'.[29]

A third engagement concerns the place of *Three Guineas* in feminist writing on peace and war. It is generally seen as a pioneering exploration of patriarchy and war. Phyllis Lassner, for example, describes it as 'the ur-text of feminist anti-war writing'.[30] Some scholars, however, have sought to position it more precisely in the evolution of feminist thinking. Yael Feldman, for example, argues that feminist thinking on patriarchy and war was already well established when Woolf came to write *Three Guineas*. Its importance resides not in its focus on patriarchy per se (nor in its identification of society as androcentric) but in its constructivist understanding of patriarchy. *Three Guineas* was a revolutionary work that shifted the discourse from its essentialist and 'maternalist' origins to a focus on the social construction of 'male' and 'female' roles. In common with her feminist predecessors Woolf was confident that the sexes differed in their propensity to aggression, but she was reluctant to put this down to innate differences. Rather, she focused on the socio-historical construction of values and identity. While she did not explicitly reject prevailing 'biological' presuppositions, often talking for example in quasi-Freudian terms of 'instinct',[31] by looking at the issue sociologically and historically she put feminist thinking on a new trajectory. *Three Guineas* is a gender analysis of peace and war *avant la lettre*.[32]

An alternative IR classic?

However, the critical value of the book as disclosed in these and other engagements should not disguise its many analytical problems. These problems, intriguingly, have gone unnoticed in feminist IR, which has tended to treat *Three Guineas* as a landmark essay or classic without going into much detail.[33] From an IR perspective the following problems are particularly salient. The book contends that competition and jealousy (as provoked by uniforms, ceremonial dress, medals, titles and other hierarchical symbols and differentiations) are emotions which 'have their share in encouraging a disposition towards war' (pp. 181, 357). But a disposition is not an action, and having a 'share' is not much use unless we know how big it is.[34] It confuses causes of war, reasons for war and morality of war (pp. 162–63). It confuses an emotional reaction (Owen's reaction against war) with a logical argument (the need for armaments to deter aggression). Woolf, indeed, relies too much on Owen's cry against war. On the strength of it she equates being in favour of war with being uncivilized. This leads to all sorts of problems. She says for example that the professions, because of the way they are constructed (breeding competitiveness, jealousy and pugnacity), produce uncivilized people and therefore war (e.g. pp. 218ff.). However, what we have here, repeated in various ways throughout the text, is not a logical argument but a false syllogism (war is uncivilized; the professions are uncivilized; therefore the professions are in favour of/are connected with/cause war – the precise formulation varies throughout). Allied with this, Woolf establishes war (and even more broadly 'fighting') as an exclusively male activity primarily through repetition, e.g. of phrases such as 'the impulses, the motives, or the morality which leads you [men] to go to war' (p. 164). This is less an argument than a mantra.

Such lack of rigour is also apparent in the repeated association of competition, the competitive spirit, aggression and 'fighting' with war. Woolf seems to be uninterested in war as a distinct category of human behaviour. There is no recognition of the diversity of war as a phenomenon, nor of the possibility that different kinds of war may require different kinds of explanation. War is merely lumped together with a range of competitive behaviours from empire-building to football (e.g. pp. 324–26).[35] Similarly, Woolf makes much of the desire for control, which she describes, but nowhere defines, as an 'infantile fixation' (pp. 345–56). However, is there not an element of 'infantile fixation' in the desire to subsume a range of subjectively undesirable behaviours under one uniform category? It is also important to note from an IR viewpoint that *Three Guineas* is almost entirely a 'second image' analysis (see Chapter 8 in this volume). The cause of war is patriarchy – what she called in one of her last essays 'subconscious Hitlerism'.[36] Her remedies include dismantling the arms industry, educating graduates to hate war, and refusing to take part in any preparations for war. However, does not this pacifist position leave the state defenceless?[37] What does one do about states that are less progressive, humane and peace-loving than 'ours', states with no wish to mend their patriarchal, hierarchical and bellicose ways? Woolf has no answer. This is one reason why many of her critics dismissed the book as naïve: it assumes the possibility of some kind of spontaneous dismantling of all the world's patriarchal structures.

Yet it would be wrong to dwell on these analytical minuses without mentioning some of the creative pluses. *Three Guineas* provides a remarkable insight into the position of women in British society in the nineteenth and early twentieth centuries. It vividly reveals the public implications of private subordination, and the many subtle forms that subordination took. It shows how ill-equipped women were to understand and contribute to public debate on war and peace as Britain approached its darkest hour. Yet it is important to note that the women in question here are not *all* women but upper-middle-class women: 'the daughters of educated men class'. Woolf had little understanding of working-class women and their plight and, according to some, little sympathy for them.[38] Arguably, therefore, her ratiocinations on women and the prevention of war are based on the experience of a small segment of the population. That said, Berenice Carroll has argued that Woolf's unflattering portrayal of working-class or poverty-stricken characters was not a product of snobbishness or lack of sympathy but the desire to illustrate graphically what an unforgiving, acquisitive, patriarchal society does to its victims.[39] In addition, it can be contended that Woolf's unwillingness to speak for *all* women is a token of both her honesty and humility. It is undeniable, however, that the tone of Woolf's comments on the working class and working-class life is frequently condescending (e.g. pp. 278, 281, 287). In common with many middle-class progressives of her age (including the English Socialist economists Sydney and Beatrice Webb and her husband Leonard) she often speaks of the working class as if it is a biological entity (e.g. pp. 401–02).

This sits uneasily with other more interesting things Woolf has to say about class. The concept of class features heavily in *Three Guineas* but although the work replicates a number of common interwar socialist tropes (e.g. the menace of the arms trade, the bellicosity of capitalism), her understanding of class is far from Marxist. Indeed, one of the contributions of the book is to de-reify the notion of social class. Woolf establishes that both she and her correspondent hail from the same 'educated class' and therefore have similar tastes, values, manners and cultural interests. However, the relative experiences, education, career prospects and wealth of the male and female members of this class differ so profoundly as to make the notion of a class little more than an 'anthropocentric ideology' (p. 369). Woolf in effect 'genders' the notion of class, showing it to be a male construction serving male interests. Acts of de-reification, indeed, collectively constitute one of the main innovations of the book. Unquestioned institutions (e.g. the family), practices (e.g. the law), and sentiments (e.g. patriotism) are problematized in terms of their potential contribution to war by providing a view of them from female eyes (e.g. pp. 155–57). The book vividly illustrates how God, nature, law and property were invoked in defence of these things, reifying and thus legitimating the gender discrimination at their core (e.g. pp. 248, 353, 359, 376).

Perhaps above all *Three Guineas* is path-breaking in feeding a series of conventional questions (e.g. how can we go about preventing war?) through the prism of gender awareness. In doing so it raised for the first time a series of novel questions for students of IR: to what extent should war be seen as a male practice? Is patriotism a masculinist ideology which legitimizes male possessiveness and dominance? What role does the state play in the reproduction of male dominance? What is the connection between patriarchy and war? *Three Guineas* does not provide convincing answers, but it was the first book to ask these questions and make the connections.

For this reason it is right to regard *Three Guineas* as a classic of IR. More precisely it is an *alternative* classic, not so much in view of its radical approach but its unorthodox form. While Woolf herself regarded it as her 'book of facts'[40] it is far from a work of social science, even broadly defined. It engages the reader emotionally and aesthetically as much as intellectually. It has more in common with *The Third of May 1808*, *Guernica*, or (even) *Et in Arcadia ego* than *Politics Among Nations* or *Theory of International Politics*. It is a pamphlet, an essay, an epistle and, above all, an ambitious and intricate work of art.

Notes

1 This chapter began as a paper delivered at the 'Women Thinkers of the Twenty Years' Crisis' workshop, University of Limerick, and the British International Studies Association (BISA) annual conference, University of Cork, December 2006. I am grateful to all those who commented on the paper and especially to Luke Ashworth and Kim Hutchings.

2 Virginia Woolf, *Three Guineas*, Oxford: Oxford University Press, [1938] 1992, p. 158. Page numbers placed in parentheses in the text refer to this edition.

3 See Christine Froula, *Virginia Woolf and the Bloomsbury Avant-Garde: War, Civilization, Modernity*, New York: Columbia University Press, 2005, p. 399. Unlike the humble penny, the guinea – the unit of currency in which professional fees and prizes in horse racing were traditionally fixed – was infused with high social status.

4 In her diary Woolf envisioned *Three Guineas* as a public letter condensing 'all the articles that editors have asked me to write during the last few years – on all sorts of subjects. Shd. Women smoke. Short skirts. War – & c.' Froula, *Woolf and the Bloomsbury Avant-Garde*, p. 260.

5 As suggested by Julia Briggs, *Virginia Woolf: An Inner Life*, London: Penguin, 2006, p. 311.

6 Briggs, *Virginia Woolf: An Inner Life*, pp. 331, 490.

7 We learn from Morag Shiach in her explanatory notes (pp. 428–31) that in 1936 Woolf signed the manifesto of the International Peace Campaign which included the statement: 'Modern war and preparations for war are hostile to the arts, and most of all to writing'. In the same year she was asked to join the committee of patrons of Newnham (women's) College, which was launching an appeal to fund new buildings. The society for helping young women find positions in the professions was probably modelled on the London and National Society for Women's Service.

8 The quote, from *To the Lighthouse*, suggests recognition that not only the institutions of society are patriarchal but language itself. See Berenice A. Carroll, '"To Crush Him in Our

Own Country": The Political Thought of Virginia Woolf', *Feminist Studies*, 1978, vol. 4, 117–18; Jane Marcus, *Virginia Woolf and the Languages of Patriarchy*, Bloomington, IN: Indiana University Press, 1987. See also *Three Guineas*, p. 366 on the 'need to find new words and new methods'.

9 The colleges of Girton, Newnham, Lady Margaret Hall and Somerville were founded between 1869 and 1879.

10 In a letter to E. M. Forster on the eve of the publication of *Three Guineas*, Woolf wrote 'We must attack Hitler in England'. Quoted in Briggs, *Virginia Woolf: An Inner Life*, p. 485.

11 By this Woolf meant loyalties to traditions, institutions, and professions vis-à-vis people.

12 Agnes Allen, 'Still a Man's World', *Saturday Review*, 27 August 1938, p. 6.

13 K. John (John Maynard Keynes?), 'The New Lysistrata', *New Statesman and Nation*, 11 June 1938, pp. 995–96.

14 Unsigned review, 'Women in a World of War', *Times Literary Supplement*, 4 June 1938, p. 379.

15 Theodora Bosanquet, review of *Three Guineas*, *Time and Tide*, 4 June 1938 (abstracted in Robin Majumdar and Allen McLaurin (eds), *Virginia Woolf: The Critical Heritage*, London: Routledge & Kegan Paul, 1975, pp. 402–03).

16 See similar comments from among others Vita Sackville-West in Brenda R. Silver, '*Three Guineas* Before and After: Further Answers to Correspondents', pp. 261–62, and Naomi Black, 'Virginia Woolf and the Peace Movement', p. 192, both in Jane Marcus (ed.), *Virginia Woolf: A Feminist Slant*, Lincoln, NE: University of Nabraska Press, 1983.

17 John, 'The New Lysistrata', pp. 995–96.

18 C. Day-Lewis, 'Virginia Woolf: Educated Man's Daughter', *The New Masses*, 9 August 1938, pp. 22–23.

19 Quoted in Silver, '*Three Guineas* Before and After', p. 267.

20 Q. D. Leavis, 'Caterpillars of the Commonwealth Unite!', *Scrutiny*, September 1938, pp. 203–14.

21 See e.g. Carroll, 'Crush Him in Our Own Country', p. 117.

22 See e.g. Theodore Dalrymple's unremittingly hostile 'The Rage of Virginia Woolf' in his *Our Culture, What's Left of It*, Chicago, IL: Dee, 2005, pp. 63–76.

23 Leonard Woolf, *Downhill All the Way: An Autobiography of the Years 1919–1939*, London: Hogarth Press, 1967, p. 27.

24 Leonard Woolf, *The Journey Not the Arrival Matters: An Autobiography of the Years 1939–1969*, London: Hogarth Press, 1967, p. 43.

25 Quentin Bell, *Virginia Woolf: A Biography*, vol. 2, St Albans: Triad and Paladin, 1976, pp. 204–06.

26 Being capable of and suited to life in the polis; having a sense of good and evil, just and unjust (Aristotle, *The Politics*, London: Penguin, 1992, pp. 13, 54, 59–60).

27 Woolf's self-description of her approach to conventional politics.

28 Carroll, 'Crush Him in Our Own Country', pp. 99–131. For a slightly different take on Woolf's indifference see Hermione Lee, *Virginia Woolf*, London: Chatto & Windus, pp. 681–82.

29 Amy M. Lilly, '*Three Guineas*, Two Exhibits: Woolf's Politics of Display', *Woolf Studies Annual*, vol. 9, 2003, 29–54.

30 In *British Woman Writers of World War II: Battlegrounds of their Own*, Basingstoke: Palgrave Macmillan, 1998, p. 29.

31 The degree to which Woolf anticipated/borrowed/abused Freudian theory is contested. See Yael S. Feldman, 'From Essentialism to Constructivism? The Gender of Peace and War – Gilman, Woolf, Freud', *Partial Answers: Journal of Literature and the History of Ideas*, 2004, vol. 2, 130–39.

32 Feldman, 'From Essentialism to Constructivism?', pp. 113–45.

33 See e.g. Cythia Enloe, *The Morning After: Sexual Politics at the End of the Cold War*, Berkeley, CA: University of California Press, 1993, p. 77; *Maneuvers: The International Politics of Militarizing Women's Lives*, Berkeley, CA: University of California Press, 2000, pp. 288–89.

34 See also ibid. pp. 192–93 where Woolf states that possessiveness and meanness (as bred supposedly by the universities) are 'connected' with war.

35 Charlotte Perkins Gilman reached the same conclusion years some years previously in works such as *The Man-Made World* (1911). Crime, rivalry, fighting and war were anti-social products of the same phenomenon: a competitive and acquisitive 'masculinism'. See Feldman, 'From Essentialism to Constructivism?', pp. 119–23. On *Three Guineas* as a 'psychopathology

of masculinism' see Sybil Oldfield, *Women Against the Fist: Alternatives to Militarism 1900–1989*, Oxford: Blackwell, 1989.

36 Woolf, 'Thoughts on Peace in an Air Raid', in *Collected Essays*, vol. 4, ed. L. Woolf, London: Chatto & Windus, 1969, p. 174.
37 On Woolf's pacifism see Black, 'Virginia Woolf and the Women's Movement', 186–97; Lee, *Virginia Woolf*, pp. 688–98.
38 See e.g.: Chambers, *The Novels of Virginia Woolf*, London: Oliver and Boyd, 1947, pp. 1–3.
39 Carroll, 'Crush Him in Our Own Country', pp. 105–07, 122–23.
40 Quoted in Carroll, 'Crush Him in Our Own Country', p. 102.

5 Power, morality and the remaking of international order: E. H. Carr's *The Twenty Years' Crisis*

Peter Wilson

One should not see *The Twenty Years' Crisis* (*TYC*) as a manifesto for political realism, still less a work recommending surrender to the immanence of power.[1] That Carr saw power as immanent in politics, especially international politics, there can be no doubt. Indeed, this was not so much a matter of 'seeing' as 'conceiving'. For Carr the immanence of power in politics was true by definition. Politics is about the clash of interests, and the clash of interests between large, powerful groups is serious politics. While it would be inaccurate to define politics 'exclusively in terms of power', Carr declared, 'it is safe to say that power is always an essential element in politics'.[2] However, the idea that Carr not only recognized the immanence of power but advocated surrender to it is one that all careful readers of this seminal contribution to International Relations (IR) must dismiss. In this chapter I try to do six things: (i) set out Carr's intentions in writing *TYC*; (ii) state its central argument; (iii) outline its main contentions; (iv) account for its classical status; (v) identify some of its shortcomings; and (vi) conclude with some thoughts on the 'surrender' thesis and why *TYC* is likely to remain an IR classic.

Aims

What was Carr aiming to do in *TYC*? In the Preface he states that his purpose is to analyse 'the underlying and significant, rather than the immediate and personal, causes of the disaster' – the disaster being the outbreak of war in 1939 (p. ix). Here we have an immediate clue to the nature of the intellectually and historically broad-ranging study to follow. Carr was not interested in what this statesman or that, whether Mussolini, Briand, Hitler or Chamberlain, said or did at this or that moment (though he was rather more interested in the sayings and doings of 'Herr Hitler'[3] than the others). Rather he was interested in the conditions which made their sayings and doings politically significant, even possible.[4] A settlement, he continued, which addressed the immediate and personal causes and not the underlying and significant, that 'destroyed the National Socialist rulers of Germany' but left untouched 'the conditions which made the phenomenon of National Socialism possible', would 'run the risk of being as short-lived and as tragic as the settlement of 1919' (ibid.). His next book was to be called *Conditions of Peace* (1942). This one could have been called *Conditions of War*.

The subtitle of the book suggests another purpose. This was to provide an introduction for students to the new academic subject of IR. In 1936 Carr resigned from the British Foreign Office, which he had served for 20 years, to take up the Woodrow Wilson Chair of International Politics at the University College of Wales, Aberystwyth.[5]

His first book on this subject, *International Relations since the Peace Treaties*, was published the following year. It was a book intended to be helpful to students. *TYC*, his second book on the subject, could be seen in the same vein. Yet his engagement with not only specialist academic literature – in political philosophy, history and international relations – but also contributions to popular debate, notably by Nobel Peace Laureate Sir Norman Angell, suggests a broader audience. One of his aims was to provide a deeper, more critical, analytical framework for popular debate (and possibly the intellectual substructure for the promotion of his own socialist utopia – but more on that in a moment).

This leads to the final aim that can be deduced from the substance and tone of the text: to reveal the folly of Versailles and the wisdom of appeasement. Carr was a junior member of the British delegation at the Versailles Peace Conference, remaining in Paris several years after. He was appalled by the harshness of the terms imposed on Germany and the manner in which the German delegation was treated. His indignation stayed with him for many years and goes some way to explain why his treatment of Hitler and the Nazi regime in the pages of the *TYC* is so mild. He was infuriated by the logic of Versailles, or at least the hypocritical way in which the principal status quo Powers (France and Britain) implemented it by keeping Germany in a position of permanent subordination. He refused to be indignant over Hitler's reoccupation of the Rhineland in 1936, seeing it as a righting of a past wrong.[6] Allied with his deep desire to avoid another war this accounts fairly efficiently for Carr's support for a policy of active accommodation of Hitler's demands. He welcomed the Munich agreement of 1938, describing it as 'the nearest approach in recent years to the settlement of a major international issue by a procedure of peaceful change' (p. 282). With its frank recognition of power realities and its appeal to an accepted canon of international morality (the principle of self-determination) the Munich agreement contained a wisdom lacking in previous conceptions of peaceful change.[7]

Main argument

The pre-1914 order had collapsed. The attempt to rebuild it on the old nineteenth-century foundations was doomed to failure. A new order could only be built on foundations able to withstand the pressures of a very different world. The nineteenth century was characterized by *laissez-faire*, free trade and liberal democracy. The twentieth century was characterized by large-scale industry, mass production, the rapid development of communications, controlled trade and mass democracy – or at least changes in the nature and scale of production necessitated corresponding changes in political organization (i.e. towards a more 'interventionist' state). This is the basic contention of *TYC* and the historical baseline from which Carr conducts his wide-ranging and multifaceted analysis. Yet textbooks over the years have tended to present the work in terms of its 'devastating critique' of 'utopian ideals' such as the League of Nations and collective security. It is certainly true that the book contains a critique in the name of 'realism' of interwar 'utopianism', and that this critique is generally held to have had a 'devastating impact' in IR.[8] However, two things should be noted. First, while Carr believed this critique to be of vital importance at the historical juncture of 1939, one should not equate it unconditionally with Carr's own position. Second, the meaning he gave to these elastic terms ultimately does not make sense unless this historical baseline is taken into account. Taking a 'realistic' view ultimately meant taking a view that was in line with prevailing *material conditions*. Looked at another way, Carr gives attention to the numerous events, theories, policies and decisions that litter the theory and practice of international relations of the interwar period. However, these are all pressed into the service of a broader historical-theoretical point. What, we may ask, is the crisis of the 20 years' crisis? It is the world economic crisis, the collapse of free trade, the failure of the League, the failure of collective security, 'the armament crisis', the international tensions of 1939. Carr depicts all these things, and more, as crises. However, the real, fundamental crisis for Carr is 'the final and irrevocable breakdown of the conditions which made the nineteenth-century order possible' (p. 303). It was the failure of the Western Powers to recognize this breakdown and adapt their policy-making and diplomacy to the needs and conditions of a new historical epoch. Hence his relative disinterest in the sayings and doings of this or that statesman. 'The breakdown of the post-War utopia', he declared, 'is too overwhelming to be explained merely in terms of individual action or inaction. Its downfall involves the bankruptcy of the postulates on which it is based' (p. 53).

Central contentions

An account, therefore, of the complex structure of *TYC* must begin with Carr's reading of nineteenth-century liberalism. Carr's argument was not, as some have assumed,[9] that nineteenth-century liberalism was invalid per se but that it was able to survive and in some cases flourish owing to a special set of material circumstances. These he described as 'the spacious conditions of the nineteenth century' (p. 297) marked by the wide availability of 'unoccupied and unexploited territories' and 'a plentiful supply of cheap labour' (pp. 77–78). Liberal principles such as 'the greatest good of the greatest number' were not universally valid. Rather they were expressions and rationalizations of the interests of a rising commercial class. Similarly, the brilliant success of liberal democracy in a limited number of countries was due not to 'certain *a priori* rational principles which had only to be applied in other contexts to produce similar results' (p. 37). Rather it was due to a 'balance of forces peculiar to the economic development of the period and the countries concerned' (ibid.).

Yet at a time when the material conditions which had sustained liberalism were breaking down everywhere an attempt was made to transplant its 'half-discarded assumptions' into the 'special field of international relations' (p. 36). Nothing better illustrated this than 'the Benthamite doctrine of the efficacy of rational public opinion'. According to this doctrine public opinion could be relied on to judge rightly on any question rationally presented to it, and once it had judged rightly it would necessarily act rightly (p. 34). This constituted one of the main intellectual pillars of the League of Nations. The whole conception of the League, Carr contended, was 'closely bound up with the twin belief that public opinion was bound to prevail and that public opinion was the voice of reason' (p. 45). In Manchuria and Abyssinia, however, public opinion proved impotent. Moreover, in practice statesmen often proved to be more reasonable than the people they represented. The 'plain men throughout the world' who in the opinion of Wilson, Cecil and other League champions possessed 'simple and unclouded views of right and wrong' sometimes took the form of a 'disorderly mob emitting incoherent and unhelpful noises'. In international affairs, according to Carr, it was undeniable that 'public opinion was almost as often wrong-headed as it was impotent' (pp. 42–51).

Underpinning nearly all nineteenth-century liberal ideas was the doctrine of the harmony of interests between individual and the community. There were two major interwar manifestations of this doctrine: the notion that no nation benefited from war, that all nations had a common interest in peace; and the notion that economic protectionism was not in the long-term interests of any country, that all nations had a common interest in free trade. Both of these 'utopian' notions were widely accepted in the Anglo-Saxon world and for a particular reason: they were, Carr asserted, the doctrines of the political and economic top dogs, of the 'haves' against the 'have-nots', the 'satisfied' against the 'dissatisfied'. The notion that war profited no one was easy to accept in countries which having fought profitable wars had no desire to encourage others to do the same. The notion that the catastrophe of 1914–18 had demonstrated the futility of war was easier for the victors to accept than the vanquished, who tended to blame their fears and insecurities not on 'war' but on the fact of losing. According to Carr, the common interest in peace masked the fact that some nations desired to maintain the status quo without having to fight for it, while others desired to change the status quo without having to fight in order to do so (p. 68). The utopian assumption of a world interest in peace masked fundamental conflicts of interest.

The same logic applied to the doctrines of *laissez-faire* and free trade. '*Laissez-faire*, in international relations as in those between capital and labour, is the paradise of the economically strong', Carr asserted (p. 77). The implication of the harmony of interest doctrine in the international economic sphere was the permanent relegation of weaker, non-industrial Powers to second-class status. The notion of a universal interest in free trade, equally favourable to all and prejudicial to none, was a mantra of League and other international economic conferences of the 1930s. Yet it was contrary to fact that economic protectionism was detrimental everywhere to those that practised it. While it might make international trade as a whole weaker, and the economic interests of Europe or the world at large might suffer, protectionism could strengthen the economy and independence of less advantaged states (ibid.). Those who elevated 'peace' and 'free trade' to the status of universal principles simply failed to understand the self-interested character of their thought.

Armed with this appreciation of Carr's understanding of liberalism, his understanding of realism begins to make sense. His account of realism begins safely enough. Machiavelli is described as the first important political realist (p. 81). Bodin, Bacon, Spinoza and Hobbes are cited as major classical influences. More controversially, however, he cites Kjellen, Spengler, Hegel and Marx as important modern influences. Hegel and Marx in particular liberated realism from the pessimism of Machiavelli and Hobbes and made it more historical, scientific and progressive. They rejected all notions of divine providence and contended that nothing existed outside the historical process, the laws of which it was the job of the realist to reveal. Progress was part of the 'inner essence' of this process. Mankind was moving with an 'iron necessity towards an inevitable goal' (Carr quoting Marx, p. 85). For Carr, therefore, realism primarily means something like 'acceptance of the entire historical process', outside of which there are no standards of judgement, and the general course of which human beings are powerless to alter (pp. 81–86). This is significant because it shows that this early account of realism is also, in comparison with later accounts, quirky. A critic might contend that it was not so much a product of a careful study of the history of political thought as something that followed ineluctably from his (precipitous) decision to frame his discussion in terms of the stark opposition between 'realism' and a bundle of liberal ideas and assumptions that he provocatively labelled 'utopianism'. Realism becomes historical and determinist precisely because utopianism is ahistorical and voluntarist (asserting e.g. the existence of certain a priori principles standing outside of history, and attaching great importance to the exercise of independent human reason).

However, as the *cognoscenti* of *TYC* know, Carr not only described realism, he also critiqued it. Realism certainly had important tasks to perform. Carr viewed the exposure by realist criticism of the hollowness of utopianism as 'the most urgent task of the moment in international thought' (p. 113). This is why, as he later admitted, *TYC* states its argument with 'a rather one-sided emphasis which no longer seems as necessary or appropriate as it did in 1939'.[10] However, a 'final resting place' could not be found in 'pure realism' (p. 113). Indeed, a thrust of *TYC* is that there are no final resting places. This is why, despite being influenced by Marx, and using some of his methods to great effect, in the final analysis Carr did not consider himself to be a Marxist. He broadly accepted Marx's analysis of the rise and fall of Western bourgeois capitalism. Indeed, realistic or objective history for Carr meant history broadly in line with Marx's materialist understanding of the historical process.[11] However, he did not share Marx's confidence in the revolutionary potential of the proletariat, nor his vision of the culmination of the historical process in a worldwide classless society. He accepted much of Marx's analysis but not his teleology.[12]

In Carr's view, 'consistent realism' lacked 'four things that appear to be essential ingredients of all effective political thinking: a finite goal, an emotional appeal, a right of moral judgment and a ground for action' (p. 113). Realism was also vulnerable to its own insight of the conditioned nature of thought. Realism, he said, is 'often' as much conditioned as any other mode of thought.[13] For example, in politics the belief that certain facts were unalterable or certain trends irresistible commonly reflected 'a lack of desire or lack of interest to change or resist them' (ibid.). So we are left with the conclusion that the determinist reading of history may not be a true/real/objective reading but a pragmatic one, being conditioned by the interests and circumstances of the (in this case 'modern realist') reader. As well as this problem of reflexivity it is important to note one further feature of Carr's critique of realism. It was impossible to be a 'pure' or 'consistent' realist, he suggests, because in some respects it is 'uncongenial or incomprehensible to the human mind' (ibid.). It went against, for example, one of the most deep-rooted human beliefs, that 'human affairs can be directed and modified by human action and human thought' (p. 117). So an important element of his critique of realism, often overlooked, is that its view of the world is not so much empirically wrong but psychologically unsustainable. The human mind, even of the most unsentimental and scientific realist, will always rebel against it.

Carr's dissatisfaction with realism carries over to his substantial treatment of international law, where again he charts a middle course. Realism held that law was merely the 'will of the state', the 'weapon of the stronger' or the 'registration of power relations' within any given community (pp. 223–27). However, according to Carr law is unsustainable if it relies for compliance exclusively on punishment. Laws that go against the conscience of the community are difficult to enforce. Furthermore, while enforcement is an essential factor in the bindingness of law, so is 'the sense of right of the community' (p. 227). It was true that there was no special sanctity in 'the rule of law' or its international counterpart *pacta sunt servanda*. This again was a utopian fallacy and delusion. It was always important to ask: what law? whose law? Law, he contended, is not an abstraction. The ethical content of law is always a function of the ends it serves. However, Carr none the less held law to be an essential ingredient of organized social life. Coherent social life was not possible without the 'element of fixity and regularity and continuity', which it provided (pp. 228–31). The chief problem with current international law was that it lacked an effective mechanism by which important rules could be peacefully changed. With the creation of the League war had been removed as a legitimate means of modifying the existing order. Yet no effective mechanism had been put in its place. As a result international law had become a 'bulwark of the existing order' to an extent previously unknown (pp. 244–45). This was the most fundamental reason, according to Carr, for the decline in respect for law. Those states desiring to change the law had no choice, in the face of the hostility to such changes from the status quo Powers, but to break it. For this reason their behaviour should not be judged as any more immoral or unreasonable than the behaviour of the status quo Powers. But crucially and contrary to the 'pure' realist view, Carr believed that it was possible to devise a mechanism whereby law could be changed peacefully, in line with what was considered 'just and reasonable' in the community of nations (pp. 278–84). Indeed, he regarded this as one of the chief tasks facing, to cite the dedication of *TYC*, 'the makers of the coming peace'. Law was not inevitably a bastion of an unjust *status quo*.

Given the collapse of the old order and the 'ignominious failure' (p. 287) of the attempt to recreate it, where lay the future? In Carr's view it lay in a socialist-inspired transformation of international order. His starting point here, interestingly, is the need for greater equality. The historical struggle between the privileged and the unprivileged had been transferred from within national communities to between them. Mitigating the inequality between nations was now the main challenge of international order. Rising to it would involve inter alia the substantial reduction of consumption in privileged nations, a 'gigantic programme of economically unremunerative expenditure', the 'increasing elimination of the profit motive from the national economy', the 'subordination of economic advantage to social ends', and the extension of these ends 'across the national frontier' (pp. 302–07). Only by such means, and the frank acknowledgement of the interdependence between economics and politics, national and international welfare, could the mistakes of the past be averted and a lasting peace built. This, too, Carr acknowledged, was utopia. However, it stood 'more directly in the line of recent advance than visions of a world federation or blue-prints of a more perfect League of Nations. Those elegant superstructures must wait until some progress has been made in digging the foundations' (pp. 307).

Classic status

'Digging the foundations': in these final words of *TYC* resides the reason why it rapidly became regarded as an IR. It was the first work in the field to call for unsentimental and systematic analysis of the facts of international relations as the vital first step to improve them. Stanley Hoffmann once described it as 'the first "scientific" treatment of modern world politics'.[14] While the meaning of scientific, as Hoffmann's inverted commas suggest, can be debated, there can be no doubt that *TYC* was the first work to grapple with a range of basic international questions – relating to the role and relationship of law, power, morality, war and order – in the spirit of science; in the spirit, that is, of detached social enquiry stripped of the liberal rationalist teleology that hitherto had informed most work on the subject. In this regard, and in particular his call for an unsentimental analysis of the role of power in international politics, Carr influenced virtually every IR scholar of significance of the next generation.[15]

Yet it is important to stress that it is not 'facts' and 'power' per se that are important but the approach taken towards them. There is a sense in which the chief contribution of *TYC*, and the main source of its classical status, is methodological. *TYC* is the first genuinely critical work of international relations. It was the first work that sought systematically to get behind conventional narratives, assumptions and wisdoms and ask: what sustains them? Carr's 'realism' is a critical tool, forged from the exotic metals (certainly for IR of the time) of Marx's concept of ideology and Mannheim's sociology of knowledge.[16] It is the means by which he sought to expose 'the hidden foundations of utopian theory' (p. 18), to unmask it as the 'disguise for the interests of the privileged Powers' (p. 118). For the purposes of this argument it does not matter that 'utopianism' is an amalgam of not necessarily compatible liberal ideas and theories. It does not matter that his understanding of 'realism' is quirky. Nor does it matter that the scholars of the subject he influenced ignored almost to a man, and indeed a woman, the quasi-Marxist implications of his employment of this 'realist' tool. What matters is that he got them to think critically in a deep sense. To ask: why does this author/actor say the things he does in the way he does? What interests and/or pragmatic purposes may he be serving? What events or policies does this theory of international relations serve to rationalize or justify? What subjective interests does this 'objective' voice serve? What particular interest does this assertion of a common interest or general harmony of interest disguise or rationalize? When it comes to assessing any idea or policy, *cui bono?*[17] The answers that Carr himself gave to these questions, directed at some of the most cherished political and economic nostrums of his day, have been regarded by many as unsatisfactory. However, in asking them he opened up a new critical vista in IR and played a decisive role in putting the discipline on a methodologically stronger and more analytically self-conscious footing.

Shortcomings

There can be no definitive statement of the shortcomings of such a wide-ranging and provocative work as *TYC*. In the following I offer five salient criticisms, not so much of his interpretation of particular events and issues, but of the structure and coherence of his argument. The strength and significance of these criticisms can only be judged by the reader, from his/her particular viewpoint. However, they are criticisms that all serious students of the book need to take into account.

First, a number of critics have objected to the moral stance of *TYC*, particularly Carr's assertion that there was essentially no moral difference between the methods and policies of the fascist Powers and those of the Western Powers. According to Carr, Nazi Germany was not doing anything in the 1930s that the UK and France would not have done if they had found themselves in the same position. A country's moral outlook was entirely a function of its position in the balance of power. Those in a favourable position used the slogans of law, security and peace to maintain it. Those in an unfavourable position used the language of justice and fairness to undermine it. Many critics, however, found it abhorrent that law, justice and morality could be reduced to questions of self-interest in this way. The logic of Carr's position was that there were no moral constraints on action. Morality was purely instrumental. Only expediency mattered. In addition, it implied that the domestic constitution and character of the state, communist, democratic or Nazi, did not matter. But according to some (and who today apart from the strict neo-realist would disagree?) this amounted to a relapse into utopianism and wishful thinking as deep as that of any of the 'utopians'.[18]

Second, Carr's concept of peaceful change has been attacked on a number of fronts. Some have found it intrinsically perplexing. How can 'yielding to threats of force' be conceived as 'a normal part of the process of *peaceful* change' (p. 277; emphasis added)? Some have found it unhelpful. How do we know, in the process of 'give and take' between 'haves' and 'have-nots' posited by Carr, when concessions to a rising Power should be halted lest the positions of the rising Power and the declining Power be merely reversed? Additionally, who is to count as a 'have' or a 'have-not' Power? Carr offers no definition but merely accepts as 'have-nots' those who said they were. But was Italy, a victor in World War One, a 'have-not' Power because *Il Duce* said she was? Was Germany, the victor in all the major diplomatic quarrels of the late 1930s, a 'have-not' because Hitler found it rhetorically convenient to portray her so?[19] This is a weakness in Carr's argument than can easily go undetected because of the skilful way in which it was constructed.

Third, Carr conceived utopianism in terms of the transplantation into international thought of the assumptions of nineteenth-century liberalism. There are several problems with this. Carr's understanding of 'nineteenth-century liberalism' tends to shift according to his particular target. Sometimes it means liberal democracy, sometimes classical political economy, sometimes the harmony of interests, sometimes Benthamism, sometimes rationalism, the meaning of these things being far from fixed. Benthamism, for example, sometimes means 'utilitarianism' and other times 'the efficacy of rational pubic opinion'. Other aspects of Bentham's thought e.g. his call for 'the emancipation of all distant dependencies',[20] are conveniently ignored. What precisely was being transplanted, therefore, is not always clear. In addition, there is more than a little selection bias in the ideas Carr deems to be representative of a broad and barely coherent liberal tradition.[21] With regard to the principal institutional manifestation of utopianism, the League of Nations, it may have been true that many of his proponents had strong faith in the efficacy of public opinion to enforce its decisions, but it was not true that they based their ideas on laissez-faire or the doctrine of the harmony of interests. In the security field, for example, they supported the League precisely because they felt that '*laissez-faire*/anarchic' doctrines would no longer work.[22]

Fourth, Carr claimed that he was laying down the foundations for a 'science' or IR. However, his twin conceptual pillars of utopianism and realism were far from stable. It was not always clear what the 'realities' were that 'realists' vis-à-vis 'utopians' took into account. Similarly, Carr sometimes opposes realism to 'the ideal' and sometimes to 'the apparent', the former being a conservative tactic (to pursue the ideal is not only futile but will make things worse), the latter being a radical tactic (behind the façade of sweetness and light lies a structure of oppression, self-interest and discrimination).[23] When it comes to 'utopia' things are even worse. Sometimes it means 'impractical', sometimes 'unverified', sometimes 'abstract', sometimes 'unprecedented', and sometimes 'false'. Connectedly, 'morality' was employed in conjunction with a staggering range of synonyms e.g. 'altruism', 'conscience', 'goodwill', 'ideals', 'self-sacrifice'.[24] In addition Carr's 'breathtaking equations'[25] (e.g. utopia: reality = free will: determinism = theory: practice = conscience: coersion = goodwill: enmity = altruism: self-seeking) suggested a fast-and-loose approach to concepts far removed from science.

Finally, Carr can be accused of committing, in the final chapter of the book, the very sin of which he accused the 'utopians': 'couching optative propositions in the indicative mood' (p. 17). Carr saw his socialist scheme for the reconstruction of the international order as a logical extension of existing historical trends: a 'progressively emerging future end' as he later put it.[26] This is what made it 'realistic'. However, the refashioning of liberalism and the recovery of capitalism after the war were soon to demonstrate that Carr's irresistible trends were far from irresistible. Carr turned out to be 'the prophet of a false collectivist dawn'.[27] His 'immanent developments' and prescriptions 'directly in the line of recent advance' (p. 307) look more and more like normative preferences dressed up in the language of fact.

Conclusion

Deep down *TYC* is a highly normative book. This is the first conclusion to be drawn from the preceding analysis. It is far from being a work of modern fatalism advocating surrender to the immanence of power. In the final analysis morality for Carr is as vital an element as power. He says, for example, that 'the *homo politicus* who pursues nothing but power is as unreal a myth as the *homo economicus* who pursues nothing but gain. Political action must be based on a co-ordination of morality and power' (p. 125). He declares that 'every solution of the problem of political change, whether national or international, must be based on a compromise between morality and power' (p. 265). He contends that while 'it is utopian to ignore the element of power, it is an unreal kind of realism which ignores the element of morality in any world order' (p. 302). Those commentators who have portrayed *TYC* as a manifesto of power have mistaken what Carr believed needed to be emphasized at a particular historical juncture for his understanding of reality *in toto*. They have also portrayed it in a way that is consistent with their own beliefs, disregarding inconvenient complexities, not least the dialectical nature of the relationship between power and morality, which Carr viewed as an engine of change, if not unequivocally of progress.[28]

Will the classical status of *TYC* endure? The first point to make is that it has not diminished in the 70 years since it was first published. Indeed, it has acquired new admirers since it was 'freed from the grip of the realists' in the 1990s.[29] A new edition with valuable additional material was published in 2001. It still regularly appears, if problematically under 'Realism', on undergraduate reading lists. Its influence, baleful or benign, assures it a prominent place in the history of the discipline. Moreover, it remains, despite its many shortcomings, one of the most original and provocative analyses of international relations in the literature, a work of rare insight and argumentative power. In this regard one should not conclude without mentioning the quality of the writing in *TYC*. It is true that Carr employed his remarkable dexterity with the English language to conceal flaws that would have been all too apparent in the work of a lesser writer. But one of the reasons why *TYC* continues to be widely read and discussed is that it is a work of considerable literary merit. There is something Hobbesian in the gravity, Swiftian in the sharpness of wit, and Burkian in the combination of coolness and passion in Carr's writing. On the literary plane alone *TYC* stands comparison with some of the finest political disquisitions in the English language.

Notes

1 The argument of Hans J. Morgenthau, 'The Surrender to the Immanence of Power: E. H. Carr' in Hans J. Morgenthau (ed.), *Dilemmas of Politics*, Chicago, IL: Chicago University Press, [1948] 1962, pp. 350–57. It has been echoed many times since, e.g. H. R. Trevor-Roper, 'E. H. Carr's Success Story', *Encounter*, 1962, vol. 18, p. 75.

2 E. H. Carr, *The Twenty Years' Crisis, 1919–1939: An Introduction to the Study of International Relations*, London: Macmillan, 1939, p. 131. Unless otherwise stated, all subsequent page numbers placed in parentheses in the text refer to this first edition.

3 Merely 'Hitler' in the second edition (1946) of Carr, *The Twenty Years' Crisis, 1919–1939*.

4 Carr later elevated this to a principle of historical research. While historical events were 'set in motion by the individual wills … the historian must go behind the individual wills and inquire into the reasons which made the individuals will and act as they did, and study the "factors" or "forces" which explain individual behaviour'. Quoted in R. J. Evans, 'Introduction', *What is History?*, London: Palgrave Macmillan, [1961] 2001, p. xviii.

5 For the imbroglio over Carr's appointment see Brian Porter, 'Lord Davies, E. H. Carr and the Spirit Ironic: A Comedy of Errors', *International Relations*, 2002, vol. 16, 77–96.

6 See Carr, 'An Autobiography', in M. Cox (ed.), *E. H. Carr: A Critical Appraisal*, London: Palgrave Macmillan, 2000, pp. xviii–xix.

7 For the background, historical and psychological, to Carr's support for appeasement see Jonathan Haslam, *The Vices of Integrity: E. H. Carr, 1892–1982*, London: Verso, 1999, Chapters 2 and 3.

8 See further my 'Myth of the First Great Debate', *Review of International Studies*, 1998, vol. 24, 1–15.

9 See e.g. Whittle Johnson, 'E. H. Carr's Theory of International Relations: A Critique', *Journal of Politics*, 1967, vol. 29, 861–84. I have reviewed the secondary literature on Carr up to 2000 in 'Radicalism for a Conservative Purpose: The Peculiar Realism of E. H. Carr', *Millennium: Journal of International Studies*, 2001, vol. 30, 123–36.

10 Preface to the second edition of Carr, *The Twenty Years' Crisis, 1919–1939*, p. x.

11 See Trevor-Roper, 'E. H. Carr's Success Story', p. 74; Evans, 'Introduction', pp. xxvi–xxxviii; and Keith Jenkins, 'Rethinking the Value of *What Is History?*' in Cox, *A Critical Appraisal*, pp. 304–21.

12 See Carr, 'An Autobiography', pp. xxi–xxii; Michael Cox, 'E. H. Carr and Isaac Deutscher: A Very Special Relationship', in Cox, *A Critical Appraisal*, pp. 125–44.

13 The word 'often' is an example of the slippery use of words of which Carr has sometimes been accused. When it came to utopianism the conditioning was 'always'. Nowhere in *TYC* does he explain how realism can sometimes be less conditioned than other modes of thought. He returned to this question, however, in *What is History?* (pp. 37–38), arguing that some degree of social transcendence was possible through critical self-awareness (which Marxists/realists possessed but liberals/rationalists/utopians did not).

14 Stanley Hoffmann, 'An American Social Science: International Relations', *Daedalus*, 1997, vol. 106, p. 43.

15 See further Peter Wilson, 'E. H. Carr's *The Twenty Years' Crisis*: Appearance and Reality in World Politics', *Politik*, 2009, vol. 12, 21–25.

16 See Charles Jones, *E. H. Carr and International Relations: A Duty to Lie*, Cambridge: Cambridge University Press, 1998, Chapter 6.

17 If not the term then the methodological stance that Susan Strange took from Carr. See her *States and Markets*, London: Pinter, 1988, pp. 63, 132, 217, and Benjamin J. Cohen, *International Political Economy: An Intellectual History*, Princeton, NJ: Princeton University Press, 2008, pp. 44–65. For Carr's attempt (one of the first) to map the relationship between international politics and ecomonics (i.e. IPE), see pp. 145–68.

18 See, for example, the views of Angell, Hayek and Crossman summarized in Wilson, 'Carr and his Early Critics: Responses to *The Twenty Years' Crisis*, 1939–45', in Cox, *A Critical Appraisal*, pp. 166–83.

19 See, for example, the views of Maddox, Hayek and Crossman, summarized in Wilson, 'Carr and his Early Critics', pp. 171–83.

20 Quoted in M. J. Smith, 'Liberalism and International Reform', in Terry Nardin and David R. Mapel (eds), *Traditions of International Ethics*, Cambridge: Cambridge University Press, 1992, p. 204.

21 See Casper Sylvest, *British Liberal Internationalism, 1880–1930: Making Progress?* Manchester: Manchester University Press, 2009, especially Chapter 2.

22 The view of Angell summarized in Wilson, 'Carr and his Early Critics', pp. 174–75.

23 See Stefano Guzzini, 'The Different Worlds of Realism in International Relations', *Millennium: Journal of International Studies*, 2001, vol. 30, 118–19.

24 The views of, *inter alia*, Woolf and Stebbing summarized in Wilson, 'Carr and his Early Critics', pp. 177–81. Woolf was so incensed with *TYC* that he wrote two replies. For an analysis see Peter Wilson, *The International Theory of Leonard Woolf*, New York: Palgrave Macmillan, 2003, Chapter 8.

25 Hedley Bull, '*The Twenty Years' Crisis* Thirty Years On', *International Journal*, 1969, vol. 24, p. 627.

26 Carr, *What is History?* p. 118.

27 Cox, 'Introduction', *Twenty Years' Crisis*, reissue, London: Palgrave Macmillan, 2001, p. lvii.

28 This is well brought out in Seán Molloy, *The Hidden History of Realism: A Genealogy of Power Politics*, New York: Palgrave Macmillan, 2006, Chapter 3.

29 The first shot in a volley of reappraisals of Carr was fired by Ken Booth in 'Security in Anarchy: Utopian Realism in Theory and Practice', *International Affairs*, 1991, vol. 67, 537–45.

6 A new politics for a global age: David Mitrany's *A Working Peace System*

Lucian M. Ashworth

In early 1965 Hans J. Morgenthau was contacted by Kurt Dreifuss of the Society for a World Service Federation. During their discussions Morgenthau recommended that Dreifuss read David Mitrany's *A Working Peace System* (*WPS* – 'this is the Functionalist approach of Mitrany, and I agree it makes sense'). Dreifuss tried in vain to track down a copy. Refusing to give up, he 'phoned Morgenthau who said "it is distressing but not surprising to me"'. Instead Morgenthau lent Dreifuss his own well-worn copy.[1] During the following year Dreifuss organized a republication of the original pamphlet in a collection that included other works by Mitrany. In his Introduction to this volume Morgenthau concluded that the very future of civilization now rested on the ability of the functional approach to overcome an obsolete and dangerous nationalism.[2]

Born in Bucharest in 1888 to a Jewish family, Mitrany left Romania at the age of 20. Enrolling at the London School of Economics in 1912, he studied sociology under L. T. Hobhouse and political science under Graham Wallas. Hobhouse and Wallas were to influence the young Mitrany in different, but compatible, ways. From Hobhouse came the idea of functions as the basis of society, while from Wallas came Mitrany's scepticism of rational plans for society that led to his emphasis on needs as an alternative basis for social organization. Becoming a British citizen after the First World War, he divided his time after that between Britain and the USA. His working life took him to Harvard, Princeton, and the offices of Unilever in London.[3]

Mitrany's first articulation of the functional approach to world order had come a decade before *WPS* in *The Progress of International Government*.[4] Yet, the functional approach to government – where the institutions of government are built up around specific functions that are perceived as being vital to the reproduction of society – was not new. Hobhouse had used it in his formulation of a liberal approach to government in 1911, and Mary Parker Follett used functional government in her 1918 book.[5] In the 1920s H. G. Wells, R. H. Tawney, G. D. H. Cole and Harold Laski had all used a functional approach to support a guild socialist alternative politico-economic system.[6] Mitrany was not even the first to apply functional government to international relations. That distinction falls to Laski. Mitrany's genius was to develop a comprehensive functional approach to international order that fused ideas of both the welfare state and international organizations that also did not ignore issues of power and national interest. *WPS* was the culmination of two decades of work on the problems of modern governance, yet it only represented a part of his larger research agenda, which included publications on the peasant social revolution, international sanctions, the adaptation of government to total war and the office of the ombudsman.[7] *WPS* was originally a policy document written for Chatham House's Foreign Press and Research Section, then part of the Foreign Office's war effort. It was published in pamphlet form in 1943 and quickly made Mitrany's name among international experts.

Ideologically Mitrany is hard to pin down, and he liked it that way. His writing on peasant agriculture displayed a strong sympathy for the anarchist ideas of Proudhon (and a dislike of the urban Marxists).[8] He worked for the liberal *Manchester Guardian* and was an enthusiastic member of the British Labour Party's Advisory Committee on International Questions. However, he was also a political advisor for Unilever. Opposed to the national planning ideas of many labour and social democratic parties, he was nonetheless an enthusiastic advocate of international planning.[9] *WPS* is best seen as a confluence of all of these positions, as well as a reaction to the failure of collective security in the 1930s. A common mistake has been to regard the pamphlet as having no theory of government, and consequently being merely a theory of 'economic integration'.[10] In fact, *WPS* is premised on a theory of government, but it is not a theory of state government. Indeed, Mitrany's political theory flows from his study of the peasant social revolution, and has strong anarchist elements to it. It is also a mistake to regard his approach as being a theory of political integration (Mitrany always strenuously denied this[11]). Rather, functional integration for Mitrany was primarily a means towards the establishment of world peace. Mitrany turned to need as the basis of a world order owing to his deep scepticism with previous world orders based on rationality. Mitrany took from Wallas the view that reason was not employed by humanity until we had used our emotions to choose the social urges and entities that we considered important. Needs, in a global context, were Mitrany's interpretation of Wallas' social urges and entities.[12]

In this chapter I first consider the argument of *WPS*. I follow this with an assessment of why it is a classic, and an analysis of the reaction to it. With a few exceptions, Mitrany's ideas are less quoted and used in International Relations (IR) today than they were up to the mid-1980s, and in European Union Studies he is usually read through the prism of neo-functionalist analysis.[13] Despite this, I conclude that the success of *WPS* lies in its broad appeal that stretches beyond the immediate concerns of 1943.

The argument of *WPS*

The initial popularity of *WPS* was in part due to its timely and provocative argument. It addressed, and rejected, the popular federal plans for world peace, while laying out a project for the development of an incremental plan for the establishment of global authorities based upon the idea of the fulfilment of human needs. The ethos of the piece was a deep pessimism with both the form of the sovereign state system and with current constitutional and legalistic plans for solving the problem of war. This pessimism was not unique to Mitrany, and in fact was a hallmark of much of interwar thinking in the UK,[14] but what was different about Mitrany was his scepticism about the possibilities of establishing a strong overarching 'political' security organization along the lines of the old League of Nations. Thus, the idea of organizing international life on the basis of function-specific organizations was a product of the lowering of expectations about what was possible at the level of global order.

Overshadowing *WPS* is the failure of the League of Nations project, and the cause of that failure, in Mitrany's view, is shared with the numerous federal schemes for world peace that were currently being bandied about in British and US circles. It was an overly constitutional and legal solution that combined rigidity with the failure to deal with the major practical problems facing humanity. The League failed not because it was a utopian vision ahead of its time, but rather because it was a rigidly formal structure that owed its shape to nineteenth-century ideas of the 'nightwatchman' state (p. 8). Calls for a federated world were of the same order, and overlooked the need for a more flexible solution capable of making constant adjustments as new problems arose.

For such a short work *WPS* covered many issues that were of contemporary relevance. Five areas stand out, four of which form the argument for the development of the fifth. First, and building on work he had done on the Tennessee Valley Authority and the New Deal while he was at the Princeton Institute for Advanced Study, was the changing role of the state from a legalistic to a service-based organization. The second concerned the failures and inherent flaws of the federalist solutions to modern world problems. Third, Mitrany saw the task facing his generation as one of practical politics, not of ideology. Fourth, was the fundamental inability of the system of states to deal with the antimony between power and sovereignty. Fifth, Mitrany advanced his functional approach as the best means to deal with all of these concerns. I will examine each of these areas in turn.

A crucial underlying assumption in *WPS*, building upon earlier work by both Mitrany and his contemporaries, was that during the first half of the twentieth century the state was going through profound changes in its form and in what it was expected to accomplish. The implications of these changes for international order were wide-ranging and often contradictory, but they suggested to Mitrany that any system of world politics based upon older principles of government would be insufficiently adaptable and thus doomed to failure. The central idea here was the change in the nature of the state from a primarily legalistic and constitutional 'nightwatchman' role, to a state based on services and the solving of practical problems of need and welfare regardless of their constitutional legality. He saw the nineteenth-century concern with the constitutional constraint of authority as a necessary stage in human development that curbed arbitrary power and defined the relationship of the individual to the state. However, this political revolution did not address the serious social concerns that were being thrown up by industrial development. It carried with it another negative legacy for the solving of twentieth-century concerns: these constitutional arrangements had been copper-fastened by rigid legal constraints that were meant to prevent their erosion, but had the unintended consequence of making further reform beyond basic rights difficult (p. 7).

The pressures for social change had led to widespread revolts against this rigid legal-constitutional order. The darker side of this revolt could be seen in communism and fascism where 'totalitarian leaders have been playing the strong card of pragmatic socialism against constitutional democracy' (p. 9). Despite this association with totalitarianism this 'trend of the times' was also strongly present in Western democratic societies, and thus defied ideological and national differences. Although little mentioned in *WPS*, Mitrany had earlier explored two major examples of this trend in democratic societies: the New Deal in the USA, and the emerging welfare state in the UK.[15] Both had faced legal-constitutional challenges. Aspects of the New Deal had been challenged by the Supreme Court, while the early British welfare state had faced House of Lords opposition in 1909. This crossing of ideological and national divides was a feature of the new politics. Where the earlier constitutional government had stressed national difference as the basis for defining individual constitutional authorities (based on peoples), the new social politics involved solving issues of human need that often could only be effectively solved through international cooperation. This gave a boost to international organizations designed to deal with special social and economic problems, and hence 'the lines of national and international evolution are not parallel, but converging' (ibid.). Thus, for Mitrany, new forms of government were developing that were centred on needs, rather than rational legal formulas. Although what Mitrany meant by need was never clearly stipulated.

This trend towards the politics of the welfare state, however, also contained within it the seeds of discord and more violent international wars. The widening of the state's involvement into fresh areas of social and economic planning, coupled with the internationalization of the global economy, meant that there were now more areas in which the state took an interest, which in turn increased the number of issue areas in which states could come into conflict with other states. As a result, the state, designed to preserve the security of a close-knit community, was now converted into a cause of conflict.[16] For many the answer to this problem with the state was some form of federation that would use familiar constitutional means to construct political entities that would make more social and economic sense. These ranged from ideas of League-like weak confederations, to full formal federal arrangements.[17] Much of *WPS* was given over to criticizing ideas of federal union, both in their continental and ideological forms. In Mitrany's view, the idea of a federal road to peace was flawed on many counts. First, federalism was strongly linked to nineteenth-century ideas of creating a single rigid constitution to deal with the problems of conflict. As a constitutional solution its concerns were not with the changing nature of world politics, but rather with the political problems found within the state (pp. 14–15). Second, rather than solving the problem of violent interstate rivalries, federations would merely create larger federal states that would be better equipped to engage in war, and more likely to exacerbate rivalries with those outside the federation. In this sense, federations would just replicate the problem of the sovereign nation state on a larger scale. Mitrany even argued that ideological unions were unlikely to reflect their ideological colours in their foreign policy, pointing out how current democracies do not always support democracy at the international level (pp. 16–18). Third, continental unions would also still have to face the problem of the fear of domination by the dominant power within the federation, thus exacerbating rivalries (p. 12). Finally, there was no necessary link between federal unions and peace. Here Mitrany quotes Coudenhove-Kalergi (the central figure in the pan-Europa movement) who dismissed the peaceful nature of a pan-European union, stressing instead its similarity with the movements for German and Italian unification. In fact, Mitrany saw the problem of conflict as worse, since a full continental union would be more likely to achieve the autarky and self-sufficiency associated with unfettered state competition (ibid.). In later publications Mitrany would also accuse the federalists of naivety for their belief that it was possible to merge modern service-orientated states.[18]

This leads us to a third theme in *WPS*, that the problem of world politics is fundamentally a problem of practical politics, rather than of ideology. This slant in Mitrany's work is often misunderstood to mean that he has dismissed the importance of ideology and cultural difference, and is instead replacing it with a grey technocratic (and therefore thoroughly undemocratic) system of global governance.[19] To begin with, this interpretation misses the underlying pessimism of Mitrany's analysis of world affairs. It is not that he underrates the power of ideology, culture and nationalism, but rather he is all too aware of how these have contributed to the global crisis faced by humanity in the early 1940s.[20] We seek practical solutions to global problems not because ideology is weak, but rather because it is far too strong. As a result, it is important not to attempt to try to regulate 'the parochial politics of its members' as federalism does by diving into constitutional matters that stir up local loyalties and ways of life (p. 15). Global governance needs to be about those practical political matters where common agreement is easier to find, and where people will not feel that their particular ways of doing things are under threat. His templates for how this was done were the earlier Public International Unions and those branches of the League system that had succeeded and survived. The goal here is to achieve what so many IR experts of the interwar period, including those now associated with the realist tradition such as E. H. Carr and C. A. W. Manning, were looking for: a means to achieving peaceful change. For Mitrany this required moving away from emotive issues such as changes in boundaries, towards solving major problems in a way that left fraught irreconcilables untouched (pp. 26–27).

For Mitrany the presence of emotive nationalisms made attempts at a legal-constitutional order obsolete. Here again we see the importance that Mitrany attached to the power of nationalism as a problem of global order. Yet, while so much of Mitrany's work was premised on the problem of nationalism as an emotive issue that was not open to rational solution, he did in the final analysis succumb to a rational solution himself. While needs-based organizations were a means by which Mitrany could confront the emotive appeal of nationalism with the arguably deeper and more primeval urges to satisfy human needs, he did assume that needs-based functional organizations would in turn replace national loyalties among populations as their success at providing services undermined the appeals of nationalism. This contains within it an assumption that human loyalties are based upon reasoned judgement and instrumental calculation.[21]

The fourth theme is the inherent flaw in the system of states that the League had left unresolved, and which remains an irritant in state relations to this day. The notion of state equality had, for Mitrany, 'in the past caused all efforts at common international action to flounder between the Scylla of power and the Charybdis of sovereignty' (p. 27). In a system of states, great powers (often representing larger swathes of humanity) have disproportionate control over the operation and management of the international system. Smaller states oppose this with the concept of the innate equality of sovereign states. There is no resolution to this antimony in a society of states, and consequently all attempts at concerted action are poisoned by it. The League suffered one of its most damaging crises over this issue when the question of permanent membership of the League Council was raised (p. 27–28). This tension between sovereign equality and power would remain as long as solutions to the world's problems revolved around state membership of organizations, and state direction of specific problems. Some support for Mitrany's case can be gleaned from the current workings of the European Union and the United Nations Security Council, where the question of the relative power of the larger members (with the bulk of the population) frequently come into conflict with the small states' claims to equality.

The final theme that emerges from *WPS* is the central issue of the whole work. Mitrany's answer to all of these developments, failed alternatives and problems is his functional alternative, and it is his presentation and defence of it that takes up over half of the pamphlet. Again, it is important to stress the fundamental pessimism behind what Mitrany suggests. The functional approach is superior not because it is an ideal form of government, but because it is the most likely to succeed. The reasons for its potential success are both that it is a practical alternative that conforms to the times, and that it leaves the question of specific goals open and flexible. Thus, Mitrany's approach to IR privileges process over goals. The functional approach is a path to be taken, not a blueprint for a fully formed better world. Here again is a marked contrast with the federalist movement, with its well thought-out goals, but fuzzy means for getting there.

The form of the functional alternative, therefore, is defined by the specific problems that it sets to solve. 'The problem of our generation', Mitrany claimed, 'is how to weld together the common interests of all without interfering with the particular ways of each' (p. 31). It was here that the constitutionalism of the federalist and League enthusiasts had come unstuck. The essential principle of the functional approach was to 'weld together' only those common interests that did not interfere with these particular ways. As a result, 'activities would be selected specifically and organised separately, each according to its nature, to the conditions under which it has to operate, and to the needs of the moment' (p. 33). Primarily this meant functions associated with needs that were fundamentally technical in nature. In terms of principles of government, therefore, the functional approach would attempt to do internationally what the new service and welfare states were doing nationally: solve specific problems through the establishment of narrowly problem-focused international organizations that would evolve as the issue itself evolved.

Mitrany never specifies what a functional organization should look like. For him such matters depended on the nature of the function and the wishes of those involved:

> The functional *dimensions* … determine themselves. In a like manner the function determines its appropriate *organs*. It also reveals through practice the nature of the action required under the given conditions, and in that way the *powers* needed by the respective authority (p. 35, emphasis in the original).

Yet, this fuzzy definition of both function and need hid a problem. The functional approach was premised on the idea that needs were prior to culture, and therefore politically uncontentious. However, there was no reason why this should be the case. In fact, while need could rather tritely be viewed as prior to culture, the actual means by which people satisfied need was often deeply culture-specific. For example, while we all need to eat, the way that we cook the food we eat is the product of culture. In this sense, the idea that functional organizations would somehow escape cultural wranglings was naïve.[22] That said, Mitrany certainly looked to existing practice for hints on the form of functional organizations. This included a diverse range of recent experiences, including wartime planning, the largely Berne-based Public International Unions, the specialized agencies of the League, as well as domestic experiences such as the New Deal or the London Transport Board. He also flagged the issue of functional representation: that these functional bodies needed to be representative of all those involved in a specific function, but on the flip side those who did not have a stake should not carry undue weight. Thus, representation and democratic control should also be dictated by the nature of the function, and not necessarily by outdated notions of constitutional legal equality (pp. 38ff.).

Reaction and significance

There are three reasons why I see *WPS* as a classic work. First, the pamphlet managed to combine topicality with a theoretical underpinning that would be of interest to future generations no longer animated by the immediate problems addressed by the text. This might explain why his work survived in IR, while work by his contemporaries such as Leonard Woolf, H. N. Brailsford and Philip Noel-Baker fared less well. Ironically, at the time when *WPS* was written Mitrany would have been far less well known, both in policy circles and to the wider public. Second, the functional approach emphasized process over specific goals. He saw the institutional details of any proposed new world, if they were to be practical and effective, as the work of those most actively involved in a function. Mitrany's goal was to lay out workable principles based on the 'trend of the times'. The only problem with this approach was that it left the question of the nature of functional organization to be filled in by later theorists, and many of these reinterpreted functional cooperation in ways that were not sympathetic to Mitrany's own world view. Yet, there were advantages to Mitrany's approach. Not tied to any particular idea of functional cooperation, his ideas as process could find themselves applied to a number of different sets of organizations. Third, his international theory represented a clear attempt to synthesize current developments in the study of domestic politics, and apply them to international problems. Many of the Anglo-US debates about international affairs in the first few decades of the century had revolved around legalistic arguments. The hope was to apply the same 'rule of law revolution' that had occurred in nineteenth-century domestic politics of Western states to the international sphere. The functional approach was an attempt to develop an international theory that took into account the shift towards service and needs that had come with the development of the welfare state. Mitrany saw himself as reconnecting the study of the international with the seismic shifts that had happened in the rest of politics. In this context, Mitrany was responsible for revolutionizing the study of international organizations.

The initial reaction to *WPS* among Mitrany's centre-left colleagues was lukewarm. Much of the criticism was based on the misperception that what Mitrany called functional cooperation referred only to economic and social cooperation, and therefore was not primarily concerned with longer-term issues of security and political cooperation. While they saw value in functional cooperation, for them the key issue was the establishment of a new 'political' League organization to control security issues. Leonard Woolf wrote that while there was a place for functional international organizations 'the necessity for a central world authority is absolute'.[23] Noel-Baker echoed Woolf's position, arguing that 'the first and indispensable condition of either peace or economic prosperity, is the creation of a strong international political organisation'.[24] Outside of the Labour Party advocates of a federal alternative were also critical of Mitrany's lack of a central political organization.[25] Yet, despite these criticisms, Mitrany's ideas of international functionalism became widely accepted in British circles. Indeed, Wilson has argued that the popularity of functionalism was partially responsible for the decline in federalist thought in the UK after 1945.[26]

Interestingly, it was outside his circle that Mitrany often found the strongest support for his ideas. E. H. Carr endorsed a functionalist solution to the problem of European order, even if he failed to cite *WPS*.[27] More direct acknowledgement and engagement with Mitrany's work came from realist scholars in the USA. While John Herz was concerned that a functionalist approach did not always take into consideration the ubiquity of conflicts over power, he believed that it could contribute to solving international problems, especially if it rested on broad public support.[28] Morgenthau was far more enthusiastic than Herz, and his work is peppered with references to functionalist solutions to global problems.[29] Later, Inis Claude's study of international organization would include a chapter-length critical analysis of the functional approach that, while sceptical of certain assumptions of Mitrany's approach, acknowledged that it 'has the great merit of appealing both to humanitarian idealism and to national self-interest',[30] Claude had neatly summarized Mitrany's appeal to classical realism: that it combined a normative approach with an (often pessimistic) acceptance of the pragmatic problems posed by current structures of political power. Mitrany was less happy about the neo-functionalist interpretation of his theories, and indeed many of the myths about what Mitrany stood for stem from writers such as Ernst Haas,[31] Leon Lindberg and Stuart A. Sheingold.[32]

Following the US republication of *WPS* in 1966, a fresh generation of students adapted the functional approach to understand the new world of détente and North-South dialogue.[33] Here, functionalism became associated with technocratic organizations, especially those within the United Nations system. This shift of focus to the UN had its roots in Mitrany's own identification of the UN as a functional system.[34] The concentration on the UN also led to a downplaying of the role of functional democracy. The functional approach continued to be a major part of the IR curriculum during the 1980s, and was also taught as a forebear of neofunctionalism in European Union studies for much longer. Since the mid-1990s Mitrany has become less popular in discussions of IR theory. An exception to this has been the interest in Mitrany from those studying the historiography of the field of IR.[35] Despite this recent neglect, there is an enduring appeal to Mitrany's ideas. His view of the shifting basis of government, and the challenge of an outdated state system, places change rather than continuity at the heart of human governance. Yet, alongside this is a pessimism about our ability to transcend our dogmatic and divisive identities.

Notes

1 Letter from Kurt Dreifuss to Louis B. Sohn, 12 March 1965, and letter from Kurt Dreifuss to David Mitrany, 1 June 1965, Box Mitrany/2, Mitrany Papers, British Library of Political and Economic Sciences, LSE, London.

2 Hans J. Morgenthau, 'Introduction', in David Mitrany, *A Working Peace System*, Chicago, IL: Quadrangle, 1966, p. 11. Page numbers placed in parentheses in the text refer to the 1943 edition. David Mitrany, *A Working Peace System*, Oxford: Oxford University Press/RIIA, 1943.

3 For further biographical information on Mitrany, written by his research assistant, see Dorothy Anderson, 'David Mitrany (1888–1975): An Appreciation of his Life and Work', *Review of International Studies*, 1998, vol. 24, 577–92.

4 London: Allen & Unwin, 1933.

5 L. T. Hobhouse, *Liberalism,* London: Williams and Norgate, 1911; Mary Parker Follett, *The New State*, London: Longman, 1918.

6 H. G. Wells, *Men Like Gods,* London: Cassell, 1923; R. H. Tawney, *The Acquisitive Society,* New York: Harcourt Brace, 1920; G. D. H. Cole, *Guild Socialism,* New York: Stokes, 1920; Harold Laski, *A Grammar of Politics,* London: George Allen & Unwin, 1925. For a full discussion of these works in relation to Mitrany's functional approach see David Long, 'International Functionalism and the Politics of Forgetting', *International Journal,* 1993, vol. 48, 355–79.

7 For a full summary of his work see Anderson, 'David Mitrany (1888–1975)'. See also Lucian M. Ashworth, *International Relations Theory and the Labour Party: Intellectuals and Policy Making 1918–1945*, London: I. B.Tauris, 2007, p. 120ff.

8 For Mitrany's work on the peasant social revolution see his 'Marx v. the Peasant', in T. E. Gregory and Hugh Dalton (eds), *London Essays in Economics: In Honour of Edwin Cannan*, London: Routledge, 1927; *The Land and the Peasant in Rumania: The War and Agrarian Reform,* London: Humprey Milford and Oxford University Press, 1930; *Marx Against the Peasant: A Study in Social Dogmatism*, London: Weidenfeld & Nicolson, 1951.

9 See David Mitrany, 'International Consequences of National Planning', *Yale Review* 1947, vol. 37, 18–31.

10 See, for example, the presentation of Mitrany in David Mutimer, 'Theories of Political Integration' in H. Michaelmann and P. Soldatos, *European Integration Theories and Approaches,* Lanham, MD: University Press of America, 1992, pp. 13–42.

11 See 'Note for Ernst Haas', 14 February 1963, from the Mitrany Papers, LSE Library archives. Mitrany once told Charles Pentland that European integration theory was a waste of time.

12 Graham Wallas, *Human Nature and Politics,* Boston, MA and New York: Houghtom Mifflin, [1908] 1916, pp. 21, 25, and Chapter 4.

13 A notable exception to this is Ben Rosamond's thoughtful analysis in his *Theories of European Integration,* Basingstoke: Palgrave Macmillan, 2000, pp. 31–36.

14 For this see Richard Overy, *The Morbid Age: Britain and the Crisis of Civilisation, 1919–1939,* Harmondsworth: Penguin, 2010.

15 See, for example, his 'The New Deal: An Interpretation of its Origin and Nature', *Agenda*, 1942, vol. 1.

16 David Mitrany, 'Memorandum on Studies in International Relations', unpublished paper dated 1933–34; David Mitrany, 'A Realistic Interpretation of Security', Lecture to the Student's International Union, 16 July 1935, pp. 4–6; David Mitrany, 'Outline for a Paper on Pacifism', no date, p. 1; all from the Mitrany Papers. British Library of Political and Economic Sciences, LSE, London. Mitrany, *Progress of International Government*, p. 42.

17 For a discussion of these debates see Peter Wilson, 'The New Europe Debate in Wartime Britain' in Philomena Murray and Paul Rich (eds), *Visions of European Unity,* Boulder, CO: Westview, 1996, pp. 39–62.

18 See also David Mitrany, 'The Functional Approach to World Organization', *International Affairs*, 1948, vol. 24, 351–53; David Mitrany, 'The Prospects of Integration: Federal or Functional?', in A. J. R. Groom and Paul Taylor (eds), *Functionalism. Theory and Practice in International Relations*, New York: Crane Russak, 1975, p. 62.

19 See, for example, Alec Stone Sweet and Wayne Sandholtz, 'Integration, Supranational Governance, and the Institutionalisation of European Polity', in Wayne Sandholtz and Alec Stone Sweet*, European Integration and Supranational Governance,* Oxford: Oxford University Press, 1998, p. 5.

20 Lucian M. Ashworth, 'Bringing the Nation Back In: Mitrany and the Enjoyment of Nationalism', in L. Ashworth and D. Long (eds), *New Perspectives on International Functionalism*, Basingstoke: Palgrave Macmillan, 1999.

21 See Ashworth, 'Bringing the Nation Back In?' Inis Claude was also critical of the extent to which functional organizations would attract loyalties. See his *Swords into Plowshares: The Problems and Progress of International Organization,* 4th edn, New York: Random House, [1956] 1971, p. 355.

22 See Lucian M. Ashworth, *Creating International Studies. Angell, Mitrany and the Liberal Tradition*, Aldershot: Ashgate, 1999, pp. 101–03.

23 Leonard Woolf, *International Post-War Settlement*, London: Fabian Society/Victor Gollancz, 1944, p. 7.

24 Philip Noel-Baker, 'Notes on Mr Dalton's Outline Sketch of the Principles Upon Which a Delcaration of Post-War International Policy Should Be Based', Labour Party International Department memo, November 1943, p. 5. William Gillies papers, Labour Party Archives, John Rylands Library, Manchester, UK.

25 See, for example, Lionel Curtis's comments in David Mitrany, 'The Functional Approach to World Organization', *International Affairs,* 1998, vol. 24, 362–63.

26 Wilson, 'The New Europe Debate in Wartime Britain', pp. 57–58.
27 E.H. Carr, *Nationalism and After*, London: Macmillan, 1945, pp. 47–74. Carr's use of Mitrany is mentioned in Ashworth, *Creating International Studies,* p. 113, and William Scheuerman, 'The (Classical) Realist Vision of Global Reform', *International Theory*, 2010, vol. 2, 260. See also Wilson, 'The New Europe Debate in Wartime Britain', pp. 42–44.
28 John H. Herz, *International Politics in the Atomic Age*, New York: Columbia University Press, 1959, 327–29. See also Scheuerman, '(Classical) Realist Vision', pp. 264–66 and Casper Sylvest, 'Realism and International Law: The Challenge of John H. Herz', *International Theory*, 2010, vol. 2, 436.
29 See also Scheuerman, '(Classical) Realist Vision', 262–64.
30 Claude, *Swords into Plowshares*, p. 386
31 For Mitrany's objection to Haas's interpretation see 'Note to Ernst Haas', 14 February 1963, From the Mitrany Papers, British Library of Political and Economic Sciences, LSE, London. For Haas's views of functionalism and neofunctionalism see Ernst B. Haas, *The Uniting of Europe: Political, Social and Economic Forces, 1950–57*, London: Stevens, 1958, and *Beyond the Nation-State: Functionalism and International Organization*, Stanford, CA: Stanford University Press, 1964.
32 Leon N. Lindberg and Stuart A. Scheingold, *Europe's Would-Be Polity*, Englewood Cliffs, NJ: Prentice-Hall, 1970, pp. 6–7.
33 James Patrick Sewell, *Functionalism and World Politics: A Study Based on United Nations Programs Financing Economic Development*, Princeton, NJ: Princeton University Press, 1966; A. J. R. Groom and Paul Taylor, *Functionalism: Theory and Practice*, London: University of London Press, 1975. Mark F. Imber, 'Re-Reading Mitrany: A Pragmatic Assessment of Sovereignty', *Review of International Studies*, 1984, vol. 10, 103–23.
34 Mitrany, 'The Functional Approach to World Organization'.
35 Cornelia Navari, 'David Mitrany and International Functionalism', in David Long and Peter Wilson (eds), *Thinkers of the Twenty Years' Crisis*, Oxford: Oxford University Press, 1995; Anderson, 'David Mitrany'; Ashworth, *Creating International Studies*; Ashworth and Long *New Perspectives on International Functionalism*; and Wilson, 'The New Europe Debate in Wartime Britain'.

7 Politics between and beyond nations: Hans J. Morgenthau's *Politics Among Nations*

Nicolas Guilhot

It is an unusually daunting task to review a work considered to be a classic in a few pages, let alone pass judgement on it. The task may be even more challenging when the work in question is unanimously considered to have 'made the field' of International Relations (IR) as we know it.[1] However, Hans J. Morgenthau's *Politics among Nations: The Struggle for Power and Peace*[2] (*PAN*) presents us with an even greater challenge, which has to do with the constantly evolving nature of the text through its successive editions. The first difficulty is to ascertain which book is under scrutiny. Is it the 1948 first edition, still very close in tone and general orientation to the previous *Scientific Man versus Power Politics* (1946), with its rather explicit and recurring rejection of the scientific method? If there ever was something akin to a founding text that 'made the field' of IR, then the original 1948 edition would certainly qualify. The book was an instant academic best-seller, immediately 'adopted as a textbook for foreign policy and international relations at Harvard, Yale, Princeton, Columbia, and Notre Dame Universities'. The following year, 90 colleges had adopted it throughout the USA, which was more than all other previous textbooks combined.[3] Generally, the book was well received, and the first reviews contributed to establishing its status as a 'realist' manifesto. In his *Review of Politics*, Waldemar Gurian saluted a 'landmark' in the US literature on international relations, and underscored Morgenthau's opposition to the 'legalistic approach' and to 'idealism and utopianism'.[4]

Yet, the academic fortune of *PAN* as a realist and scientific approach to politics may be deceptive, for the first edition of *PAN* did not include the 'Six Principles of Politics Realism', the compulsory reading of most introductory courses in IR. Should we then look instead at the second edition, published in 1954, with its more ambitious claims of theory-building and its explicit endorsement of realism? Or perhaps later editions, coping with the consequences of the thermonuclear revolution?[5] At the time of writing, *PAN* has gone through seven editions, the latest one established in 2006. And there seems to be just as many Morgenthaus as there are editions of *PAN*: contrasting with the early reception of the book that established him as the consummate realist thinker, the current Morgenthau revival tends to bring out the moral, ethical and even utopian dimensions of his thought, thus challenging the realist monopoly over the interpretation of his thought, or destabilizing the very notion of what constitutes 'realism'.[6]

The difficulty is also compounded by the long gestation period of the book. We now know, thanks to the work of Christoph Frei, that the basic layout of *PAN* and its core arguments were already in place in the 1930s, long before Morgenthau became the founding father of IR. *PAN*, then, is Morgenthau's *magnum opus*, a gigantic work in progress, a geological sedimentation of successive intellectual layers, each reflecting a particular historical context and a specific stage in Morgenthau's rich intellectual biography.[7] Written by an émigré scholar who lived through the collapse of the old European world and reflected upon it from the shores of a new hegemonic power which he regarded as lacking the tragic sense of history that alone sustained political wisdom, *PAN* is also a book in which the twentieth century is thinking aloud, trying to draw from its past possible lessons for an uncertain future. The following, therefore, only offers a glimpse of various themes that run through the book.

Beyond the 'Six Principles of Realism'

Rather than shunning the ambiguity of *PAN*, it is preferable to see it as a constitutive element that provides a point of entry into its formidable architecture. The evolving nature of this book reflects a deep-seated tension characteristic not only of Morgenthau's own thinking, but more generally of IR theory as a whole. This tension is best captured by comparing the first edition of *PAN* with subsequent ones. Every student of IR is familiar with one of the latter. With the introduction of the 'Six Principles of Realism' in 1954, *PAN* became a book that 'purport[ed] to present a theory of international politics' – not only a theory, but a 'rational theory', the possibility of which was warranted by the fact that politics is 'governed by objective laws' (pp. 3–4, fourth edition). Although Morgenthau was cautious to insist that the theory must be judged by its pragmatic value, he nevertheless suggested that it must satisfy formal criteria of internal consistency and logical conformity with its own premises.

This concern with theory, scientific laws and rationality, which certainly did a great deal to define the discipline for generations of students, is deceptive. It is nowhere to be found in the 1948 edition, which establishes humbler goals and scrupulously avoids making any concession to the idea that a science of politics is possible or even meaningful.[8] The best a scholar of politics can do, Morgenthau wrote, is not to unveil the laws of politics but to 'trace the different tendencies which, as potentialities, are inherent in a certain international situation' (p. 6). Far from following the scientific method having currency in the natural sciences, the realist student of international relations needs instead a:

> creative imagination … capable of that supreme intellectual achievement which consists in detecting under the surface of present power relations the germinal developments of the future, in combining the knowledge of what is with the hunch as to what might be, and in condensing all these facts, symptoms, and unknowns into a chart of probable future trends which is not too much at variance with what actually will happen (p. 116).[9]

What goes under the name of 'theory' in *PAN* is thus a phenomenology of power, a casuistic exercise aiming at 'detecting' or 'distinguishing' political phenomena rather than articulating them under eternal laws. The book is replete with nomenclatures, typologies, taxonomies and other types of distinctions – between sources of power, between imperialisms, etc. This phenomenological acuity, which consists in recognizing, within the uninterrupted jetstream of events, the basic 'underlying forces' that determine it, is a talent that belongs to the scholar as much as to the seasoned politician. The theory of international politics, as Morgenthau understood it, could be not separated from the exercise of sound political judgement, and thus from a given historical context.

Against the positivistic and scientistic readings of realism and against ambiguous formulations owing to Morgenthau himself, it is important to emphasize that *PAN* does not purport to turn international politics into a science.[10] If what is called for is 'creative imagination' rather than the detached calculations of the scientist, it is because for Morgenthau each historical situation is 'unique', and cannot be derived from an axiomatic set of principles. The antiscientific thrust that provides the *basso continuo* of *PAN* stems from the powerful echoes that Weimarian *Wissenssoziologie* finds in Morgenthau's work. If there cannot be a scientific knowledge of history – and, for that matter, of politics – it is because knowledge itself is historical, as Morgenthau never tired of repeating.[11] While the cornerstone of science in the 1950s was its value-neutrality, 'no study of international politics … can be disinterested in the sense that it is able to divorce knowledge from action and to pursue knowledge for its own sake' (p. 7), since the observer is also a participant existentially engaged in the situation he describes. Knowledge is historically situated and indexed to a specific situation.[12] Of course, the kind of knowledge offered in *PAN* is no exception, and it too is rooted in a particular historical configuration, as the book's explicit purpose is 'to reflect on international politics in the United States, as we approach the mid-twentieth century' (p. 8). The adoption of Morgenthau as the tutelary figure of a discipline eager to pass as a social 'science' has made us forget that its founding text was explicitly claiming its historical situatedness.

Human nature as a historical horizon

In Morgenthau's insistence on the historical and therefore finite nature of human reason, we can recognize one of the touchstones of realism, namely its staunch opposition to all politics claiming to fulfil the meaning of history. Here, realism targets indiscriminately all philosophies of history, whether they belong to Marxism, liberalism, their scientific variants, reactionary visions of 1,000-year empires, or the pretence of modern nationalism to realize universal morality. In *PAN*, the charge is mostly levelled against the latter ('the nationalistic masses of our times meet in the international arena, each group convinced that it executes the mandate of history' – p. 249, fourth edition), but the critique of the theories of imperialism in Chapter 5 is also a critique of the intellectual temptation, plaguing much of the 'scientific' study of politics, to formulate laws of history.[13]

Yet, Morgenthau's theory of international politics stops short of being a pure historical relativism. While knowledge cannot escape its historical condition, one thing remains unaffected by the vicissitudes of history, and that thing is human nature. To the extent that Morgenthau can speak of 'laws' of politics and other historical regularities, it is because his realism is essentially an anthropology. To the extent that he postulates an unchanging human nature located outside of history, Morgenthau's anthropology is where his general approach to politics remains most indebted to a theological vision of man as a mixed creature, driven by a 'lust for power' but also capable of moral aspirations that most often exceed his capacities.[14] In *PAN*, this basic anthropological setup is, however, deployed in a different way, which downplays the theological motives. Morgenthau foregrounds the biological components of human nature as a set of 'elemental bio-psychological drives' described as 'the drives to live, to propagate and to dominate' that are 'common to all men' (p. 17). It is this biological substratum that provides the only invariable mechanism in history and that is constantly expressed in political life, as men – and the states they form – seek to pre-serve their power, increase it, or simply display it. Whatever 'laws' of international politics Morgenthau claims to expound are rooted in this underlying reality, as the *same* drives, the *same* forces correlate in ever-changing combinations. In this respect, the famous 'Six Principles' opening the book from the second edition onwards are unambiguous: the 'laws' governing politics are 'objective' only because they 'have their roots in human nature' (p. 4, fourth edition). They are not political laws or historical laws *per se*: they are natural laws. Similarly, it is this drive for power that defines the concept of 'interest' specific to the study of politics and outlined in the second principle (p. 5, fourth edition).

The biological nature in which Morgenthau grounds the possibility of a rational understanding of politics also betrays his indebtedness to Freud and Nietzsche, who located in irrational drives the principle of interpretation of the social world. For Morgenthau too, these drives constitute the basic stuff of which society is made, as 'the struggle for existence and power … is the raw material of the social world' (pp. 50–51). Acting as a true clinician, the student of international relations must read in political phenomena the symptoms of these underlying forces, which are known and in limited number. Potentially dangerous and destabilizing, these drives must be kept under check by social institutions. Morgenthau follows a rather Freudian understanding of institu-tions as instances that repress or channel drives in order to make social life possible, and projects it upon the international sphere. There too, a number of social and cul-tural institutions operate to tame power drives (the balance of power, international law) or to provide them with an outlet (colonial conquest), thus ensuring a relative peace within the European space.

Against this backdrop, *PAN* appears as an imposing effort to come to terms with a double crisis: the crisis of *rationalism*, including its political variants, such as Wilso-nianism, and the crisis of the *institutions* that traditionally ensured the relatively peaceful socialization of power-driven actors. Morgenthau composes *PAN* precisely when these institutions no longer succeed in performing this function. As a new inter-national order takes shape following the World War II, neither the 'self-regulatory mechanism of the social forces which manifests itself in the struggle for power on the international scene, that is, the balance of power', nor the 'normative limitations upon that struggle in the form of international law, international morality, and world public opinion' seem 'capable of keeping the struggle for power within peaceful bounds' (p. 9).

Power unleashed: politics after the balance of power

Several factors explain the exhaustion of the 'moderating and restraining' influence of the balance of power. First, with the rise of modern nationalism, individual nations no longer saw their policy goals as limited interests detached from moral values, but con-sidered them as having universal moral significance, thus giving rise to dangerous 'political religions'. Second, the divisions between the victors of the World War II and the subsequent formation of two antagonistic blocs led by 'two giants eyeing each other with watchful suspicion' (p. 285) have given rise to a new balance of power, which, Morgenthau claims, lacks the flexibility of the old balance to the extent that the extreme concentration of power characterizing it is such that shifting alliances by smaller players would be unable to affect it. Morgenthau also dedicates a few pages – too few – to the 'disappearance of the colonial frontier' and to decolonization. The 'wide expanses of three continents: Africa, the Americas, and the part of Asia border-ing on the Eastern oceans' (p. 278) allowed European powers to satisfy their hunger for land, resources and manpower without endangering the relative balance prevailing in Europe. Land grabs also made policies of compensation between great powers possible and usually successful. However, while in the past great powers could, thus, 'deflect their rivalries from their own mutual frontiers to the periphery and into politically empty spaces' (pp. 282–84), the closure of the colonial space, the anticolonial revolu-tions, and the formation of Cold War blocs gradually expanded the balance of power beyond the European space until it spanned the entire globe.

The concept of the balance of power is arguably a master concept in the realist tra-dition, to which Morgenthau gave its *lettres de noblesse* in *PAN*. It is important to note, however, that Morgenthau offers no apology for the balance of power and that he uses the term in different ways.[15] When the concept is first introduced, it is associated with a generic notion of 'equilibrium' as a self-regulatory mechanism, also found in other disciplines such as economics or the life sciences (p. 125). However, Morgenthau also makes clear that such a mechanistic understanding of the balance is insufficient. A purely power-based balance would require a constant assessment of how much power the other participants in the balance can muster, yet this assessment is impossible, Morgenthau suggests, since power comes in different and generally incommensurable forms.[16] Thus, deprived of moral substance, the balance of power is fundamentally 'uncertain', and this uncertainty has disastrous consequences: a purely mechanical balance would be highly unstable, since each player, uncertain about the actual dis-tribution of power, would constantly seek to increase his own power and secure his position by acting preemptively, thus creating a situation in which 'preventive war' becomes 'a natural outgrowth of the balance of power' (p. 155). More importantly, Morgenthau understands the balance of power as a *European* reality, the effectiveness of which was dependent upon a *specific historical configuration*. He explicitly considers the balance to be only an 'instrumentality' which, in order to operate successfully to the benefit of all, requires the existence of an underlying moral community. Such a moral community existed in the seventeenth and eighteenth centuries, when dynastic ties, a cosmopolitan aristocracy and a community of Christian rulers configured Europe as a single *respublica*, where the understanding of the balance was rooted in a shared moral code (pp. 160–61). In the absence of such a community, the balance of power remains 'inadequate' or simply impossible to establish. One cannot over-emphasize this point too much: the balance of power, for Morgenthau, can only oper-ate within a *community* of values. Only then does the balance exert its 'restraining' influence, as one's way of life is never what is at stake in disputes occurring within a moral community of states.[17]

The other institutions 'civilizing' the drive for power – international public opinion and international law – do not fare better. If, according to Morgenthau, the degree of cultural and social variance found in the modern world prevents the emergence of a universal moral code, the same cause makes the formation of a world public opinion impossible. Here again, the main culprit is modern nationalism, whose corrosive influ-ence did not only dissolve the ties making the international society of the eighteenth century, but also made the nation state the sole receptacle of moral allegiances. Inter-national law cannot guarantee peace either, since the decentralized character of its judicial and enforcement functions means that political differences may in many cases evolve into 'tensions' that are not amenable to legal arbitrage. Its effectiveness, thus, 'do[es] not depend primarily upon legal considerations', but on the actual distribution of power (p. 229). In other words, international law was efficient only as long as it relied on the balance of power as its decentralized enforcement mechanism. Trained as a legal scholar, Morgenthau had written extensively during the interwar period against the positivist hegemony in the analysis of international law. In his last article published as a lawyer, he had defended a sociological (i.e. realist) understanding of international law on the basis of its functional relationship to social forces and cultural-normative spheres, which displaced the centre of gravity of the analysis outside the legal element itself. As a result, law became a mere *function* of underlying social configurations: 'Where there is no community of interests or balance of power, there is no international law.'[18]

Besides, to the extent that it is not grounded in a political and cultural community, international law lacks the dynamic mechanisms of legislation and jurisdiction that ensure its capacity to effect change in a domestic setting and thus satisfy those who seek to transform the *status quo*. As a result, international law is essentially a conservative force, which provides the international status quo with 'ideological disguises and moral justifications' (p. 342).

Morgenthau the cosmopolitan?

Morgenthau's analysis of the crisis of the mid-twentieth century thus leads him back time and again to the problem of international ethics. Balance, law, public opinion: all possible means of restraining national power must be rooted in some form of moral community. One of the most surprising aspects of *PAN* is that, while the book has become a classic of realism, it ends up embracing a cosmopolitan vision of international politics and calling for the establishment of the *civitas maxima*. It is indeed on the basis of a domestic analogy that Morgenthau approaches the problem of world peace in the twentieth century: only the political unification of humanity into a world state can overcome the ineffectiveness of international law, give rise to a genuine world public opinion and reactivate balancing under the form of internal checks and balances. In other words, the founding text of IR theory calls for nothing short of the abrogation of IR altogether.

This cosmopolitan vein has been recently foregrounded by a number of commentators, eager to see in Morgenthau 'an idealist in disguise', to quote Stanley Hoffmann.[19] There is no doubt that his vision of a world state owed much to Hans Kelsen.[20] Morgenthau made clear that the notion of 'state' was 'but another name for … the legal order which determines the conditions under which society can employ its monopoly of organized violence for the preservation of order and peace' (p. 396). The world state adumbrated in *PAN* would thus provide the 'legal continuity' of world society, and result in a unified legal system resembling the Kelsenite vision of a seamless pyramid of positive legal relations flowing from a *Grundnorm*. In some interpretations, this cosmopolitan vision has been sufficient to cast Morgenthau as a liberal reformer, and if there is any clear trend in the current revival of Morgenthau, it is definitely in favour of a more nuanced, less 'realist', as it were, understanding of this towering figure of IR.[21] This interpretation certainly recovers an intellectual complexity that was rapidly overshadowed by a reductive understanding of the book, partly encouraged by Morgenthau.[22] A subtle shift, thus, occurred in the 1950s: while realism received almost no mention in the first edition of *PAN*, the second edition introduced the 'Six Principles' and identified Morgenthau's theory with realism.[23] As a result, normative and moral concerns became less central, resulting in a distorted image of realism in general, and of Morgenthau in particular.

Yet, Morgenthau's cosmopolitanism is highly ambivalent. It should be noted that, contrarily to his assertive style in most of the book, he stops short of endorsing the proposal of the world state in the first person, and limits himself to restating an 'argument' that has been 'advanced from time to time' (p. 483, fourth edition), as a sympathetic but external observer.[24] More importantly, his disquisition on the world state is not fully consistent with his overall conception of politics – something Morgenthau could not ignore but chose not to address. He knew the world state would amount to 'humanity politically organized' (p. 400) – but what would be 'political' about this organization? Morgenthau subscribed to a concept of the political partially elaborated in critical dialogue with Carl Schmitt and entailing the ever-present possibility of existential conflict: the 'political' was a dimension of the human condition structured by primordial distinctions between friend and foe.[25] For the same reason, political existence was not something that humanity as a whole was capable of, since it was deprived of an enemy. Morgenthau was too familiar with Schmitt's critique of humanity as a depoliticizing concept to ignore the contradiction in the terms implied in the idea of 'humanity politically organized'. Also, the world state collides with another key tenet of Morgenthau's vision of man: provided humanity was thus united, where would the lust for power find outlets, given that for Morgenthau it is built into the bedrock of human nature? Would not a world state require the creation of a new man, as any realist would immediately object? The advocacy of a world state, it seems, was fundamentally at odds with his vision of man and politics. Why did he endorse it, then?

Rather than raising logical or principled objections to the cosmopolitan project, Morgenthau chose instead to outline only the *empirical* hurdles paving the way towards the establishment of a world state. As a result, the world state remains in *PAN* an abstract necessity: 'in no period of modern history was civilization more in need of permanent peace and, hence, of a world state, and … in no period of modern history were the moral, social, and political conditions of the world less favorable for the establishment of a world state' (p. 402). The Augustinian accents of this passage are telling, for they suggest that the *civitas maxima* may not be a more concrete perspective than the *civitas dei*. What, then, is the proper conduct for those who wish to prepare the conditions for the creation of a world state? What would foster its eventual emergence? The answer Morgenthau provides is, to say the least, surprising: traditional state diplomacy, with its cadre of professional diplomats insulated from social and democratic pressures, operating in relative secrecy, and taking into their own hands the destiny of peace.

'Whoever invokes humanity wants to cheat', Schmitt famously wrote.[26] It is difficult to shake off the suspicion that Morgenthau's advocacy of the world state may fall under this category. Also, it is tempting to think that he refrained from developing a radical, principled critique of cosmopolitanism as a tactical concession, in order to harness its normative appeal to his own realist vision of diplomacy, which owed very little to cosmopolitan ideals. For the distant possibility of the unification of humanity is adumbrated only as a justification for the reinstatement of traditional state diplomacy, under the pretext that 'the mitigation and minimization of those political conflicts which in our time pit the two superpowers against each other' is a first step towards the establishment of a true world community. Notwithstanding Morgenthau's finesse in conducting his argument, it is hard to square the cosmopolitan vision of a world community with the vision of diplomacy that closes *PAN*, a vision that extols eighteenth-century political intrigues. Some of the fundamental rules of diplomacy that Morgenthau enunciates at the end of the book are simply incompatible with a cosmopolitan vision, however construed (e.g. 'the objectives of foreign policy must be defined in terms of the national interest and must be supported with adequate power'). A close ally of Morgenthau, Waldemar Gurian was not fooled by this passage: Morgenthau, he wrote concisely, 'is not an advocate of the world state'.[27]

Yet, we must leave open another possibility. Just as Morgenthau the legal scholar warned his readers that the letter of international law could remain the same while its meaning could change, we must again see *PAN* as a text that resonated with different historical contexts and meant different things at different times – including for Morgenthau himself. While there is little doubt that in 1948 Morgenthau endorsed the perspective of a world state for purely instrumental reasons, the situation may well have been different by the late 1950s and early 1960s. As Campbell Craig has shown, the thermonuclear revolution gradually led Morgenthau to revise some essential tenets of realism: the incapacity of even the most powerful state to prevent the annihilation of its citizenry in case of nuclear war signalled the demise of the most basic justification of sovereignty, namely protection; the meaninglessness of nuclear 'victory' made the defence of the national interest in an anarchic world based on the possibility of nuclear war problematic; finally, the nuclear bomb itself united humanity in a 'common fear of atomic destruction'.[28] The bomb thus provided a *material, anthropological* basis for the gradual demise of the nation state and the effective unification of humanity. From that moment on, the realist analysis of world conditions merged with the 'utopian approaches to politics in general' and called for the creation of a world state.[29] Being fundamentally an ideology of survival, realism in the nuclear age meant striving to overcome the multiple sovereignties that maintained the world under the menace of nuclear annihilation. By the time of the third edition (1960) therefore, despite its unchanged wording, the section of *PAN* dedicated to the world state took an entirely new meaning and reflected a historical limit of realism.

Conclusion

It is probably impossible to pronounce a summary judgement about *PAN*, because of the scope of the book, but also because Morgenthau's purpose was not to build a systematic theory. As a result, he was able to weave together strands of thought that were not always congruent and reflected the superposition of different contexts and different intellectual traditions. In the luxuriance of the book, just as in the complexity of Morgenthau's biography, it is possible to find a mixture of elements that can be interpreted in one way or another: a critique of nationalism, but also a critique of democracy and its deleterious effects upon foreign policy; an appeal to the 'rational element' in IR, but also a sustained rejection of rationalism; reformist ideas, but also an unrestrained *amor fati*, which is the unmistakable mark of all conservative thought and always legitimates the authority of tradition ('what exists must have something to be said in its favor; otherwise it would not exist', p. 63). As a result, Morgenthau's realism has been alternatively described as a reconstruction of liberalism (Michael Williams), a conservative theory of politics (Martti Koskenniemi), or an extension of Weimarian progressive culture into international affairs (William Scheuerman in his most recent work) – when it has not just been pigeonholed into a simplistic version of power politics. In the end, it is highly implausible that the interpretation of Morgenthau's politics and of his vision of IR will ever command agreement among scholars. The question may simply be undecidable, and the meaning of *PAN*, as with any other 'classic', can be recovered only through the careful study of its reception and its uses. In the meantime, the interpretation of Morgenthau and *PAN* will remain the turf upon which the battles over the identity of the discipline are fought, and a good indication of its current state and future direction.

Notes

1 Robert Jervis, 'Hans Morgenthau, Realism, and the Scientific Study of International Relations', *Social Research*, 1994, vol. 61, 853–54, at p. 853.
2 Hans J. Morgenthau, *Politics among Nations: The Struggle for Power and Peace,* New York: Knopf, 1948. Unless otherwise stated page numbers placed in parentheses in the text refer to this first edition.
3 Christoph Frei, *Hans J. Morgenthau: An Intellectual Biography*, Baton Rouge, LA: Louisiana State University Press, 2001, p. 73. Besides Frei and Scheuerman, see also Alfons Söllner, 'German Conservatism in America: Morgenthau's Political Realism', *Telos*, 1987, vol. 72, 161–72.
4 Waldemar Gurian, 'Reviews – International Politics', *The Review of Politics*, 1949, vol. 11, 255–59, at pp. 255–56.
5 The evolution of Morgenthau's thinking about nuclear war is analysed in Campbell Craig, *Glimmer of a New Leviathan: Total War in the Realism of Niebuhr, Morgenthau, and Waltz*, New York: Columbia University Press, 2003.
6 For a few examples of this current Morgenthau revival, see for instance Anthony F. Lang (ed.), *Political Theory and International Affairs: Hans J. Morgenthau on Aristotle's the Politics*, Greenwood, CT: Praeger, 2004; A. J. H. Murray, 'The Moral Politics of Hans Morgenthau', *The Review of Politics*, 1996, vol. 58, 81–107; William Scheuerman, 'Was Morgenthau a Realist? Revisiting Scientific Man vs. Power Politics', *Constellations*, 2007, vol. 14, 506–30; William Scheuerman, *Hans Morgenthau: Realism and Beyond*, Cambridge: Polity Press, 2009; Vibeke Schou Tjalve, *Realist Strategies of Republican Peace: Niebuhr, Morgenthau, and the Politics of Patriotic Dissent*, New York: Palgrave Macmillan, 2008; Michael C. Williams, 'Why Ideas Matter in International Relations: Hans Morgenthau, Classical Realism, and the Moral Construction of Power Politics', *International Organization*, 2004, vol. 58, 633–65; Michael C. Williams (ed.), *Realism Reconsidered: The Legacy of Hans J. Morgenthau in International Relations*, Oxford: Oxford University Press, 2007. I analyse some of the reasons behind this revival in the Introduction to Nicolas Guilhot (ed.), *The Invention of International Relations: Realism, the Rockefeller Foundation and the 1954 Conference on Theory*, New York: Columbia University Press, 2011.
7 *PAN* is composed of 32 chapters divided into ten sections. Section I ('Theory and Practice of International Politics') clarifies the approach followed by Morgenthau and distinguishes it from the social scientific ideal of reducing politics to a social physics. Section II focuses on the concept of power and on the expression of power politics in the international arena (status quo, imperialism, policy of prestige). The book then explores the predominant – i.e. national – form that power takes in the contemporary world (Section III), and the different devices that have been used to contain national power: the balance of power (Section IV), international morality and public opinion (Section V); international law (Section VI). Section VII is an intermezzo taking stock of the state of world politics after 1945 and of the paralysis of the traditional limitations of power. Sections VIII and IX concentrate on Morgenthau's devastating critiques of the various means to achieve peace through law, from disarmament conferences to the UN, or peace through transformation, from the utopias of the world state to the cultural activism of UNESCO. The last section, focusing on 'peace through accommodation', advocates the restoration of traditional diplomacy as the most promising, albeit imperfect, way to ensure a modicum of peace and stability.

8 On the anti-scientific drive of early realism, see Nicolas Guilhot, 'The Realist Gambit: Postwar American Political Science and the Birth of IR Theory', *International Political Sociology*, 2008, vol. 2, 281–304.

9 This dimension is not entirely absent from the 'Six Principles': while Morgenthau compares a rational theory of IR to a 'portrait', he still mentions that it will never overlap perfectly with the 'photographic picture' of reality (pp. 7–8, fourth edition)

10 One could object to the title of Chapter 2, 'The Science of International Politics'. However, under this misleading title, the chapter is essentially a reflection upon the limits of rationalism, and it is entirely possible that Morgenthau deliberately chose to misrepresent his argument in order to surf the enthusiasm of the times for the social science project. As he had acknowledged earlier, 'no political thinker can expect to be heard who would not, at least in his terminology, pay tribute to the spirit of science'. Hans J. Morgenthau, *Scientific Man vs. Power Politics*, Chicago, IL: University of Chicago Press, 1946, p. 31. A similar reading of *PAN* can be found in Oliver Jütersonke, 'The Image of Law in *Politics among Nations*', in Williams, *Realism Reconsidered*, pp. 93–117.

11 For a discussion of realism's uneasy relation to science, see 'The Realist Gambit'.

12 On this issue, see Peter Wilson's chapter on Carr and Casper Sylvest's contribution on Herz in this volume.

13 Immediately after the previous quotation, Morgenthau adds a beautiful and incisive conclusion: 'Little do they know that they meet under an empty sky from which the gods have departed'.

14 On this theme, see Roger Epp, 'The Ironies of Christian Realism: The End of an Augustinian Tradition in International Politics,' in Eric Patterson (ed.), *The Christian Realists: Reassessing the Contributions of Niebuhr and His Contemporaries*, Lanham, MD: University Press of America, 2003, pp. 199–232; Nicolas Guilhot, 'American Katechon: When Political Theology Became IR Theory', *Constellations*, 2010, vol. 17, 224–53. The influence of Niebuhr on both Morgenthau and IR in general is important. See Daniel Rice, 'Reinhold Niebuhr and Hans Morgenthau: A Friendship with Contrasting Shades of Realism', *Journal of American Studies*, 2008, vol. 42, 255–91. On Niebuhr and Morgenthau's vision of politics after 1945, see Tjalve, *Realist Strategies of Republican Peace*.

15 On this point, see in particular Richard Little, 'The Balance of Power in *Politics among Nations*', in Williams, *Realism Reconsidered*, pp. 137–65, as well as the discussion in Scheuerman, *Hans Morgenthau*.

16 See the discussion about the 'uncertainty of the balance' (p. 151).

17 The non-mechanistic nature of Morgenthau's theory of the balance of power is also underscored by Michael Williams, 'Why Ideas Matter in International Relations', pp. 651–52.

18 Hans J. Morgenthau, 'Positivism, Functionalism, and International Law,' *American Journal of International Law*, 1940, vol. 32, 260–84, at p. 275.

19 Stanley Hoffmann, 'Notes on the Limits of Realism', *Social Research*, 1981, vol. 48, 653–59, at p. 657.

20 Jütersonke, 'The Image of Law', p. 109.

21 In particular Scheuerman, *Hans Morgenthau*, and Williams, *Realism Reconsidered*.

22 According to Stefano Guzzini, its reception was initially rather 'one-sided' and overlooked its anti-Hobbesian aspects. Guzzini, *Realism in International Relations and International Political Economy*, London: Routledge, 1998, p. 24.

23 Scheuerman, *Hans Morgenthau*.

24 While writing the sections of *PAN* dedicated to world government, Morgenthau had certainly on his mind the United World Federalists, led by Cord Meyer, and the more utopian Committee to Frame a World Constitution based at the University of Chicago.

25 On this issue, see Martti Koskenniemi, *The Gentle Civilizer of Nations: The Rise and Fall of International Law, 1870–1960*, Cambridge: Cambridge University Press, 2002; Hans-Karl Pichler, 'The Godfathers of "Truth": Max Weber and Carl Schmitt in Morgenthau's Theory of Power Politics', *Review of International Studies*, 1998, vol. 24, 185–200; William Scheuerman, *Carl Schmitt: The End of Law*, Lanham, MD: Rowman & Littlefield, 1999; Williams, 'Why Ideas Matter in International Relations'.

26 Carl Schmitt, *The Concept of the Political*, Chicago, IL: Chicago University Press, 2007, p. 54.

27 Gurian, 'Reviews – International Politics', p. 257.

28 Hans J. Morgenthau, 'What the Big Two Can, and Can't Negotiate', *The New York Times*, 20 September 1959, quoted in Craig, *Glimmer of a New Leviathan*, p. 107.

29 Hans J. Morgenthau, University of Maryland address, March 1961, quoted in Craig, *Glimmer of a New Leviathan*, p. 108. On the issue of the world state, see in particular Hidemi Suganami, *The Domestic Analogy and World Order Proposals*, Cambridge: Cambridge University Press, 1989 and Danilo Zolo, *Cosmopolis: Prospects for World Government*, Cambridge: Polity Press, 1997.

8 The enduring logic of the three images: Kenneth N. Waltz's *Man, the State, and War*

Brian C. Schmidt

There is little need to belabour the question of whether Kenneth Waltz's *Man, the State, and War: A Theoretical Analysis* (1959, *MSW*) is a classic text of International Relations (IR).[1] No matter how one defines the term, *MSW* unequivocally is a classic. Although much of Waltz's fame derives from his landmark book, *Theory of International Politics* (1979),[2] establishing structural realism or neo-realism as a dominant paradigm, Waltz's exposition of the 'third image' – the anarchy among states – in his earlier book lays the foundation for the systemic theory of realism that he develops later. Waltz himself attributes the durability of *MSW* 'to the continuity of international politics', which he argues is best explained by the enduring 'anarchic structure of international politics' (p. xi). The fact that *MSW* not only remains in print, but continues to be widely read by both undergraduate students and senior scholars is a testimony to the significant contribution that the book makes to the study of international politics. By developing three distinct images or, if you like, three distinct levels of analysis, for investigating the cause of war, Waltz makes a profound and lasting contribution to the field and it is incredibly difficult to imagine how IR would have evolved if he had not written this book.

The chapter begins with a short overview of the main arguments and content of *MSW*. The overview provides additional justifications for designating the book a classic work of IR. Next, I situate the text within the disciplinary history of IR and highlight the unique contribution that Waltz makes to the field. While a greater appreciation of the significance of the text can be gained by situating it in the history of IR, its status as a classic is strengthened further by the fact that it continues to serve as a foundation for new research in the field. In the last section, I consider some of the critiques of Waltz's *MSW*.

The three images and the cause of war

Although Waltz recollects that '*MSW* did not present a theory of international politics', but instead laid 'the foundation for one', the insightful typology that he developed for organizing the answers that thinkers throughout the ages put forth to explain the causes of war has proved to be an invaluable contribution to the field (p. ix). As the story goes, Waltz was under extreme pressure as a doctoral student at Columbia University to prepare quickly for his minor field comprehensive examination in IR (his major field was political theory). Professor William T. R. Fox informed Waltz that the exam would cover the entire field rather than be limited to a predetermined set of topics. In the midst of wading through the vast IR literature at Columbia's Butler library, a flash of insight led Waltz to realize that he could organize the material into three different levels of analysis that corresponded to the manner in which scholars have approached the study of international politics (p. viii). Not only did classifying the material according to whether individuals (first image), states (second image) or the international system (third image) were identified as the principal cause of international conflict prove useful in preparing for the comprehensive examination, but this would become the foundation of his doctoral dissertation and eventual book that critically examined the ideas that thinkers throughout history have offered to explain the reasons for the recurrence of war.

Waltz, at the urging of his wife, decided to refer to his classificatory scheme as images rather than levels of analysis. In the Introduction to the book, Waltz explained that the 'three estimates of cause will subsequently be referred to as images of inter-national relations ... with each image defined according to where one locates the nexus of important causes' (p. 12). Years later in the Preface to the 2001 edition, Waltz indi-cated that his use of the term image was apt 'because one cannot "see" international politics directly, no matter how hard one looks, and because developing a theory requires one to depict a pertinent realm of activity' (p. ix). Similar to a theory, an image is a filtering mechanism whereby the analyst views the world in a particular manner. David Singer, however, popularized the level of analysis terminology in his 1961 essay 'The Level-of-Analysis Problem in International Relations', which he pub-lished shortly after reviewing *MSW*.[3] Together, Singer and Waltz helped to specify the international system as a unique level of analysis and contributed to one of the field's endless debates on whether students should focus on the individual parts (states and individuals) or the system as a whole.

By systematically examining the timeless question of what is the cause of war, *MSW* achieved the venerable distinction of being a classic text of IR. Its status as a classic is not only a consequence of the question that Waltz posed, but also due to the manner in which he investigated the answer by surveying the ideas of classic political philosophers such as St Augustine, Hobbes and Rousseau as well as modern social scientists in the fields of psychology and anthropology. Waltz organized the answers according to 'three headings: within man, within the structure of the separate states, within the state system', which he referred to, respectively, as the first, second and third image (p. 12). Waltz described the chapters in his book as 'essays in political theory'. He wrote: 'this description is justified partly by the mode of inquiry – we proceed by examining assumptions and asking repeatedly what differences they make – and partly by the fact that we consider a number of political philosophers' (p. 2). It should be emphasized that Waltz did not limit all of his attention to investigating the cause of war. He also considered the various prescriptions that thinkers offered for achieving a condition of peace. Waltz insightfully argued that there was an intimate connection between under-standing the cause of war and explaining how peace can be achieved, and he devoted considerable attention to analysing the prescriptions that logically followed from each of the three images.

According to Waltz, those who adhere to the first image believe that the cause of war is to be found in the nature and behaviour of mankind. The evil of war is directly attributed to the evil or limited capacities of man. If this is indeed the case, then the attainment of peace requires changing the nature and behaviour of man. Waltz divided the first image into pessimists, who believe that human nature cannot be changed, and optimists, who believe human beings can be sufficiently reformed to reduce the incidence of war. The distinction made between first image pessimists and optimists underscored Waltz's dual interest in understanding both the cause of war and the pre-conditions of peace. In the case of the first image, it can be argued that while Waltz is dismissive of the notion that human nature can adequately explain the cause of war, he is even more critical of the idea that man can be reformed to achieve peace.

This is clearly the case with Waltz's scathing criticism of first image optimists, which is where he placed behavioural social scientists. Although he is generally critical of the notion that human nature can explain the recurrence of war, which he argues is the view of first image pessimists such as St Augustine, Reinhold Niebuhr and Hans J. Morgenthau, Waltz dismisses the idea that human beings can be sufficiently reformed to achieve peace. His basic criticism of the first image pessimists, which, in hindsight, foreshadowed the transition from the human nature realism of Morgenthau to struc-tural realism, is that the same nature has to explain a wide range of behaviours. Waltz concluded that if human nature is a constant, it cannot explain variations in war and peace. The redeeming quality of the pessimists, for Waltz, is their recognition that since the nature of man cannot be altered, political solutions are needed to reduce the inci-dence of war. This recognition was missing from the optimists who advanced the logic of their argument about human nature being responsible for the cause of war to finding the best means through which to modify man's bellicose behaviour. Waltz dismisses the various proposals that behavioural social scientists provide to alter the nature of man. Not only are the proposals that Waltz selectively reviews judged to be preposterous, but he faults all of the first image optimists for their failure to consider the larger political framework in which individual human beings act. The first image optimists, according to Waltz, 'betray a naivete in politics that vitiates their efforts to construct a new and better world' (p. 39).

The second image includes thinkers who argue that defects within polities, states or societies are responsible for the incidence of war. According to this explanation, good states, those without defects, are pacific while bad states, those that, by definition, possess defects, are bellicose. In this section of the book, Waltz surveys the ideas of a range of thinkers who claim that the cause of war is rooted in the flawed internal structure of particular types of states. Here again, Waltz is equally concerned with the prescriptions that second image thinkers such as Karl Marx and Immanuel Kant pro-vide for turning 'bad' states into 'good' states. While he devotes an entire chapter cri-ticizing the second image view of the Marxists, Waltz first turned his attention to the thought of the nineteenth-century liberals and provided a damning indictment of what we now call the democratic peace thesis (theory).

According to nineteenth-century liberals and their present-day followers, a world composed of liberal democracies would be a world at peace. The logic of their argu-ment, and, for Waltz, second image thinkers more generally, is that internal, domestic conditions determine external behaviour. Second image thinkers provide an 'inside-outside' explanation in which state behaviour is determined by causal developments at the national level. Nineteenth-century liberals argued that democracies were inherently peaceful. The answer that they provided to the problem of war was to convert the trouble-making non-democracies into peaceful democracies. In this case, Waltz had less of a problem with non-interventionist liberals such as Kant and Cobden than with interventionist liberals such as Wilson and Paine, who were willing to use force in order to promote democracy. Reluctant to wait on the forces of history, interventionist lib-erals argued that the historical process could be speeded up if democracies took it upon themselves to eliminate non-democracies. Waltz took issue with this argument and levelled a number of dire warnings that US foreign policy-makers have obviously ignored. Democratization by force, Waltz argued, was based on a number of 'utopian assumptions that are frightening in their implications'. He claimed 'the state that would act on the interventionist theory must set itself up as both judge and executor in the affairs of nations'. Also, while believing to have a just cause, Waltz reasoned that so too would the target state. Waltz cited A. J. P. Taylor to underline the following realist point: 'Bismarck ... fought "necessary" wars and killed thousands; the idealists of the twentieth century fight "just" wars and kill millions' (pp. 113–14).

Waltz concluded that both liberal and Marxist theories shared the same basic problem of trying to infer international outcomes on the basis of generalizations made about one specific pattern of state and society. Finally, after four chapters, we learn that 'the international political environment has much to do with the ways in which states behave' and thus why first and second image theories are essentially flawed (p. 122). The third image, according to Waltz, provides the most insightful explanation of the cause of war because it focuses on the framework of state action. According to Waltz, the anarchical structure of the international system is the permissive cause of war because there really is nothing to prevent one state from attacking another state. The tragic condition of the international system means that the requirements of state action are imposed by the circumstances that all states confront. In explicating the third image, Waltz focused on the political thought of Jean-Jacques Rousseau and, in doing so, popularized his fictitious story of the stag hunt to countless students. Waltz reasoned that sovereign states in an anarchical system face a similar set of constraints as the hungry men that Rousseau described in the state of nature. In both scenarios, Waltz argued that the structure of the situation provided a more determinative explanation of the resulting conflict than does a detailed analysis of the motivations and character of the actors themselves. Waltz concluded that 'among states as among men there is no automatic adjustment of interests' and 'in the absence of supreme authority, there is then constant possibility that conflicts will be settled by force' (p. 188).

For Waltz, the implications of the third image are profound. After clarifying his argument that international anarchy is the underlying explanation of the cause of war, Waltz proceeded to illustrate how the logic of the third image could be used to explain a number of additional regularly repeating patterns of behaviour, including the widespread use of tariffs and the balance of power. Waltz demonstrated how the practice of balancing was intimately connected with the logic of the third image. He used game theory to show 'that the balance of power is not so much imposed by statesmen on events as it is imposed by events on statesmen' (p. 209). While Waltz went to great lengths to impress the reader with the intellectual merits of the third image, he did not spend much time on the corresponding prescriptions for peace. As a realist, there was not much Waltz could say as world government, the logical remedy for international anarchy, appeared to be an idealist pipe dream. Yet, to be fair to Waltz, he found all of the images' respective remedies for peace to be utopian. Nevertheless, there is no denying that the inadequacies of the prescriptions that followed from image one and two proved to be much more damning to Waltz than those that followed the third image.

In the Conclusion, Waltz considered the distinct possibility that all three images were needed to understand a complex international outcome such as war. He admitted that 'no single image is ever adequate' and for this reason 'prescriptions directly derived from a single image are incomplete because they are based upon partial analyses' (pp. 225, 230). In terms of providing a general explanation of the cause of war, however, which is what Waltz set out to investigate, he made a strong case for the anarchical state system. The third image tells us why war may occur at any point in time; namely, that there is nothing to prevent it from happening. Waltz recognizes, however, that international anarchy cannot provide a specific explanation of a particular war. He concedes that the immediate causes of war are to be found in the first and second images. It is the specific acts by individuals and states that are the efficient cause of war, but the international system provides the permissive cause of all interstate wars. Waltz, of course, would go on to develop the logic of third image into a full-blown theory of international politics that he argued could explain important international outcomes without the need for variables associated with the first and second images. Yet, in *MSW*, Waltz concluded that:

> the third image describes the framework of world politics, but without the first and second images there can be no knowledge of the forces that determine policy; the first and second images describe the forces in world politics, but without the third image it is impossible to assess their importance or predict their results (p. 238).

The long road to a theory of international politics

When Waltz finished the manuscript in 1954, which he originally submitted as his doctoral dissertation at Columbia University entitled 'Man, the State, and the State System in Theories of the Causes of War', IR was in the early stages of what Stanley Hoffmann described as the 'long road to theory'.[4] The initial quest for a theory of international politics was, in part, a response to the perceived crisis that the field was facing after World War II. This crisis, like later crises, was about the status of IR as an autonomous field of inquiry and the closely related questions regarding its proper scope, subject-matter and analytical focus. At this crucial point in time, there was a noticeable split in the field between those who were inspired by the behavioural movement taking place in political science to create a comprehensive 'scientific' theory of politics and those who insisted that IR needed its own unique theory of international politics.[5] In this regard, it is difficult to read *MSW* without situating it within the context of the behavioural revolution that was deeply impacting the social sciences.

Although Waltz was aware of the pressing need for a systematic, empirical theory, at this point in his career he argued that familiarity with political philosophy was of crucial importance for developing a theory of international politics. Contrary to those championing behaviouralism in the 1950s, many of whom were increasingly dismissive of political philosophy on the grounds of it being antiquarian, Waltz argued that the ideas of classical political theorists were directly relevant to the pressing issues of the present, especially with respect to the problem of how to achieve peace. Rather than shunning political theory, Waltz embraced it arguing that 'traditional political philosophy, concentrating as it does upon domestic politics, is relevant to the student of international relations' (p. 10). Waltz not only defended the study of political philosophy as being an integral element of political science, but he rejected the bifurcation that Martin Wight would later make between, on the one hand, a rich tradition of political theory and, on the other hand, an impoverished tradition of IR theory.[6] *MSW* was Waltz's explicit attempt to demonstrate the relevance of political theory to understanding the causes of war. His defence of political theory was also on display in a paper that he presented at a seminar held at the Institute of War and Peace Studies of Columbia University in 1957 devoted to examining theoretical aspects of international relations. Waltz had served as the rapporteur for the very first seminar on theory of international politics that was held in Washington, DC, in 1954 and sponsored by the Rockefeller Foundation.[7] In his paper entitled 'Political Philosophy and the Study of International Relations', Waltz not only defended political philosophy as an aid to dealing with present problems, but he accentuated the importance of political theory in developing a general theory of international relations.[8] By arguing that there was intimate relationship between political theory and systematic theory, Waltz was attempting to prevent the divorce that would eventually occur in the discipline between normative and positive theory.

Waltz's displeasure with the early proponents of the behavioural notion of science was noticeable in *MSW*, and this was noted in some of the reviews of the book. His critique of the idea that science could be applied to the social realm to solve social ills was consistent with the powerful argument that Morgenthau had provided in *Scientific Man Versus Power Politics*.[9] Reviewers who were sympathetic to behaviouralism accused Waltz of unfairly misrepresenting their views and providing a distorted and biased account of the behavioural literature. Waltz's decision to dedicate an entire chapter to the behavioural sciences was not made solely to reveal the implications of the first image. As in other sections of the book, such as the chapter on Marxism, Waltz created a straw man to help prove the point that he was attempting to make. In his review of *MSW*, Paul Hammond observed that the decision to focus on the work of social psychologists provided Waltz with a tempting target 'for it shows scholars and scientists at their worst, carrying their disciplines onto unfamiliar territory where they were bound to be misused'. However, by only examining 'those contributions at their worst', Hammond criticized Waltz for not thoroughly examining the potential contribution that the behavioural disciplines could make to the study of war.[10]

This was similar to the criticism that David Singer raised in his review of *MSW*. While Singer acknowledged that some behavioural scientists did provide rather simplistic solutions to the problem of war, he charged that 'Waltz commits an even greater sin than that of naïve optimism and exuberance, by reinforcing this stereotype of irrelevance and incompetence in the minds of the political scientists who constitute the bulk of his readership'.[11] From Singer's perspective, behaviouralism held great promise in IR's quest for theory and Waltz's rejection of the 'scientific study of man' merely reinforced existing pedagogical and ideological taboos in the field. While beginning his review favorably, writing that *MSW* was 'a welcome and valuable addition to the literature', Singer concluded rather harshly:

> by his hasty rejection of the usefulness of the behavioural sciences, and his heavy reliance upon the traditional political philosophers, Waltz seems to succumb to, and strengthen, such taboos, thus inhibiting his own search for the answers that he posed in *Man, the State, and War*.[12]

Perhaps Waltz heeded some of Singer's criticism as *Theory of International Politics* replaced political philosophy with social science.

Conclusion

There is no denying that Waltz's theoretically informed framework for investigating the cause of war and peace has withstood the test of time. The three images are part of the vernacular of IR and have proven to be just as useful today as they were when Waltz utilized them to pass his comprehensive exam. This is not to say that Waltz's three images have not been criticized, rejected or modified. There is an abundance of secondary literature that criticizes nearly every aspect of Waltz's classificatory framework. Yet, as Hidemi Suganami acknowledges, 'the status of a scholarly text is not necessarily undermined by the number of errors it has subsequently been alleged or found to contain'. With respect to *MSW*, he writes that 'the very act of engaging critically with *Man, the State, and War*, as I, among others, have done, reinforces the status of the book as a classic'.[13] The fact that it remains almost impossible to investigate theoretically the issue of war and peace in IR without referencing *MSW* is yet another indication of its status as a classic.

Waltz's tripartite classificatory framework for investigating the cause of war has been the target of a broad and extensive critique. Some have challenged the intellectual merits of searching for a general explanation of war. While commending Waltz for rejecting monocausal explanations of war, K. J. Holsti faults those who continue to search for the cause of war without giving any consideration of the issues that lead men to fight in the first place. For Holsti, to leave issues out of the investigation is to ignore politics.[14] Those who pursue the cause of war through the route of quantitative inquiry, especially those involved with the Correlates of War Project, argue that 'social scientists need to know a fair amount about the *correlates* of war before we can speak with much authority about its *causes*'.[15] Identifying the factors that can be empirically proven to increase the probability of war and inductively integrating them to understand the steps to war is argued to be a more fruitful path to knowledge than a general philosophical search for the cause of war.[16] In this regard, the scientific study of war has expanded Waltz's levels-of-analysis framework to include war-prone dyads, regions and systems. Suganami comments that while Waltz's tripartite scheme 'reflects a very common view of how modern political life is organised ... it is neither necessary nor sensible to squeeze every causal factor of war into three places'.[17]

Critics have identified numerous problems with Waltz's exposition of each of the three images. Some of this criticism is derived from the perception, especially after reading *Theory of International Politics*, that Waltz's analysis is biased against the first and second image in order to help make the case for the superiority of the third image. Waltz, for example, is accused of unfairly dismissing the first image on the basis of his contentious claim that human nature, which he argues is a constant, cannot explain variations in war and peace. Yet, it is questionable whether human nature is a constant and, moreover, the crucial 'within man' category is personality, which is variable. Waltz, as Suganami points out, discusses both human nature and personality traits.[18] In their plea for IR scholars to consider the impact of individuals on international politics, Daniel Byman and Kenneth Pollack charge that Waltz inappropriately dismisses the first image by defining it 'solely in terms of an ineffable quality shared among all humans' thus constructing a straw man. Byman and Pollack develop a number of hypotheses on personality traits and argue that 'because personalities differ, it is entirely possible that variance in the traits of individuals explains differences in international relations'.[19]

Waltz is also perceived as giving little credence to second-image, 'inside-out' explanations of the cause of war. While all the responsibility cannot be assigned to Waltz, Jack Levy notes that among political scientists 'domestic political variables are not included in any of the leading theories of the causes of war; instead they appear only in a number of isolated hypothesis and in some empirical studies that are generally atheoretical and noncumulative'.[20] In *Theory of International Politics*, Waltz characterizes theories of international politics that concentrate causes at the national level as being 'reductionist' because 'the whole is understood by knowing the attributes and the interactions of its parts'.[21] Second image theories can, according to Waltz, at best help explain why a particular war broke out; they cannot provide an explanation for the recurrence of war. Waltz argues that only the third image, which locates the cause of war at the international level, provides the underlying explanation for war. By privileging the international system as the permissive cause of war, Waltz is often accused of creating a sharp dichotomy between domestic and international politics that rests on the distinction that he makes between hierarchical and anarchical systems.[22] The deeply held assumption among IR scholars that anarchy is the distinguishing feature of international politics that accounts for the periodic outbreak of interstate war is one of Waltz's enduring legacies. Waltz's role in perpetuating the assumption that international politics is anarchic, has not, however, escaped critical scrutiny.[23]

Although Waltz did privilege the third image when he developed his theory of international politics, it is difficult to deny the conclusion of *MSW* that all three images are necessary to understand the cause of war. Not only did he acknowledge that no single image is ever adequate by itself, but he carefully considered the argument that all causes may be interrelated. It is not overly controversial to suggest that some of the profound insights that Waltz provided in *MSW* have been overlooked as a consequence of the popularity of *Theory of International Politics*. As a true classic, however, we have the good fortune of having the opportunity to re-read *MSW* in the quest to understand why war continues to be an enduring feature of international politics.

Notes

1 Kenneth N. Waltz, *Man, the State, and War: A Theoretical Analysis*, New York: Columbia University Press, [1959] 2001. Page numbers placed in parentheses in the text refer to this edition.
2 See also Anders Wivel's chapter in this volume.
3 J. David Singer, 'The Level-of-Analysis Problem in International Relations', in Klauss Knorr and Sidney Verba (eds), *The International System: Theoretical Essays*, Princeton, NJ: Princeton University Press, 1961, pp. 77–92.
4 Stanley Hoffman, 'International Relations: The Long Road to Theory', *World Politics*, 1959, vol. 11, 346–77.
5 Nicolas Guilhot (ed.), *The Invention of International Relations Theory*, New York: Columbia University Press, 2011.
6 Martin Wight, 'Why Is There No International Theory?', *International Relations*, 1960, vol. 2, 35–48.
7 Brian C. Schmidt, 'The Rockefeller Foundation Conference and the Long Road to a Theory of International Politics', in Guilhot (ed.), *The Invention of International Relations Theory*, pp. 79–96.
8 Kenneth N. Waltz, 'Political Philosophy and the Study of International Relations', in William T. R. Fox (ed.), *Theoretical Aspects of International Relations*, Notre Dame, IN: University of Notre Dame Press, 1959, pp. 51–67.

 9 Hans J. Morgenthau, *Scientific Man Versus Power Politics*, Chicago, IL: University of Chicago Press, 1946.
10 Paul Y. Hammond, review of Kenneth N. Waltz, *Man, the State, and War*, in *Political Science Quarterly*, 1960, vol. 75, 448–50, at p. 449.
11 J. David Singer, 'International Conflict: Three Levels of Analysis', *World Politics*, 1960, vol. 12, 453–61, at p. 455.
12 Singer, 'International Conflict', p. 461.
13 Hidemi Suganami, 'Understanding Man, the State, and War', *International Relations*, 2009, vol. 23, 372–88, at p. 386.
14 Kalevi J. Holsti, *Peace and War: Armed Conflicts and International Order 1648–1989*, Cambridge: Cambridge University Press, 1991.
15 Daniel S. Geller and J. David Singer, *Nations at War: A Scientific Study of International Conflict*, Cambridge: Cambridge University Press, 1998, p. 2.
16 John A. Vasquez (ed.), *What Do We know about War?*, Lanham, MD: Rowman & Littlefield, 2000.
17 Suganami, 'Understanding Man, the State, and War', p. 382.
18 Suganami, 'Understanding Man, the State, and War', p. 380.
19 Daniel L. Byman and Kenneth M. Pollack, 'Let Us Now Praise Great Men: Bringing the Statesman Back In', *International Security*, 2001, vol. 25, 107–46, at p. 112.
20 Jack S. Levy, 'Domestic Politics and War', in Robert I. Rotberg and Theodore K. Rabb (eds), *The Origin and Prevention of Major Wars*, Cambridge: Cambridge University Press, 1989, p. 79.
21 Kenneth N. Waltz, *Theory of International Politics*, New York: Random House, 1979, p. 18.
22 Robert O. Keohane (ed.), *Neorealism and its Critics*, New York: Columbia University Press, 1986.
23 See e.g. Helen Milner, 'The Assumption of Anarchy in International Relations: A Critique', *Review of International Studies*, 1991, vol. 17, 67–85.

9 The conditions and consequences of globality: John H. Herz's *International Politics in the Atomic Age*

Casper Sylvest

Columbia University Press published not one but two classics of International Relations (IR) in 1959. The best-known is undoubtedly Kenneth N. Waltz's *Man, the State and War*, which fleshed out the three images that generations of scholars and their students have since deployed to make sense of war and international politics. Despite its popularity and favourable reception at the time, the second book has not achieved quite the same status. *International Politics in the Atomic Age* (*IPAA*) by John H. Herz (1908–2005) is nevertheless a classic by virtue of its groundbreaking analysis of the nuclear revolution and its impact on the theory and practice of world politics.[1] Whereas Waltz's work foreshadowed a new systematic and social scientific brand of (neo-)realism, *IPAA* was the first sustained and durable attempt to ponder what realism might mean in the atomic age.

In the early twenty-first century classical realism is back in vogue. For a variety of reasons, including the perceived sterility of neo-realism, the need for a refined critique of ideological crusading, and a push to reorientate IR theory and realism towards some of the most pertinent political, democratic and normative challenges of contemporary global politics, a growing literature harks back to the rich and tension-ridden analyses of international politics formulated by realists during the mid-twentieth century.[2] As part of this development the social and political thought of Herz has been accorded more attention in recent years.[3] Like other contemporary realists, the starting point for Herz was an understanding of international politics as conflictual and hostile to liberal programmes for reform. This involved developing sophisticated theories and strategies for understanding and navigating the perilous waters of international politics; strategies which respected the workings of politics and guarded against its pitfalls while also, significantly, sketching the imperfect ways in which some progress might after all be achieved. Working with the forces of social life and not against them, judiciously combining moderation and power for socially useful purposes, and respecting the value of diplomacy and the *Fingerspitzengefühl* (intuition) of practical experience were (and are) some of the mantras of this brand of realism.

Although post-war realists prided themselves on their useful concepts and theoretical insights, in our modern vocabulary of (US) social science, realism of this sort was as much vision or ideology as theory. The 1950s and 1960s was a crucial period in the development and eventual bifurcation of US political science into a behavioural and eventually rationalist standard and the increasingly isolated domain of political theory. With realists at the helm, IR tried for some time to avoid being steamrolled by the move to science.[4] This was ultimately a futile project as the defensive tone of Herz's preface to *IPAA* testifies. Here he characterized the book as 'old-fashioned' and

sardonically admitted that he had not used IBM machines, conducted interviews or surveys, and that the text was free from graphs, diagrams and statistical figures: 'It is
simply the product of the application to problems and subject matter at hand of
whatever intelligence was available' (p. v). Armed with these old-fashioned tools, Herz
embarked on an analysis that deserves its classics label precisely by virtue of its ability
to connect a realist analysis with humanist, liberal values under the condition of
'globality' (p. 317) that nuclear weapons inaugurated but which have since been reinforced by a range of crises related to climate change, environmental degradation,
population growth and energy.

This chapter seeks to make this case by first providing a brief introduction to Herz,
his German-Jewish background and to his best-known contribution to IR theory: the
concept of the security dilemma. I then turn to a summary of *IPAA*, its structure and
arguments, before ending with a discussion of the reception of the book and its
contemporary relevance.

In a dilemma: realism for liberal purposes

Hans Hermann Herz, who changed his first name to John upon immigrating to the
USA, was born in 1908 into a Jewish middle-class family in Düsseldorf, Germany. He
received a liberal education at the local high school and at a string of excellent German
universities. As an adolescent with vague social-liberal political ideals he formed lasting
and important friendships with a Zionist and a Marxist. Until the spring of 1933,
however, when Herz lost his newly acquired job at the local court, his political interests
lost out to more intellectual pursuits in the study of law, jurisprudence, philosophy,
history and the arts. National Socialism, increasing anti-Semitism, and ever dimmer
professional prospects provoked a political awakening on Herz's part. Help came from
his *Doktorvater* (Doctoral supervisor) at the University of Cologne, the prominent
positivist legal theorist Hans Kelsen, under whom Herz had written a dissertation
about the identity of states and its implications for the edifice of international law. As a
Jew, Kelsen ended up in Geneva in neutral Switzerland and in 1935 Herz followed suit
and began a diploma that combined his interest in international law with his ambition
to break into the study of politics and international affairs. The Geneva years were
tremendously important for Herz's intellectual development but also politically dis-
heartening. European statesmen appeased Hitler and the sanctions regime of the
Geneva-based League of Nations disintegrated irrevocably during the mid-1930s. Herz
fought both developments with his pen, in journals of the peace movement and in his
Diploma on 'National Socialist Doctrines of International Law'.[5]

In the summer of 1938 Herz left Europe for the USA. Seeking an academic career,
Herz ended up in Princeton's newly formed Institute of Advanced Study as a colleague
and acquaintance of Albert Einstein. In the build-up to World War II, Herz began his
research into the nature and workings of (international) politics to be published more
than a decade later, following government work in the Office of Strategic Studies, and
after Herz had secured a position at Howard University in Washington. *Political Realism
and Political Idealism* developed the concept of the security dilemma with which Herz
is associated. This concept is crucial for understanding the depth and implications of
the analysis provided in *IPAA*. The dilemma begins not from first image claims about
the limitations or qualities of human nature, but rather from a social context marked
by fear and uncertainty. If this context is also marked by the absence of centralized

authority (as in international politics), the actions of one agent easily give rise to suspicion, competition and a quest for security, which often spurs feelings of insecurity in other actors that in turn strengthens the original dilemma.[6] The concept has much purchase, theoretically and practically. It helps us to understand why relations between states with benign intentions can deteriorate and, for example, issue in arms races or wars, and in analysing empirical developments it leads us to focus on the importance and structural effects of actor perceptions and rationales. It is somewhat ironic that this *social* and *structural* account of international politics barely received a mention in Waltz's effort to supersede classical realism and develop a structural realist theory.[7]

While the dynamics of the security dilemma constrained attempts to rationally mould political relationships, Herz's first book also made a strong case for charting a middle course between the unacceptable alternatives of cynical realism and naive, ineffectual idealism.[8] Whereas the latter lacked insight into the logic of the security dilemma, on its own the former was ultimately unfruitful as a political philosophy. So while acknowledging the security dilemma, Herz sought a *via media* that gave realism practical prominence and yet prioritized the values of a broadly utilitarian liberal ideology. Realizing liberal political ideals was a piecemeal business that required respect for the autonomous logic of politics. The idealist notion that one can 'balance the books' of politics or that it is somehow possible to reach a consensus that satisfies everyone, had to be substituted with an understanding of the deep, moral problems associated with political action. Sometimes, Herz admitted, the end does justify the means. And this is exactly 'the paradox, the danger, and ultimately the tragic guilt involved in a life of action'.[9] On the other hand, the notion that one should resign to any form of determinism was morally, politically and intellectually unacceptable. For Herz, it was all about balancing the visions of realism and idealism in the particular social context that the security dilemma gave rise to in international politics. Realizing liberty, change, progress, reform and other cardinal values of liberalism may not be likely, and certainly not guaranteed, but viewed through the lens of the security dilemma it cannot be ruled out. Human wisdom and volition are unreliable and feeble factors in world politics, but they are not doomed to hopelessness.

The diagnosis

Writing in the late 1950s, any sound analysis of international politics, according to Herz, had to begin from and try to make sense of the nuclear revolution and its impact on humanity, social life and political organization. *IPAA* was designed and written with this objective in mind. In essence the argument of the book is that some of the fundamental characteristics of the international *system*, particularly territoriality and the notion that (great power) war is winnable, are fundamentally challenged and transfigured by the invention of thermonuclear weapons and intercontinental delivery vehicles. In this context, the concept of the national interest became (even more) unstable and mysterious, if not empty. The atomic age literally meant a globalization of human existence – a contraction of time and space – that in turn globalized threats to security and liberty. Consequently, the *structure* of international politics was undergoing a dramatic change.[10] Universal destructivity undermined the claims of almost any political authority to offer protection and security. Humanity was placed in a new, precarious and potentially catastrophic condition, which was only exacerbated by the ineptness of traditional analytical and political tools, including the time-honoured

perspective and practice of power politics. The double task thrown up by these developments was to analyse, assess and conceptualize the nature, extent and consequences
of this change in international politics and to begin the task of charting possible routes of
escape.

The structure of *IPAA* reflects this argument. The first two parts of the book deal
with the rise of traditional international politics from the seventeenth century and with
the challenge of this system provided by the H-bomb, and the 'accumulated and accumulating effect' of modern science and technology (p. 12). The penetration of the atom
led, in short, to the perforation of the 'hard shell' of the state, because there were no
appropriate means of defence against nuclear weapons. This in turn invalidated the
security contract (see below) on which this form of authority was based. The third and
final part of *IPAA* was Herz's attempt to confront this predicament and the reconfigured
security dilemmas it involved.

The account of the rise of modern international politics placed much emphasis on
the concept of territoriality, which emerged as a specific solution to a political problem
during the seventeenth century: how could the more than 300 states in the Holy Roman
Empire – structures of political authority that technically were under the suzerainty of
the nominal unity of Pope and Emperor – be considered sovereign? How, in other
words, could sovereignty be defined in a way that accommodated the hotchpotch of
juridical and political allegiances in the Holy Roman Empire *and* respected the de facto
authority of 'states'? Herz found the answer in a short essay by G. W. Leibniz (1646–
1716), which summarized some of the most important findings of *Caesarinus Für-
stenerius* (1677). According to Leibniz, sovereignty may not be absolute in the Hobbesian
sense, but it did signify *ability* to participate in European affairs and (more importantly) de facto *control* of a territory. This sociological formula bound sovereignty,
independence and power to 'an underlying pattern of statehood' without compromising
the ethereal *majesté* of the Holy Roman Empire. Territoriality gradually turned states
into hard, impenetrable shells, while their interaction made them part of a larger collective structure. This was, according to Herz, the bedrock of modern international
politics.

Informing this conception of the state was a version of the social contract: protection
and security was the currency that made citizens obey state authority. Seen in conjunction with the development of modern science and technology (what Herz was later
to term the civilizational process),[11] the trend towards ever larger units could be
understood in terms of persistent recalibrations of the relationship between technologies of destruction and the protection offered by the predominant forms of political
authority. Just like the gunpowder revolution challenged the small state and city-states,
the nuclear revolution spelled the end of the security contract on which the nation state
was based. Herz did not argue that territorially based states did not, in fact, continue to
play an important role in international politics, only that their underlying rationale had
been eroded with the development of the H-bomb. What distinguished this situation
from earlier adjustments to the balance between protection, political authority, the size
of units and increased technology-based destructivity was that the end of the cycle had
been reached (p. 13). In effect, the world had closed. The dangers of Cold War tensions, based on the nation state system and extended territoriality, could perhaps logically
be countered by a world state, but that appeared decidedly impractical at the height of
superpower confrontation. Other means of stabilizing and reforming the world (of
states) had to be identified.[12]

In advancing this argument, Herz idealized, romanticized even, the limited but fundamentally important norms that buttressed and moderated international politics in the passing age of territoriality. Like Morgenthau's analysis of the golden age of the balance of power or the English school's perspective on the institutions that are essential for the stability and reproduction of an international society,[13] Herz's conception of power politics went far beyond the mechanical. At the same time, idealizing the power politics of a bygone age was also a rhetorical strategy that served to underline the radical nature of the change that Herz sought to identify. Here lies a key strength of *IPAA*. While some of its arguments about the obsolescence of hard security shells or the omnicidal character of nuclear weapons appear as second nature to us, in the late 1950s with the Cuban Missile Crisis lurking in the future such arguments struggled to advance beyond the one-worldist slogans of the peace movement ('one world, or none'). Herz trod a fine line between pointing to the essential unpredictability, indefiniteness and hectic flux beneath the apparently stable order of international politics, while insisting that something fundamental was being transformed. Indeed, Herz argued that these developments amounted to 'the most radical change in the nature of power and the characteristics of power units since the beginning of the modern state system or, perhaps, since the beginnings of mankind' (p. 22).

A perspective that took into account the apparent stability, new challenges and an underlying, conceptual *systemic* crisis was characteristic of Herzian analysis. Indeed, the messy world of real international politics only reinforced the acute danger of the situation, since outmoded analytical tools prevented scholars and policy-makers from grasping change. In this context Herz shrewdly examined the preconditions and logics of bipolarity and deterrence, accepting their apparent stability while warning against their underlying fragility. The Herzian analysis of (ideological) bipolarity as stable, *qua* being 'a rigid and perpetually endangered equipoise' (p. 166) that only faintly resembled a balance of power system, in some ways anticipated Kenneth Waltz's later analysis but also took much more seriously the danger of nuclear weapons.[14] Similarly, drawing on Robert Oppenheimer's famous image of 'two scorpions in a bottle' (p. 14), Herz foreshadowed critiques of deterrence as being capable of achieving stability within narrowly defined parameters but also as ultimately unreliable as a general principle of international order.[15] The reasoning behind this verdict was (and is) that effective deterrence requires at least 'a minimum of rationality, self-restraint, and ability to subordinate immediate "national" interests to overall world interests in the avoidance of destruction on the part of the powers' (pp. 209–10). Fear and uncertainty make this kind of rationality implausible. People and politics enter the equation, and with that a never-ending game of second-guessing intentions. Stability becomes mere hope. The overall effect of these insights was to underline the seriousness of the situation and the limited visibility of observers and practitioners. To Herz it was, then:

> [n]o wonder that international politics, not only in its actualities but also in its concepts and terminologies, is confused, and that present-day man in the world exists as in a maze. At no time in modern history has security meant so much to him; at no time has there seemed less hope of retrieving it (p. 223).

However, if security is so decisive in the atomic age, why can it not be provided? The answer is simple: the security dilemma. Fear, uncertainty about the intentions of others and the offensive capability lodged in every claim for necessary defensive military measures, can easily conspire to produce mistrust and suboptimal outcomes. In fact, the security dilemma reached its most poignant manifestation in the pinched ideological bipolarity of the Cold War (p. 241).

Paths to survival

And yet, *IPAA* was more than a doomsday scenario of realism. The fact that in the atomic age 'power can destroy power from center to center' (p. 108), gave fear and worst-case scenarios a special place in the configuration of international politics. Living on the knife-edge of fear could result in preventive warfare and quests for world hegemony. However, here the poignancy of the security dilemma produced a paradox that allowed a ray of light into the otherwise grey mental landscape of nuclear winter: not only was the attempt to achieve security from attack or dominance often counterproductive, it was potentially *self-destructive*, since the means to security could eradicate the end and then some. The alternative to mutual accommodation was mutual destruction (p. 243).

It was against this background that Part III of *IPAA* offered a two-tiered sketch of how international politics could be brought back from the brink of auto-destruction. The first and most immediate task was to conduct 'a holding operation', which mobilized the entire edifice of classical realist virtues. The aim was to create a balance – a *modus vivendi* – between the two superpowers, and that entailed a recognition of the impurity of politics, the need for quid pro quos, and an acceptance that some (containable) realms of 'low-intensity' or proxy conflicts had to be left to themselves as safety valves. Apart from this it was diplomacy, statesmanship, empathy, gradual build-up of trust and a sober assessment of power relations – the cardinal virtues of classical realism – that carried the burden (Chapter 11). One discerns parallels to other realist aphorisms here: to Carr's notion that stability in human affairs is like the stability of the bicycle or the spinning top, to Kissinger's formula of acting as if your intuition was already experience or, more mysteriously, to Morgenthau's equation of political wisdom and fortuity.[16]

The second and much more extensive task was to rethink our options in the shadow of the nuclear threat. This was dependent on (what became known as) *détente* and an amelioration of security concerns. Few and certainly not Herz, expected this to happen in 1959. In fact, Herz often characterized himself as an ingrained pessimist. He felt a duty to investigate how a more constructive and lasting peace could be envisaged in the atomic age, and it was this sense of duty, apparently, more than any expectation about the prospects of this project materializing, that powered the most controversial chapters of the book. The straw that Herz held on to was a frail, positive element hidden in the threat of universal destruction. On the other hand, Herz seems to have got carried away just a little during the research process. He came to argue, indeed, that a liberal internationalist project could no longer, in the new circumstances, be dismissed as *prima facie* utopian. And while the starting point of this analysis was nuclear weapons, other problems quickly pointed in the same direction – the population explosion and its consequences for resource depletion and the earth's environment also contributed to the condition of globality (pp. 316–19). Arguably, the third part of *IPAA* evinces the case of the professional realist, for whom distancing himself from utopianism is so customary, that when he gradually warms to solutions that are traditionally associated with one-worldism, he relabels them or takes shelter in the uniqueness of the nuclear age (e.g. p. 309).

In the wake of the nuclear revolution, the project of universalism was based on a realization that *in the long run* national interest and universal idea(l)s were inseparable. It was based, in short, on *an ethics of survival*: despite competing value claims among humans, survival is a truly universal value. To many readers (past and present), this prompts questions about what, if anything, realism can then mean. Again, it is worth directing attention to the red thread running through Herz's *oeuvre*: the attempt to harness realist insights for more sophisticated attempts to realize the values of humanist liberalism. The conceptualization of the security dilemma as a *social* condition made this possible. The nuclear revolution and the identification of 'the combined population-resources problem' (p. 316) did not spell an end to this vision; if anything, and to the disappointment of some realist colleagues, it intensified Herz's liberal longings. In the first instance this was a case for 'divesting nations of their nuclear power', a move (perhaps the only one) that could potentially restore the impermeability and future of the nation state (p. 339). In the long run, however, *IPAA* was the first step towards broadening the concept of security to include issues relating to the environment, climate, poverty and resource depletion. For Herz, discovering globality and the oneness of the world permanently upset the balance between the real, the possible and the necessary.

Reception and relevance

In his autobiographical writings and in personal letters, Herz described *IPAA* as a sort of best-seller for Columbia University Press.[17] As sales figures of academic books go, there is something to this. The original hardback sold 3,195 copies in the four years following publication and the paperback edition that became available in 1962 ran through eight or nine printings and sold nearly 25,000 copies during the next 12 years.[18] The reception of the book was overwhelmingly positive and it received fine reviews in the press. The *New York Times* described *IPAA* as 'a lucid, extremely interesting analysis of the nature of international politics in the present age'.[19] More importantly perhaps, academic peers were generally appreciative. C. A. W. Manning, for example, thought it 'a momentous book, a portentous book, an earnest, honest, authentic book, a book which hits the target', adding wryly 'It remains, if and while there is still time, for someone to hit the bull'.[20] Herz's claim to have escaped utopianism attracted disbelief from reviewers, who singled out the concept of the 'planetary mind' that, ironically, speaks almost directly to contemporary debates.[21] Such remarks notwithstanding, most reviewers were decidedly positive in their appreciation. Most glowingly, Martin Wight called *IPAA* 'one of the two or three most distinguished books on international politics since 1945'.[22]

Wight's verdict is underscored by the obvious contemporary relevance of Herz's vision of globality, security and politics. First, Herz's groundbreaking theorization of the nuclear revolution and (what is now termed) violence interdependence[23] challenges an underlying (normative) assumption of most realist theory in IR; namely, that great power war is a possible and acceptable way of deciding conflicts in international politics. If this assumption is no longer valid, what can and should realism be?[24] Secondly, the dominant trope in academic discourse of recent decades, globalization, has outlasted the overblown claims sometimes made in its name and achieved a strong foothold in the study of IR and political studies more widely. With the range and intensity of the truly global problems now confronting us – themes Herz so discerningly identified a half-century ago – global governance, government and reform are squarely back on the academic and political agenda.[25] The history of international thought is strewn with liberal prescriptions on this issue. Most contemporary realists, however, ignore these discussions or habitually dismiss them as idealist pie-in-the-sky thinking. Alongside some of the other classical realists, whom he influenced in global directions, Herz's ideas provide an internal challenge to the realist oblivion and have become a central source of inspiration in the revival of 'one-world' thinking.[26]

Finally, Herz provided a useful conceptual apparatus for empirically analysing contemporary global security issues. For example, the security dilemma is a useful prism for understanding the renewed competition between interdependent but sovereign actors in international politics over scarce resources. This perspective could also shed light on the risk of (re)militarized energy policies and a new rush for territorial control among great powers. Furthermore, it is a distinct strength of this realism that it is attuned not only to the connection of these dynamics to global problems like climate change and inequality but also to the normative questions that arise. While Herz's last writings are marked by deep pessimism, he did point to some modest (and characteristically realist) ways in which the distrust afflicting international politics could be modified. This was a precondition for another central concern of his realism: mitigating or perhaps in some respects transcending the security dilemma when survival is at stake. Should the general paralysis that seems to plague our political response to global problems continue, however, it is likely that we will be forced to turn to another of Herz's suggestions – that of an interdisciplinary 'survival research' focusing on the matrix of culture, politics, security, technology and ecology. The aim of this 'discipline' should be a balanced and habitable planet. Its tasks should be to determine elite political interests, ascertain the most politically important links between those aspects of contemporary social life that our knowledge-economy serves to keep separate, and to formulate ('superdisciplinary') policies 'for safeguarding the human future in the face of all the threats involved'.[27] Apart from the nuclear peril, the ageing Herz came to place much emphasis on the ecological crisis stemming from a dangerous combination of population growth, resource depletion and anthropogenic climate change. Appealing to the conscience of all scientists, a deeply concerned and desperate Herz sought greater insight into the economic, social and political requirements of a habitable world, making no secret of the significant consequences such a perspective would have across the globe and for the contemporary Western lifeworld.

The atomic age inaugurated the necessity of thinking politics, security and survival on a planetary scale. With *IPAA*, Herz made the first, sustained attempt to come to grips with this insight. Only slowly, it appears, are we coming round to his perspective.

Notes

1 John H. Herz, *International Politics in the Atomic Age*, New York: Columbia University Press, 1959. Page numbers placed in parentheses in the text refer to this edition. On Waltz, see Brian C. Schmidt's chapter in this volume.
2 For a good overview, see Duncan Bell, 'Introduction: Under an Empty Sky – Realism and Political Theory', in Bell (ed.), *Political Thought and International Relations: Variations on a Realist Theme*, Oxford: Oxford University Press, 2008, pp. 1–25.
3 See, in particular, *International Relations*, 2008, vol. 22, special issue commemorating the centenary of the birth of Herz, as well as Peter Stirk, 'John H. Herz: Realism and the Fragility of the International Order', *Review of International Studies*, 2005, vol. 31, 285–306;

Christian Hacke and Jana Puglierin, 'John H. Herz: Balancing Utopia and Reality', *International Relations*, 2007, vol. 21, 367–82; Ken Booth, *Theory of World Security*, Cambridge: Cambridge University Press, 2007; William E. Scheuerman, 'Realism and the Critique of Technology', *Cambridge Review of International Affairs*, 2009, vol. 22, 563–84; Casper Sylvest, 'Realism and International Law: The Challenge of John H. Herz', *International Theory*, 2010, vol. 2, 410–45; Jana Puglierin, *John H. Herz: Leben und Denken zwischen Idealismus und Realismus, Deutschland und Amerika*, Berlin: Duncker and Humblot, 2011; Casper Sylvest, 'Technology and Global Politics: The Modern Experiences of Bertrand Russell and John H. Herz', *International History Review*, 2013, vol. 35, 121–42.

4 See particularly Nicolas Guilhot, 'The Realist Gambit: Postwar American Political Science and the Birth of IR Theory', *International Political Sociology*, 2008, vol. 2, 281–304. For general discussion of the development and competing identities of political science, see John G. Gunnell, *The Descent of Political Theory*, Chicago, IL: Chicago University Press, 1993; Emily Hauptmann, 'Defining Theory in Postwar Political Science', in George Steinmetz (ed.), *The Politics of Method in the Human Sciences*, Durham, NC: Duke University Press, 2005, pp. 207–32; Ira Katznelson, *Desolation and Enlightenment*, New York: Columbia University Press, 2003.

5 Eduard Bristler, *Die Völkerrechtslehre des Nationalsozialismus*, Zürich: Europa, 1938. The dissertation was written in English and later published (under pseudonym in German). See also John H. Herz, *Vom Überleben*, Düsseldorf: Droste, 1984.

6 John H. Herz, *Political Realism and Political Idealism*, Chicago, IL: Chicago University Press, 1951; John H. Herz, 'Idealist Internationalism and the Security Dilemma', *World Politics*, 1950, vol. 2, 157–80. See also Robert Jervis, 'Cooperation Under the Security Dilemma', *World Politics*, 1978, vol. 30, 167–214; Charles L. Glaser, 'The Security Dilemma Revisited', *World Politics*, 1997, vol. 50, 171–201; Ken Booth and Nicholas J. Wheeler, *The Security Dilemma: Fear, Cooperation and Trust in World Politics*, Basingstoke: Palgrave Macmillan, 2008; Shiping Tang, 'The Security Dilemma: A Conceptual Analysis', *Security Studies*, 2009, vol. 18, 587–623.

7 The most prominent defender of offensive neorealism, John J. Mearsheimer, does pay tribute to Herz's structural argument. See John J. Mearsheimer, *The Tragedy of Great Power Politics*, New York: Norton, 2001, e.g. p. 36.

8 E. H. Carr made a very similar point in *The Twenty Years' Crisis*. See Peter Wilson's chapter in this volume.

9 Herz, *Political Realism and Political Idealism*, p. 143.

10 In Herzian vocabulary, structure was shorthand for the fundamental characteristics of international politics in a given era, whereas the system referred to the ways in which the units of this domain organized their relations (p. 7).

11 John H. Herz, 'The Civilizational Process and its Reversal', in Herz, *The Nation-State and the Crisis of World Politics*, New York: McKay, 1976, pp. 195–225.

12 These considerations led Herz to modify the thesis about the territorial state that informed *IPAA*. It was first advanced in John H. Herz, 'Rise and Demise of the Territorial State', *World Politics*, 1957, vol. 9, 473–93, and revised in John H. Herz, 'The Territorial State Revisited – Reflections on the Future of the Nation-State', *Polity*, 1968, vol. 1, 11–34.

13 See the chapters by Nicolas Guilhot and Andrew Hurrell in this volume.

14 See Kenneth N. Waltz, 'The Stability of a Bipolar World', *Daedalus*, 1964, vol. 93, 881–909; Kenneth N. Waltz *Theory of International Politics*, New York: McGraw-Hill, 1979. See also the critique in Campbell Craig, *Glimmer of a New Leviathan: Total War in the Realism of Niebuhr, Morgenthau, and Waltz*, New York: Columbia University Press, 2003.

15 *IPAA*, Chapter 8, which also includes a sceptical analysis of graduated deterrence and ideas about limited nuclear war (pp. 200–3). See also Nicholas J. Wheeler, '"To Put Oneself into the Other Fellow's Place": John Herz, the Security Dilemma and the Nuclear Age', *International Relations*, 2008, vol. 22, 493–509.

16 E.H. Carr, *Conditions of Peace*, London: Macmillan, 1942, p. xxiii; Henry Kissinger, *A World Restored: Metternich, Castlereagh and the Problems of Peace 1812–1822*, Boston, MA: Houghton Mifflin, 1957, p. 328; Hans Morgenthau, *Scientific Man versus Power Politics*, Chicago, IL: University of Chicago Press, 1946, p. 187.

17 Herz, *Vom Überleben*, p. 169.

18 The sales figures explain the publisher's failed attempt to publish a new, second edition in the late 1960s and early 1970s. Herz was unhappy with his terms and royalties. Time constraints also played a part. The detailed sales figures and related correspondence can be found in John H. Herz Papers, M. E. Grenander Department of Special Collections and Archives, State University of New York at Albany, Box 40, Folder: 'Correspondence with Publishers, 1957–75' (the papers are uncatalogued; the reference is to the temporary organization of the papers).

19 August Heckscher, 'The Old Order Changeth – But Old Ways of Thinking Remain', *New York Times*, 29 March 1959; see also Charles C. Price, 'Permeability on a Bipolar Planet', *Saturday Review*, 28–29 March 1959, pp. 29–30.

20 C. A. W. Manning, Review of *IPAA*, *International Affairs*, 1960, vol. 36, p. 75.

21 See, for example, Campbell Craig, 'The Resurgent Idea of World Government', *Ethics and International Affairs*, 2008, vol. 22, 133–42.

22 Martin Wight, Review of *IPAA*, *American Political Science Review*, 1960, vol. 54, p. 1057. See also Erich Hula, Review of *IPAA*, *Social Research*, 1960, vol. 27, 323–24; Arnold Wolfers, Review of *IPAA*, *Political Science Quarterly*, 1959, vol. 74, 437–38.

23 Daniel H. Deudney, *Bounding Power: Republican Security Theory from the Polis to the Global Village*, Princeton, NJ: Princeton University Press, 2007.

24 See particularly Craig, *Glimmer of a New Leviathan*.

25 In these debates the problems as well as the solutions vary widely. See e.g. Luis Cabrera, 'World Government: Renewed Debate, Persistent Challenges', *European Journal of International Relations*, 2010, vol. 16, 511–30; W.E. Scheuerman, *The Realist Case for Global Reform*, Cambridge: Polity, 2011.

26 See particularly Craig, *Glimmer of a New Leviathan*, p. xv; Sylvest, 'Realism and International Law'; Scheuerman, *The Realist Case*. Dan Deudney's republican security theory points in some of the same directions but is largely dismissive about Herz's contribution. Deudney, *Bounding Power*, pp. 249–52 and the critique in W.E. Scheuerman, 'Deudney's neorepublicanism: One-world or America first?', *International Politics*, 2010, vol. 47, 523–34. See also Brent J. Steele's chapter on *Bounding Power* in this volume.

27 John H. Herz, 'On Human Survival: Reflections on Survival Research and Survival Policies', *World Futures*, 2003, vol. 59, 135–43, at pp. 140, 139.

10 Realism meets historical sociology: Raymond Aron's *Peace and War*

Bryan-Paul Frost

Henry Kissinger claimed that Raymond Aron's *Peace and War: A Theory of International Relations* had established a 'new standard' in the field.[1] While acknowledging that no 'book on such a vast subject can be final', he nonetheless predicted that 'henceforth, international theorizing will require reference to Aron'. *Malheureusement*, this was one of Kissinger's statements that did not prove prophetic.[2] First published in 1962, *Peace and War* generally received critical acclaim throughout France. This was no mean feat given Aron's decidedly conservative and anti-communist credentials. Once the book made it across the Atlantic and onto US shores, however, its reception had markedly cooled.[3] This is perhaps best illustrated in a review by another classic author, Hans J. Morgenthau: while admitting that the book contained 'political analysis of the very first order,' he more or less politely dismissed it as a 'contribution to the advancement of theoretical knowledge'.[4] Certainly *Peace and War* is mentioned in perfunctory footnotes listing famous and/or influential books in the tradition of classical realism, but to all intents and purposes, John Hall's comment about the work remains as true today as it was when he wrote it in 1981: 'one suspects that [*Peace and War*] is more quoted than read.'[5] In other words, Aron's magisterial, 800-page tome is cited, but not studied.

Although there are likely many reasons that account for this neglect, Stanley Hoffmann captured a large measure of the truth when he asked why Morgenthau's classic exercised such an enormous influence on the field of International Relations (IR) whereas Aron's influence was decidedly more muted:

> One of the many reasons why Raymond Aron's monumental *Peace and War* – a book far more ambitious in its scope and far more sophisticated in its analyses than *Politics Among Nations* – incited no comparable reaction from scholarly readers may well have been the greater judiciousness and modesty of Aron's normative conclusions. Humane sceptics invite nods and sighs, not sound and fury; and sound and fury are good for creative scholarship. Moreover, Aron's own scholarship was overwhelming enough to be discouraging; Morgenthau's was just shaky enough to inspire improvements.[6]

Similar remarks could be directed towards a more contemporary classic, namely Kenneth N. Waltz's *Theory of International Politics*. Waltz criticizes both Aron and Hoffmann for rejecting the possibility of developing a general theory of international relations similar to that found in economics. More specifically, Waltz argues that they both fail to appreciate or grasp neorealism's key insight 'that international politics can be thought of as a system with a precisely defined structure': this is 'neorealism's fundamental departure from traditional realism'. Consequently, Aron and Hoffmann are much more likely to privilege the unit (or even individual) level of analysis when explaining international outcomes and to downplay systemic causes: in the words of Aron (which are cited by Waltz), 'the principal actors have determined the system more than they have been determined by it' (p. 95).[7] In short, we may surmise that one of the reasons *Peace and War* suffers relative neglect in comparision to other classic works in the field is because it did not 'deliver the goods' that so many academics were hoping for: Aron failed to construct a parsimonious, deductive and predictive theory of international politics.

The role of theory

Aron could not agree more, and would more than likely have taken this censure as high praise: not only did he fail to construct such a theory, but the leitmotif of *Peace and War* can be read as a refutation of the possibility of such a theory ever being developed. The reason Aron's theoretical conclusions are modest to the point of being disappointing is that he did not set out primarily to *explain* international relations but to *understand* them. Aron consistently maintained that it was impossible to explain the totality of international politics through a single concept such as 'power' or the 'configuration of forces', and he was therefore never persuaded or tempted by the behaviourist (or positivistic) revolution in the social sciences that became so fashionable in the 1950s and so influential beyond. Instead of a doctrine or theory in the behaviourist sense, Aron offers his readers a way of thinking about, or a general approach to, political phenomena, the hallmarks of which are modest expectations, tentative conclusions, and (at best) probabilistic causal relations. Even if one agrees that Aron's sober procedure remains closer to the actual texture of international politics than more grandiose theorizing, it is by that same token easy to see how the latter could capture and excite the imagination of future social scientists.

Rather than making bold pronouncements about what his theory would accomplish, Aron begins the book with a warning (or reminder) to his readers that will be repeated and demonstrated throughout concerning 'the limits of our knowledge' (p. 4). The limits are not so much a lack of historical evidence or information (although Aron certainly means this as well) but rather the inherent limits of theoretical knowledge itself. As there has never been a single goal or objective which all states pursue (be that in any given historical epoch or across different epochs), then any attempt to claim that there is such a transhistorical, overarching end (whether it be 'power', 'security' or the 'national interest') will inevitably result in vague, exaggerated, or downright false oversimplifications. This is not to say that efforts at conceptualizing international relations are fruitless – on the contrary, Aron is at pains to point out that all political units must be mindful of the alternatives of war and peace, and that 'the risk of war obliges [states] to calculate forces or means'. However, the alternatives of war and peace do not and cannot tell the theorist what specific goals political units will pursue, and in the absence of this, the theorist is relatively constrained in what he can say or predict: 'lacking a single goal of diplomatic behaviour, the rational analysis of international relations cannot be developed into an inclusive theory' (pp. 16–17). These early cautionary remarks reach a crescendo at the end of Chapter 3, Part I (the last of the three chapters that articulate his fundamental theoretical concepts before he turns to the development of typical diplomatic systems in Chapters 4–6). Here Aron most fully develops the difference between economic behaviour and diplomatic-strategic behaviour, and in so doing he clarifies why the former has had (and will continue to have) far more 'success' when it comes to theory. Although Aron admits that '*homo economicus* exists only in our rationalizing reconstruction', that reconstruction resembles a 'concrete economic subject' far more accurately than any imagined or postulated *homo diplomaticus* resembles any historical diplomat. The concrete economic subject more often than not does seek a single objective (the 'maximization' of some quantity, whether it be income, profit or production) while diplomats do not. In other words, there is no comparable variable in international relations that serves the same function as 'utility' in economics, and to claim that there is would be to create a 'caricatured simplification of certain diplomatic personages at certain periods' and not the much sought-after 'idealized portrait of the diplomats of all ages'. Aron's humble conclusion is that '*there is no general theory of international relations comparable to the general theory of economy*' (pp. 90–93). While the necessity of calculating forces or means makes it possible to elaborate a conceptual framework, the multiplicity of goals (or the indeterminacy of diplomatic-strategic behaviour) prevents the articulation of theories similar to those in economics.

However, Aron did not merely argue that constructing a general theory was doomed to failure, he also saw that it was potentially politically dangerous. Of particular concern to Aron was to caution theorists against believing that they could transform international relations into an operational or predictable science; in this spirit of caution, he engaged in an extended analysis of game theory at the end of the book (pp. 767–87). While not denying its potential usefulness in helping to clarify certain aspects of diplomatic-strategic conduct, Aron emphasizes that it is not possible to quantify mathematically a concrete situation: the number of players changes, the possible courses of action are virtually endless, the stakes of the game alter during the course of a conflict, the information with which leaders make decisions is never complete or perfect, and so forth. Moreover, the very attempt at mathematical quantification is likely to lead theorists to ignore or distort a whole range of critical variables that are notoriously impossible or difficult to quantify – e.g. glory, justice, prestige or religion – and yet which are so often decisive in understanding a given event. What gives these criticisms their urgency is Aron's keen awareness that diplomats will inevitably use and be influenced by theoretical knowledge, and that such mathematically inspired or oriented models are likely to result in misunderstanding and misguided policies: diplomats may become prisoners of a certain theoretical outlook, unable to comprehend the genuine motivations of allies and enemies, and to propose innovative solutions in times of crisis.[8] Theory and theoretical models might be useful in helping to clarify or pinpoint the unique character of a particular event or historical epoch, but no theorist should foist upon the diplomat the dangerous illusion that theoretical knowledge and quantification can sharply reduce uncertainty, ambiguity and risk. One might say that theorists who engage in or encourage such hopes are not only poor theorists but they also fail in their civic duty as political educators. In a clear nod to Pascal, Aron once remarked: 'To approach human affairs in the spirit of geometry is catastrophic.'[9]

In order to flesh out more completely why Aron came to these conclusions, it is useful to remind readers who are unfamiliar with his life and background that he was not a political scientist nor an IR theorist *per se*. Rather, when Aron received his doctorate in 1938, he was considered by many to be the most promising philosophy student of his generation. Entitled *Introduction to the Philosophy of History* (and published that same year), Aron defended his dissertation before a sceptical jury, breaking as he did with the reigning neo-Kantian, historical positivism of his professors.[10] His own philosophy of history was pessimistic – even relativistic – arguing that there was a plurality of possible historical interpretations, and that there could never be one overarching explanation or determination of the past (especially of the Marxist variety). Some later called it the first existential philosophy of history in France.[11] Now, despite the fact that Aron later retracted some of the more extreme and obscure claims that he made in the *Introduction*, he nevertheless always affirmed that his 'postwar works constitute a logical, if not necessary, continuation of the basic question raised in the *Introduction à la philosophie de l'histoire*'.[12] This 'basic question' was: What are the characteristics and limitations of valid historical knowledge? The answer to this question was of more than scholarly interest to Aron. Rather, it animated his entire adult life; for the issues raised in the *Introduction* concerned the dialectical relationship of history and politics – of how individuals, hoping to understand themselves through understanding the past, could nevertheless live and act and justify their decisions in the world.[13] At all events, during and after World War II, Aron became a true polymath – a genuine Renaissance man – and over the course of his life he wrote on subjects ranging from philosophy to sociology, economics to ethics, ideology to history, education to nuclear weapons, and of course political science and international relations. These were not amateur essays and books, and they were read and studied by a wide variety of people, including France's political leaders, from President Charles de Gaulle downwards. Thus, while Aron was clearly knowledgeable about international relations, and while he wrote *Peace and War* in order to conceptualize concretely and sharpen his own understanding of world affairs (as well as to provide his readers with the analytical tools necessary to make better sense of current events), this was only one of a vast array of subjects of which he was conversant, and which grounded and influenced his thinking. This rejection of narrow specialization – an all-too-common feature of twentieth- (and indeed twenty-first-) century scholarship and academic life – contributed to his aforementioned modesty when it came to theory and theoretical conclusions. On the one hand, Aron was far too thoughtful a student of history (both ancient and modern) to claim à la Marx and others that it was deterministic and could largely be comprehended through a single variable or conceptual prism; and on the other hand, he was far too versed in philosophy to believe that any one system had all the answers (although he certainly privileged some philosophers over others). Aron's philosophy of history had inured him from seeking easy answers, both practically and theoretically, in a world as complex as the twentieth century. This in turn made his analysis more subtle and supple (if by the same token it made it more frustrating for those who demanded more concrete and useful results). Aron's philosophically grounded history, or historically grounded philosophy, could never accept unidimensional explanations.

Given such theoretical restraint, the question naturally arises as to how Aron conceived of theory and what purpose it served. Drawing on Part I of *Peace and War* ('Theory: Concepts and Systems') as well as two other relevant essays, Aron suggests that there are at least **three elements from which any theory in the social sciences** is composed. First, and most generally, every theory requires a definition of the class of phenomena being investigated, an attempt to make clear the 'horizons considered to be fundamental'.[14] Second, a theory contains an analytical framework, a framework that includes the elaboration of fundamental concepts (e.g. force, power, strategy and

diplomacy) as well as systems and types of systems (e.g. the general patterns of relations established between political units capable of being implicated in a general war).
And third, and more specifically, theory suggests certain 'effect phenomena' or 'determined factors', those principal elements (e.g. factors of power, choice of objectives) and
recurrent situations (e.g. the frequency and types of war and peace) of international
politics for which sociological analysis seeks to discover the 'cause phenomena' or
'determinants' (pp. 17, 177–80). Quite clearly, Aron's understanding of theory is not
going to provide a rigorously interconnected series of hypotheses. Instead, he prefers to
stay close to the actual texture of international relations – for what good is a theory in
the social sciences that is so thoroughly divorced from political life that it no longer
resembles it, or which seeks to impose on its subject matter a conformity or regularity
that distorts the subject matter itself? This rejection of what might be called a 'thesis-
driven' understanding of international relations theory has led some theorists to claim
that Aron does not really have a 'theory' of international relations at all, or more
broadly that Aron's 'theory' is for the most part only a conceptual framework.[15] Now
Aron is aware of these objections, and he asks whether or not his analysis should be
classified as a 'theory' or a 'conceptualization':

> It all depends on what we expect of a theory, of the model of a theory (in physics
> or in economics) to which we refer. Such a conceptual analysis seems to me to
> fulfil some of the functions that we can expect from a theory: it defines the essen-
> tial features of a sub-system; it provides a list of the main variables; it suggests
> certain hypotheses about the operation of the sub-system, depending on whether it
> is bipolar or multipolar, homogeneous or heterogeneous.[16]

What we can say is that while Aron's theory is not a system of interconnected
hypotheses, it does allow a theorist to enumerate the key elements of international
relations – the cause and effect phenomena – from which such hypotheses can be generated. It seems that Aron thought it more important to make certain that his analytical framework helped to elicit the right questions about international relations, that it
allowed individuals to see the plurality of factors animating international politics.
Aron's theoretical framework will suggest hypotheses, but never prescribe them.

Realist historical sociology

The above remarks ought in no way to suggest that readers of Part I of *Peace and War*
will find themselves in alien territory – far from it. Throughout his conceptual analysis,
both in this book and elsewhere, Aron sounds many familiar themes in the very broad
tradition of (classical) realism: he affirms the anarchic nature of the international
system; maintains that states must therefore closely monitor their relative power, force,
and collective capacity for action vis-à-vis other states; and he concludes that international politics is animated by the omnipresent possibility of peace or war between
nations. In this respect, Aron makes no claim to originality here, and simply follows the
well-trodden path of philosophers, jurists, diplomats and soldiers before him, from
Grotius to Vattel, and Montesquieu to Clausewitz. To unearth Aron's thoughtfulness,
one must dig a bit deeper. Three examples must suffice. In the first place, Aron always
emphasizes what might be loosely termed 'moral' considerations in his conceptual framework. For example, when Aron begins to delineate the specific focus of international

relations, he stresses the fact that the alternatives of war and peace often (if not always) involve a claim to justice: international relations deal with '*the relations between political units, each of which claims the right to take justice into its own hands and to be the sole arbiter of the decision to fight or not to fight*' (p. 8). Although some may claim that all politics is ultimately 'power' politics, Aron adds that all political claims inevitably contain a greater or lesser degree of justice, and that these assertions must be properly weighed, assessed and appreciated by a prospective theorist. War (and peace) rarely take place outside the arena of justice and morality, even if those claims are not always as robust as one would hope, and are often mixed with other, less 'noble' motives. None the less, the distinctive arena of international relations can never be severed irrevocably from considerations of justice and morality: wars between political units cannot be explained by or reduced to mere self-interest or the accumulation of power because the human beings who represent their political units do not always act in this fashion. In the second place, Aron is continually reformulating his own assumptions in manifold ways, as if to remind his readers that there is not – and cannot be – a single, privileged historical perspective. For example, when Aron discusses the goals or ends that states seek, he argues that at the most general level of abstraction or conceptualization, they have sought three objectives: security (either by increasing their own force or weakening a rival's), power (the ability of imposing one's will on another), and glory (to be recognized by others in a certain way or for a certain quality). Aron nicely distinguishes these three goals from one another (the first of which he calls a 'material' objective, the latter two 'moral' ones) by contrasting three famous French leaders. 'Clemenceau sought the *security*, Napoleon the *power*, Louis XIV the *glory* of France'.[17] As the chapter proceeds, Aron reconceptualizes these objectives as he deepens his analysis of them. The ternary series security, power and glory could also be reformulated as space (to conquer more territory), men (to conquer more subjects), and souls (to convert others to a political, social, or religious idea), or again as body (to accumulate material objectives such as space or resources or force), heart (to satisfy a state's *amour propre* by prevailing over its rivals), and mind (to spread an idea of which the state represents a unique incarnation) (pp. 72–77).[18] To codify these variables mathematically would be a nightmare; to ignore them would be to mistake a dream for reality. And finally, in the third place, Aron centres much of his attention on the unit (and individual) level of analysis. More specifically, he argues that it is imperative for a theorist to be cognizant of a state's regime, for it is only here that one will discover its conception of justice and its overarching political objectives. Certainly Aron is attuned to whether any particular international system is bi- or multipolar, and he is aware of the dynamics that often prevail within such systems. None the less, it is the compatibility or conflict among the regimes of the major powers in any given international system (or sub-system) that is most decisive in influencing the character of that system. As Aron observes (perhaps thinking of Germany in the 1930s): 'A change of regime within one of the chief powers suffices to change the style and sometimes the course of international relations' (p. 95). This makes Aron's theorizing much more akin to classical philosophers such as Thucydides and Aristotle than it does to many a contemporary theorist. At the end of the day, all three of these examples punctuate the fact that Aron does not believe (in common with Waltz and others) in a 'theory of undetermined behaviour', one that divorces the political unit's intentions from the forces it possesses. Aron thus rejects any 'science that gives to the forms of behavior it studies explanations *contrary* to or *divorced* from the meaning understood by the participants' themselves.[19]

In Part II ('Sociology: Determinants and Constants'), Aron looks to establish pro-positions of a general nature, relative '*either to the action which a certain cause pro-duces … or to regular series or patterns of development*' (p. 178). Sociology investigates two types of causes, which he distinguishes as material and moral. Material or physical causes are space (geography), population (demography), and resources (economics), whereas the moral or social determinants are nations 'with their regimes, civilizations, [and] human and social nature' (pp. 178–80). Each chapter examines one of these variables in its manifold complexity, and Aron's discussion ranges from Montesquieu's climatic determinism in *The Spirit of the Laws* to modern psychological theories of aggression and war. Part III ('History: The Global System in the Thermonuclear Age') might be described as an enormous case study of the Cold War up until the early 1960s. Aron pinpoints two significant differences between the postwar system and all previous ones: the '*technological revolution*' both in weapons and industry, and the '*global extension of the diplomatic field*', origin of both real heterogeneity (diversity of the principles of state legitimacy, dimensions of the political units) and of juridical homogeneity (United Nations, equality and sovereignty of states)' (p. 371). But how-ever significant these differences are, they have neither changed the nature of human beings nor that of the political units involved; diplomacy in the international system can still be understood in the context of Clausewitz and the general theoretical frame-work elaborated in Part I. Although Parts II and III are probably skimmed or skipped over by many if not most scholars today, both parts do have the benefit of highlighting Aron's distinctive methodological approach, namely historical sociology. According to Aron, the distinguishing characteristic of historical sociology is its emphasis on 'com-parative study', by which he means an investigatory method that attempts to isolate and highlight probabilistic causal relations through a rigorous comparison within and across different historical periods. In this respect, the historical sociologist is continuously required to glide back and forth between an analysis of the structural determinants of behaviour (i.e. the macro or sociological or systemic causes that exert an influence on international politics) and the concrete study of a given diplomatic constellation (i.e. the micro or historical or unit/individual level causes that influence decision-making). Aron notes that theorists who focus primarily on the former factors to the neglect of the latter are likely to commit two related errors: 'they tend to establish "causes" where, at most, there are trends, and they do not take account of all the factors involved but exaggerate the influence of those that are considered.' One might say that one of the great virtues of historical sociology is that it compels a theorist to give due consideration and weight to the authentic *political* perspective of those actors whose decisions are the object of theoretical or scientific investigation. Certainly theorists must avoid privileging the micro level of analysis to the exclusion of everything else, for then they are likely to deny that there are any recurrent, systemic patterns of behaviour. Nevertheless, the greater problem or temptation that Aron saw in his day was that theorists tended to ignore or discount what the historical actors themselves said influ-enced them to act in a certain way, especially when it came to the regimes they had self-consciously chosen to serve and defend.[20] In sum, Aron is the champion of case study-based analysis.

Whether a theorist admitted it or not, Aron was keenly aware that 'normative implications are inherent' in every theory in the social sciences, and he was forthright enough to detail his own in Part IV ('Praxeology: The Antinomies of Diplomatic-Strategic Conduct' – p. 575). Aron's normative conclusions – or 'morality of prudence' – emerge from his attempt to transcend and thereafter to moderate what he sees as the two 'praxeological problems' confronting leaders: the '*Machiavellian problem*' of the legitimate recourse to force (what he later christens a 'morality of struggle') and the '*Kantian problem*' of collective security and universal peace (or a 'morality of law' – pp. 577, 608–09). Neither a morality of struggle nor a morality of law can, on its own, provide a leader with a consistent *and* responsible principle of diplomatic-strategic conduct. On the one hand, even though states share certain norms of behaviour and principles of legitimacy, they continue to reserve the right to use force as they see fit, and the diplomat who neglects to calculate the balance of power in the hope of upholding international law fails in his duty. On the other hand, states have rarely considered every recourse to arms to be legitimate, and they have often sincerely aimed at promoting and defending higher goals and values. Aron is neither a cynic nor an idealist, and he is able to avoid both a vulgar Machiavellianism and a naive Kantianism. The bellicose character of international politics cannot be transcended, only moderated, but such moderation can come neither from opportunism divorced from reflection upon higher principles and goals, nor from the single-minded pursuit of heartfelt convictions divorced from considerations of the consequences of those actions. Only a morality of prudence considers and weighs both of these antinomies when it comes to deciding the best course of action. Such a morality will eschew the pursuit of grandiloquent and 'limitless' objectives such as 'making the world safe for democracy' in favour of achieving more modest but concrete goals just as much as it will reject the exercise of pure power politics to obtain all of one's objectives when honorable compromises and the 'limitation of violence' are also available (p. 585). The morality of prudence is therefore a morality of responsibility, and prudent diplomats, unlike those acting from conviction alone, always take into consideration the likely consequences of their decisions and act accordingly.

Peace and War in the future

This essay has attempted to limn the layers, contours and dynamics of Aron's distinctive approach to international relations in general, and *Peace and War* in particular, in order to assist individuals in wading through this weighty volume. It stands as a refuge for those who delight in complexity, nuance and admissions of uncertainty and doubt. Not surprisingly, Aron never created a 'school of thought' or cultivated 'disciples', and this might also explain why the book is not as famous or influential as it otherwise might have been. Many contemporary scholars, of course, continue to find his work inspiring – but those who do so most authentically continue to heed Aron's injunction that there never was, and never will be, an 'Aronian school of thought'.[21] One might speculate that *Peace and War* will never take centre stage when it comes to international relations theorizing, but as long as there are people who are dissatisfied with or have doubts about the latest theoretical fashions, and especially those theories that claim to explain almost everything in a neat and tidy package, then Aron's opus will likely always remain in print and be consulted with profit. Perhaps the last words in this essay should be those of Kissinger himself, which help to underscore *Peace and War*'s distinctive contribution to international relations and why it deservedly remains a classic, albeit a somewhat neglected one: *Peace and War* 'is not a book for those striving for ready-made solutions. However, Aron does better than give us answers – he teaches us which questions are significant'.

Notes

1 Raymond Aron, *Peace and War: A Theory of International Relations*, trans. R. Howard and A. B. Fox, Garden City, NY: Doubleday & Co, 1966, reissued (with a new introduction by Daniel J. Mahoney and Brian C. Anderson) by Transaction Publishers, New Brunswick, NJ, 2003. It was originally published as *Paix et guerre entre les nations*, Paris: Calmann-Lévy, 1962. For those not familiar with the French original, all page references (in parentheses) and quotations in the text and notes will be to the English-language edition, and all emphasized words in quotations are contained in the original.

2 Henry Kissinger, 'Fuller Explanation', *New York Times Book Review*, 12 February 1967, p. 3.

3 For a summary of the French and American responses, see Robert Colquhoun, *Raymond Aron: The Sociologist in Society, 1955–1983*, vol. 2, London: Sage Publications, 1986, pp. 191–97. Colquhoun's two-volume intellectual biography also contains a fine index of the copious secondary literature on Aron through the mid-1980s as well as a bibliography of his voluminous corpus. See also Perrine Simon, *Raymond Aron: bibliographie*, Paris: Julliard, 1986. For those interested in Aronian scholarship after this time, perhaps the best places to begin would be through such associations and institutions as the *Société des Amis de Raymond Aron* and the *Centre de Recherches Politiques Raymond Aron* at the École des Hautes Études en Sciences Sociales in Paris. New editions of his works continue to be published in France and elsewhere (in the USA, notably through Transaction Publishers), and the scholarship on all aspects of his thought shows no sign of diminishing.

4 Hans J. Morgenthau, Review of *Peace and War*, *American Political Science Review*, 1967, vol. 61, p. 1111. Witness also the appraisal by Oran R. Young, who concluded that 'In terms of the criteria of theory Aron's book is a clear-cut failure, albeit a failure of heroic proportions'. See 'Aron and the Whale: A Jonah in Theory', in Klaus Knorr and James N. Rosenau (eds), *Contending Approaches to International Politics*, Princeton, NJ: Princeton University Press, 1969, pp. 129–43, at p. 143.

5 John Hall, *Diagnoses of Our Time: Six Views on Our Social Condition*, London: Heinemann Educational Books, 1981, p. 164.

6 Stanley Hoffmann, 'An American Social Science: International Relations', *Daedalus*, 1977, vol. 106, 41–60, at p. 45.

7 See Kenneth N. Waltz, 'Realist Thought and Neorealist Theory', *Journal of International Affairs*, 1990, vol. 44, 21–37, at p. 30, and *Theory of International Politics*, New York: Random House, 1979, p. 47.

8 According to Hall, *Diagnoses of Our Time*, p. 173, this is precisely what Aron said happened in Vietnam. The USA employed and became trapped by a false theoretical understanding of the conflict, and it treated the 'situation under the aegis of a strategic theory designed to deal with a superpower'. Consequently, the USA failed to see the actual 'stakes' involved in the war and was unable to imagine or devise an effective response.

9 Raymond Aron, *On War*, trans. T. Kilmartin, New York: W. W. Norton, 1968, pp. 117–18.

10 Raymond Aron, *Introduction to the Philosophy of History: An Essay on the Limits of Historical Objectivity*, trans. G. J. Irwin, Boston, MA: Beacon Press, 1961. Perhaps not surprisingly, his thesis was greeted with enthusiasm by many of his peers and colleagues, in no small part because the looming world war seemed an absolute refutation of there being any necessary and inherent 'progress' or 'reason' in history. It should be noted that by this time, Aron had already published two books on German sociology and historical philosophy, effectively introducing thinkers like Max Weber to a wider French, academic audience. See *Essai sur une théorie de l'histoire dans l'Allemagne contemporaine: La philosophie critique de l'histoire*, Paris: Vrin, 1938, and *German Sociology*, trans. M. Bottomore and T. Bottomore, Glencoe, IL: Free Press, 1957.

11 Raymond Aron, *Thinking Politically: A Liberal in the Age of Ideology*, trans. James and Marie McIntosh, intro. D. J. Mahoney and B. C. Anderson, New Brunswick, NJ: Transaction Publishers, 1997, pp. 44–45.

12 Raymond Aron, 'Introduction', in Miriam Bernheim Conant (ed.), *Politics and History: Selected Essays by Raymond Aron*, New York: The Free Press, 1978, p. xix.

13 See Raymond Aron, *Memoirs: Fifty Years of Political Reflection*, trans. G. Holoch, New York: Holmes & Meier, 1990, pp. 36–47, 79–85.

14 Raymond Aron, 'Theory and Theories in International Relations: A Conceptual Analysis', in Norman D. Palmer (ed.), *A Design for International Relations Research: Scope, Theory, Method, and Relevance*, Philadelphia, PA: The American Academy of Political and Social Science, 1970, pp. 55–66, at p. 55.

15 See, for example, Charles A. McClelland, 'Conceptualization, Not Theory', in Palmer, *A Design for International Relations Research*, pp. 72–75.

16 Raymond Aron, 'What Is a Theory of International Relations?', *Journal of International Affairs*, 1967, vol. 21, pp. 193–94.

17 It is also worth mentioning in this context that Aron thus avoids reifying the state and treating it as a 'rational actor' pure and simple. There is no doubt that Aron often speaks of a state acting, and he was acutely aware that a state's traditions and customs will obviously affect the way its leaders act and the goals that they seek. However, at the end of the day, he also recognized that states do not behave independently of their decision-makers, and this means that the individual level of analysis enjoys a priority in Aron's theoretical framework that is often missing in realist and especially neorealist theories.

18 Another example of this occurs in Chapter 6 (pp. 150–73), where Aron takes peace as his conceptual starting point rather than the possibility of war. He then develops a fourfold typology: peace by equilibrium, by hegemony, by empire and by terror, the latter being characteristic of the Cold War.

19 See Hoffmann, 'An American Social Science', p. 52, as well as Hoffmann, *The State of War: Essays on the Theory and Practice of International Politics*, New York: Praeger, 1965, p. 25.

20 Raymond Aron, 'Conflict and War from the Viewpoint of Historical Sociology', in *The Nature of Conflict: Studies on the Sociological Aspects of International Relations*, Paris: UNESCO, 1957, pp. 177–203, at p. 193.

21 See Aron, *Thinking Politically*, pp. 253–54. For a small sampling of such contemporary scholars, see Daniel J. Mahoney, *The Liberal Political Science of Raymond Aron*, Lanham, MD: Rowman & Littlefield, 1992; Brian C. Anderson, *Raymond Aron: The Recovery of the Political*, Lanham, MD: Rowman & Littlefield, 1997; Murielle Cozette, 'Realistic Realism? American Political Realism, Clausewitz and Raymond Aron on the Problem of Means and Ends in International Politics', *Journal of Strategic Studies*, 2004, vol. 27, 428–53; and Reed M. Davis, *A Politics of Understanding: The International Thought of Raymond Aron*, Baton Rouge, LA: Louisiana State University Press, 2009.

11 Towards a liberal realism: Inis L. Claude's *Power and International Relations*

J. Samuel Barkin

Inis L. Claude's *Power and International Relations*[1] is an analysis of the role of inter-national organization in securing peace among the great powers, particularly in a world of bipolar confrontation and nuclear weapons. He compares three international systems for maintaining the peace: the balance of power; collective security; and world government. He concludes that the balance of power is the most realistic, but that its reliability as a mechanism for maintaining the peace is enhanced by being embedded in the United Nations (UN), which provides both an institutional structure for and a symbolism of pacific dispute resolution. As such, the argument is clearly realist in its focus and assumptions, but more sympathetic to international institutions and international cooperation than are most realist arguments.

A classical realist orientation with a focus on, and sympathy for, international organizations and the symbolism of cooperation is a hallmark of Claude's work. His career spanned the Cold War, with most of his major works published in the 1960s, and with a core focus on the relationship among international organizations, the structure of the international system, and the maintenance of international peace and security. *Power and International Relations* fits neatly within this focus, although with a greater stress on the international system, and less on international institutions as organizations, than some of his other work. It was recognized at the time, and continues to be recognized, as a classic conceptual analysis of the balance of power.

Power and International Relations is a fascinating book, and was well received at the time of publication. Among other indicators, it won the American Political Science Association's Woodrow Wilson Award for best book on government, politics, or inter-national affairs in 1963. However, in some respects it has not aged well in the half-century since it was first published. While the title suggests a general treatment of power in international relations, the book itself focuses on military power, and in par-ticular on the prevention of great power, and nuclear, war. As such, much of the dis-cussion is dated, since the security concerns at the height of the Cold War, with its bipolar system and its persistent threat of nuclear war, are very different from those of today. In addition, the project preceded what has been called the second great debate in International Relations (IR), and the development of positivist methodologies.[2] It is an exercise in big thinking of the old school, focusing more on thoughtful and reasoned argument than on methodological precision. At the same time, many of the details of the argument remain relevant for the contemporary analysis of international security structures, and the conclusions are prescient, foreshadowing some more recent devel-opments both in international relations theory and in the practice of contemporary international politics.

The argument

Claude sets out to examine the problem of power and war in a world of intense bipolar competition in which both superpowers, the USA and the Soviet Union, were developing sufficient nuclear forces to destroy civilization, and in which two world wars had been fought within the past half-century. His goal is to analyse the three major schools of thought predominant at the time regarding how to constrain national power and restrain states from going to war, in order to determine which has the most promise. The three schools of thought focus on the balance of power, collective security and world government.

He begins by defining power very narrowly, much more so than many of his contemporary IR theorists, as military force. Power is thus for him a measure of the ability to wage war in the short term, rather than a measure of longer-term military potential (which would include economic potential, as Hans J. Morgenthau does[3]) or of the ability to change the behaviour of others (which would include power over opinion, as E. H. Carr does[4]). He sets out by asking what the three schools of thought can tell us about how states can be restrained from using their existing military capabilities to wage major war, given that in a nuclear world another world war could be unconscionably destructive. He assumes that the nation state will remain for the foreseeable future the core focus of political decision-making and of political loyalties, and therefore that it will remain the central actor in international politics.

The focus on military power and on states suggests a realist analysis, and in many ways *Power and International Relations* fits into the classical realist tradition (although its focus on system structure foreshadows neorealism, in much the same way as does Kenneth Waltz's *Man, the State, and War*, published three years previously[5]). This fit is reinforced by Claude's frequent stress on the importance of politics rather than law and formal institutional structure. However, he is much more willing than most realists to criticize the concept of the balance of power, and is much less willing to write off as 'utopian' attempts to create other structural constraints on war. His is therefore a more nuanced, liberal and internationalist version of classical realism than the works that tend to be read as the classics of the genre today, such as Morgenthau's *Politics Among Nations* or John H. Herz's *Political Realism and Political Idealism*.

Claude addresses the three schools of thought on a continuum from the least to the greatest centralization of power, and in order of their historical development in the modern state system. By either measure, the first to be addressed is the balance of power. His primary criticism of the balance of power as a school of thought concerns its imprecision. He identifies several potential meanings of the concept: a situation; a policy; and a system. In any of the three meanings, furthermore, the term 'balance' is used both to refer to an equilibrium, in which power across states and alliances is relatively equal, or as a disequilibrium, in which threats to states, or to the peace, are overmatched. What is worse, theorists of the balance of power often use these meanings interchangeably, often without being clear about which of the meanings they refer to. (Claude in fact gives several examples where different meanings are used within the same sentence.) In the end, he concludes that for many IR theorists the concept of the balance of power is a symbol of respectability rather than a term of substantive content. 'It is a test of intellectual virility, of he-manliness in the field of international relations.'[6]

The only use of the term that Claude finds useful in a discussion of the problem of power and war is as a system, in which individual attempts to maximize power cancel each other out and result in an equilibrium of military capability. This can happen either automatically (this is the version of the balance of power system that Waltz was later to use as the foundation of neorealism[7]), or manually, as the result of policies by specific states or statespeople designed to create equilibrium (this use being distinct from balance of power as a specific foreign policy, in that it refers to systemic results rather individual policy). Examples of a manually operated system include the British self-conscious propensity in the eighteenth and nineteenth centuries for keeping continental Europe divided, or the complex equilibria designed and managed by diplomats such as Metternich.[8]

The problem that Claude has with the balance of power understood in this way is that as a system it has historically not worked all that well at preventing war. He quotes Morgenthau as arguing that the system has in the past been a success in preventing the rise of a single imperial power, and then suggests that this is an 'uncertain, unreal, and inadequate system' and that it is 'necessary to take a somewhat stricter view than Morgenthau's of the nature of international order'.[9] In response to Morgenthau's claim that small nations owe their independence to the balance of power, Claude responds that according to this argument 'the preservation of weak states depends upon an equilibrium, the absence of an equilibrium, or sheer luck; it can hardly be regarded as a clear tribute to the equilibrating efficiency of a balance of power system'.[10] While his critique saves its most pointed ire for Morgenthau, it effectively covers the range of realist thinking at the time of writing. He concludes that while a balance of power system has some utility in constraining war, and has the advantage that statespeople can draw on previous practice in operating the system, it is prone to spectacular failures. Furthermore, the classical European balance destroyed in World War I could no longer be reconstructed, and it was by no means clear how to construct an effective new balance for a bipolar and nuclear world.

The second school of thought, the one to which by his own admission Claude is most sympathetic, is collective security. He has two primary goals in his discussion of this approach to constraining power and preventing war. The first is to debunk the claim that collective security is an exercise in idealism that fails to take power into account.[11] This claim is often made by classical realists. More recently the claim has become embedded in the story of the first great debate and its opposition of realism and utopianism that has become so central to the history that IR as a discipline tells about itself.[12] Claude shows, through an extensive review of the works of scholars and statespeople in what he calls the Wilsonian school (because President Wilson was its most famous proponent, not its key thinker), that their work was not based on the assumption that power could be ignored, but rather on the conclusion that the balance of power had failed. The logic of the Wilsonian argument was that, in a world of total war, great powers would come to recognize that any threat to the stability of the international system was a threat to their national interest, and they needed an institutional structure through which to act on that recognition. The idea of collective security was sold to the US public in more idealist language than this because its proponents felt that the public at large would respond better to idealist than to realist language, not because its proponents were themselves idealists. Claude's second goal in his discussion of collective security is to show that a collective security system has in fact never been tried in the modern state system. Such a system requires the participation of all of the great powers, and an agreement by those powers that collective action will be taken against any of them that disturb the international peace. The League of

Nations did not fit this bill, because at least two great powers did not participate at any one time (the USA throughout, Germany and the Soviet Union for most of the League's history). Furthermore, the UN, Claude argues, was never intended to oversee a real collective security system. The veto given to permanent members of the Security Council means that the body can never authorize action against the great powers. The UN, therefore, was designed as a mechanism for preventing lesser powers from threatening international security, not for replacing the balance of power as a mechanism for preventing great power war. Claude's conclusion is that collective security is a promising system in principle, but that the requisite political conditions do not yet exist to put such a system in place.

The third school of thought, the one to which Claude seems least sympathetic, is world government. He argues that the logic of proposals for a supranational authority capable of preventing war was insufficiently thought through. He criticizes proponents of world government on three grounds. First, they have an inadequate theory of the role of the state. The concept of world government is built on the idea of the state as holder of the monopoly of force in a polity, but in practice states never actually hold such a monopoly. Second, they are conceptually unclear about whether the subjects of a world government would be individuals or states. Third, they propose systems of law without recognizing that law cannot function purely as a deterrent, it needs to be based on a collective political consensus. As such, Claude argues that world government in the context of the modern state system is structurally flawed and politically implausible.

This section is the weakest in the book. Claude seems at times to be stretching to ridicule an idea he does not like, rather than engaging in measured analysis. The discussion of states and the monopoly of force is a good example. It points to several versions of Max Weber's definition of the state, without actually looking at Weber's original, with its nuanced elaboration.[13] States (as opposed to governments – Claude confuses the two in this section of the book) do in fact claim monopolies of legitimate violence in support of a political order. A world government could presumably do the same, in a way that limits even if it does not eliminate organized violence. Similarly, even if a world government were not completely effective in eliminating violence among groups (and it would probably not be), this is not the question that Claude started with. He set out to address the question of great power war, and a world government that prevented great powers from amassing large armies and major nuclear forces could in fact presumably prevent this specific form of organized violence. A world government capable of doing so may create a different sort of monster, but this is not an argument that Claude pursues.

The overall conclusion that Claude draws is that each of the three schools of thought has something to contribute to solving the problem of power and war in international relations. Balance of power theory recognizes that states have control over the means of power, and will be reluctant to give it up. Collective security theory recognizes that some increase in the political centralization of the international system is necessary in response to the increasing destructiveness of contemporary power, while at the same time recognizing the centrality of states to the system. World government theory, while it does not provide an answer to the question of power and war in international relations, usefully restates the question. It asks not how conflict among groups can be prevented, but how it can be 'resolved or contained by political rather than violent means'.[14] He also concludes that, rather than creating a system of collective security, the most important aspect of the UN is taming the balance of power system, both by providing impartial dispute resolution of a kind that does not exist in a 'pure' state system, and by changing what he calls the symbolism, what in the terminology of contemporary IR would be called the norms,[15] of war in the international system. This conclusion does not appear to draw directly on the arguments made earlier in the book. Rather, it hints at a new approach to understanding the problem of power and war, one that fore-shadows both some of Claude's later work,[16] and the ideational turn in IR that began a quarter of a century after *Power and International Relations* was written.

Strengths and weaknesses

Power and International Relations is a masterful analysis of the theories of balance of power and collective security, if less so world government. It shows a level of nuance in reading these schools of thought that has for the most part been lost in the contemporary trend to parsimonious, 'scientific' theories of IR. The critical analysis of the balance of power remains one that realists for the most part fail to address adequately,[17] and the discussion of the theory of collective security is one that should remain required reading as an antidote to the realism/idealism dichotomy that can still be found in contemporary IR.[18] There are, however, some weaknesses in the argument. Ironically, many of these are of the same sort that Claude criticizes so effectively in the three schools of thought that he analyses. His own use of terms, while clearer and better defined than 'balance of power,' can be imprecise. For example, he clearly defines power at the beginning of the book as referring only to military capabilities, but later seems to use the term in a broader sense, to mean material capabilities more broadly, or even the ability to influence others' behaviour. He also speaks of force in places, without being clear about how force is different from power as he has defined it. This terminological slippage is common in the IR literature, but seems more pointed in a work that criticizes terminological imprecision in others.

Similarly, there is slippage in the topical focus of the book as well. Claude notes in the Introduction that he focuses on the threat of major war in a nuclear era. However, he often seems to be talking about the use of force more broadly, for example at the level of civil disturbance rather than nuclear conflagration. And at times he seems to be speaking of the maintenance of order in international politics, a much wider issue than that of great power war. True, great power war in a nuclear era is a threat to the international order. However, the converse is not necessarily true – threats to the international order do not necessarily bring great power war. His observation about the UN, that given veto powers in the Security Council it is a vehicle for maintaining an existing balance of power rather than a real collective security system, tells us a lot about the structure of the contemporaneous (and contemporary) international political order. However, it tells us little about great power war.

Finally, the book relies too often on semantic rather than substantive arguments. If the goal of the analysis is to determine which school of thought gives us the most useful ideas for the prevention of war, then drawing the best of the ideas from each school seems a reasonable analytical route to follow. Too often, however, Claude dwells on minor inconsistencies and logical contradictions within individual works. With authors who remain central to the IR canon, such as Morgenthau, this can be informative for today's reader, to the extent that contemporary debates continue to draw on these works. However, the majority of the objects of these critiques are outside the contemporary canon. An example can be found in the section on world government, in which Claude points out at some length the weaknesses of Albert Einstein's arguments on the subject. Einstein's was at the time an active voice in the world government movement, but he was never (nor did he claim to be) an IR scholar. Critiquing his arguments on the subject, therefore, makes for better polemics than scholarship. And this style of criticism seems a little unfair given than Claude himself is not in the end willing to propose specific governance structures for the international system. There is no perfect system of governance for the international system, so expecting perfection from others is unreasonable. Nor does it seem reasonable for Claude to expect perfect logical and terminological consistency in others when he does not provide it himself.

Contemporary relevance

In some ways *Power and International Relations* seems dated and of limited relevance to the contemporary international scene, not surprising in a work that is more than half a century old. In other ways, it does a good job of pointing out how both international governance and academic IR have changed. The book is old enough that its predictions about change in the international system have already been tested. Some have been proved wrong, but more have been proved right. Since the depths of the Cold War the world of international politics has changed in fundamental ways. The world is no longer bipolar. In fact, in terms of military power it is arguably as unipolar as it has been at any point in the modern state system. Major war among the great powers, while not inconceivable, certainly is not high on anyone's list of current major threats to international security. In this sense, the basic frame for the book is, for the moment, obsolete. Furthermore, the greatest fear motivating the book, nuclear conflagration, has receded. The USA and Russia each individually retain the ability to destroy civilization at the push of the button, but we no longer worry much that they will do so. This development puts into question a core underlying premise of the book, that a focus strictly on the built instruments of military force is an adequate starting point for understanding key patterns in international politics.

Another premise that Claude gets wrong is with respect to arms control and disarmament. He dismisses the possibility that negotiated arms reductions would have much impact on international politics as being something so unlikely that it does not merit much discussion. While arms control treaties have certainly not been a panacea, they are (arguably) far from irrelevant. They have functioned both to reduce nuclear stockpiles to small fractions of what they once were, and to act as lubricants to the improvement in superpower relations during the latter part of the Cold War.

Reading *Power and International Relations* is a useful reminder of how much, and in what ways, not only international politics but also IR has changed. The book is a state-of-the-art review of the international security literature at the time. This is true of its substance and its style. It was written near the end of the dominance of what might be called the diplomatic history style, and what has been called the classical approach of IR scholarship.[19] On the one hand, the style can be annoying to a contemporary reader, inasmuch as it is replete with references to people and events that no longer hold resonance. On the other hand, it displays a deep familiarity with the actual practice of international politics that often seems lost in the methodological focus of more recent IR scholarship. Beyond style and method, the book is also a useful reminder that the world in which IR is studied has changed every bit as much as the way in which we study it. Security studies as a whole has expanded considerably from the Cold War focus on military capabilities and major power war, but the neorealism that remains in some ways at the core of the field (rhetorically, at least) is still rooted in the bipolarity and nuclear confrontation of the Cold War. Reading IR written in, rather than about, the coldest of the Cold War is a useful corrective to strong claims that international politics is much as it ever was.

Despite being set in a different era of international politics, however, *Power and International Relations* effectively foreshadows some key developments both in the role of the UN in issues of war and security, and in IR theory. Most importantly, perhaps, the conclusion to the book, while it does not use the specific term, discusses the development of multilateralism as an institution.[20] This can be seen in Claude's discussion both of the developing role of the UN as a forum for dispute resolution, and of changes in the norms of war. The combination of the two has made war between states much more exceptional than in the classical balance of power period, and has made wars of territorial expansion rare. As multilateralism has developed it has been less focused on the Security Council and General Assembly than Claude envisioned, and has involved the nebulous UN system more broadly, but the core insight of his conclusions remains sound. This insight also informs some of his later work, such as his work on the legitimation function of the UN.[21]

In part through this link, *Power and International Relations* additionally foreshadows some of the recent trends in IR theory. These include the ideational and normative turn of the past quarter of a century, associated most closely with constructivism. They also include recent attempts to resurrect the contextual and prudential aspects of classical realism, which collectively have been referred to as 'reflexive realism'.[22] Claude's attempt to take military power seriously, to focus on politics rather than institutions and constitutions, but at the same time to question the received wisdom in realist scholarship about the conclusions to be drawn from those premises, is one that reflexive realists have perhaps paid less attention to than they should.

Contemporary impact

Power and International Relations has not had an enormous impact on contemporary IR theory. The argument of the book fits broadly into the classical realist school of thought, and seems intended to speak to that literature. However, this school of thought has largely been displaced in security studies by more self-consciously methodological and positivist work. Even the seminal works of classical realism, such as Morgenthau's *Politics Among Nations* or Carr's *The Twenty Years' Crisis*, are read, and assigned to graduate students, less frequently than used to be the case. However, they are often cited as the classics of the school of thought. *Power and International Relations*, being an internal critique of a school of thought that is no longer at the centre of the discipline, is therefore neither a good example of classical realism, nor a clear departure from it. And the basic question that Claude asks in the book, about avoiding great power nuclear war, is no longer central to security studies.

It none the less continues to be cited in the IR literature. Google Scholar identifies approximately 600 citations, which continue at a rate between five and ten a year. It continues to be cited for its discussion of the multiple and mutually contradictory meanings of the balance of power. However, while Claude's critique of the terminology and efficacy of the balance of power literature is one of the best examples in the literature, it was not (as Claude notes in the book) particularly original. The more original part of the discussion of the balance of power in *Power and International Relations* is the focus on the systemic aspect, but in the contemporary literature Kenneth Waltz gets most of the credit for introducing a systemic model of the balance of power to IR theory.

Power and International Relations is also cited for its discussion of collective security from a critical but sympathetic perspective. While the book was prescient in foreshadowing the current literature on multilateralism and the role of norms in international security, the contemporary literature on these subjects does not draw heavily on it. The constructivist methodologies that these literatures generally draw on do not fit much better with Claude's style of argument than do the positivist claims of much of the contemporary field of security studies. As such, *Power and International Relations* is cited in the contemporary literature more for specific elements of its argument than for it overall theme or its conclusions. Nonetheless, the book remains a valuable read. It is accessible and engaging, and sheds some much-needed light on terms and concepts that remain central to contemporary security studies, but that are built on assumptions too often taken for granted. To the student of the history of the international scene, either diplomatic or intellectual, the book is an excellent review of both international politics and international relations and security studies theory at the height of the Cold War. To the student of international organization, it offers an important viewpoint on the development of the UN system from the goals of its designers to its current role in international politics. And to the student of international security, it offers an excellent reminder of just how much the world has changed in the past half-century.

Notes

1 Inis L. Claude, Jr., *Power and International Relations*, New York: Random House, 1962.
2 On the 'great debates' framing, see Yosef Lapid, 'The Third Debate: On the Prospects of International Theory in a Post-Positivist Era', *International Studies Quarterly*, 1989, vol. 33, 235–54.
3 Hans J. Morgenthau, *Politics Among Nations: The Struggle for Power and Peace*, New York: Alfred A. Knopf, 1948.
4 E. H. Carr, *The Twenty Years' Crisis, 1919–1939: An Introduction to the Study of International Relations*, New York: Harper & Row, 1964.
5 Kenneth Waltz, *Man, the State, and War*, New York: Columbia University Press, 1959.
6 Claude, *Power and International Relations*, p. 39.
7 See Kenneth Waltz, *Theory of International Politics*, Reading, MA: Addison-Wesley, 1979; and the Chapter by Anders Wivel in this volume.
8 See, for example, Carsten Holbraad, *The Concert of Europe: A Study in German and British International Theory 1815–1914*, London: Longman, 1970.
9 Claude, *Power and International Relations*, p. 69.
10 Claude, *Power and International Relations*, p. 68.
11 A seminal version of this claim can be found in Carr, *The Twenty Years' Crisis*.
12 See Brain Schmidt (ed.), *International Relations and the First Great Debate*, London: Routledge, 2012.
13 Max Weber, *Economy and Society*, Berkeley, CA: University of California Press, 1978, e.g. p. 56.
14 Claude, *Power and International Relations*, p. 271.
15 See, for example, Peter J. Katzenstein (ed.), *The Culture of National Security: Norms and Identity in World Politics*, New York: Columbia University Press, 1996.
16 For example, Inis L. Claude, Jr., 'Collective Legitimization as a Political Function of the United Nations', *International Organization*, 1966, vol. 20, 367–79.

17 For an example of a recent volume on the balance of power theory that continues the terminological pathologies that Claude discusses see T. V. Paul, James J. Wirtz, Michel Fortmann (eds), *Balance of Power: Theory and Practice in the 21st Century*, Stanford, CA: Stanford University Press, 2004. For an excellent recent analysis see Richard Little, *The Balance of Power in International Relations*, Cambridge: Cambridge University Press, 2007.

18 For a further discussion of this dichotomy see J. Samuel Barkin, *Realist Constructivism: Rethinking International Relations Theory*, Cambridge: Cambridge University Press, 2010.

19 Hedley Bull, 'International Theory: The Case for a Classical Approach', in Klaus Knorr and James Rosenau (eds), *Contending Approaches to International Politics*, Princeton, NJ: Princeton University Press, 1969, pp. 20–38.

20 On multilateralism as an institution, see John Gerrard Ruggie, 'Multilateralism: The Anatomy of an Institution', *International Organization*, 1992, vol. 46, 561–98.

21 Claude, 'Collective Legitimization as a Political Function of the United Nations'.

22 See for example Brent J. Steele, '"Eavesdropping on Honored Ghosts": From Classical to Reflexive Realism', *Journal of International Relations and Development*, 2007, vol. 10, 272–300.

12 The joke's on you: International Relations and Stanley Kubrick's *Dr. Strangelove*

Henrik Bliddal

Without a doubt, Stanley Kubrick's *Dr. Strangelove or: How I Learned to Stop Worrying and Love the Bomb*, first shown in US theatres in January 1964, is a true film classic.[1] While some conservative voices decried it as downright dangerous owing to its characterization of US politicians and military officers as impotent, in every sense of the word, it was widely praised and became a big box office success.[2] It was nominated for 14 awards, winning four (although none of the four Oscars for which it was nominated). In the latest instalment of '100 Years … 100 Movies', a list of the top 100 US movies, compiled by the American Film Institute, it ranks as the 39th greatest movie of all time, and the popular Internet Movie Database rates it as the 34th best film in movie history.[3]

To include it in a volume on classics of International Relations (IR) is surely more controversial. However, if one accepts the validity of this volume's concept of an 'alternative classic', then *Dr. Strangelove* is, in fact, a rather uncontroversial choice. It is extensively used in IR and Political Science classrooms around the world. I even suspect that *Dr. Strangelove* finds its way more often onto IR curricula than some of the books presented in this volume. In other words, there is no more 'classic' way of introducing students to key aspects of international relations via film than with *Dr. Strangelove*.

Today, the use of audiovisual and other unconventional material is becoming ever more widespread, despite the fact that 'traditional' teaching and learning, with the blackboard at the centre, still prevail in many universities. Movies provide simultaneous stimulation of multiple senses, ground abstract concepts, engage emotions, contextualize historical events, and, maybe most importantly, facilitate an active-learning environment, moving from an 'instructional model' of memorization, towards a 'learning paradigm'.[4] In this sense, *Dr. Strangelove* offers 'lessons about war, politics, and history' and can be used as 'a teaching aid for classes in introductory international relations, foreign policy, defense policy, causes of war, organizational politics, and Cold War history'.[5]

Still, *Dr. Strangelove* is much more than just a tool for teaching. It is also a critical intervention, however unorthodox. Kubrick carries the logics of the balance of power and deterrence to their extremes (and beyond), uncovering their inconsistencies, as he sees them. He exposes the gendered dimension of foreign policy and international relations as well as dysfunctional in-fighting so often found in bureaucracies and domestic politics. Kubrick does so by employing a satirical lens in this 'nightmare comedy' where a runaway General sends his nuclear bombers to attack the Soviet Union, in the end leading to the destruction of 'all human and animal life on Earth' (43 min.). He unsettles preconceived notions of international politics and, thus, invites the viewer to engage critically with their logical foundations, in a way that still resonates today.[6]

To show that *Dr. Strangelove* is both a formidable teaching and learning tool and can be used to critically engage with prevalent themes in IR theory, this chapter will, first, briefly summarize *Dr. Strangelove's* plot, and place it in its historical, political and IR context. Second, it will focus on two dominant themes of the movie through the use of selected scenes and their relation to theoretical concepts: the balance of power and deterrence. By focusing on these two themes, I do not intend to diminish the importance of other themes and currents in the movie. It presents an excellent opportunity to delve into discussions on bureaucratic and organizational politics, for example. Quite frankly, I am perplexed that it took a further 20 years for feminist IR to have an impact on the discipline, when *Dr. Strangelove* provided such a poignant critique of the position of women in security politics. Where are the women, Cynthia Enloe asks?[7] In *Dr. Strangelove's* 1964, they are the naïve secretaries that warm the beds of Generals, and the playmates ('Miss Foreign Affairs') that adorn the erotic magazines of nuclear bomber pilots. Nowhere are they to be seen in the 'War Room'. What about the men? They are the war-lusting Generals who blame their impotence on communist plots; the officers who find their hidden desires in the nylons and lipsticks of a B-52 survival kit and ride into orgasm on the back of a nuclear bomb; and the national elite who cannot wait for the end of the world where they get to rebuild the human race by breeding prodigiously on a 10-to-1 female-to-male ratio. An important study linking *Dr. Strangelove* and gender studies of IR is hidden in plain view here.[8]

Politicizing nuclear weapons in times of turmoil

The basic plot of *Dr. Strangelove* is simple, and the central locations and characters are few. When the gun-toting Brigadier General Jack D. Ripper (Sterling Hayden) orders his B-52 nuclear bombers to attack the Soviet Union, his goal is to force the US government to direct an all-out nuclear attack before the Soviet Union can respond and retaliate. He complicates the task of averting a nuclear war between the two superpowers by not sharing the three-letter recall code for the bombers with anyone. The situation worsens when the Russian Ambassador, who is called to sit with the President (Peter Sellers) and his aides in the 'War Room', reveals that the Russian leaders are only days away from unveiling a novel Doomsday Machine. Unable to keep up with the arms race, the communist leadership has built what they deem to be the ultimate deterrer of a US nuclear attack. The Doomsday Machine, which is made up of especially powerful and 'dirty' nuclear bombs, will automatically annihilate the world in the case of a nuclear attack on Russian soil. Unable to recall the planes, the US and Russian leaders agree to shoot down the bombers. And even though a pragmatic British liaison officer (also Peter Sellers) at the B-52 base eventually does succeed in cracking the recall code, a lone bomber continues to make its way into Russian territory because it cannot receive the recall signal due to a damaged communications unit. The stage is irrevocably set for nuclear apocalypse.

Since the late 1950s Kubrick had become deeply troubled by the prospect of nuclear war. After releasing *Lolita* in 1962, he therefore fixed his sights on making a movie tackling this issue. He had been an avid reader of books on nuclear weapons for some time already, studying much of the blooming literature of the so-called Second Wave of deterrence theory of the late 1950s[9] and building up a research library of over 70 books,[10] underscoring Jack Nicholson's later verdict that Kubrick gave 'new meaning to the word meticulous'. It was Alastair Buchan, one of the founders of London's International Institute for Strategic Studies (IISS), who recommended Peter George's novel *Red Alert*, to which Kubrick soon bought the film rights. In a late-night revelation, Kubrick decided to depart from his original idea of producing a nail-biting thriller based on the book and instead turned to comedy.[11] He felt that a satirical perspective would better convey the dangers and absurdities that he saw in the two superpowers' reliance on nuclear arsenals to keep each other in check. It turned out to be a wise if controversial decision.

The political context of *Dr. Strangelove's* release was a sensitive one. The Cuban Missile Crisis had taken place just over a year previously, and US President John F. Kennedy was assassinated on 22 November 1963. To release a black comedy about the end of the world at this point in history was surely a risky proposition. Unsurprisingly, Cold War sensitivities were at the heart of some harsh criticisms levelled against the movie. Bosley Crowther, a critic at the *New York Times*, wrote that it was 'a bit too contemptuous of our defense establishment for my comfort and taste' and later followed up by pronouncing it, among other things, 'malefic and sick', 'close to being irresponsible' as well as 'defeatist and destructive'.[12] Mockery of the US military establishment, for which Kubrick harboured an 'intense dislike',[13] was not as widespread as it would soon become with the intensification of the war in Vietnam. Lewis Mumford, a cultural critic of architecture and literature, defended Kubrick in the pages of the *New York Times*. For him the movie was 'the first break in the catatonic Cold War trance that has so long held our country in its rigid grip'.[14] Robert Brustein, the renowned theatrical critic and playwright, argued in the *New York Review of Books* that it 'may well be the most courageous movie ever made', where 'a subterranean vibration becomes a series of earthquakes, shattering cultural platitudes, political pieties, and patriotic ideals with fierce, joyous shocks'.[15]

Despite, or precisely because of, being released at a delicate time, *Dr. Strangelove* made an immense impact on critics, the movie business, and, in particular, young people. James Naremore argues that with *Dr. Strangelove* 'Kubrick had moved ahead of the cultural curve, tapping into a youth audience that would sustain him over the next decade no matter what the critics said'.[16] Henceforth, the movie became part and parcel of the US (and international) movie canon and, indeed, the public consciousness. For example, Ronald Reagan, in one of his first requests as President, wanted to see the 'War Room' that he knew so well from Kubrick's movie. Of course, no such thing existed.

Despite the wickedly ironic disclaimer that 'none of the characters portrayed in this film are meant to represent any real persons living or dead', displayed prominently at the start of the movie, moviegoers could not help but see resemblances to well-known public figures of the early 1960s.[17] This undoubtedly gave the movie an added relevance. In General Ripper's persona, none-too-subtle nods were made towards Curtis LeMay, the father of the controversial fire-bombing campaign in Japan during World War II and later head of Strategic Air Command, the US nuclear weapons command. President Merkin Muffley was modelled on Adlai Stevenson, the Democratic presidential candidate who lost out to Dwight D. Eisenhower. However, a great deal has been made of the character of Dr. Strangelove. Peter Sellers, in his third virtuoso performance of the movie, plays the German nuclear scientist and adviser on deterrence whose Nazi convictions gradually come to the surface as nuclear annihilation draws closer. Parallels have been drawn to numerous public figures of the time: Wernher von Braun, the former Nazi scientist who helped the USA fly to the moon; Edward Teller, one of the chief scientists behind the H-bomb and a right-wing hawk; Henry Kissinger, at the time an expert on nuclear weapons policy; and, most strongly, Herman Kahn, a provocative strategist who argued in *On Thermonuclear War* that a 'usable' nuclear war-fighting capability was the most credible deterrent.[18] For the people that influenced the character of Dr. Strangelove, the association certainly was not a positive one. Even so, Kubrick had, for example, built 'a sort of friendship with [Kahn] and constantly picked his brain for information about nuclear strategy',[19] highlighting how closely Kubrick wanted the movie to conform to deterrence theory in order to expose its weaknesses, as he perceived them.

Realist theory in overdrive: the balance of power and deterrence in *Dr. Strangelove*

As with the overwhelming majority of movies dealing with political themes at the time, *Dr. Strangelove's* historical backdrop was the intense competition of the Cold War between East and West. The feeling of a permanent high-stakes crisis between the two blocs permeates the whole fabric of the movie. Competitive behaviour not only dominated the arms race between the USA and the Soviet Union, but also the economic, the cultural and even the sporting arenas. The ability of Kubrick and the cast to play with the absurdities of the Cold War are remarkable.

In this regard, Peter Sellers, in particular, delivers a virtuoso performance in his three roles as Dr. Strangelove, Lionel Mandrake (the British liaison officer to the crazed General Ripper) and Merkin Muffley (the weak, indecisive, and therefore, of course, 'effeminate' US President). In one of Peter Seller's many improvised takes in the movie, he, in his role as President Muffley, brilliantly pokes fun at the notion of superpower competition in *every* domain. When President Muffley calls the Russian Premier Kissof for the first time to tell him that the rogue General Ripper has sent nuclear bombers to attack the Soviet Union, a competition of sorts ensues in the extent to which each statesmen expresses his sorrow about the whole episode. Neither is willing to concede that the other might be sorrier than the other. Only after delicate negotiations is 'equilibrium' reached:

> President Muffley: 'I'm sorry, too, Dmitri. I'm very sorry. [*Premier Kissoff's answer, whose voice you never hear in the movie*] Alright, you are sorrier than I am. But I am sorry as well. [*Kissoff's answer*] I am as sorry as you are, Dmitri. Don't say you're more sorry than I am because I am capable of being just as sorry as you are. So we're both sorry, alright? [*Kissoff's answer*] Alright (42 min.).

The costly endeavour of keeping up with the other side also provides the impetus for the Russian leaders' decision to build the Doomsday Machine, which to them appears as a cheap balancing strategy in the light of ever-increasing demands from the population for everyday commodities. The Doomsday Machine is the ultimate equalizer: once it has been built, the Russian leadership can concentrate on its internal problems instead of buying yet more arms. This argument is presented by the Russian ambassador De Sadeski in the 'War Room':

There were those of us who fought against it, but in the end we could not keep up in the Arms Race, the Space Race and the Peace Race. At the same time, our people grumbled for more nylons and washing machines. Our Doomsday scheme cost us just a fraction of what we had been spending on defense in a single year. But the deciding factor was when we learned your country was working along similar lines, and we were afraid of a Doomsday Gap. (48 min.)

This Doomsday Gap mirrors the hysteria of the times (and later years): the 'bomber gap' of the mid-1950s; the 'satellite gap' after the launch of Sputnik by the Soviet Union in 1957; and the 'missile gap' that helped John F. Kennedy to win the presidency. These presumed gaps all turned out to be chimerical, but only after they had had enormous impact on US politics, triggering increased defence spending.

The viewer is shown the absurdity, in Kubrick's mind, of such 'gap debates'. This culminates when it becomes clear that the last bomber will deliver its payload and trigger the Doomsday Machine. Echoing Herman Kahn's real-world call to use abandoned mines as shelters in nuclear war,[20] Dr. Strangelove recommends shuffling off several hundred thousand of the US elite into mine shafts, in order to 'preserve a nucleus of human specimen' (1h 24 min.). General Turgidson, the President's chief military adviser in the movie, immediately jumps in 'to look at this thing from a military point of view'. He fears that 'the Ruskies stashed away some big bombs and we didn't, [and] when they come out in a hundred years, they could take over'. He refuses to believe that a devastated world would 'cause a change in Soviet expansionist policy'. Rather, the USA should 'be increasingly alert to prevent them from taking over other mine-shaft space in order to breed more prodigiously than us, thus, knocking us out through superior numbers when we emerge'. At the same time, the Russian Ambassador De Sadeski proves that it is not only Turgidson who thinks about the 'time after', when he proceeds to take pictures of the 'Big Board', where the locations of important US military installations can be seen. In other words, in *Dr. Strangelove's* world balancing is ubiquitous and ever-present, even when the world is doomed.

If the balance of power provides the backdrop, deterrence takes front and centre place on Kubrick's stage, and this is where the movie excels. Instead of ridiculing deterrence outright or launching a frontal assault, Kubrick takes a decidedly more effective and, at first, oblique tack. Indeed, the problems faced by the protagonists could have been taken straight out of a textbook. Carol Cohn once argued that 'learning the language [of defence intellectuals] is a transformative, rather than additive process' whereby you 'enter a new mode of thinking', leading to 'a serious quandary':

> If we refuse to learn the language, we are virtually guaranteed that our voices will remain outside the 'politically relevant' spectrum of opinion. Yet if we do learn and speak it, we not only severely limit what we can say but also invite the transformation, the militarization, of our own thinking.[21]

Cohn had 'no solutions to this dilemma'. Kubrick, at least at some level, seems to have been at once aware of this predicament *and* managed to find a way out of it: satire. Introducing the satirical element allows Kubrick to take the ideas behind the concept of deterrence just far enough so that they crash in on themselves. Speaking the language of deterrence, he thus provides a critical commentary that effectively undermines deterrence as a strategy in the mind of the audience.

It is Dr. Strangelove who provides a definition of deterrence that would not have been ill-placed in an IR book of the period: 'Deterrence is the art of producing in the mind of the enemy the fear to attack' (49 min.). This is not too far from Glenn Snyder's definition from 1961, for example: deterrence is 'discouraging the enemy from taking military action by posing for him a cost and risk outweighing his prospective gain'.[22] Faced with a perceived mutual threat, policy-makers in the Soviet Union as well as in the USA made nuclear deterrence the cornerstone of their policies towards each other in order to avoid military conflict. Although it seems hard to fathom for a contemporary audience, the motto adorning General Ripper's Burpelson Air Force Base – 'Peace is our Profession' – was indeed the motto of Strategic Air Command (49 min.). Kubrick was terrified, like so many others, that something could go wrong, as it nearly had during the Cuban Missile Crisis.[23] How could a situation where both sides threatened wholesale destruction, which in turn would have assured mutual destruction, be stable? This was one of the key policy questions asked during the Cold War.[24] In the movie, stability clearly breaks down as the renegade General Ripper takes matters into his own hands and orders a first strike on the Soviet Union in order to push the US government into an all-out attack before the other side can react. This scenario might seem outlandish to today's audience. Still, the movie was prefaced with the sentence that '[i]t is the stated position of the U.S. Air Force that their safeguards would prevent the occurrence of such events as are depicted in this film'.[25] While the intention of this was certainly ironic, some in the audience were probably reassured by this statement.

A key element in deterrence theory is credibility. Only if both sides believe that the other means what it says can deterrence be stable. In Patrick Morgan's words, '[t]o have credibility [in the Cold War] it was necessary to be able to do unacceptable damage, to have proper forces for that purpose, and have the opponent conclude that you had the will to carry out your threat'.[26] All else being equal, the third component of credibility is the most critical one. To have the right capabilities to do unacceptable damage is one thing, but to convince an opponent that you have the *will* to carry out the threat is another. As Nobel Laureate Thomas Schelling pointed out in his seminal book *The Strategy of Conflict*, '[i]n case a threat is made and fails to deter, there is a second stage prior to fulfilment in which both parties have an interest in undoing the commitment. The purpose of the threat is gone, its deterrence value is zero, and only the commitment exists to motivate fulfilment'.[27]

Dr. Strangelove takes up the question of credibility in several scenes, but two stand out. First, the reason why General Ripper can send his planes to the Soviet Union in the first place is because President Muffley had devolved some command and control functions to his base commanders under 'Plan R', a fact that the President seems to have forgotten. General Turgidson therefore has to remind him that 'Plan R is an emergency war plan, in which a lower echelon commander may order nuclear retaliation after a sneak attack if the normal chain of command has been disrupted' (24 min.). This mechanism was put into place in order 'to be a sort of retaliatory safeguard' because 'Senator Duff made that big hassle about our deterrent lacking credibility'. The logic behind this, of course, is that if the Russian side could take out the President and those next in the line of command, no retaliatory strike could be made in time, creating the slight possibility that the Russians could undertake a first 'decapitating' strike.[28] The risk of a renegade General was apparently overlooked in this scheme.

Another key event is the building of a Russian Doomsday Machine, which aims to minimize any 'meddling' after a first strike. Again, Schelling was one of the first to identify this problem:

> The credibility of the threat before the act depends on how visible to the threatened party is the inability of the threatening party to rationalize his way out of his commitment once it has failed its purpose. It is essential, therefore, for maximum credibility to leave as little room as possible for judgment or discretion in carrying out the threat.[29]

Kubrick follows the logic of this argument to its conclusion. The Doomsday Machine replaces discretion with automaticity. When President Muffley asks 'how is it possible for this thing to be triggered automatically and at the same time impossible to untrigger', Dr. Strangelove explains:

> Mr. President, it is not only possible, it is essential. That is the whole idea of this machine, you know. … [B]ecause of the automated and irrevocable decision-making process which rules out human meddling, the Doomsday Machine is terrifying, simple to understand, and completely credible and convincing (49 min.).

In other words, Kubrick wants to show the audience that the goal of absolute credibility is unachievable, and that the various policy recommendations to increase it – for example, Kahn's push to develop war-fighting nuclear capabilities – can never rule out the possibility that something might go wrong.

Another important debate in the literature on deterrence revolves around communication of threats, for 'both the threat and the commitment have to be communicated'.[30] In deterrence strategy, an inherent tension of communicating too much or too little exists. If one side gives away too much information about its forces, doctrine, and so on, the adversary might think that he can outsmart the other side, creating the possibility of a first strike. However, if too little communication is exchanged, then the other side cannot make proper threat assessments. This problem of communication is also laid bare in *Dr. Strangelove*. Had the Russians communicated to the Americans that they had built an automatic Doomsday Machine, it would have been suicidal for General Ripper to have sent his nuclear bombers. Dr. Strangelove himself puts the question to De Sadeski: 'The only one thing that I don't understand, Mr. Ambassador, is that … the whole point of the Doomsday Machine is lost if you keep it a secret. *Why didn't you tell the world, eh?*' (51 min.). De Sadeski's unfortunate answer is that '[i]t was to be announced at the Party Congress on Monday. As you know, the Premier loves surprises'.

The movie provides great springboards for other sub-themes of nuclear deterrence, for example the debate on two main schools within deterrence thinking: the massive retaliation school and the war-fighting school.[31] The adherents of the former believe that the threat of massive retaliation is the best option to deter the adversary, i.e. where all-out attack is the only option, and are exemplified in the Russians and their Doomsday Machine. The second school is represented through the idea of getting as many people into mine shafts as possible in order to survive a nuclear confrontation were it to occur. In sum, it is no wonder that this movie is shown so often in classes on deterrence theory and strategy.

Conclusion: the continued relevance of *Dr. Strangelove*

Even after Kubrick's death in 1999, *Dr. Strangelove* stood out among the copious amounts of praise heaped upon his oeuvre. James Christopher of *The Times*, for example, called it his 'most perfectly realized film'.[32] Kubrick's movies will, therefore, certainly remain a staple of film studies and attract the continuing admiration of film aficionados. However, two decades after the ending of the Cold War, it is an entirely legitimate question to ask whether *Dr. Strangelove* will continue to be watched by IR scholars and students.

The *Washington Post's* Stephen Hunter, while acknowledging that *Dr. Strangelove* is a 'still-brilliant meditation on man's tendencies toward self-incineration', for one, points out that it 'had one small flaw: It was wrong. Or rather, MAD [Mutual Assured Destruction] was right: The world didn't end, we didn't blow ourselves up, unless I slept through the event'.[33] Of course, the absence of nuclear annihilation is not necessarily proof that MAD was right. Whether (or how much) nuclear weapons kept the super-power confrontation cold is still a matter of considerable debate.[34] In this context alone, *Dr. Strangelove* remains relevant.

What is more, questions about nuclear deterrence are once again central to strategic debates. For example, could the international community live with a 'nuclear' Iran, i.e. do the tenets of nuclear stability also apply to states that, as some argue, exhibit 'irrational' decision patterns? Other important real-world developments have sparked renewed interest in deterrence theory as well. In 1999 a senior NATO diplomat was quoted as saying that the Alliance's nuclear weapons had 'been put in a small box somewhere in the corner, and that is where they should stay.'[35] However, in 2012 NATO published a new Deterrence and Defence Posture Review, the result of a thorough year-long study of NATO's deterrence and defence needs, during which the role of nuclear weapons in NATO was hotly debated. The issue of NATO's planned missile defence system, and Russia's concerns, cannot be fully understood without referring to deterrence theory. Even the discussion between the 'war-fighting' school and minimalist deterrence has re-emerged forcefully in the pages of *Foreign Affairs*.[36] As astonishing as it might seem, *Dr. Strangelove* still addresses all of these issues. Of course, other themes have emerged in today's deterrence literature in which Kubrick's movie has less to add. For example, the so-called fourth wave in deterrence research is concerned with how to deal with asymmetric threats, such as terrorists,[37] and cyber space has introduced altogether different dynamics to deterrence strategies.[38]

Ultimately, an overriding quality of *Dr. Strangelove* is that, while it is a Cold War movie par excellence, it is so much more. If one wants to draw a parallel to the world of books, the difference between *Dr. Strangelove* and other Cold War movies is akin to the difference between books of IR theory and of 'current events'. While the Fareed Zakarias of this world will continue to produce best-sellers, it is unlikely that readers will pick them up in ten years' time (let alone 50), other than historians or people browsing through bargain bins. *Dr. Strangelove* speaks to an audience whose interests are very far from being confined to the Cold War, and thus, as long as the themes dissected so brilliantly in the movie remain relevant, so will *Dr. Strangelove*.

Notes

1 *Dr. Strangelove or: How I Learned to Stop Worrying and Love the Bomb*, directed by Stanley Kubrick, 95 min., Columbia Pictures and Hawk Films, 1964. References placed in parentheses in the text are to this movie.

2 In 1994, when it was shown in theatres again, its total lifetime gross was US $9,440,272 in the USA (Internet Movie Datebase (IMDB)), *Box Office/Business for Dr. Strangelove or: How I Learned to Stop Worrying and Love the Bomb*. Available at: www.imdb.com/title/tt0057012/business (accessed 10 November 2011).

3 American Film Institute (AFI), *AFI's 100 Years ... 100 Movies 10th Anniversary Edition* (2007). Available at: www.afi.com/100years/movies10.aspx (accessed on 10 November 2011). IMDB, *Dr. Strangelove or: How I Learned to Stop Worrying and Love the Bomb*. Available at: www.imdb.com/title/tt0057012/ (accessed on 10 November 2011).

4 Lynn M. Kuzma and Patrick J. Haney, 'And ... Action! Using Film to Learn about Foreign Policy', *International Studies Perspectives*, 2001, vol. 2, 33–50.

5 Dan Lindley, 'What I Learned since I Stopped Worrying and Studied the Movie: A Teaching Guide to Stanley Kubrick's *Dr. Strangelove*', *PS: Political Science & Politics*, 2001, vol. 3, 663–67, at p. 663.

6 Cynthia Weber uses movies to disrupt certain IR 'myths', i.e. the foundational assumptions underlying theories or traditions that they rely upon to appear true. By stepping into the world of movies, she wants to unsettle 'common truths' that are taken for granted in order to expose similar ones found in IR theories. Cynthia Weber, *International Relations Theory: A Critical Introduction*, 3rd edn, London: Routledge, 2009. However, *Dr. Strangelove*, as a satire, is a movie that already wants to unsettle 'common truths' and, thus, may not suitable for this particular move.

7 Cynthia Enloe, *Bananas, Beaches and Bases: Making Feminist Sense of International Politics*, London: Pandora, 1989, p. 7. See also Alexandra Hyde and Marsha Henry's chapter in this volume.

8 For an example of how gendered discourse permeates the world of nuclear weapons see Carol Cohn, 'Sex and Death in the Rational World of Defense Intellectuals', *Signs*, 1987, vol. 12, 687–718.

9 On the 'three waves of deterrence theory', see Robert Jervis, 'Deterrence Theory Revisited', *World Politics*, 1979, vol. 2, 289–324.

10 James Naremore, *On Kubrick*, London: BFI and Palgrave Macmillan, 2007, p. 119.

11 *Inside the Making of Dr. Strangelove* (4 min.), found on the 2003 Collector's Edition DVD of *Dr. Strangelove*.

12 Quoted in Naremore, *On Kubrick*, p. 122.

13 Robert Gregg, *International Relations on Film*, Boulder, CO: Lynne Rienner, 1998, p. 7.

14 Quoted in Naremore, *On Kubrick*, p. 122.

15 Robert Brustein, 'Out of This World', *The New York Review of Books*, 5 March 1964. Available at: www.nybooks.com/articles/archives/1964/feb/06/out-of-this-world/?pagination=false (accessed 10 November 2011).

16 Naremore, *On Kubrick*, p. 123.

17 Before the opening scene. Interestingly, this does not feature on the 2003 DVD.

18 Herman Kahn, *On Thermonuclear War*, Princeton, NJ: Princeton University Press, 1960.

19 Naremore, *On Kubrick*, p. 124.

20 Kahn, *On Thermonuclear War*, pp. 88ff.

21 Cohn, 'Sex and Death in the Rational World of Defense Intellectuals', p. 716. Recall also Martin Wight's words that debates of international theory, including on nuclear weapons, are 'constantly bursting the bounds of the language in which we try to handle it'. Martin Wight, 'Why Is there no International Theory', *International Relations*, 1960, vol. 2, 35–62, at p. 48.

22 Glenn Snyder, *Deterrence and Defense: Toward a Theory of National Security*, Princeton, NJ: Princeton University Press, [1961] 1981, p. 35.

23 For a detailed discussion of near-disasters, see Scott D. Sagan, *The Limits of Safety: Organizations, Accidents, and Nuclear Weapons*, Princeton, NJ: Princeton University Press, 1993.

24 Patrick M. Morgan, *Deterrence Now*, Cambridge: Cambridge University Press, 2003, pp. 15, 20ff.

25 Before the opening scene. This does not feature on the 2003 DVD, either.

26 Morgan, *Deterrence Now*, p. 16.

27 Thomas C. Schelling, *The Strategy of Conflict*, Cambridge, MA: Harvard University Press, [1960] 1981, p. 39.

28 For a discussion on predelegated authority and devolution of authority, see Paul Bracken, 'Delegation of Nuclear Command Authority', in Ashton B. Carter, John D. Steinbrunner,

Charles A. Zraket (eds), *Managing Nuclear Operations*, Washington, DC: Brookings Institution Press, 1987, pp. 352–72.

29 Schelling, *The Strategy of Conflict*, p. 40.

30 Schelling, *The Strategy of Conflict*, p. 38.

31 Proponents of the massive retaliation school included leaders such as Eisenhower and Khrushchev and analysts like Charles Glaser. War-fighting was a preferred option for policy-makers such as James Schlesinger, Paul Nitze and Harold Brown and for analysts like Herman Kahn and Colin Gray. See Morgan, *Deterrence Now*, pp. 22ff.

32 James Christopher, 'Kubrick: A Cinematic Odyssey', *The Times* (London), 8 March 1999.

33 Stephen Hunter, 'Through a Lens, Darkly; Stanley Kubrick Looked at the Silver Screen and Saw a Thousand Shades of Gray', *The Washington Post*, 8 March 1999.

34 See, for example, Morgan, *Deterrence Now*, pp. 1–41.

35 *The Economist*, 'Knights in Shining Armor? A Survey of NATO', 24 April 1999.

36 See, for example, the debate in the pages of *Foreign Affairs*, which was started by Daryl Press and Keir Lieber, 'The Nukes We Need: Preserving the American Deterrent', *Foreign Affairs*, 2009, vol. 88, 39–51.

37 See Jeffrey W. Knopf, 'The Fourth Wave in Deterrence Research', *Contemporary Security Policy*, 2010, vol. 31, 1–33.

38 For an example of an analysis of how cyber security affects traditional security strategies, see Paul Cornish, David Livingstone, Dave Clemente, and Claire Yorke, *On Cyber Warfare*, London: The Royal Insititute of International Affairs, 2010.

13 The virtue of uncertain advice: Robert Jervis' *Perception and Misperception in International Politics*

Shiping Tang[1]

In *Perception and Misperception in International Politics* (*P&M*),[2] displaying 'prodigious learning' in his early to middle thirties,[3] Robert Jervis was able to weave (social) psychology, the history of science and technology (e.g. pp. 165–72, 195–201) and, of course, diplomatic and international histories, into a marvel.

P&M solidified the status of political/social psychology of international politics as a legitimate field of inquiry in International Relations (IR).[4] Yet, *P&M* is much more than an importation of psychology into IR. It touches upon a host of key IR issues, puzzles and concepts that remain essential for understanding IR. *P&M* offers extensive, profound and enlightening, yet often uncertain (in the positive sense of the word), insights into some of the most central problems in IR.

Jervis's classic is not just dry stuff for IR scholars only. Like his other works, *P&M* speaks loudly (although not always unambiguously) to policy-makers. Each chapter in *P&M* contains a wealth of information that alerts policy-makers to the profound ambiguities, difficult trade-offs and psychological obstacles in making strategic decisions: indeed, most of the chapters have a section entitled 'implications for decision-making' or 'suggestions'. It is not an overstatement that Jervis's works offer far more (albeit demanding) advice than most of the policy-oriented books that purport to offer clear-cut solutions to pressing problems.[5] Decision-makers do themselves (and all of us) a disservice by ignoring his witty, subtle, but never certain, teaching. It is a safe bet that, after reading Jervis, all of us (including decision-makers) will probably be left with a slightly deflated (or at least, a less inflated) ego, because one of Jervis's cardinal messages is that our perceptions and judgements are marred by many biases and errors that are hard to avoid.[6]

The rest of this short appraisal of *P&M* consists of the following. Section I introduces the volume's structure. Section II singles out the volume's major contributions. Section III offers a critique of the volume. I conclude with some observations on the future of a psychological approach to IR and political science in general as well as on the future of social psychology itself.

Before I move on to the specifics, however, I would like to emphasize two key messages that Jervis has been trying to convey to IR (and the broader social sciences) that unfortunately have long been underappreciated in the post-Waltzian rush towards theoretical parsimony and the quest for firm answers. The first message is an insistence on the need for a multi-levelled and systemic *rather than structural* approach towards social sciences (especially pp. 18–31, emphasis added).[7] At the onset of *P&M* (p. 6), Jervis explicitly states that his approach will be 'eclectic' ('too eclectic for some tastes', in his own words), and this ability to eclectically draw from a wide range of literature, in addition to IR and political sciences, has been a hallmark of Jervis's long and distinguished career. This eclectic approach, already apparent in his *Logic of Images*,[8] anticipates his most interesting work, *System Effects*.[9] In my view, scholars who draw from a wide literature and consider more factors at different levels will always be more sophisticated than scholars who tend to reason simplistically under the cover of seeking parsimony.

The second message is Jervis's appreciation of the complexity of social systems and. thus. his refusal to give clear-cut answers to many questions: for him, it is simply self-evident that there cannot be firm and definitive answers to many questions, because social life is simply too complex. This message, undoubtedly not very popular, was most explicitly articulated in *System Effects*,[10] although both *Logic of Images* and *P&M* already underscore the message, however implicitly.

Finally, a specific caveat regarding *P&M* is in order. Jervis has always taken signalling and reading signals (i.e. perception and misperception) to be two sides of the same coin.[11] Indeed, his original plan was to study both signalling and perception, and he decided to work on the two sides separately only after the task had turned out to be too large. For Jervis, therefore, *Logic of Images* and *P&M* are part of the same (ongoing) project, and we do ourselves a service by reading the two texts together, despite the fact that *P&M* has received far greater attention than *Logic of Images*.

The structure and scope of *Perception and Misperception*

On the first page of *P&M* (p. 3), Jervis posed the central questions for his book:

> What are the causes and consequences of misperception? What kinds of perceptual errors commonly occur in decision-making? How are beliefs about politics and images of other actors formed and altered? How do decision-makers draw inferences from information, especially information that could be seen as contradicting their own views?

Affirming that decision-makers' perceptions do matter for understanding important issues in international politics, Jervis then goes on to show that 'many important differences in policy preferences are traceable to differences in decision-makers' perceptions of their environment and that there are important differences between reality and shared or common perceptions' (pp. 14–15). Methodologically, Jervis relied on a two-step model: first establishing decision-makers' perceptions as the immediate or proxy indicators for their decisions and then relating those perceptions to reality, or at least to the information available to decision-makers. Of course, this was done on the understanding that psychological factors are not the only factors that influence decision-makers' perceptions: other factors such as international and domestic politics are legion, but they have to be put to one side in order to concentrate on the already huge task in hand (pp. 28–31).

After the short introductory chapter, *P&M* is divided into four major parts. Part I, 'The Setting', comprises three chapters. Chapter 1 deals with perception as part of the 'level of analysis' problem (i.e. viewing IR from the individual, state, and systemic levels). Chapter 2 introduces the question of how the behaviour of others is perceived, with a special focus on intentions that paves the way for the discussion in Chapter 3. Chapter 3, undoubtedly the most cited part of the whole book, explores the contrast between the deterrence model and the spiral model, which centres on the intentions of the adversary. This chapter anticipates another of Jervis's seminal articles, 'Cooperation under the Security Dilemma'.[12] This chapter also identifies reassurance as a process that builds cooperation and trust between states (see below).

Part II, 'Processes of Perception', comprises four chapters. Chapter 4 introduces 'cognitive consistency' as a major source of misperceptions, emphasizing the impact of (relatively) deeply held preconceptions on our perceptions. Chapter 5 deals with the impact of our immediate concerns on our processing of incoming information, regardless of whether there is communication between the objects we wish to learn about and ourselves. Building on the discussion in previous chapters, Chapter 6 explores a key topic: 'how decision-makers learn from history'. The chapter also contains a tantalizing appendix on the impact of domestic politics and training on perception and judgement, which Jervis unfortunately did not develop further in the book. Chapter 7 discusses the possibility and the means of attitude change, in light of the fact that we tend to maintain, if not strengthen, our existing perceptions and judgements even in possession of discrepant information.

Part III, 'Common Misperceptions', focuses on several important misperceptions and their sources. This part again has four chapters. Chapter 8 addresses the agency of others as centralized or coherent: we often see the behaviour of others as more centralized, planned, coordinated and therefore often more wicked and threatening than they actually are. Chapter 9 underscores our tendency to overestimate our importance as causes of others' *desired* behaviours or as target of their *undesired* behaviours. Chapter 10 explores the impact of desires and fears on perception. Finally, Chapter 11 singles out cognitive dissonance as a major source of cognitive distortion after we have committed to a particular policy or behaviour, especially when things have not turned out as expected or desired.[13]

Part IV is a short concluding chapter that gives some advice on how to minimize misperceptions, recognizing that total avoidance is impossible.

The lasting impact of *Perception and Misperception*

To some extent, *P&M* is unique among classics of IR: unlike many others, *P&M* does not offer a grand theory or a sweeping narrative about international politics. Instead, *P&M* elaborates and touches upon a host of key IR issues, puzzles and concepts. At the very least, these include uncertainty, intentions versus interests and resolve (pp. 48–54), the security dilemma/spiral model, deterrence, trust and trustworthiness (p. 44), reassurance attempts and programmes (p. 82), signalling, reading signals (i.e. perceptions and misperceptions), the commitment problem (pp. 44–45), objective and subjective incompatibility of interest (pp. 75–76), concern for reputation of resolve (pp. 102–7), the domino effect as positive feedback (pp. 58–62, 100–107),[14] sunk costs and sticking with a bad policy (Chapters 4 and 11). It even anticipates 'framing' and 'loss aversion' (pp. 51–52, 393–99) as captured by prospect theory.[15]

Owing to its broad canvas and nuanced arguments, *P&M* is not an easy target for critics. Rather, *P&M* opened up a vast new territory for exploration and inspired an ever-growing literature, directly and indirectly: *P&M* is an ideal launching pad for understanding the psychological dimensions in international politics. Indeed, many dissertations and monographs have been written to tease out, criticize, refine and develop some of the themes that emerged from *P&M*.[16] Below, I focus on those fundamental concepts and notions in *P&M* that have been the most influential and received the most attention.

The security dilemma, the spiral model and intentions

Jervis's discussion of the spiral model and the security dilemma in Chapter 3 of *P&M* and 'Cooperation under the Security Dilemma' have turned the security dilemma and the spiral model into some of IR's key concepts.[17] They also inspired an extensive literature on the security dilemma as a possible cause of ethnic conflict,[18] although this literature has been saddled by much conceptual confusion that was not cleared up until very recently.[19]

Building upon Osgood's 'gradual reciprocation in tension-reduction' (GRIT),[20] Chapter 3 of *P&M* also laid part of the foundation for understanding reassurance as a cooperation and trust-building process and how mistrust can form between two benign states and prevent them from achieving cooperation.[21] This chapter also provides a key platform for bringing arms control into reassurance and cooperation-building.[22]

Chapter 3 makes it clear that gauging the intentions of others is a key task for states. This key emphasis laid part of the theoretical foundation for the school of defensive realism.[23] Jervis also noted that intentions interact with interest and resolve (pp. 48–49). His discussion, thus, points to the need for a more fine-grained differentiation of four internal dimensions (capabilities, interests, intentions and resolve) and the external environment when it comes to understanding an actor's behaviour (or non-behaviour), which was taken up recently.[24] Relatedly, Jervis also developed a typology of states based on their willingness to take risks (pp. 48–54). Even more strikingly, Jervis's insistence that states can change their types anticipates the possibility of 'identity changes', long before constructivism became fashionable, as he wittily noted later.[25]

Cognition, emotion and learning in war and peace

A central theme from *P&M* has been that nothing can be more off the mark than assuming decision-makers to be capable of digesting and synthesizing vast amounts of information in a cool-headed fashion, especially in times of crisis. This theme too has inspired a growing literature, and it tends to be more empirical in orientation. With in-depth investigations of historical cases, these works provided more robust evidence that faulty perceptions and judgements often do lead to misguided decisions, resulting in the escalation of international crises and unfulfilled cooperation.

Building on Jervis's discussion about cognitive closure and dissonance, Lebow showed that many international crises originated in or escalated to war owing, in no small part, to decision-makers' irrational cognitive closure and urge to reduce cognitive dissonance under the influence of stresses and emotions.[26] Larson inquired into the origins of containment policy as a shifting of beliefs and attitudes by examining the belief systems and schemas of key US decision-makers in the early days of the Cold War.[27] Bringing political consideration firmly into the picture, Farnham examined Franklin Roosevelt's reading into and coping with the looming threat posed by Hitler's Germany both before and after the Munich Crisis.[28]

Taking Jervis's discussion about learning from history and the psychological literature on heuristics as a starting point,[29] Khong explored how historical events shaped analogies (as a form of heuristics) which in turn shaped perception of interests and choices of strategies by key US decision-makers in the months leading up to the fateful escalation in Vietnam in the summer of 1965.[30] Reiter, critically building upon Jervis and Khong, explores how small states' choice of allies is based on learning from their past experiences with both quantitative and qualitative methods.[31]

Examining costly US interventions in the Third World and their aftermaths, Hopf identified the misplaced belief in domino effects by US decision-makers as a key factor that had propelled the USA into those interventions.[32] Mercer's *Reputation in International Relations* focuses on reputation as images of others based on their past behaviour. His central argument is that much of decision-makers' concern for their reputation for resolve during conflict, or their belief in the 'domino theory', may be unfounded.[33]

Although not directly influenced by, but certainly encouraged by *P&M*, McDermott deployed prospect theory to examine the conditions under which US decision-makers are more or less willing to take risks during foreign policy crises.[34] More recently, Taliaferro has applied prospect theory to understand why leaders persisted with dead-end policies despite mounting evidence that their policies were doomed.[35]

Things to desire in *Perception and Misperception*

Classics are classics not because they are faultless. Perhaps the most glaring omission in *P&M* is an all too evident lack of attention to emotion, as Jervis himself recognized and readily admitted later.[36] Although *P&M* mentions ego and decision-makers' political motivation from time to time (e.g. pp. 382n2, 400n37, Chapter 10), its core approach is cold cognitive, conforming to the mood of psychology of its time: its only focused discussion on emotion being in Chapter 10 concerning desires and fear. Indeed, Jervis himself, on the opening page, singled out that 'more attention is paid to emotional than to cognitive actors' as a major fault of the psychology literature of the era, as if emotions and perceptions can be separated.[37]

Yet, it is apparent from even Jervis's own discussion in *P&M* that much of what he had to say cannot operate without emotions (pp. 68–94, Chapters 4, 5, 9 and 11). Without egocentrism and ethnocentrism (i.e. group feelings), there can be no self-interest and national interest. Without egocentrism and ethnocentrism, it is hard to understand why we tend to have little empathy for the interests, intentions and demonstrations of resolve of others, and why even genuinely aggressive states tend to put much of the blame on the other side and neglect the possibility that one's own behaviour has been a cause of undesired reactions of others. Without decision-makers' egos and the motivated biases derived from them, it is hard to explain why they tend to resist trade-offs when facing difficult choices and stick with doomed policies while dismissing disconfirming information along the way: these biases are motivated, both emotionally and materially (cf. Chapters 4 and 11).[38]

Likewise, without fear, it is hard to understand the salience of the enemy image and, in turn, the commitment problem (e.g. pp. 310–11).[39] Without fear, it is hard to understand the differential perceptions of malignant and benign intentions. Without fear and ego, it is hard to understand why we tend to overestimate our importance as the cause of desired behaviour of others and as the target of their undesired behaviour (pp. 343–55).[40] Finally, without emotions, it is hard to understand post-decisional emotional conflict and stress.[41] To put it bluntly, without emotions such as fear, honour and ethnocentrism, it is hard to understand international politics and the broader social world, as Reinhold Niebuhr pointed out long ago.[42]

A second fault of *P&M* lies in its not entirely consistent use of concepts, labels and categories. Most prominently, Jervis did not neatly tie up all the loose ends on the security dilemma and the spiral model.[43] As such, many have extended and expanded, if not bent, the security dilemma and the spiral model to the degree of abusing the concept, resulting in much confusion which was not redressed until very recently.[44]

Finally, although Jervis was extremely careful when grafting psychological literature to IR, he often uses evidence from domestic scenarios (e.g. labour negotiations and congressional hearings) to illustrate situations in IR. This is not always valid: anarchy does make a difference.[45]

The future of psychology in international politics

Building on the works of George, Jervis, Janis and many others, studying the psychological dimensions of IR has become a thriving (sub-)field within IR and the field has grown alongside psychology. Yet, the field is not without its challenges. To begin with, the psychological literature has been very fragmented, as psychologists themselves have acknowledged. This means that when explaining a complex social fact, we need more than just a few psychological traits. Yet, too often, many psychology-based works on IR (and on political issues in general) tend to single out one or two psychological traits in order to explain some fairly complex social facts, often without combining them with political factors (e.g. domestic politics). Alternatively, they tend to pit different psychological traits against each other as if our brains always operate using one circuit at a time. This not only oversimplifies complex social facts but results in the fallacy of 'over-psychologizing' of which Jervis gave warning. To better understand political decisions, we need to synthesize politics and psychology more organically and rely on more than one or two psychological traits, despite the methodological obstacles.[46] In the same vein, we also have to resist the temptation to pit rational reasoning against psychological logic or to pit different psychological traits against each other.

Second, even if we want to look into how the interaction between cognition, emotion and politics shapes decision-makers' perceptions and decisions in the real world, this may prove to be a very difficult, if not impossible, task. Khong as well as Lebow and Stein came closest because they were able to interview some key decision-makers at times of crisis, but their successes may be difficult to repeat.[47] When this is the case, perhaps IR theorists should become less elite-centric and shift to focus on the interaction between cognition, emotion and politics at the popular level. On this front, the interaction of politics and collective memories in intrastate and interstate reconciliations may be a fertile ground for developing new ideas.[48]

Third and related to the second, a key challenge for the psychological study of IR is to link psychological factors with big issues. On this front, constructivism's emphasis on identity and identity changes is an obvious trial field.[49] As Jervis rightly pointed out,[50] however, much of constructivism for years has been very structural, ignoring psychological factors altogether. Yet, whereas realism as a mostly materialist approach can somewhat afford to ignore the real processes of ideational change and the transformational power of ideas in human society, constructivism cannot, preaching as it does the transformational power of ideas. Structural constructivism (without psychology) is thus an oxymoron. We need to bridge the gap between macro-social (material and ideational) changes and psychological changes. On this front, Norbert Elias's magnum opus *The Civilizing Process,*[51] which masterfully weaves together psychological changes and macro-social changes (both material and ideational), should be a constant source of inspiration.

Finally, IR theorists have not been shy about borrowing from the psychological literature. However, can IR theorists contribute to social psychology, theoretically? Some have been trying to do this by formulating new theories that promise to integrate many dispersed psychological theories and to advance new hypotheses regarding our psychology that are testable in experimental settings.[52] At the same time, we also need psychologists to draw from IR and the broader political sciences and sociology literature. So far, social psychologists have almost exclusively drawn inspirations from each other, and the dialogue between social psychology and political sciences or sociology has mostly been a one-way street. Yet, social psychology cannot expect to mature by working mostly with college sophomores. Instead, social psychologists have a great deal to gain by learning from and cooperating with political scientists and sociologists because the latter know a lot about how individuals, from key decision-makers to voters, think and act in *important* real life situations. And in this regard *P&M* has shown the way.

Notes

1 The author thanks Jon Mercer, Xiaoyu Pu, Jiwu Yin and, most importantly, the always enlightening and modest Bob Jervis himself, for their critical comments. All errors and omissions are the author's own.

2 Robert Jervis, *Perception and Misperception in International Politics*, Princeton, NJ: Princeton University Press, 1976. Page numbers placed in parentheses in the text refer to this edition.

3 I simply cannot resist plagiarizing Karl Popper's words for Donald T. Campbell's classic paper, 'Evolutionary Epistemology', without citing either Popper or Campbell. For Jervis's fascinating reflections on his own intellectual career, see Robert Jervis with Thierry Balzacq, 'The Logic of Mind: Interview with Robert Jervis', *Review of International Studies*, 2004, vol. 30, 559–82. See also 'Theory Talks with Robert Jervis', *Theory Talk*, 12. Available at: www. theory-talks.org/2008/07/theory-talk-12.html (accessed on 24 August 2012). For a touching tribute to Jervis (plus Bruce Bueno de Mesquita and Peter Katzenstein) by Rose McDermott (one of Jervis's students), see 'Great Mentors', *Perspectives on Politics,* 2010, vol. 43, 713–15.

4 Other important contributions came from Kenneth Boulding, Joseph De Rivera, Merton Deutsch, Alexander George, Margaret Hermann, Irving Janis, Herbert Kelman, Robert North and Charles Osgood, none of whom can be cited here owing to space limitations.

5 For Jervis's own take on how his thinking on policy issues and theoretical issues mutually benefit each other, see Robert Jervis with Thierry Balzacq, 'The Logic of Mind: Interview with Robert Jervis'.

6 Jervis himself certainly would like to think that his former students 'who serve in the government or who as academics have gone in for temporary stints understand that they may be wrong, and are wiser for this' (Robert Jervis, personal communication with the author, 11 October 2011).

7 By 'systemic', I mean an approach that considers interaction among many factors at different levels. For a more detailed discussion about the systemic approach, see Robert Jervis, *System Effects: Complexity in Political and Social Life*, Princeton, NJ: Princeton University Press, 1997.

8 Robert Jervis, *Logic of Images in International Relations*, Princeton, NJ: Princeton University Press, 1970.

9 Jervis, *System Effects: Complexity in Political and Social Life*; and Jervis and Balzacq, 'The Logic of Mind: Interview with Robert Jervis', p. 571. He reaffirmed this take in personal communication with the author (June 2006), when he was preparing a new preface for the Chinese translation of *System Effects: Complexity in Political and Social Life*.

10 Thus, if you come to look for definitive answers in Jervis, *Logic of Images in International Relations, Perception and Misperception in International Politics* and especially *System Effects: Complexity in Political and Social Life*, you would be disappointed. Indeed, when I first discussed *System Effects: Complexity in Political and Social Life* with my fellow graduate students, they could not conceal their disbelief: 'That book has no [specific] theory!' My reply was: 'Well, *System Effects* is not about small theories, it is about a perspective for understanding the social world!' I shall refrain from summarizing what systemic effects are here, not only because there is no way that I can summarize what systemic effects are, but also because I hold *System Effects: Complexity in Political and Social Life* to be a required reading for any student of human society: There is no replacement for reading the text itself.

11 Robert Jervis, 'Signaling and Perception: Drawing Inferences and Projecting Images', in Kristen Monroe (ed.), *Political Psychology*, Mahwah, NJ: Lawrence Erlbaum, 2002, pp. 293–312, at pp. 295–96. See also Jervis and Balzacq, 'The Logic of Mind: Interview with Robert Jervis', pp. 560–61.

12 Robert Jervis, 'Cooperation under the Security Dilemma', *World Politics*, 1978, vol. 30, 167–214.

13 Cognitive consistency (Chapter 4) and evoked sets (Chapter 5) operate before a decision or behavior. Cognitive dissonance (Chapter 11) operates after a decision or behavior, especially when the outcome turns out to be undesired. In this sense, Chapter 11 should immediately follow Chapters 4 and 5.

14 See also Jervis, *System Effects: Complexity in Political and Social Life* (Chapter 4); Robert Jervis and Jack Snyder (eds), *Dominoes and Bandwagons: Strategic Beliefs and Great Power Competition in the Eurasian Rimland*, New York: Oxford University Press, 1991.

15 Amos Tversky and Daniel Kahneman, 'Prospect Theory: An Analysis of Decision under Risk', *Econometrica,* 1979, vol. 47, 263–91; and Amos Tversky and Daniel Kahneman, 'The Framing of Decisions and the Psychology of Choice', *Science*, 1981, vol. 211, 453–58.

16 I limit my discussion to those works that are more directly inspired by Jervis's *Logic of Images in International Relations* and *Perception and Misperception in International Politics*. Not surprisingly, some of the works were written by Jervis's former students (e.g. Barbara Farnham, Ted Hopf, Chaim D. Kaufmann, Rose McDermott and Jonathan Mercer).

17 See Charles L. Glaser, 'Political Consequences of Military Strategy: Expanding and Refining the Spiral and Deterrence Models', *World Politics*, 1992, vol. 44, 497–538; Ken Booth and Nicholas Wheeler, *The Security Dilemma: Fear, Cooperation, and Trust in World Politics*, New York: Palgrave Macmillan, 2008; and Shiping Tang, *A Theory of Security Strategy for Our Time*, New York: Palgrave Macmillan, 2010, especially Chapters 2 and 3. See also Casper Sylvest's chapter on Herz in this volume.

18 See, for example, Barry Posen, 'The Security Dilemma and Ethnic Conflict', *Survival*, vol. 35, 27–47.

19 Shiping Tang, 'The Security Dilemma and Ethnic Conflict: Toward a Dynamic and Integrative Theory of Ethnic Conflict', *Review of International Studies*, 2011, vol. 37, 511–36.

20 Charles A. Osgood, *An Alternative to War or Surrender*, Urbana, IL: University of Illinois Press, 1962. Briefly, GRIT means one side takes some initial conciliatory steps to reduce tensions between itself and another state. If the other state responds positively, then the two states may end up in an improved relationship. In more formal terms, GRIT is based on the logic of reassurance and costly signaling.

21 Deborah W. Larson, *Anatomy of Mistrust: US-Soviet Relations during the Cold War*, Ithaca, NY: Cornell University Press, 1997; Andrew Kydd, *Trust and Mistrust in International Relations*, Princeton, NJ: Princeton University Press, 2005; and Tang, *A Theory of Security Strategy for Our Time: Defensive Realism*, Chapter 5.

22 See, for example, Glaser, 'Political Consequences of Military Strategy'; Charles L. Glaser, 'Realists as Optimists: Cooperation as Self-help', *International Security*, 1994–95, vol. 19, 50–90; and Tang, *A Theory of Security Strategy for Our Time*, Chapter 5.

23 Shiping Tang, 'Fear in International Politics: Two Positions', *International Studies Review*, 2008, vol. 10, 451–70; and Tang, *A Theory of Security Strategy for Our Time*. Very briefly, defensive realism does not assume all states to be malignant. As such, a defensive realist state does not believe that offensive strategies are the only viable security strategy: cooperation is also a viable option.

24 Shiping Tang, 'Outline of a New Theory of Attribution in IR: Dimensions of Uncertainty and their Cognitive Challenges', *Chinese Journal of International Politics*, 2012, vol. 5, 299–338.

25 Jervis with Thierry Balzacq, 'The Logic of Mind: Interview with Robert Jervis', pp. 559–63. Unfortunately, whereas constructivists tend to forget that states' identity change is nothing peculiar, some of Jervis's more materialist fellow realists tend to deny that state identities can change at all or that such changes matter.

26 Richard Ned Lebow, *Between Peace and War: The Nature of International Crisis*, Baltimore, MD: Johns Hopkins University Press, 1981.

27 Deborah W. Larson, *Origins of Containment: A Psychological Explanation*, Princeton, NJ: Princeton University Press, 1985.

28 Barbara Rearden Farnham, *Roosevelt and the Munich Crisis: A Study of Political Decision-Making*, Princeton, NJ: Princeton University Press, 1997.

29 See also Ernest R. May, *Lessons of the Past: Uses and Misuses of History*, New York: Oxford University Press, 1975. On heuristics and biases, see Amos Tversky, Thomas Gilvoch and Daniel Kahneman (eds), *Judgment under Uncertainty: Heuristics and Biases*, Oxford: Oxford University Press, 1982. See also Thomas Gilvoch, Dale Griffin and Daniel Kahneman (eds), *Heuristics and Biases: The Psychology of Intuitive Judgment*, Cambridge: Cambridge University Press, 2002.

30 Yuen Foong Khong, *Analogies at War: Korea, Munich, Dien Bien Phu, and the Vietnam Decisions of 1965*, Princeton, NJ: Princeton University Press, 1992.

31 Dan Reiter, *Crucible of Beliefs: Learning, Alliances, and World Wars*, Ithaca, NY: Cornell University Press, 1996.

32 Ted Hopf, *Peripheral Visions: Deterrence and American Foreign Policy in the Third Word*, Ann Arbor, MI: University of Michigan Press, 1994. See also, Jervis and Snyder (eds), *Dominoes and Bandwagons*.

33 Jonathan Mercer, *Reputation in International Politics*, Ithaca, NY: Cornell University Press, 1996. See also Jervis and Snyder, *Dominoes and Bandwagons*; Daryl Press, *Calculating Credibility*, Ithaca, NY: Cornell University Press, 2005; and Shiping Tang, 'Reputation, Cult of Reputation, and International Conflict', *Security Studies*, 2005, vol. 24, 34–62.

34 Rose McDermott, *Risk Taking in International Politics: Prospect Theory in American Foreign Policy*, Ann Arbor, MI: University of Michigan Press, 1998.

35 Jeffrey Taliaferro, *Balancing Risks: Great Power Intervention in the Periphery*, Ithaca, NY: Cornell University Press, 2004.

36 Jervis with Balzacq, 'The Logic of Mind: Interview with Robert Jervis', pp. 564–65. Jervis, of course, has since corrected this important omission. See Robert Jervis, Richard Ned Lebow and Janice Gross Stein, *Psychology and Deterrence*, Baltimore, MD: John Hopkins University Press, 1985; Robert Jervis, 'Understanding Beliefs', *Political Psychology*, 2006, vol. 27, 641–62. For recent attempts of synthesizing emotion and cognition, see Jonathan Mercer, 'Rationality and Psychology in International Politics', *International Organization*, 2005, vol. 59, 77–106.

37 Of course, the expulsion of emotion from psychology in the 1950–60s was a reaction against psychology's earlier excessive focus on emotion.

38 For a classic statement on the 'totalitarian' ego, see Anthony G. Greenwald, 'The Totalitarian Ego: Fabrication and Revision of Personal History', *American Psychologists*, 1980, vol. 35, 603–18. For motivated biases in our reasoning, see Ziva Kunda, 'The Case for Motivated Reasoning', *Psychological Bulletin*, 1990, vol. 108, 480–98.

39 See also Jervis, *Logic of Images*, pp. 90–96.

40 Shiping Tang, 'The Social Evolutionary Psychology of Fear (and Trust): Or Why Is International Cooperation Difficult?', unpublished manuscript.

41 Irving Lester Janis and Leon Mann, *Decision Making: A Psychological Analysis of Conflict, Choice, and Commitment*, New York: Free Press, 1977, Chapters 11 and 12. See also, Lebow, *Between Peace and War*; and Jervis, 'Understanding Beliefs', esp. 652–57.

42 Reinhold Niebuhr, *Moral Man and Immoral Society: A Study in Ethics and Politics*, New York: Charles Scribner's Sons, [1932] 1960, xx–xxv, pp. 89–93. See also Richard Ned Lebow, *A Cultural Theory of International Relations*, Cambridge: Cambridge University Press, 2008; and Shiping Tang, 'Reconciliation and the Remaking of Anarchy', *World Politics*, 2011, vol. 63, 711–49.

43 See Jervis, 'Cooperation under the Security Dilemma'; and *P&M*.
44 See Tang, *A Theory of Security Strategy for Our Time*.
45 Tang, 'Reputation, Cult of Reputation, and International Conflict'.
46 See, Janice Gross Stein, 'Building Politics into Psychology: The Misperception of Threat', *Political Psychology*, 1988, vol. 9, 245–71; Barbara Farnham, 'Political Cognition and Decision-Making', *Political Psychology*, 1990, vol. 11, 83–111; and Tang, 'Reconciliation and the Remaking of Anarchy'.
47 Khong, *Analogies at War*; Richard Ned Lebow and Janice Gross Stein, *We All Lost the Cold War*, Princeton, NJ: Princeton University Press, 1994. For an earlier important discussion on the methodological challenges of testing psychological hypotheses that addresses only part of the broad challenge, see Chaim D. Kaufmann, 'Out of the Lab and into the Archives: A Method for Testing Psychological Explanations for Political Decision Making," *International Studies Quarterly*, 1994, vol. 38, 557–86.
48 Tang, 'Reconciliation and the Remaking of Anarchy'.
49 See, for example, Ted Hopf, *Social Construction of International Relations: Idendities & Foreign Policies, Moscow, 1955 & 1999*, Ithaca, NY: Cornell University Press, 2002.
50 Jervis with Balzacq, 'The Logic of Mind: Interview with Robert Jervis', pp. 562–63.
51 Norbert Elias, *The Civilizing Process*, revised edn, trans. Edmund Jephcott, Oxford: Blackwell, [1939] 1994.
52 Lebow, *A Cultural Theory of International Relations*; and Tang, 'Social Evolutionary Psychology of Fear (and Trust)'.

14 Probing the institutional fabric of world politics: Hedley Bull's *The Anarchical Society*

Andrew Hurrell

Hedley Bull frequently used the term 'classical' in his own lectures and writings. The term, he said, did not refer to a particular period but should rather be understood in the sense proposed by Matthew Arnold, namely the degree to which a work provided 'most excellent exposition' of a particular issue or of an enduring question.[1] The status of *The Anarchical Society* as a classic text in this sense is clear. It provides the most systematic and powerful exposition of the view that together states form an international society, and it develops this idea as a powerful vantage point from which to analyse and assess the possibilities of order in world politics. At the core of the book is the question: to what extent does the inherited political framework provided by the society of sovereign states continue to provide an adequate basis for order? *The Anarchical Society* does not seek to provide a purely descriptive or narrative account of international events or developments, nor is it directly concerned with the explanation of international relations. Rather, it provides an interpretation of how international relations have changed and how those changes should be evaluated from the perspective of a particular set of values, above all the pursuit of order.[2]

Bull's concern with order and institutions would seem to connect with the debates on multilateralism, international institutions and global governance that have been so prominent during the period since the end of the Cold War. But Bull's focus is less on explaining particular institutions and more on assessing and evaluating the overall character of institutionalization in world politics, the normative commitments inherent in different ways of governing the globe, and the adequacy of existing institutions for meeting practical and normative challenges. *The Anarchical Society* remains a fundamental teaching text. It is one of the most important and most-cited works of the so-called English School of International Relations.[3] Its pedagogical value rests on the quality of Bull's writing and analysis – its intellectual rigour, its clarity of exposition, and its capacity to unsettle established and comfortable positions.

The first section of this chapter will elaborate this claim in more detail and provide a brief overview of the main arguments of the book. The following section will consider two other ways in which the book can be said to be a classical text: as emerging from, and taking forward, a set of 'classical traditions' of thought on international relations, and as representing a 'classical approach' to how international relations should be studied. The third section explores some of the major criticisms of the book. The final section examines the book's contemporary relevance and considers the charge of outdatedness.

What is *The Anarchical Society* all about?

The central question that lies at the heart of Hedley Bull's writing concerns the nature and possibility of order in international life. As is well known, the intellectual framework for this enquiry is provided by the concept of international society:

> A *society of states* (or international society) exists when a group of states, conscious of certain common interests and common values, form a society in the sense that they conceive themselves to be bound by a common set of rules in their relations with one another, and share in the working of common institutions (p. 13, emphasis in the original).[4]

In developing this idea of international society, the book asks three kinds of questions. There are, first of all, *analytical and definitional* questions: what do we mean by order and what are the minimum conditions that would have to exist before any society could be meaningfully so described? Then there are *historical* questions: how far can one isolate an acceptance of these conditions in the historical practices of the society of states that developed first in Europe and then became global in the course of the nineteenth and twentieth centuries? And finally there are *evaluative and normative* questions: how can this idea of international society be evaluated against other models, ideas and proposals for international or world order and how is it to be judged in moral terms?

Bull begins the book with an analytical discussion of the meaning of order. On the one hand, social order can be understood in the sense of stable and regular patterns of human behaviour. In this depiction it is contrasted with chaos, instability, or lack of predictability. On the other hand, social order requires the existence of a particular kind of purposive pattern that human beings have infused with meaning, that involves a particular set of goals, objectives and values, and that leads to a particular outcome. If order is to be understood in terms of some purposive pattern, what sorts of purposes, goals and objectives might be relevant to international life? Bull defined social order as '[a] pattern [in the relations of human individuals or groups] that leads to a particular result, an arrangement of social life such that it promotes certain goals or values' (pp. 3–4).

His analysis of these 'certain goals and values' always tended to point in a constrained and minimalist direction. Bull's classic study of order in world politics concentrated on the common framework of rules and institutions that had developed within the anarchical society of states. It was *anarchical* in that there was no common power to enforce law or to underwrite cooperation; but it was a *society* in so far as states were conscious of common rules and values, cooperated in the working of common institutions, and perceived common interests in observing these rules and working through these institutions. It was, however, a necessarily thin and fragile society in which the three fundamental goals of international social life were limited to the preservation of the society of states itself, the maintenance of the independence of individual states and the regulation – but not elimination – of war and violence among states and societies.[5]

From this point of view, interstate cooperation and international law could never be expected to provide a stable and universal peace but only to mitigate the inevitable conflicts that would arise from the existence of a multiplicity of separate sovereign states. The relevant question was not: how might human beings create forms of international society or schemes of international cooperation that embodied all their aspirations for justice or which universalized some particular conception of the good society? It was rather: how might states and other groups do each other the least possible harm and, in an age of total war and nuclear weapons, survive as a species? So the core goals of international social order were survival and coexistence, and the political framework was made up of the core institutions of a pluralist international society – international law, the concert of great powers, the balance of power, diplomacy and war.

The middle part of the book devotes a chapter to each of these 'institutions' of international society. Here it is important to note the differences between Bull's approach and that of many other writers, especially those emerging from the realist tradition. Take, for example, the balance of power. For realists, the balance of power is a mechanical arrangement or a constellation of forces that pushes and shoves states to act in particular ways from outside, regardless of their intentions.[6] For Bull, it should rather be understood as a conscious and continuing shared practice in which the actors constantly debate and contest the meaning of the balance of power, its ground rules, and the role that it should play. Equally, great powers are to be studied not simply in terms of their material power or the degree to which they can impose order on weaker states or within their spheres of influence on the back of crude coercion, but rather in terms of the extent to which their role and their managerial functions are perceived as being legitimate by other states.[7] Power remains central to Bull's analysis of international relations, but power is a social attribute. To understand power we must place it side by side with other quintessentially social concepts such as prestige, authority and legitimacy. International society is therefore centrally concerned with norms and institutions. However, this does not necessarily lead to a cosy or cooperative Grotianism concerned solely with the promotion of law and morality as is so often mistakenly assumed.

The Anarchical Society and the classical tradition

Bull was committed to the view that the international system cannot be viewed in terms of a decentralized anarchic structure in which states as 'functionally undifferentiated' units vary only according their relative power capabilities – as neo-realist theorists insist. Central to the international system is a historically created, and evolving, structure of common understandings, rules, norms and mutual expectations. Notions of state sovereignty, international law or war cannot simply be assumed, and international relations cannot be analysed or taught as part of an abstract 'game' independent of its human or historical origins. It grows out of its past, although never fully outgrows it.

It follows from this that understanding international relations will involve coming to terms with the patterns and traditions of thought developed over time by both practitioners and theorists. Hence the importance within *The Anarchical Society* of Bull's use (which he took from Martin Wight) of the three traditions of thinking about order: the Hobbesian, the Grotian and the Kantian.[8] They are central to the way in which Western theorists have conceived of international relations and they continue to shed light on the most fundamental questions concerning the nature of international order. Hence *The Anarchical Society* can be seen as a classical text that reflects a view of the field as united around a common set of questions and a shared stock of historical ideas, especially theoretical ideas about the nature of the questions and the sorts of answers that have been given and that can be given. The core of the academic study of international relations (IR) should therefore involve a thorough knowledge of this intellectual heritage and of the classic works within it. Failure to address or to engage with this heritage is to waste time and effort reinventing the wheel.

A further way in which the term classical has been applied to Bull has to do with his views of how international relations should be studied. For some, this has to do with Bull's polemical attack in the 1960s on what he saw as the misguided attempts to develop scientific theories of international relations in favour of 'an older tradition of historical and philosophical reflection'.[9] There is no doubt that *The Anarchical Society* does in some broad sense reflect this kind of 'classical approach'. As Tim Dunne puts it: 'Rather than "operationalizing" concepts and formulating "testable" hypotheses, the emphasis upon contending concepts is driven by the search for defining properties that mark the boundaries of different historical and normative orders.'[10] However, exactly how is not especially clear and we need to recognize that Bull's criticism of 'scientific' approaches was muddled – not least because Bull shared much of the aspiration for theory and a good deal of the understanding of what science was all about.[11]

A more enduring feature of Bull's classical approach goes beyond any particular set of methodological or theoretical debates. As is exemplified in *The Anarchical Society* Bull had a very clear view of the role of the academic. For Bull, it is the duty of the academic to ask and pursue unfashionable questions and to be highly sceptical of all purveyors of conventional wisdom. The logic of theoretical enquiry demands analytical and critical distance, including distance from the temptations of power and from the requirements to give policy advice or to be 'policy relevant'. Bull had himself worked as a policy adviser and, as noted above, believed that the ideas of practitioners constituted an important focus for study. Indeed, the cast list of the three traditions includes the ideas of many statespersons. In addition, his work clearly reflected the preoccupations and outlooks of this time. However, Bull believed none the less in what might call the inner morality of intellectual or academic enquiry. As he wrote at the end of *The Anarchical Society*: 'The search for conclusions that can be presented as "solutions" or "practical advice" is a corrupting element in the contemporary study of world politics, which properly understood is an intellectual activity and not a practical one' (p. 308).

Criticism and evaluation

One test of a classic is the extent to which it provokes debate and becomes a reference point, even among those who reject its claims and arguments. From the earliest reviews this applied to *The Anarchical Society*. It was seen by one reviewer as 'that rarest of books: it is not the last but the first word on its subject'.[12] There are at least five broad areas of critical discussion and debate.

The first comes mostly from within those associated with the English School and concentrates on different ways in which Bull's work should be understood. On the one hand, some commentators have seen the great virtue of Bull's approach to lie in its intellectual pluralism and its occupation of a 'middle ground' between realists and liberals. From this point of view we can best understand international relations as a never-ending conversation between the Hobbesians, the Grotians and the Kantians, and in terms of the constantly shifting interplay of power, norms and interests. On the other hand, others argue that the core of Bull's contribution lies not in this openness and pluralism but rather in the idea of international society itself. From this point of view, taking forward Bull's legacy should involve developing the idea of international society – for example by unpacking further the distinction between pluralist and solidarist conceptions of international society; pressing us to think hard about the role of culture and shared moral ideas within different historical international societies; and developing Bull's insights into the shifting boundaries of international society, especially in the transition from an originally European to a global international society.

A second area of critical discussion concerns the similarities and differences between Bull and the sorts of constructivist scholarship that has been so influential in the past 20 years. Almost all constructivists make at least a passing reference to Bull and various writings have sought to compare Bull and the English School explicitly with constructivism.[13] Constructivism is far from a unified position and is becoming ever less so. Yet there are a number of claims that unite much constructivist writing on international relations, including the view that international norms are constitutive as well as regulative; the claim that norms, rules and institutions create meanings and enable or make possible different forms of social action; and the idea that many of the most important features of international politics are produced and reproduced in the concrete practices of social actors. It is evident that Bull was deeply committed to the centrality of norms and institutions in international politics and to the notion that society is constituted through diverse political practices built around shared, intersubjective understandings – that is, understandings that exist between and among actors. Equally, Bull's core definition of international society highlights *shared* conceptions of interests and common values and the *shared consciousness* of being bound by legal and moral rules.

However, for those who have sought to understand constructivism in social scientific terms Bull's work is insufficiently rigorous. He does not tell us enough about when and how we might identify the existence of an international society and how we should operationalize his own central distinction between an international system on the one hand and an international society on the other. He tells us that norms matter but does not give us a theoretically convincing account of how, where and why.[14] At the other end of the constructivist spectrum, critical constructivists argue that Bull's emphasis on norms and intersubjective understandings is not pushed far enough, and that he stays too close to the all-too-often self-serving purposes of practitioners. Although ideas and language matter, Bull's philosophical realism distinguishes him from many more strongly reflectivist or discursive constructivists (and still more from post-modernism). Bull rejected the notion that international relations could be ever studied *solely* in terms of shared understandings rather than in terms of the interaction between material and social facts. For Bull, ideas mattered to the extent that they are taken up and acted upon by powerful states, and the relevance of particular norms and institutions would always have to be linked to the underlying distribution of material power. Finally, in contrast to more self-consciously critical constructivists, Bull believed that brute material facts and cold power politics could act as a powerful check on both the aspirations of practitioners and the methods of the analyst.

A third area of critical discussion comes from those who support the importance of a social and historical account of international relations but who find Bull's approach inadequate. Yes, there is a proper concern for history but what we find in *Anarchical Society* is a strangely narrow and old-fashioned history. As Keene puts it: 'It was a political, legal and diplomatic history of international society, not a social history of international politics, law and diplomacy.'[15] Even looking narrowly at the institutions of international society we do not learn much about the historical or sociological operation of, say, international law or diplomacy. Stronger criticisms come from those historical sociologists who deny that international society can be meaningfully studied without a much deeper engagement with capitalist modernity and with the changing character of the state and of the social relations embodied in the state. How can such a statist theory of international relations that claims to talk about history and society say so little about the nature of the state and how it has evolved through time?[16]

A fourth dimension of the critical debate relates to the treatment of normative questions in *The Anarchical Society*. On this account, Bull (and the English School more generally) had opened up a fertile realm of classical political thought, but conceived of 'classical theory' in narrow and impoverished ways. The result was to cut off IR from the far richer traditions of political and social theory to which it is necessarily intimately connected, and to downplay or ignore a range of fundamental questions about state, community, nation that could never be satisfactorily addressed solely from the perspective of the society of states.[17] Equally, as the global agenda was changing, surely there was a pressing need was to broaden and deepen the subject by bringing debates on international and global justice into closer contact with the ever-expanding and far more sophisticated world of political theory and political philosophy.[18]

The fifth area of criticism has to do with the charge of outdatedness, and it is to this important issue that the chapter now turns.

Contemporary relevance

For many readers *The Anarchical Society* is outdated.[19] Bull's emphasis on the great powers, on the balance of power and war as an institution of international society; his use of the writings of Grotius, Hobbes and Kant; and his central concern with the ideas and practices of classical European state system of the eighteenth and nineteenth centuries – all this seems far removed from the study of contemporary world politics. Much of Bull's thinking was evidently shaped by the concerns of the Cold War, by the dangers posed by nuclear weapons, and by the problems of managing nuclear deterrence. In the latter part of *The Anarchical Society* he considers many of the claims made at that time that international relations were undergoing fundamental change. He was deeply sceptical about many of these arguments, for example that economic interdependence was undermining the role of the state and transforming world politics. His emphasis on continuity seemed then, and seems much more now, to downplay the dynamic forces at work in global politics and to fail to recognize the extent to which the international system has been moving decisively 'beyond Westphalia'.[20] For many readers the dramatic and far-reaching changes associated with globalization make it very difficult to accept Bull's prescriptive bottom line, namely that a thin pluralist international society of states remains the best available means of upholding world order.

There is undoubtedly much in *The Anarchical Society* that seems hard to reconcile with the changes that have taken place in global politics after the Cold War. Bull had, after all, expressed little interest in formal international institutions, including the United Nations. He believed that what he saw as the deeper 'institutions' of the balance of power, war, the great powers, diplomacy and international law were of more abiding importance.[21] In *The Anarchical Society* he was critical of 'Kantian' optimism about the spread and impact of liberal democracy – the set of claims that would develop into democratic peace theory. The impact of economic globalization and political democratization, the increased importance of transnational civil society, the increased density, scope and range of international institutions, the multiple problems that result from the break-up of states and ethnic self-assertion – all these factors have developed to such a point that, for many commentators, Bull's narrow focus on the society of states is now wholly inadequate and outdated.

One possible response is simply to view Bull's rather sober and sceptical conclusions as a line in the sand against which the claims for change and transformation can be judged. Pedagogically it makes great sense for students to read Bull alongside the many works of the 1990s and early 2000s that stressed the idea of systemic transformation, especially in the context of globalization. Which parts of Bull's picture still hold? Which do not? And why? Bull did not ignore change, and as noted the latter sections of *The Anarchical Society* consider many different forms of change and many alternative paths to world order. However, Bull did advocate sobriety in analysing change. He argued consistently that many of the contemporary trends and features which appear novel – from transnational corporations to the privatization of violence in the form of terrorist groups or warlords – look more familiar when approached from a sufficiently long historical perspective. Equally, he suggested that we can gain much from comparing the present with previous epochs of change – hence his suggestive, if underdeveloped, idea about 'neo-medievalism'. This involves the idea that, either generally or in particular regions such as Europe, we might be witnessing a return to an order characterized not by nation states but by multiple and overlapping authorities, jurisdictions and identities.

We might therefore simply see *The Anarchical Society* as providing a classical exposition of how to think about claims for change. Bull, after all, never argued that states were the only legitimate objects of study in world politics, nor that they are, or would necessarily remain, in 'control'. He was in fact rather pessimistic about the prospects for international society. Thus, in response to a reader's comments on *The Anarchical Society*, he wrote: 'I am not sure that it is correct to say ... that in the book I see "an international society emerging". I think I rather argue that international society exists but is in decline.'[22] The reasons for this decline have to do partly with the unprecedented expansion in the normative ambitions of international society, and partly with the erosion of its political foundations. Equally, he was perfectly aware of the potentially transformative nature of what has come to be called globalization. However, he was less sure that these new elements provided an adequate basis for order (or, for that matter, justice) within international society.

A second response is to use the conceptual categories developed in *The Anarchical Society* as a means of capturing some of the major changes that have taken place in recent international relations. Hence many within the English School have sought to develop Bull's distinction between pluralist and solidarist versions of international society. They have also suggested that Bull's own thinking on international society was moving in a more solidarist direction towards the end of his career or that his thinking can be interpreted in proto-solidarist terms.[23] Substantively they have argued that, contrary to the statism and the scepticism expressed in *The Anarchical Society*, a consensus was in fact developing within post-Cold War international society around such solidarist norms as humanitarian intervention or the responsibility to protect.[24] In still more strongly progressivist mode, but still owing much to Bull's work, others have explored how the changing conditions of global politics may be opening political and moral spaces for the transformation of the political community.[25]

In similar vein one might pick up on the under-exploited intellectual resources of *The Anarchical Society* – for example, taking on board the degree to which regionalism has become an important characteristic of contemporary world politics but examining and comparing these 'regional international societies' within the framework of Bull's ideas and concepts. Or thinking through the notion of 'world society' whose importance Bull stresses but which is left underdeveloped in his work, and the complex ways in which the international society of states and the ever denser and more politically active world society relate to each other.[26]

Yet a third possibility is to argue that he was often right both in the questions he asked about change and in many of his conclusions. Asking the right questions is often by far the hardest element of any intellectual project. Bull, for example, was constantly fascinated with the boundaries of international society, with the criteria for membership, and with the idea that as society deepens so questions of membership become more important. This led him to ask about the position of those groups that lay on or beyond the historical boundaries of international society, such as pirates, mercenaries, heretics, infidels and barbarians. Twenty years ago it might have seemed rather quaint to assign a book on international politics that included discussion of such groups. Today the importance of pirates, mercenaries, heretics and barbarians can hardly be doubted.

Clearly Bull's arguments cannot simply be replayed and there are very important differences of emphasis and of empirical application. Yet as the claims of the post-Cold War period concerning globalization have been subjected to scrutiny and criticism, the pattern of argumentation that we see both in Bull's work as a whole and in many of his substantive conclusions recur: that the historical novelty of current globalizing forces has been exaggerated; that the decline in the role of the state has been overdone; and that understandings of order built around power and the major powers have by no means wholly disappeared from the global stage. More importantly, his emphasis on the dual challenge of managing power and mediating between conflicting values remains fundamental to understanding both the limits of solidarism in the contemporary world and the continued importance of older-style pluralist mechanisms of order.[27] Faced by more troubled times, therefore, we should recognize the continued importance of Bull's realism and his scepticism.

It cannot be overemphasized that Bull's preoccupation in *The Anarchical Society* is not with world politics in general, but with the nature and possibilities of international order. As noted above, Bull never argued that states were the only legitimate objects of study in world politics. And he was perfectly aware of the potentially transformative nature of what has come to be called globalization. However, he was less sure that these new elements provided an adequate basis for order (and still less for justice) within international society. It is certainly the case that, even within its own terms, Bull's conception of interstate order was too starkly divorced from the social and economic structures within which states and societies are embedded. It is also the case that, as often noted, his work tended to downplay political economy, and his view of the state's capacity to control the direction and scope of either the national economy or global capitalism was strained, even in the mid-1970s. Moreover, any contemporary analysis of order and governance needs to place order within the state system against the other two arenas within which all social order needs to be understood: civil society on the one hand (including what is now termed transnational civil society), and economic markets on the other.

Yet, it remains plausible to argue that alternative global frameworks for order are either incoherent and contested (for example transnational civil society), or efficient but highly unstable (as in the case of markets and the global economy). Yes, the past 35 years have seen an intensification of economic and social globalization, but the inequalities and discontents of globalization have led to increased political strains both internationally and within many states. In addition, they have fatally undermined any notion that globalization will lead easily or unproblematically to shared values, resilient institutions, or to a meaningful global moral community. Yes, the density of the norms, rules and institutions of international society has increased tremendously, often pushing in a liberal direction. Yet, Bull's scepticism may still be merited: whose solidarist or liberal order? How stable and how legitimate can a liberal order be when it depends so heavily on the hegemony of the single superpower whose history is so 'exceptionalist' and whose attitude to international law and institutions has been so ambivalent? How will international society confront its current triple challenge: a power transition driven by the rise of new emerging powers; a structural transition in the scope of cooperation as governments have to face a series of complex and often interconnected global challenges; and a cultural transition as both state power and the dynamics of the global capitalist economy move beyond the West?

So we are still left with Bull's concern with the disjuncture between the vaulting normative ambitions of contemporary international society and its precarious power-political, institutional and cultural foundations. Although sometimes seen as optimistic, complacent, or even nostalgic, Bull was constantly worried by what he called 'premature global solidarism' – that too many hopes, too many demands, and too many moral claims were being placed on the still thin fabric of international society. Contemporary readers will disagree as to whether Bull's own conclusions remain valid, but his questions and the framework for analysing provided by *The Anarchical Society* remain one of the most important points of departure for any study of order in world politics.

Notes

1 Matthew Arnold, *Culture and Anarchy* (1869) in *Arnold's 'Culture and Anarchy' and Other Writings*, Cambridge: Cambridge University Press, 1993. For a discussion of Arnold's notion of culture as 'the best that has been thought and said', see Stefan Collini, *Matthew Arnold: A Critical Portrait*, Oxford: Oxford University Press, 2008.
2 On this point see Edward Keene, 'International Society as an Ideal Type', in Cornelia Navari (ed.), *Theorising International Society: English School Methods*, Basingstoke: Palgrave Macmillan, 2009, pp. 104–23.
3 For a succinct recent account see Tim Dunne, 'The English School', in Christian Reus-Smit and Duncan Snidal (eds) *The Oxford Handbook of International Relations*, Oxford: Oxford University Press, 2008, pp. 267–85. For longer studies see Andrew Linklater and Hidemi Suganami, *The English School and International Relations: A Contemporary* Reassessment, Cambridge: Cambridge University Press, 2006; Barry Buzan, *From International to World Society? English School Theory and the Social Structure of Globalization*, Cambridge: Cambridge University Press, 2004; and Richard Little and John Williams (eds), *The Anarchical Society in a Globalized World,* Basingstoke: Palgrave Macmillan, 2006. For a discussion of where Bull fits within the English School see Tim Dunne, *Inventing International Society: A History of the English School*, New York: St Martin's Press, 1998. For a full bibliography see the English School website. Available at: www.polis.leeds.ac.uk/research/international-relations-security/english-school/ (accessed 17 December 12). For a recent collection of articles concentrating more directly on Bull himself see Coral Bell and Meredith Thatcher (eds) *Remembering Hedley*, Canberra: ANU e-press, 2008.
4 Hedley Bull, *The Anarchical Society: A Study of Order in World Politics*, Basingstoke: Palgrave Macmillan, 2012. Page numbers placed in parentheses in the text refer to this fourth edition.
5 One important influence on Bull's understanding of order was his Oxford tutor, the legal theorist H. L. A. Hart, and his notion of a 'minimum content of natural law'. See H. L. A. Hart, *The Concept of Law*, Oxford: Oxford University Press, 1981. For a more detailed

analysis of Bull's views, see Kai Alderson and Andrew Hurrell (eds), *Hedley Bull on International Society*, Basingstoke: Palgrave Macmillan, 2000, Chapters 1–3; Robert Ayson, *Hedley Bull and the Accomodation of Power*, Basingstoke: Palgrave Macmillan, 2012.

6 See, for example, Robert Jervis, 'A Political Science Perspective on the Balance of Power and Concert', *American Historical Review*, 1992, vol. 97, 716–24.

7 On the importance of legitimacy in the context of unequal power see Ian Clark, *Hegemony in International Society*, Oxford: Oxford University Press, 2011.

8 Martin Wight, *International Theory: The Three Traditions*, eds. Gabriele Wight and Brian Porter, Leicester: Leicester University Press, 1991. See also Hedley Bull, 'Martin Wight and the Three Traditions of International Relations', *British Journal of International Studies*, 1976, vol. 2, 101–16.

9 Hedley Bull, 'International Theory: The Case for the Classical Approach', *World Politics*, 1966, vol. 18, 361–77.

10 Dunne, *Inventing International Society*, p. 271.

11 Patrick T. Jackson, *The Conduct of Inquiry in International Relations. Philosophy of Science and its Implications for the Study of World Politics*, London: Routledge, 2011, p. 6.

12 Michael Mandelbaum, 'Review of *The Anarchical Society*', *Political Science Quarterly*, 2007, vol. 92, 574–75.

13 See Tim Dunne, 'The Social Construction of International Society', *European Journal of International Relations*, 1995, vol. 1, 367–90; and Christian Reus-Smit, 'Imagining Society: Constructivism and the English School', *British Journal of Politics and International Relations*, 2002, vol. 4, 487–509.

14 See for example, Martha Finnemore, 'Exporting the English School?' *Review of International Studies*, 2001, vol. 27, 509–13.

15 Edward Keene, 'The English School and the British Historians', *Millennium: Journal of International Studies*, 2008, vol. 37, 387.

16 Justin Rosenberg, 'The International Imagination: IR Theory and "Classic Social Analysis"', *Millennium: Journal of International Studies*, 1994, vol. 23, 85–108.

17 See for example, Chris Brown, *Sovereignty, Rights and Justice*, Cambridge: Polity, 2002.

18 See Andrew Hurrell and Terry MacDonald, 'Ethics and Norms in International Relations', in Walter Carlsnaes, Thomas Risse and Beth Simmons eds, *Handbook of International Relations*, London: Sage, 2012.

19 For a recent example see Ian Hall, 'Taming the Anarchical Society', *e-International Relations* (5 July 2012). Available at: www.e-ir.info/2012/07/05/taming-the-the-anarchical-society/ (accessed 9 July 2012).

20 For claims about change and transformation see David Held and Anthony McGrew (eds), *The Transformations Reader*, 2nd edn, Cambridge: Polity Press, 2003.

21 For a recent critique of this position see Peter Wilson, 'The English School Meets the Chicago School: The Case for a Grounded Theory of International Institutions', *International Studies Review*, 2012, vol. 14.

22 Bull's letter to Shaie Selzer, Macmillan Publishers. 14 November 1975. Bull's Papers, Bodleian Library, Oxford.

23 See, for example, Tim Dunne and Nicholas Wheeler, 'Hedley Bull's Pluralism of the Intellect and Solidarism of the Will', *International Affairs*, 1996, vol. 72, 91–107.

24 See, for example, Nicholas Wheeler, *Saving Strangers: Humanitarian Intervention in International Society*, Oxford: Oxford University Press, 2000. Note that Bull examined the possibilities of change in norms concerning intervention well before the subject became fashionable. See Hedley Bull (ed.), *Intervention in World Politics*, Oxford: Oxford University Press, 1984.

25 See, for example, Andrew Linklater, *The Transformation of Political Community: Ethical Foundations of the Post-Westphalian Era*, Cambridge: Polity Press, 1998.

26 Both of these issues are examined in Buzan, *From International to World Society*. On the former issue see also Barry Buzan and Ana Gonzalez-Pelaez (eds), *International Society and the Middle East: English School Theory at the Regional Level*, London: Routledge, 2009. On the latter issue see also Ian Clark, *International Legitimacy and World Society*, Oxford: Oxford University Press, 2007.

27 See Andrew Hurrell, *On Global Order: Power, Values and the Constitution of International Society*, Oxford: Oxford University Press, 2007.

15 A circumspect revival of liberalism: Robert O. Keohane and Joseph S. Nye's *Power and Interdependence*

Thomas C. Walker[1]

Classic works in International Relations (IR) can emerge in a variety of ways. Some classics introduce a new paradigm that explains complex phenomena better than previous efforts. Others revive neglected but important ideas and claims. Still others hit the tenor of the times and speak to immediate challenges facing global politics. Robert O. Keohane and Joseph S. Nye's *Power and Interdependence* (*PI*), first published in 1977, is indeed a classic for all of these reasons.[2] Unlike some of the works discussed in this volume, Keohane and Nye's work was promptly hailed as a classic. Two of the leading IR journals published article-length reviews of *PI* shortly after its publication. In *International Organization*, Kal Holsti surmised that this book may 'prove to be one of the most significant writings in international relations theory of the past two decades'.[3] In an extensive review published in *World Politics,* Stanley Michalak referred to *PI* as 'a groundbreaking work ... that will have a long-term impact on the ways in which teachers and scholars conceptualize international phenomena'.[4] Both of these reviewers were prescient. The themes and puzzles presented in *PI* continue to shape our thinking on globalization, international trade, regime formation and change, non-state actors as well as the nature of power and military force in the global realm.

PI was an early collaboration between two young scholars who would both become ranked among the most influential in the field of IR. When IR scholars were recently asked 'whose work has had the greatest influence on the field of IR in the past 20 years' Robert O. Keohane was ranked first and Joseph S. Nye was ranked sixth.[5] Their high standing in the field rests in no small part on the enduring influence of *PI* and the ways in which it deviated from the standard realist approach. The degree of realist dominance in the decades prior to *PI* cannot be overstated. In the mid-1950s Hans J. Morgenthau's *Politics Among Nations,* the subject of Chapter 7 in this volume, was 'used by more North American university-level instructors than all competing texts in international politics combined'.[6] The discipline's reliance on realist theory was rigorously documented by John Vasquez. Vasquez demonstrated how realist theory informed more than 90 per cent of the hypotheses tested by IR scholars up to the 1970s.[7] In this context of realist dominance, Keohane and Nye offered a timely contrast. The events of the 1970s seemed to shake the foundations of political realism. The US inability to prevail in Vietnam despite overwhelming military capabilities was particularly troubling for many political realists. Power, especially military power, was not as fungible as realists had expected. The oil embargo initiated by the Organization of Petroleum Exporting Countries (OPEC) in 1972 further highlighted the changing nature of power in the global system by demonstrating how militarily weak states could still wield considerable influence. The global economic crisis brought on by the collapse of the Bretton Woods system showed that even the hegemon was vulnerable in an interdependent world. Finally, the emergence of new issues of global environmental management and questions of global governance of seabed resources raised a new set of problems that realism could not address. Collectively, these real-world events posed serious challenges to the realist paradigm. *PI* effectively responded to this series of crises that beset world politics in the 1970s. In their Preface to the first edition, Keohane and Nye admit that they 'soon became uneasy about this one-sided [realist] view of reality, particularly about its inadequate analysis of economic integration and of the roles played by formal and informal international institutions' (p. v). Keohane and Nye set out to address these inadequacies by clarifying the concept of complex interdependence and to show how complex interdependence contributes to the rise of international regimes in a variety of issue areas. Their case studies examined international monetary affairs and global management of the oceans. They also devoted chapters to the cooperative bilateral relationships between the USA and Canada and the USA and Australia. These cases demonstrate how growing interdependence undermines the efficacy of military power and imposes layers of complexity on global politics that are not acknowledged by realism.

I will begin reviewing the central claims and contentions made in *PI* and how these claims challenged mainstream IR in the 1970s. I will then critically explore Keohane and Nye's later efforts to graft *PI* onto neorealist theory rather than highlighting how their ideas challenge realist expectations. I argue that this obscures the close relationship between *PI* and long-standing liberal internationalist themes in IR. I conclude by exploring the significant and enduring legacy of *PI* in the study of IR.

Reintroducing interdependence and globalization

While the central themes of *PI* have a long provenance in IR (see Chapters 2 and 6 on Norman Angell and David Mitrany in this volume), Keohane and Nye's book is one of the earliest efforts to systematically analyse the processes that later came to be known as globalization. While their first sentence might seem clichéd today, it was surprisingly novel in 1977: 'We live in an era of interdependence' (p. 3). Interdependence is accelerating owing to both technological advances and increasing levels of trade. The 'remarkable advances in transportation and communications technology' allow easy exchange of ideas, goods and people. Since the end of World War II, Keohane and Nye note, world trade in the industrialized world 'has grown by more than 7 percent per year and has become a larger proportion of gross national product for most major countries of Europe and North America' (p. 39). They characterize complex interdependence along three dimensions. First, foreign policy in this era of interdependence is distinct owing to the multiple and layered channels connecting societies. States are not the unitary or sole actors as realists have assumed. With greater ease and greater frequency, bureaucrats as well as non-governmental elites meet to negotiate and coordinate global understandings and policies. These new layers of interaction are more complicated and multifaceted than realists tend to acknowledge. The outcomes of these interactions often have consequences for domestic politics as well as international. As Keohane and Nye argue, '[t]ransnational communications reinforce these effects. Thus, foreign economic policies touch more domestic economic activity than in the past, blurring the lines between domestic and foreign policy … Parallel developments in issues of environmental regulation and control over technology reinforce this trend' (p. 26). States are neither as unitary nor as sovereign as realists would have them be. Domestic political outcomes can increasingly be linked to policies and actions emanating from abroad.

A second characteristic of complex interdependence is the absence of hierarchy among issues. 'The agenda of interstate relations', Keohane and Nye note, 'consists of multiple issues that are not arranged in a clear or consistent hierarchy' (p. 25). Military security does not dominate the agenda. The old realist distinction between high politics (i.e. concerns with power and security) and low politics (i.e. all other non-security issues including trade, finance and the environment) holds no longer. The two have become overlapping and intertwined. So the realist's exclusive emphasis on high politics is insufficient in this age of interdependence.

The first two characteristics relate directly to the third characteristic of interdependence: the diminishing importance of military force. Not only is force more costly but it will rarely achieve a wide range of political objectives. This results from the diversity of issues and levels of economic interdependence shared by states across the world. Keohane and Nye argue that 'employing force on one issue against an independent state with which one has a variety of relationships is likely to rupture mutually profitable relations on other issues' (p. 29). This drives up the costs of using force. The diminishing importance of military force is especially relevant in 'Western democracies' where 'popular opposition to prolonged military conflicts is very high' (p. 29). Keohane and Nye's emphasis on democracies in an interdependent world is an important but underdeveloped aspect of *PI*.

A world characterized by complex interdependence, therefore, demands different points of emphasis than those offered by political realism. More attention must be devoted to questions of international management and cooperation. This places international organization and international regimes as prominent pieces in Keohane and Nye's model. Domestic politics must also be taken into account. Similar to the realist neglect of international organization and regimes, Keohane and Nye note how the 'realist approach deprecates domestic politics by suggestions that the national interest must be calculated in terms of power, relative to other states, and that if it is not, the result will be catastrophic' (p. 43). Domestic political interests, frequent and multi-layered interactions across state boundaries, overlapping issues that often lack hierarchy and the decreasing efficacy of military power are hallmarks of complex interdependence. Cooperation and international regimes will prove to be vital to managing such a complex system.

An early analysis of international regimes

Prior to the publication of *PI*, questions concerning fungible aspects of power, the interplay between domestic and international politics, the roles of international organization and the importance of international regimes were largely marginalized in the study of IR. This may have been a result of their association with interwar idealism or utopianism. Any efforts towards global governance or management were frequently dismissed by realists as utopian efforts akin to the failures of the 1930s. In their evaluation of studies of international regimes, Stephan Haggard and Beth Simmons note that all societal notions of international politics had long suffered 'from a lingering taint of idealism'.[8] One of Keohane and Nye's most notable achievements was to bundle these neglected features of global politics into one work. After the publication of *PI*, elements of liberal internationalism such as international regimes were no longer marginalized by students of IR. The 'taint' was gone.

Keohane and Nye's analysis of international regimes may be the most lasting contribution of *PI*. Four years before Stephen Krasner presented the enduring definition of international regimes as 'implicit or explicit principles, norms, rules, and decision-making procedures around which actors' expectations converge in a given issue area of international relations,'[9] Keohane and Nye defined international regimes in this way: 'By creating or accepting procedures, rules, or institutions for certain kinds of activity, governments regulate and control transnational and interstate relations. We refer to these governing arrangements as *international regimes*' (p. 5). As interdependence increases, so too does the value of ordering mechanisms like international regimes. By popularizing the concept of international regimes, Keohane and Nye provided a language for understanding politics in an interdependent world that challenged the realist language of anarchy.[10]

Keohane and Nye present several models of how international regimes endure and evolve. They are dissatisfied with the pure power or structural explanations of regime formation and change. This is especially true in the management of the global economy. Military power, according to Keohane and Nye, 'provides only a small part of the explanation' (p. 47). While powerful states will make the rules, a richer understanding of international regimes demands analysis of the issues at hand. To navigate a world characterized by complex interdependence, they develop a model of 'issue structuralism' where no clear issue hierarchy exists and traditional power relationships may not determine outcomes. As a result, both regime effectiveness and distributions of power tend to vary across issues. The oil resource issue and the power wielded by OPEC clearly informed this model. Keohane and Nye never argue that the distribution of power is unimportant to international regimes. They do, however, argue that military power grows less important with the passage of time and increasing interdependence: 'Regimes are established and organized in conformity with distributions of capabilities, but subsequently the relevant networks, norms, and institutions will themselves influence actors' abilities to use these capabilities' (p. 55). In the end, their discussion of international regimes is a perfect reflection of the book's title. While *power* remains an important factor in establishing and maintaining regimes, it must be complemented with an appreciation for the variety of issues facing states in a world of *interdependence*.

Case studies: democracies in an interdependent world

To further demonstrate how power and interdependence shape world politics, Keohane and Nye turn to a series of case studies. They begin their first case studies with broad historical overviews of international regimes in money and oceans. Their discussion of the monetary regimes from 1920 though the early 1970s will be familiar to most students of IR. They chart the decline of international trade during the interwar period owing to the absence of any international regime and the absence of a hegemonic power willing to lead. Then they turn to US efforts to sustain trade in the postwar period. For a book published in 1977, Keohane and Nye provide an excellent treatment of the demise of the Bretton Woods system and international efforts to forge a new regime based on flexible exchange rates and special drawing rights. Their discussions of the international regime(s) involving the oceans are more wide-ranging. Ocean issues range from the largely successful efforts to manage the problem of piracy to the unsuccessful efforts to establish an international regime to regulate the extraction of natural resources from the seabed. In some ways the two issue areas that they selected are not congruent and are therefore difficult to compare. For instance, the monetary issue that revolves around stable exchange rates and free trade is a positive-sum game where coordination and cooperation will benefit all parties (i.e. provide a public good), according to the economic logic of free trade. Issues involving extraction of seabed resources, on the other hand, can be viewed as largely a zero-sum game where resources are finite and their extraction by one state leaves less for another. This may explain in part why the international regime regarding monetary issues is relatively strong. Any regimes involving Law of the Sea and other ocean management issues, on the other hand, have met with considerably less success than monetary issues.

After tracing out how these issues have evolved since World War I, Keohane and Nye demonstrate how under conditions of complex interdependence realist models provide poor explanations. They chronicle the importance of domestic political coalitions along with transnational elite networks working along multiple and layered channels. In the absence of a hierarchy of issues, military force has limited utility. Given the case selection, these findings are not completely unexpected.

Keohane and Nye broaden their empirical analysis by turning to cases of bilateral relationships. They begin by exploring the past 50 years of Canadian–US relations. This is followed by an examination of Australian-US relations. Keohane and Nye consciously adopt a series of cases that 'seemed most likely to fit the three ideal conditions of complex interdependence' (p. 165). These cases possess varying and layered channels connecting actors, the absence of issue hierarchy and a low salience of military force. Their case selection reflects a certain methodological savvy. They note that they 'have chosen two cases that differ in their approximation of complex interdependence while being similar in other ways'. While both are English-speaking, former British colonies with similar forms of government, the 'Australian case is much further than the Canadian case from complex interdependence' (p. 166). Once again, the evidence drawn from their case studies fall into the category of 'most likely' and tend to support the expectations of complex interdependence.

Keohane and Nye wrote *PI* in an era during which the logic of case selection was hardly discussed. Their cases – composed entirely of liberal, democratic states – are poor reflections of international politics generally.[11] By concentrating on the behaviours of liberal democracies and ignoring authoritarian regimes (which composed a slight majority of regimes at the time of writing), their empirical purview comprises only a subset of international relations. Keohane and Nye repeatedly acknowledge this point and admit that 'the case studies are not representative of all of world politics' (p. 60). However, they fail to justify their exclusive focus on relations between democratic states. They never address why and how the forces wrought by complex interdependence might be uniquely appropriate for liberal, democratic states. This is part and parcel of Keohane and Nye's reluctance to develop the obvious connections between their work and the liberal tradition in the study of IR. While their case studies reflect a clear liberal bias (i.e. consisting exclusively of behaviours of liberal, democratic states), they never address the obvious connections between their ideas and the well-established claims of liberal international theory.

Liberal internationalism from a safe distance

From a broad theoretical perspective, *PI* is a work seeped in the tradition of liberal internationalism. Keohane and Nye's assumptions as well as their empirical claims can be traced back to the thought of early Enlightenment liberals like Thomas Paine and Immanuel Kant. One of the staples of early liberal thought, as reflected in Chapter 2 on Norman Angell, is how trade will foster understandings and interdependence. This, in turn, will encourage peaceful relations between trading states. In *Perpetual Peace,* Kant argued that international trade 'cannot exist side by side with war'. Owing to a 'mutual self-interest' created by trade, 'states find themselves compelled to promote the noble cause of peace, though not exactly from motives of morality, and wherever in the world there is a threat of war breaking out, they [trading states] will try to prevent it by mediation'.[12] For Kant, the state is the central actor in the relationship between trade and peace. Paine offers a similar vision but one where interdependence has more multilayered channels connecting individuals, societies and states. In *Rights of Man,* published four years prior to *Perpetual Peace,* Paine argued that international trade creates a 'pacific system, operating to cordialize mankind, by rendering nations, as well as individuals, useful to each other … If commerce were permitted to act to the universal extent it is capable, it would extirpate the system of war.'[13] Paine also associated the expansion of trade to the decreasing utility of military force: 'The idea of conquering countries, like the Greeks and Romans, does not now exist; and experience has exploded the notion of going to war for the sake of profit.'[14] While written nearly 200 years prior to *PI,* these early liberal views align neatly with those of Keohane and Nye. Collectively, they compose the foundational principles of the liberal internationalist vision that reaches back to the Enlightenment.

Surprisingly, Keohane and Nye do not explore many of the linkages between complex interdependence and liberal internationalism. Instead, they make a sustained effort to develop 'potentially complementary models' to political realism (p. 4). In their Afterword, published with the second edition in 1989, they confess that 'Liberalism as a traditional theory escaped mention entirely' despite the fact that the 'concept of complex interdependence is clearly liberal'. Then they highlight how they sought to link 'realist and neorealist to liberal concerns with interdependence' (pp. 247–48, 254). Their effort to link *PI* to neorealism, in their 1989 Afterword, is perhaps the most surprising feature to the contemporary reader. This is most apparent when they reflect upon the influence that their ideas have had on the field. Keohane and Nye find it ironic that 'the result of our synthetic analysis in *Power and Independence,* and of subsequent work such as Keohane's *After Hegemony,* has been to broaden neorealism and provide it with new concepts rather than to articulate a coherent alternative theoretical framework for the study of world politics' (p. 251). Much of this 'alternative theoretical framework' already existed in various strains of liberal internationalism that pass through the work of Angell (see Chapter 2) and Mitrany (see Chapter 6) and back to Paine and Kant. Keohane and Nye failed to relate well-established liberal international themes to their discussions of complex interdependence.

We might speculate why liberal internationalism escaped mention in *PI.* Given the dominance of realism in the 1970s, the decision to distance their ideas from liberal internationalism may have been strategic. Any direct assault on traditional *realpolitik* or the realist paradigm may have led to a quick dismissal of their ideas.[15] Every liberal critic of realism faced this possibility. When Norman Angell was writing his liberal manifesto *The Grand Illusion,* the topic of Chapter 2 in this book, he was warned by friends to give up this sort of frontal attack on *realpolitik* lest he become 'classed with cranks and faddists, with devotees of Higher Thought who go about in sandals and long beards, live on nuts'.[16] In a field dominated by political realism, as IR was in the

1970s, there were few fates worse than being associated with the likes of Norman Angell and Lord Cecil – two of the favourite liberal whipping boys to E. H. Carr, Hans J. Morgenthau and other leading realists. The taint of idealism, as noted above, could prove ruinous. Keohane and Nye may have been understandably cautious about tempering their critique of realism. Yet, this measured and accommodating approach to realism provides both strength and weakness to the work. While it successfully avoids any quick dismissal by realists by not launching so-called paradigm wars, which are rarely fruitful in IR, the work never established some of its obvious connections to the liberal internationalist tradition in IR.

Turning to a counterfactual view, had Keohane and Nye integrated *PI* with classical liberal internationalism, the book would have been strengthened on several fronts. First, the causal processes of how complex interdependence might foster peaceful relations and change the nature of global politics are underdeveloped. Does peace-through-interdependence result from the efforts of states, as Kant imagined? Or does it result from the multilayered societal exchanges and learning as Paine theorized? While Keohane and Nye would probably argue that both sets of processes are important, greater attention to theories of liberal internationalism would have placed the possible causal processes in a clearer light. Second, more sustained attention to liberal internationalist theory would have forced some discussion of the role of democratic governance – which stands as the pillar of liberal internationalism. With their intensive case studies on Australia, Canada and the USA, Keohane and Nye's ideal examples of complex interdependence all involve democratic states. Yet they never broach the question of whether democratic rule is a necessary condition to their theoretical expectations. Third, their efforts to complement realism rather than to challenge it obscured some of the obvious disagreements between liberals and realists on questions of trade, peace and interdependence. Political realists have long been critical of any association between trade and peace. For Morgenthau, 'free trade became the shibboleth of liberalism'. Morgenthau concluded that the growing importance of economics and trade in world politics does not maintain peace but 'is a source of conflict and war'.[17] In a chapter written in 1970 and aptly entitled 'The Myth of National Interdependence', Kenneth Waltz challenged the liberal enthusiasm for trade and cooperation. Trade might actually contribute to conflict by intensifying interactions. In *Theory of International Politics,* addressed in Chapter 16 of this volume, Waltz concluded rather pointedly that 'the myth of interdependence both obscures the realities of international politics and asserts a false belief about the conditions that promote peace'.[18] In their Afterword, published after Waltz's seminal work, Keohane and Nye still evade these clear disagreements between their theoretical claims and those made by many realists. Had Keohane and Nye integrated *PI* with a broader liberal internationalism, its departure from realism would have been better appreciated and a clearer test between realist expectations and liberal expectations could have been evaluated.

Conclusion

Despite this requisite and speculative quibbling, *PI* stands as a true classic by virtue of its influence and legacy in the study of IR. While *PI* certainly revived many neglected aspects of liberal internationalism, it is difficult to label this as an exclusively liberal work. As the title suggests, realist elements of power must be examined with liberal elements of interdependence. In their Afterword, Keohane and Nye reflect on how *PI* 'consistently asks, without dogmatic presuppositions, *under what conditions* liberal or realist theories will provide more accurate accounts of world political reality' (p. 252, emphasis in the original). In the end, this work provided IR with a new research programme and new concepts which political realism had long ignored. Each of the authors went on individually to develop ideas first put forth in *PI.* From their discussions of power, Nye developed the concept of soft power more fully in *Bound to Lead,* published in 1990. As opposed to material capabilities, soft power rests on 'the attraction of one's ideas or on the ability to set the political agenda in a way that shapes the preferences that others express'.[19] The origins of soft power, a concept now ingrained in the discourse of IR, can be clearly discerned in *PI.* Keohane followed up their seminal ideas of international regimes in his masterful book, *After Hegemony,* published in 1984.[20] This work could also merit inclusion as a classic of IR. Keohane and Nye's discussion of global governance working along informal and interdependent networks sparked a generation of research on the topic, most notably Anne-Marie Slaughter's extensive study demonstrating how transnational networks shape global politics across a variety of issues.[21] Their focus on how trade and interdependence can transform relations between states remains prominent in the liberal research programme. Recent works by Michael Mousseau and Erik Gartzke provide systemic evidence that supports the expectations of Keohane and Nye. Trade, as liberals have long predicted, is strongly associated with peace, which Gartzke refers to as the Capitalist Peace.[22] Both Mousseau and Gartzke argue that the complex networks created by trade may be a more powerful explanation for the liberal peace than democratic governance. This claim, like many others in *PI,* will continue to be evaluated by students of IR. Finally, Keohane and Nye's influence on broad studies of interdependence and globalization would be impossible to summarize. However, few would challenge the claim that Keohane and Nye's work was at the forefront. In the end, this work stands as one of the earliest and most sustained efforts to address how multifaceted concepts like globalization and interdependence are changing the nature of world politics. These efforts will continue to shape the discipline and they are far more advanced due to the contribution of Keohane and Nye's seminal study, *PI.*

Notes

1 I would like to thank Robert O. Keohane and Jonathan M. DiCiccio for helpful and insightful comments about an earlier draft of this chapter.
2 Robert O. Keohane and Joseph S. Nye, *Power and Interdependence* (2nd edn), Glenview, IL: Scott, Foresman and Co, 1989. All page numbers placed in parentheses in this review refer to the second edition, which contains all of the original 1977 text but also presents two new concluding chapters; an Afterword in which Keohane and Nye respond directly to several critics of the first edition and a short chapter on international regimes entitled 'Two Cheers for Multilateralism'. With these two exceptions, the first and second editions are identical.
3 Kal Holsti, 'A New International Politics? Diplomacy in Complex Interdependence', *International Organization,* 1978, vol. 32, 513–30, at p. 524.
4 Stanley Michalak, 'Theoretical Perspectives for Understanding International Interdependence', *World Politics,* 1979, vol. 32, 136–50, at p. 136.
5 Richard Jordan, Daniel Maliniak, Amy Oakes, Susan Peterson and Michael Tierney, 'One Discipline or Many? TRIP Survey of International Relations Faculty in Ten Countries', Teaching, Research, and International Policy (TRIP) Project, The Institute for the Theory and Practice of International Relations, The College of William and Mary, Williamsburg, VA, February 2009, p. 43.

6 William Scheuerman, *Hans Morgenthau: Realism and Beyond*, Cambridge: Polity Press, 2009, p. 102.

7 John Vasquez, in *The Power of Power Politics*, New Brunswick, NJ: Rutgers University Press, 1983, showed how realism dominated up until the 1970s. For an updated analysis of realism's hold on the field of IR, see Thomas Walker and Jeffrey Morton 'Re-Assessing the "Power of Power Politics" Thesis: Is Realism still Dominant?', *International Studies Review*, 2005, vol. 7, 341–56. Walker and Morton show a decline in realist influence, especially in the 1990s.

8 Stephan Haggard and Beth Simmons, 'Theories of International Regimes', *International Organization*, 1987, vol. 41, 491–517, at p. 491.

9 Stephen Krasner, 'Structural Causes and Regime Consequences: Regimes as Intervening Variables', *International Organization,* 1982, vol. 36, 185–205.

10 While Keohane and Nye did not coin the phrase 'international regime', they did popularize it. In the Afterword to the second edition, Keohane and Nye acknowledge their debt to John Ruggie's earlier work published in 1975 (p. 250). See John Ruggie, 'International Responses to Technology: Concepts and Trends', *International Organization*, 1975, vol. 29, 557–83.

11 For recent discussions of the logic of case selection, see Gary King, Robert Keohane and Sidney Verba, *Designing Social Inquiry: Scientific Inference in Qualitative Research*, Princeton, NJ: Princeton University Press, 1994, and Alexander George and Andrew Bennett, *Case Studies and Theory Development in the Social Sciences*, Cambridge, MA: MIT Press, 2005.

12 Immanuel Kant, 'Perpetual Peace: A Philosophical Sketch', in Hans Reiss (ed.), *Kant's Political Writings*, Cambridge: Cambridge University Press, 1970, p. 114.

13 Thomas Paine, *Rights of Man*, Baltimore, MD: Penguin Books, 1969 [1791–92], p. 234.

14 Thomas Paine, 'Letter to the Abbé Raynal', in Daniel E. Wheeler (ed.), *Life and Writings of Thomas Paine*, New York: Vincent Park and Company, [1782] 1908, p. 240. For a more thorough overview of Paine and Kant in IR, see Thomas C. Walker, 'Two Faces of Liberalism: Kant, Paine, and the Question of Intervention', *International Studies Quarterly,* 2008, vol. 52, 444–68.

15 For a discussion of how challenges to the dominant paradigm are often dismissed in IR, see Thomas C. Walker, 'The Perils of Paradigm Mentalities: Revisiting Kuhn, Lakatos, and Popper', *Perspectives on Politics*, 2010, vol. 8, 433–51.

16 Cited in John Mueller, *Retreat from Doomsday: The Obsolescence of Major War*, New York: Basic Books, 1989, p. 30.

17 Hans Morgenthau, *Scientific Man vs. Power Politics*, Chicago, IL: University of Chicago Press, 1946, p. 81; p. 86.

18 Kenneth Waltz, 'The Myth of National Interdependence', in Charles Kindleberger (ed.), *The Multinational Corporation*, Cambridge, MA: MIT Press, 1970; and Kenneth Waltz, *Theory of International Politics,* New York: Random House, 1979, p. 158.

19 Joseph S. Nye, *Bound to Lead: The Changing Nature of American Power*, New York: Basic Books, 1990.

20 Robert O. Koehane, *After Hegemony: Cooperation and Discord in the World Political Economy,* Princeton, NJ: Princeton University Press, 1984.

21 Anne-Marie Slaughter, *A New World Order,* Princeton, NJ: Princeton University Press, 2004.

22 Michael Mousseau, 'The Social Market Roots of Democratic Peace', *International Security,* vol. 33, 52–86; and Erik Gartzke, 'The Capitalist Peace', *American Journal of Political Science*, 2007, vol. 51, 166–91.

16 The politics of international theory: reading Waltz 1979 as a classic

Anders Wivel[1]

No book on international relations has generated more debate over the past three decades than Kenneth Waltz's *Theory of International Politics* (hereafter *TIP*) published in 1979.[2] Today, the book is widely regarded as a modern classic.[3] It continues to be extensively cited in the study of international relations by admirers as well as critics, and few university students would be able to take an introductory course on international relations without becoming acquainted with Kenneth Waltz's so-called neorealist – or structural realist – theory, although many will only learn about the theory from textbooks, often written by authors critical of Waltz's theory, and only a small minority will read the book cover-to-cover.

TIP leaves us with no testable hypotheses about the nature or processes of international relations. Its methodological assumptions are complex, at times foggy, and its sparse and minimalist framework has been proven partly irrelevant and partly wrong, even by scholars taking their point of departure in realist assumptions. Yet the book has had an enormous impact on thinking about international relations, and it continues to be an indispensable starting point for anyone wishing to discuss, develop or apply a realist perspective on international relations.

Despite its continued importance to the study of international relations, the position of Waltz's structural realist theory within the discipline of International Relations (IR) is changing. Neorealism no longer plays a central role in the debates regarding how to explain and understand international relations or what the discipline of IR is or ought to be.[4] One would be hard pressed to find a recent article in any one of the top ten journals on international relations, which uses neorealism as its analytical framework. Instead 'Waltz 1979' has become a standard reference in modern realism, rather like 'Carr 1939', 'Morgenthau 1948' – or 'Waltz 1959': everybody knows it, few have read it, and virtually no one uses it as point of departure for analysing international relations.

In 1979, following a decade of political, normative and academic obscurity, *TIP* marked the cool, calm and collected return of realism to the centre stage, in both practical-political and scholarly debates about international relations. During the next two decades neorealism played a major role in debates about how to explain and understand international relations[5] before being edged out by a new generation of 'post-neorealist' realists.[6] The result for neorealism was, however, not marginalization but canonization. Attacks became fewer and further between and celebrations of the contribution made by Waltz are now the order of the day.[7] *TIP* has become a classic.

How to write an IR classic (Don't worry, it's easy)

What does it take to write an IR classic? Using neorealism as a prism, it is possible to identify five rules.

1. Ask big questions of both academic and real-world importance

Neorealism seeks to explain the occurrence of war, not the outbreak of any particular war.[8] This is a genuine puzzle: why do wars occur? Throughout history there has been a sustained effort among policy-makers and populations to avoid or at least limit the occurrence of wars. For political elites and populations all around the globe, answering this question could help to prevent immense human suffering and huge material costs. For IR scholars, explaining war constitutes the primary *raison d'être* of their academic discipline. It is no coincidence that the world's first Department of International Politics was founded in Aberystwyth, UK, just after the end of the World War I in 1919, and that its chair was named after US President Woodrow Wilson, who only a year earlier had made his famous 'Fourteen Points' speech outlining his vision for a peaceful world order.

2. Stay focused and stick to your stump speech

One of the most important reasons for the success of *TIP* is that Waltz has a simple message, and that he is determined to get it across. The basic logic of the theory is simple and easy to understand: the international system is anarchic, i.e. in contrast to domestic society the international system is characterized by the lack of monopoly on the legitimate use of force (pp. 103–04). Thus, 'in anarchy there is no overarching authority to prevent others from using violence, or the threat of violence, to dominate or even to destroy them'.[9] For this reason, '[t]he international imperative is "take care of yourself"!' (p. 107). States take care of themselves by seeking to provide for their own security. Thus, the primary goal of states in anarchy is to survive. Waltz acknowledges that this is a 'radical simplification' and that '[b]eyond the survival motive, the aims of states may be endlessly varied', but he maintains that assuming that states seek primarily to survive is a useful assumption, because '[s]urvival is a prerequisite to achieving any goals that states may have, other than promoting their own disappearance as political entities' (pp. 91–92). This view of international politics has two specific consequences for state behaviour. First, states are 'like units' in the sense that they are autonomous political units performing the same basic functions such as defence, judicial tasks, policing, monetary policy, etc. (pp. 95–97). Few states dare to outsource these core functions to other states, because they fear that this will create dependency. Even when cooperating on other issues each state tends to focus on relative gains, because in anarchy a disproportionate gain by a cooperation partner may be used to threaten or destroy the state (p. 105). Thus, cooperation is difficult unless special provisions are made in order to compensate those states that are disadvantaged, and unless rules are made in order to allow for renegotiation of international treaties.[10] Second, states tend to balance power, either by internal means, i.e. armament, or by external means, i.e. alliances (pp. 117–21). The most important threat to state survival in anarchy is the power of other states, and therefore states must constantly strive to prevent others from achieving a dominant position. Since the publication of *TIP*, Waltz has stayed on course defending these points, both when debating his own work with critics,[11] and when analysing the international system in the aftermath of the Cold War.[12]

3. Challenge the orthodoxy, politically and academically, but stay safely within the dominant discourse

Almost by definition, realism is 'a hard sell' in liberal societies, because of its claim that the struggle for power, not ideological differences or ethical considerations, is at the heart of all international relations, even for liberal democracies.[13] Moreover, realism advances a pessimistic, almost fatalistic, view of international relations, which contrasts with the expectation of both the electorate and political elites in modern societies that the primary task of politicians is to solve problems and actively face the challenges that confront the societies they govern. Kenneth Waltz is often applauded for his thought-provoking ideas that go against the political and academic grain,[14] and there is definitely some truth in this. Waltz has argued that the spread of nuclear weapons may enhance peace, because the destructive power of these weapons will create an incentive to avoid military conflict,[15] that the USA is no different from other great powers and that ideas matter little to its foreign policy,[16] and that terrorism has left the basic characteristics of international relations virtually untouched, because it does not threaten state survival.[17] However, compared to post-World War II realists, such as Hans J. Morgenthau and Reinhold Niebuhr, who took their point of departure in a distinctively conservative and European conception of man and a traditionalist view of social science, Waltz represents a realist perspective that is much more synchronized with both political and academic discourse in the USA. Politically, *TIP* refrains from explicating a particular view of man, leaving it philosophically antiseptic and compatible with US liberalism.[18] Academically, Waltz clearly distinguishes his own neorealist 'theory' from realist 'thought',[19] thereby signalling that his own work – in contrast to the work of past realists – meets the contemporary standards of philosophy of science (p. 1).[20] Acting as an agent provocateur within the discourse, rather than challenging the discourse in itself, is not necessarily a bad idea. Part of the secret to *TIP*'s success is that Waltz has managed to keep his provocations within the political and academic mainstream.

4. Provide only general answers

The devil is in the detail. Avoid the devil. According to Waltz, international structure does not determine state behaviour, but '[s]tructures shape and shove'[21] 'by rewarding some types of behaviour and punishing others'.[22] For this reason, neorealism is a theory of consistency and continuity. 'A constancy of structure explains the recurrent patterns and features of international-political life' (p. 70), and for this reason, neorealism 'deals in regularities and repetitions'.[23] In sum, it is a theory of constraints[24] that does not explain 'why state X made a certain move last Tuesday' (p. 122), but simply aims to tell us a few big and important things about international relations. This position allows Waltz to discuss the big and enduring questions about international relations, but without ever exposing his own theory to falsification. In fact, this was one of the major points of criticism raised by Robert Keohane in the scholarly debate following the publication of *TIP*: 'realism does not provide a satisfactory theory of world politics, if we require of an adequate theory that it provides a set of plausible and testable answers to questions of state behaviour under specified conditions'.[25] The general nature of the theory means that we can never falsify neorealism. The theory is a rather blunt instrument if we are to understand or explain the complexities of world politics or the foreign policy of individual countries. Still, this should not detract from the heuristic value of the theory. By radically simplifying the complexity of international relations into a few abstract assumptions, neorealism helps us to understand some of its basic dynamics.

5. *Float like a butterfly, sting like a bee*

In academic debates – as in boxing – you need to be light on your feet and strong in your punch. After initially outlining his understanding of theory (Chapter 1), Waltz devotes three chapters of *TIP* (Chapters 2, 3 and 4) to mapping the efforts to create a theory of international politics thus far and to explain why they failed. Next, Waltz outlines his own theory and its implications for how we understand international relations and explains why it is the only genuine theory of international politics (Chapters 5 to 9). By following this procedure, Waltz engages in a discussion with some of the most prominent scholars at the time of the publication of the book. Additionally, it allows him to map the discipline of international relations and to assess its blind spots, and thereby position his own theory as a solution to the problems identified in the existing literature. Thus, Waltz is strong in his punch both when identifying the limitations of other approaches and the contribution of his own work. However, he is much more evasive during the subsequent discussions of his neorealist theory, when he seems mainly to defend and repeat his initial positions.[26] As noted by one sympathetic critic discussing the lack of bold hypotheses in *TIP*, 'Waltz seems preoccupied with building grand fortifications in its defence, rather than exposing it to constant danger'.[27]

How to succeed as an IR classic (unfortunately this is partly out of your control)

The style and content of a theory do not alone make it a classic. As the title of the book signals, *TIP* does not offer a specific analysis of the Cold War, but a general theory of international relations. However, the political and academic context of the book has been important to its success. Kenneth Waltz published *TIP* in the context of superpower rivalry between the USA and the Soviet Union, and the major assumptions, conclusions and debates of the book appear to be coloured by the experience of the Cold War.

Two arguments, in particular, spoke to a Cold War audience. First, Waltz made a clear distinction between bipolar systems – international systems with only two superpowers – and multipolar systems – international systems with more than two great powers. He argued that bipolar systems were the more stable of the two, because shifting alliances had little impact on the balance of power in a bipolar system, owing to the overwhelming relative power of the two superpowers (p. 170–76). Still, war between the superpowers was not ruled out, because of the risk of overreaction. For many observers this analysis had direct relevance for understanding the Cold War between the USA and the Soviet Union. In particular, the end of détente and the beginning of the Second Cold War at the time of the publication of *TIP* provided a fertile ground for a theory focusing on superpower rivalry and its consequences for international security. Second, Waltz argued that the destructive power of nuclear weapons could help keep wars 'cold'. Thus, while the anarchic structure of the international system created an ever-present risk of conflict, nuclear weapons helped to reduce this risk by raising the cost of conflict between nuclear powers (p. 188).[28] At the same time, nuclear weapons reinforced bipolarity by raising the threshold for great power status, because of the technological and economic costs associated with becoming a nuclear power (pp. 180–83).

In addition, the claims made in *TIP* played a central role in two of the most important scholarly debates on international relations in the late 1980s and early 1990s. Neorealists and neoliberal institutionalists debated the consequences of international anarchy.[29] Proponents of the two perspectives agreed that states were the primary actors in international relations, first and foremost in pursuing their own interests. However, neoliberals found that actors with common interests would aim to maximize absolute gains; not relative gains as argued by the neorealists.

In a second debate, critical theorists, constructivists, and poststructuralists – sometimes grouped together under the heading 'postmodern' approaches by realists[30] – attacked neorealists for being the primary exponents of a 'backward discipline' more generally,[31] and an outdated and highly problematic conception of security more specifically, because of the neorealist focus on the military security of states.

None of the combatants in these debates were able to declare victory. The neorealism versus neoliberalism debate resulted in a rationalist research programme on international institutions learning from both approaches. The neorealism versus postmodernism debate seemed at first to mainly galvanize the positions of both camps. However, it also spurred a growing realist *and* postmodernist interest in classical realism and how it compares with neorealism.

The logic(s) of anarchy: polarity and history in a neorealist world

The anarchic structure of the international system creates a strong incentive for self-help behaviour characterized by relative gains seeking (in order to avoid power deficits vis-à-vis other states) and power balancing (in order to avoid domination by the strongest state in the system) thereby maximizing the chance of survival. However, according to neorealism '[a]narchy is what polarity makes of it'[32] in the sense that the relative distribution of capabilities in the system (measured as the number of systemic great powers, i.e. polarity) conditions the likelihood of balancing, and therefore also the likelihood of war. For this reason, *TIP* is concerned with the determinants of polarity as well as the consequences of particular polarities. Pole status depends on 'combined capabilities', i.e. 'how [potential pole states] score on *all* of the following items: size of population and territory, resource endowment, economic capability, military strength, political stability and competence' (p. 131). Using these criteria enables us to distinguish between multipolar systems – unstable because of shifting alliances and the omnipresent danger of miscalculation among the many actors, and bipolar systems – stable because the overwhelming power of only two actors makes shifting alliances insignificant for the balance of power (but at the same time susceptible to overreaction by the two superpowers following each other's every move).

However, looking at the international system since 1991, the most important category seems to be missing. The current international system is neither bipolar, nor multipolar, but unequivocally unipolar when measured by Waltzian standards.[33] This has important consequences for neorealist balance of power logic. According to *TIP*, '[b]alance of power politics prevail wherever two, and only two, requirements are met: that the order be anarchic and that it be populated by units wishing to survive' (p. 121), but as noted by Wohlforth '[i]n any system there is a threshold concentration of power in the strongest state that makes a counterbalance prohibitively costly. This is what it means to call a system "unipolar"'.[34] Thus, whereas the logic of anarchy creates strong incentives to balance, the logic of unipolarity has the opposite effect. This leaves contemporary realists retaining Waltz's focus on the nature and consequences of international structure with a need to discuss and conceptualize unipolarity and its consequences for international relations. The general dynamics of international anarchy identified in *TIP* remain the starting point for these discussions, but their main concern is the re-conceptualization of balancing under unipolarity, typically in the form of so-called soft balancing defined as 'coalition building and diplomatic bargaining within international institutions, short of formal bilateral and multilateral military alliances'.[35]

Current unipolarity may not be the only historical anomaly challenging neorealist logic. *TIP* is based on a particular reading of history positing that '[t]he texture of international politics remains highly constant, patterns recur, and events repeat themselves endlessly' (p. 66). Diplomatic historians and IR scholars have challenged this reading by pointing to the multiple anomalies from neorealist expectations present in international history.[36] This does not necessarily undermine the logic of the theory, but it does challenge Waltz's claim that he has constructed a theory that is universally applicable across time and space.

New ideas Waltz in: neoclassical realism and the study of foreign policy

Waltz's insistence that *TIP* is strictly a theory of international politics, not foreign policy (p. 122),[37] has spurred an interest in how to combine Waltz's assumptions on international structure with explanatory variables such as domestic politics and the perceptions and intentions of leaders. Today the realist perspective on international relations is highly influenced by so-called neoclassical realists, who attempt 'to combine structural factors with domestic politics in order to explain foreign policy'.[38] Neoclassical realists open the 'black box' of the state and thereby return to a richer and more inclusive understanding of realism found in earlier formulations of the perspective. This development is not necessarily a contrast or challenge to neorealist theory,[39] but it does accentuate the need to explicate how neorealism may contribute to our understanding of foreign policy.

How may *TIP* contribute to realist theorizing on foreign policy? Neorealism tells us little about foreign policy per se but focuses instead on explaining 'international outcomes – phenomena that result from the interaction of two or more actors in the international system [such as] international cooperation, arms races, crisis bargaining, aggregate alignment patterns, and the war-proneness of the international system'.[40] The theory tells us about structural pressure, and the opportunities and limitations that follow for state action, but it tells us little about how states actually respond to these pressures (p. 73). Thus, *TIP* identifies the systemic demands on state external behaviour, but it does not tell us if and how these are met by the supply of foreign policy.

Still, foreign policy and international politics are not two distinct realms, 'since foreign policy is a constituting element *of* international politics',[41] and a structural theory is of little use if structural pressure does not affect state behaviour. Thus, it should come as no surprise that neorealism has led to hypotheses about foreign policy. For instance, the imbalance of power between the USA and its allies following the Cold War has led to hypotheses about the foreign policy of a largely unrestrained power.[42] More controversially, it may be argued that the neorealist conceptions of competition and socialization, and in particular the interaction between these processes, can lead to hypotheses about foreign policy. As noted by Waltz, 'competition spurs the actors to accommodate their ways to the socially most acceptable and successful practices. Socialization and competition are two aspects of a process by which the variety of actors is reduced' (p. 77). From this starting point, neorealism may be used to generate hypotheses about the successful adaption of democratic states to systemic constraints,[43] the decision of European states to strengthen the institutions of the European Union,[44] and which foreign policy roles will be acceptable for particular states.[45]

Alternatively, *TIP* may be used as a minimalist starting point to which we gradually add complexity. Neorealism remains the basic theory providing us with our most fundamental hypotheses (e.g. states tend to balance power in an anarchic system), but neoclassical realism is used either to explain empirical deviations from these theoretical expectations, or it serves as a specification of the unspecified neorealist explanations:[46] structures 'shape and shove',[47] but they do not explain foreign policy.[48] By constructing a theory, which acknowledges the primacy of the international system, while at the same time theorizing variations in the impact of the international systemic structure on state behaviour, i.e. the variations in 'the relative importance of systemic versus domestic and individual level variables',[49] we may be able to explain foreign policy in a way which allows us to distinguish between general and context specific variations. In accordance with neorealist logic states may be seen as the primary actors (p. 93)[50] and members of the foreign policy executive as reflecting state interests. Variations in foreign policy may stem from domestic legislatures, interest groups, societal actors as well as external pressure and the ability of foreign policy makers to obtain and process information about their external environment.[51] Starting from 'a "top-down" conception of the state, where systemic forces ultimately drive external behaviour',[52] *TIP*'s understanding of international structure may be used as a starting point when adding first and second image variables in order to explain foreign policy by gradually adding complexity to the parsimonious starting point.[53] If used in this way *TIP* may be instrumental in ameliorating an 'identity dilemma' between the equally unattractive options of either restricting relist analysis to neorealist core assumptions and ending up with indeterminate explanations, or combining structural factors with other variables and ending up with a collection of *ad hoc* arguments which are indistinct from other theoretical perspectives.[54]

The future of *TIP* and neorealism

The style and content of Waltz's theory unite to make it a powerful, if imperfect, basis for analyses of international politics and foreign policy. For this reason, *TIP* is likely to retain a strong position within the realist perspective in the years to come. In addition, there is not a great deal of competition in the market for general theories of international relations. Whereas IR scholars of the post-World War II era were generally concerned with understanding the nature of international relations in general, the discipline is becoming increasingly specialized and compartmentalized into subfields and subcultures with only a very small minority of scholars making their own attempt at a theory of international politics. At the same time the object of inquiry continues to be international relations as a whole, and this creates a desire to understand international relations as such rather than a small segment of it.[55] Thus, demand for general theories exceeds supply.

TIP remains a strong contender for meeting this demand in the future. Neoclassical realists may have overtaken its position as the coolest thing in realism, but at the same time, despite its flaws and shortcomings, Waltz's 1979 book has become a classic.

Notes

1 An earlier version of this chapter 'From Cool to Classic: Learning from Waltz (1979)' appeared in *Politik*, 2009, vol. 12, 42–47. A subsequent version of the paper benefited from presentations at the International Studies Association Catalytic Research Workshop 'Bridging the Transatlantic Divide: European and American Realism Reconsidered' in Montreal, Canada, 15 March 2011, and at an International Relations research seminar at the Department of Political Science, University of Copenhagen, Denmark, 12 April 2011. I thank all participants at these events and, in particular, Barry Buzan, Balkan Devlen, Birthe Hansen, Lene Hansen, Peter Viggo Jakobsen, Steven E. Lobell, Hans Mouritzen, Ulrik Pram Gad, Alexander Reichwein, Norrin M. Ripsman, Jeffrey W. Taliaferro and Ole Wæver.
2 Kenneth N. Waltz, *Theory of International Politics*, New York: McGraw-Hill, 1979. Page numbers placed in parentheses in the text refer to this edition.
3 Chris Brown, 'Structural Realism, Classical Realism and Human Nature', in Ken Booth (ed.), *Realism and World Politics*, London: Routledge, 2011, pp. 143–57, at p. 143; cf. Ken Booth, 'Realism Redux: Contexts, Concepts, Contents', in Booth (ed.), *Realism and World Politics*, pp. 1–14, at pp. 3–6; Randall Schweller, 'The Progressiveness of Neoclassical Realism', in Colin Elman and Miriam Fendius Elman (eds), *Progress in International Relations Theory*, Cambridge, MA: MIT Press, 2003, pp. 311–47, at p. 313; Stephen M. Walt, '"A Few Big and Important Things": The Enduring Legacy of Kenneth Waltz', *Politik*, 2005, vol. 8, 48–51.
4 Today, even realists taking their point of departure in neorealism are few and far between as exemplified by Randall Schweller's (somewhat exaggerated) claim that neoclassical realism represents the 'only game in town for the next and the current generation of realists' (Schweller, 'The Progressiveness of Neoclassical Realism', p. 345). For a notable exception to this trend, see Birthe Hansen, *Unipolarity and World Politics*, London: Routledge, 2011.
5 David A. Baldwin (ed.), *Neorealism and Neoliberalism*, New York: Columbia University Press, 1993; and Robert O. Keohane (ed.), *Neorealism and Its Critics*, New York: Columbia University Press, 1986.
6 Stephen G. Brooks, 'Dueling Realisms', *International Organization*, 1991, vol. 51, 445–77; Annette Freyberg-Inan, Ewan Harrison and Patrick James (eds), *Rethinking Realism in International Relations*, Baltimore, MD: The Johns Hopkins University Press, 2009; Steven E. Lobell, Norrin M. Ripsman and Jeffrey W. Taliaferro (eds), *Neoclassical Realism, The State, and Foreign Policy*, Cambridge: Cambridge University Press, 2009; Brian Rathbun, 'A Rose by Any Other Name: Neoclassical Realism as the Logical and Necessary Extension of Structural Realism', *Security Studies*, 2008, vol. 17, 294–321; Gideon Rose 'Neoclassical Realism and Theories of Foreign Policy', *World Politics*, 1998, vol. 51, 144–72; and Anders Wivel, 'Explaining Why State X Made a Certain Move Last Tuesday: The Promise and Limitations of Realist Foreign Policy Analysis', *Journal of International Relations and Development*, 2005, vol. 8, 355–80.
7 See e.g. the contributions to Booth (ed.), *Realism and World Politics*; and Andrew K. Hanami (ed.), *Perspectives on Structural Realism*, Basingstoke: Palgrave Macmillan, 2003.
8 Walt, '"A Few Big and Important Things"', p. 49; and Kenneth N. Waltz, 'The Origins of War in Neorealist Theory', in Robert I. Rotberg and Theodore K. Rabb (eds), *The Origin and Prevention of Major Wars*, Cambridge: Cambridge University Press, 1988, pp. 39–52.
9 Joseph M. Grieco, *Cooperation among Nations*, Ithaca, NY: Cornell University Press, 1990, p. 38.
10 Cf. Grieco, *Cooperation among Nations*.

11 Kenneth N. Waltz, 'Reflections on Theory of International Politics: A Response to My Critics', in Robert O. Keohane (ed.), *Neorealism and Its Critics*, pp. 322–45; and Kenneth N. Waltz, 'Evaluating Theories', *The American Political Science Review*, 1997, vol. 91, 913–17.
12 See e.g. Kenneth N. Waltz, 'The Emerging Structure of International Politics', *International Security*, 1993, vol. 18, 44–79; Kenneth N. Waltz, 'Structural Realism after the Cold War', *International Security,* 2000, vol. 25, 5–41; and Kenneth N. Waltz 'The Continuity of International Politics', in Ken Booth and Tim Dunne (eds), *World in Collision*, New York: Palgrave Macmillan, 2002, pp. 348–53.
13 John Mearsheimer, *The Tragedy of Great Power Politics*, New York: Norton, 2001, pp. 22–27.
14 Hans Mouritzen, 'Kenneth Waltz: A Critical Rationalist between International Politics and Foreign Policy', in Iver B. Neumann and Ole Wæver (eds), *The Future of International Relations*, London: Routledge, 1997, pp. 66–89; Booth, 'Realism Redux'; and Walt, '"A Few Big and Important Things"'.
15 Kenneth N. Waltz, 'The Spread of Nuclear Weapons: More May Be Better?', *Adelphi Papers*, 171, London: International Institute for Strategic Studies, 1981.
16 Kenneth N. Waltz, 'America as a Model for the World? A Foreign Policy Perspective', *PS: Political Science and Politics*, 1991, vol. 24, 667–70.
17 Waltz, 'The Continuity of International Politics'.
18 Keith L. Shimko, 'Realism, Neorealism and American Liberalism', *The Review of Politics*, 1992, vol. 54, 281–301, at p. 299.
19 Kenneth N. Waltz, 'Realist Thought and Neorealist Theory', *Journal of International Affairs*, 1990, vol. 44, 21–37.
20 In contrast, Ole Wæver argues that Waltz's view of theory contrasts with the mainstream view, but that few have noticed, see Ole Wæver, 'Waltz's Theory of Theory: The Pictorial Challenge to Mainstream IR', in Booth, *Realism and World Politics*, pp. 67–88.
21 Waltz, 'Reflections on Theory of International Politics', p. 343.
22 Robert Gilpin, *War and Change in World Politics*, Cambridge: Cambridge University Press, 1981, p. 85.
23 Waltz, 'The Origins of War in Neorealist Theory', p. 39.
24 Rathbun, 'A Rose by Any Other Name', p. 296.
25 Robert O. Keohane, 'Theory of World Politics: Structural Realism and Beyond', in Keohane (ed.), *Neorealism and Its Critics*, pp. 158–203, at p. 159.
26 E.g. Waltz, 'Reflections on Theory of International Politics'; and Waltz, 'Evaluating Theories'.
27 Mouritzen, 'Kenneth Waltz', p. 79.
28 Cf. also Waltz, 'The Spread of Nuclear Weapons'.
29 Cf. Baldwin, *Neorealism and Neoliberalism*.
30 Cf. John J. Mearsheimer, 'The False Promise of International Institutions', *International Security*, 1994/95, vol. 19, 5–49; and Stephen M. Walt, 'The Renaissance of Security Studies', *International Studies Quarterly*, 1991, vol. 35, 211–39.
31 Jim George, *Discourses of Global Politics: A Critical (Re)Introduction to International Relations*, Boulder, CO: Lynne Rienner, 1994.
32 Richard Little, *The Balance of Power in International Relations*, Cambridge: Cambridge University Press, 2007, p. 190.
33 Hansen, *Unipolarity and World Politics*; Kenneth Waltz and James Fearon, 'A Conversation with Kenneth Waltz', *Annual Review of Political Science*, 2012, vol. 15, 1–12, at p. 7; and William C. Wohlforth, 'The Stability of a Unipolar World', *International Security*, 1999, vol. 24, 5–41.
34 William C. Wohlforth, 'U.S. Strategy in a Unipolar World', in G. John Ikenberry (ed.), *America Unrivalled*, Ithaca, NY: Cornell University Press, 2002, pp. 98–118, at pp. 103–4.
35 T. V. Paul, 'Soft Balancing in the Age of U.S. Primacy', *International Security,* 2005, vol. 30, 46–71, at p. 58; cf. Robert Pape, 'Soft Balancing against the United States', *International Security*, 2005, vol. 30, 7–45; Birthe Hansen, Peter Toft and Anders Wivel, *Security Strategies and American World Order*, London: Routledge, 2009; T. V. Paul, James J. Wirtz and Michael Fortmann (eds), *Balance of Power: Theory and Practice in the 21st Century*, Stanford, CA: Stanford University Press, 2004; Stephen M. Walt, 'Alliances in a Unipolar World', *World Politics*, 2009, vol. 61, 86–120. For a useful overview of scholarly debates on unipolarity since the end of the Cold War, see Hansen, *Unipolarity and World Politics*, pp. 14–18.

36 Cf. e.g. Barry Buzan and Richard Little, 'Waltz and World History: The Paradox of Parsimony', in Booth (ed.), *Realism and World Politics*, pp. 288–305; John G. Ruggie, 'Continuity and Transformation in the World Polity: Towards a Neo-Realist Synthesis', *World Politics*, 1983, vol. 35, 261–85; and Ernst R. May, Richard Rosecrance and Zara Steiner (eds), *History and Neorealism*, Cambridge: Cambridge University Press, 2010.
37 Cf. also Kenneth N. Waltz, 'International Politics is Not Foreign Policy', *Security Studies*, 1996, vol. 6, 54–57.
38 Wivel, 'Explaining Why State X Made a Certain Move Last Tuesday', p. 360.
39 Schweller, 'The Progressiveness of Neoclassical Realism'; and Rathbun, 'A Rose by Any Other Name'.
40 Jeffrey W. Taliaferro, 'Security Seeking under Anarchy: Defensive Realism Revisited', *International Security*, 2001, vol. 25, 128–61, at p. 133.
41 Hans Mouritzen, 'Past versus Present Geopolitics: Cautiously Opening the Realist Door to the Past', in Freyberg-Inan, Harrison and James (eds), *Rethinking Realism in International Relations*, p. 165. Cf. Colin Elman, 'Horses for Courses: Why *Not* Neorealist Theories of Foreign Policy?', *Security Studies*, 1996, vol. 6, 7–53; Jennifer Sterling-Folker, 'Realist Environment, Liberal Process, and Domestic-Level Variables', *International Studies Quarterly*, 1997, vol. 41, 1–25.
42 Stephen M. Walt, 'Alliances in a Unipolar World'; and Waltz 'America as a Model for the World?'.
43 Michael C. Williams, 'The Politics of Theory: Waltz, Realism and Democracy', in Booth (ed.), *Realism and World Politics*, pp. 50–63.
44 Anders Wivel, 'The Power Politics of Peace: Exploring the Link between Globalization and European Integration from a Realist Perspective', *Cooperation and Conflict*, 2004, vol. 39, 5–25.
45 Cameron G. Thies, 'States Socialization and Structural Realism', *Security Studies*, 2010, vol. 19, 689–717.
46 Norrin M. Ripsman, Jeffrey W. Taliaferro and Steven E. Lobell, 'Conclusion: The State of Neoclassical Realism', in Lobell, Ripsman and Taliaferro (eds), *Neoclassical Realism, the State, and Foreign Policy*, pp. 280–90, at p. 281; and cf. Schweller, 'The Progressiveness of Neoclassical Realism'.
47 Waltz, 'Reflections on Theory of International Politics', p. 343.
48 Colin Elman, 'Realist Revisionism', in Freyberg-Inan, Harrison and James (eds), *Rethinking Realism in International Relations*, pp. 63–75.
49 Ripsman, Taliaferro and Lobell, 'Conclusion: The State of Neoclassical Realism', p. 282.
50 Cf. also Kenneth N. Waltz 'Foreword', in Booth (ed.), *Realism and World Politics*, p. xv.
51 Ripsman, Taliaferro and Lobell, 'Conclusion: The State of Neoclassical Realism', pp. 280–83.
52 Jeffrey W. Taliaferro, Steven E. Lobell and Norrin M. Ripsman, 'Introduction: Neoclassical Realism, the State, and Foreign Policy', in Lobell, Ripsman and Taliaferro (eds), *Neoclassical Realism, The State, and Foreign Policy*, 1–41, at p. 25.
53 Cf. Keohane, 'Theory of World Politics: Structural Realism and Beyond', p. 188; and Schweller, 'The Progressiveness of Neoclassical Realism', p. 317. Cf. Hans Mouritzen and Anders Wivel, *Explaining Foreign Policy: International Diplomacy and the Russo-Georgian War*, Boulder, CO: Lynne Rienner, 2012.
54 Stefano Guzzini, 'The Enduring Dilemmas of Realism in International Relations', *European Journal of International Relations*, 2004, vol. 10, 533–68; cf. Jeffrey W. Legro and Andrew Moravcsik, 'Is Anybody Still a Realist?', *International Security*, 1999, vol. 24, 5–55; and John A. Vasquez, 'The Realist Paradigm and Degenerative versus Progressive Research Programs: An Appraisal of Neotraditional Research on Waltz's Balancing Proposition', *American Political Science Review*, 1997, vol. 91, 899–912.
55 Mouritzen, 'Kenneth Waltz', p. 77.

17 The cosmopolitan turn: beyond realism and statism in Charles R. Beitz's *Political Theory and International Relations*

William Smith[1]

The normative study of international relations has gone from being a marginal concern to a dynamic research agenda.[2] This agenda – often labelled 'international political theory' – focuses on 'the moral dimension of international relations and the wider question of meanings and interpretation generated by the discipline'.[3] It not only addresses the traditional issue of warfare, but also examines the full range of moral duties owed by states and individuals to each other. The rise of international political theory can be associated with a broader revival in political theory, epitomized by the publication of John Rawls's *A Theory of Justice*.[4] This work defends principles of social justice for domestic institutions that regulate social activity. The book presents only a brief argument about international relations, with Rawls apparently rejecting the application of these principles to the international realm. Its publication did, however, inspire subsequent authors to explore this issue in greater depth, prompting an explosion of interest in arguments for and against applying principles of social justice to international relations.[5]

The insight that debates about social justice are relevant to international relations is the chief intellectual legacy of the arguments presented by the US political theorist Charles R. Beitz (born 1949) in *Political Theory and International Relations* (*PTIR*).[6] The first edition of *PTIR* appeared in 1979 and a revised edition, with a new afterword that clarifies and amends the arguments, appeared in 1999. An earlier version of the book had been prepared by Beitz as a doctoral dissertation, under the supervision of Thomas Scanlon and Dennis Thompson, while studying on the political philosophy programme at Princeton University, USA.[7] It is difficult to overestimate the impact that *PTIR* had on subsequent debates in international political theory. This is due in part to the way in which the book maps the hitherto uncharted terrain of the normative literature on international relations.[8] It is also, and more importantly, owing to its substantive conclusions, particularly its extension of Rawls's theory of justice from the domestic to the global realm. Given the significant developments in the field since the initial publication of *PTIR*, its continued status as a landmark text is a testament to the originality of its claims.[9]

This chapter explores the enduring significance of *PTIR* for reflection on the normative dimensions of international relations. The organizing theme is the book's presentation of a *cosmopolitan* alternative to the realist and statist paradigms that, according to Beitz, dominate modern thinking about international morality. The central insight of realism is associated with the claim that states should pursue their national interests over and above other moral principles. The central insight of statism, or 'the morality of states', is that states should treat each other as autonomous entities with moral rights analogous to those of individuals. These perspectives are rejected in *PTIR* in favour of a cosmopolitan theory that treats the interests of individuals as prior to interests of states. This chapter explores *PTIR*'s call for a 'cosmopolitan turn' in international political thought through: (i) summarizing its central arguments; (ii) surveying prominent responses to it in the subsequent literature; and (iii) evaluating its legacy as an attempt to lay the groundwork for a cosmopolitan political theory.

The arguments: from scepticism to cosmopolitanism

The book begins with the observation that normative issues in international relations, with the exception of warfare, have not been a central concern for modern political theory. This neglect, according to Beitz, is particularly regrettable in light of the emergence of a range of problems – such as increasing interconnectivity, inequalities as well as food and energy shortages – that do not directly relate to warfare (pp. 3–4). The challenges that confront theorists attempting to address this agenda include the widespread belief that moral judgements have no place in international affairs, the lack of a rich tradition of thought in this area and the unsettled nature of moral convictions about international politics compared to intuitions about domestic problems (pp. 5–6). The aim of Beitz's enquiry is, notwithstanding these obstacles, to 'help lay the groundwork for a more satisfactory normative political theory' (p. 6).

This aim is pursued throughout the three sections of the book. The first is a critical investigation of realist scepticism about the prospects for realizing moral principles in international relations (p. 15). Beitz devotes considerable attention to reconstructing a plausible defence of realism, in order to create a clear target for his criticisms. The account of realism on which he focuses is based upon an analogy between individuals in the state of nature and states in international relations. The lack of a shared political authority is said to undermine the case in favour of acting according to moral principle in both realms, because in its absence agents cannot be sure that their moral actions will not be exploited by others (pp. 28–32). The state of nature analogy, according to Beitz, plays two roles in realism: an *explanatory* role that predicts state behaviour through reference to structural features of the global realm; and a *normative* role that prescribes state behaviour through defending the pursuit of the national interest as the overriding aim of foreign policy (p. 35). His argument challenges both of these roles. First, he argues that structural features of the global realm do not support the state of nature analogy. The analogy, in order to mirror the situation of persons in the state of nature, must presuppose that the actors in international politics are states, who enjoy relatively equal power, are independent of each other and have no reliable expectations of reciprocal compliance with norms in the absence of a coercive authority. These presuppositions cannot be supported in light of significant non-state actors in the international realm, the fact of massive power asymmetries between states, extensive interconnectivity across borders and existing mechanisms for encouraging compliance with international norms (pp. 35–50). Second, Beitz argues that the case for national interest as a basis for foreign policy cannot vindicate the wide range of actions typically defended by realists. His argument draws on a distinction between actions that aim to preserve the lives of citizens and actions that aim to preserve territorial borders, political and economic institutions and cultural traditions. The moral weight accorded to human life supports the former as a legitimate aim of foreign policy, but the latter incorporates goals that do not appear to be necessary conditions of preserving life and therefore lack the overriding importance accorded to them by realists (pp. 50–63). This argument rests on the cosmopolitan intuition, which emerges as a central theme of the book, that 'it is the rights and interests of *persons* that are of fundamental importance from the moral point of view, and it is to these considerations that justifications of principles for international relations should appeal' (p. 55).

The second section of the book examines the major alternative to realism as a framework for reflection on international norms, which Beitz characterizes as the 'morality of states' (p. 8). Once again, a considerable part of his discussion is taken up with the task of reconstructing a plausible interpretation of this framework. The morality of states, like realism, is based upon an analogy between persons and states, but its basic claim is that persons and states have comparable moral rights to treatment as autonomous agents. The autonomy of states has been presented by thinkers such as Christian Wolff and J. S. Mill as supporting derivative rights to non-intervention and self-determination (p. 68). It is worth noting at this point that Beitz favours a broad definition of intervention, which would incorporate forms of interference embracing military, diplomatic and economic. His rationale for this broad definition is to differentiate questions of definition and justification, such that different forms of intervention can be assessed on their moral merits in particular circumstances (p. 74). The morality of states, then, departs from realism by conceptualizing the international realm as being subject to moral principles, but those principles are limited to mutual recognition of states as autonomous agents. The central objection that Beitz raises against this tradition is that its analogy between states and persons cannot withstand scrutiny. The reason is that states are comprised of a plurality of individuals and are consequently not 'organic wholes with the unity and integrity of persons'. In fact, Beitz argues that 'it is because all persons should be respected as sources of ends that we should not allow all states to claim a right of autonomy' (p. 81). The right of autonomy should be conditional upon the conformity of state institutions with 'appropriate principles of domestic justice' (p. 80). It is no accident that Beitz does not specify the content of these principles, as he wants to leave open the possibility that different principles of justice might be appropriate for different societies (pp. 104–05). He does, though, suggest that, at a minimum, the appropriate principles of justice will specify certain forms of treatment that are incompatible with respect for persons as autonomous agents (p. 81). This undermines the claim that states enjoy an unrestricted right of non-intervention: 'the non-intervention principle cannot be interpreted properly without considering the justice of the institutions of the states involved in particular instances of (potential) intervention' (p. 121). It likewise suggests that the right to self-determination should be treated as a means to the promotion of just institutions, such that claims for national independence depend, at least in part, on 'the extent to which granting independence would … help to minimize injustice' (p. 102). These conclusions again recall the cosmopolitan idea that it is not the rights of states, but the interests of individuals – secured by appropriate principles of justice – that should be central to international political theory.

This intuition is brought to the fore in the third section, which offers a cosmopolitan alternative to realism and morality of states. This alternative is 'cosmopolitan' in that 'it is concerned with the moral relations of members of a universal community in which state boundaries have a merely derivative significance' (p. 182). The argument proceeds from an internal critique of Rawls' influential 'two-stage' approach to justice. The first stage involves representatives of *persons* – deliberating behind a veil of ignorance that denies them knowledge of their character, skills and attributes – selecting principles to regulate the basic structure of their self-sufficient society. These representatives select an 'equal liberties principle' that guarantees rights for all citizens, and a 'difference principle' that ensures economic inequalities operate to the greatest benefit of the least advantaged citizens in society.[10] The second stage involves representatives of self-sufficient *societies* – deliberating behind a veil of ignorance that denies them knowledge about the identity, resources and power of their society – selecting principles to regulate their mutual relations.[11] These representatives select principles that guarantee the sovereign equality of all societies but not principles that limit economic inequalities between them. Beitz challenges this approach in two ways. First, he contends that, even if societies are self-sufficient, the second stage would generate principles that limit international inequalities. This is because, behind the veil of ignorance, representatives would want to ensure that their society does not suffer as a result of the morally arbitrary distribution of global natural resources. They would thus agree to a resource redistribution principle to ensure that the wealth generated through natural resources is distributed equitably between societies (pp. 136–43). Second, he contends that we should, in any case, reject the 'two-stage' procedure on the grounds that it is implausible to treat societies as being self-sufficient. This more radical line of argument is based on Rawls's claim that the aim of justice is to regulate social cooperation that generates benefits and burdens for participants. Beitz contends that there is extensive cooperation at the global level, which should be regulated by principles of justice chosen by representatives of a global citizenry. He suggests that the global order should be regulated according to the same principles of justice that Rawls defends for the domestic level, including a global difference principle to ensure international inequalities operate to the greatest benefit of the least advantaged global citizens (pp. 143–54). The idea is that the global realm resembles domestic society to such a degree that the justification of principles of justice applies in both contexts. The upshot is that 'it is wrong to limit the application of contractarian principles of social justice to the nation-state; instead these principles ought to apply globally' (p. 128).

The reaction: realism, statehood and global justice

The arguments of *PTIR* have provoked a great deal of debate and discussion. There is widespread agreement that Beitz has established a new agenda for normative reflection on international relations.[12] There is also an appreciation of the style of *PTIR*, with Nicholas Rengger commenting that 'Beitz's book is avowedly a work in the tradition of analytical political philosophy, but it is written with a grace and a freedom from technicality which is not always observable in other examples of this genre'.[13] The substantive debate has focused upon the success of Beitz's critiques of realism and statism and, to a greater extent, the cogency of his alternative proposals for global justice.

First, let us consider the reception of Beitz's critique of realism. Although Beitz touches on several aspects of realist thought, the bulk of his discussion focuses on debunking the analogy between persons in the state of nature and states in the international realm. The force of his critique has been noted by several commentators, who commend Beitz for challenging the realist temptation to assume that the mere nonexistence of political authority in the international realm is sufficient to warrant its categorization as a state of nature.[14] The significance of this critique is all the more notable given that, as Chris Brown observes, the use of the state of nature as a means of framing the international realm is a recurring, and perhaps regrettable, motif of

International Relations scholarship.[15] Acknowledging the force of Beitz's argument, though, does not imply that we should accept his repudiation of realism. The concern, raised by Brown, is that Beitz focuses on the Hobbesian strand of realist thought at the expense of alternative and potentially more fertile strands. Brown identifies such a strand with certain ideas of Morgenthau and Niebuhr. This strand does not conceptualize states as Hobbesian rational actors, but is instead marked by 'a scepticism about the capacity of human beings to remake the world, based on both a strong sense of the existence of evil, and a feeling for the tragic aspects of the human condition'.[16] The neglect of this strand, according to Brown, stacks the deck in Beitz's favour, because realist perspectives that accept states as rational actors might, shorn of their mistaken assumptions about the state of nature, prove to be more hospitable to ambitious programmes for global reform.[17] This criticism of Beitz may be a little harsh. It is, for instance, difficult to see how he, or indeed anyone, could reconstruct and subject to critical scrutiny the kind of intuitive acceptance of evil and tragedy that Brown associates with realism. It does, though, demonstrate that there is rather more to realism than the Hobbesian themes stressed by Beitz, which in turn recommends a certain degree of caution about rejecting its sceptical counsels out of hand.[18]

The second section of *PTIR* has generated less critical discussion than either of the other two sections. This, as Beitz notes in a recent essay, is somewhat surprising, given that his critique of the morality of states is 'at least as much at odds with conventional conceptions as the distributive cosmopolitanism adduced later on'.[19] It is also surprising in light of the continued prominence of these, or similar, views in contemporary discussions.[20] A recent attempt to remedy this neglect is provided by David Miller.[21] He advances several claims, the most relevant of which relate to Beitz's argument that the autonomy of a state should be treated as conditional on the compliance of its institutions with 'appropriate principles of justice' (pp. 81ff.). The advantage of this formulation, as Miller concedes, is that it allows a degree of flexibility about the conceptions of justice that might obtain in different societies. This allows scope for societies to determine their own institutional arrangements, thus, granting moral leeway to depart from the institutions familiar to liberal societies (pp. 104–05). The disadvantage, however, is that it raises some practical difficulties about which conception of justice should apply in deliberating about the merits of various forms of intervention. It also fails to address the problem of partial compliance with appropriate principles, or to put the point another way, the extent to which societies can depart from justice without triggering possible intervention by outside agents. The worry is that, as Miller puts it, 'Beitz tries to make the idea of social justice do too much work'.[22] A more general objection, which Beitz has since acknowledged, relates to the manner in which the morality of states tradition is mapped. As Beitz observes in the Afterword to the revised edition, his account runs together a wide range of views, from 'absolutist' doctrines that admit of no limits to self-determination to more 'liberal' accounts that make state autonomy conditional upon respect for human rights or other moral principles (p. 214). This admission, if sound, has implications for the adequacy of the manner in which Beitz maps the field of competing options in international political theory (pp. 214–16). It also recalls an earlier point about his discussion of realism, in that the morality of state tradition may contain more plausible variants than the representatives that Beitz focuses on in his analysis.[23]

The third section of *PTIR* has been the most significant in terms of its impact on subsequent debates. This is because many of the arguments in favour of applying principles of justice to the global realm, particularly those that proceed from Rawls's theoretical framework, 'first see the light of day here'.[24] Although some commentators have endorsed Beitz's position, others have disputed his attempt to use Rawls's ideas as the basis for radical claims about global justice.[25] This line of attack is pursued by Brian Barry. He argues that, for Rawls, principles of justice only apply in contexts of social cooperation where two conditions are met. First, social cooperation must be a collective enterprise to provide public goods that all can enjoy or insurance schemes for mutual aid. Second, the regulation of this collective enterprise through principles of justice should be mutually beneficial to all relevant parties. Barry does not believe that either of these conditions is met in global interaction as described by Beitz. Global trade may create certain benefits for trading parties, but it is not, Barry contends, a cooperative enterprise aimed at providing public goods or mutual aid. Also the regulation of global trade according to principles of justice would not, he argues, be mutually beneficial for all parties, but would instead place significant burdens on wealthy trading partners who must bear the costs of a global difference principle with redistributive effects. It should be noted that Barry *does* accept that the global realm should be subject to principles of social justice. His complaint against Beitz is that it is not possible to defend this idea by appealing to Rawls's concept of social cooperation, because – according to a proper interpretation of that concept – it is impossible to say that cooperation of the relevant sort exists in the global realm.[26]

These debates took another turn with the publication of *The Law of Peoples*, in which Rawls offered a critical response to Beitz's cosmopolitan reading of his theory.[27] In order to appreciate this response, let us recall an important feature of Beitz's argument. Beitz supports *either* a resource redistribution principle *or* a global difference principle. The either/or formulation is important, because Beitz does not support the implementation of *both* of these principles. In fact, given his rejection of the assumption that states are self-sufficient, he believes that the case in favour of the second principle supersedes the first. He defends a resource redistribution principle in order to show that, even if we accept Rawls's implausible assumptions about self-sufficiency, we should accept some principle of global justice. In *The Law of Peoples,* Rawls rejects the case for both of Beitz's proposed principles. First, he suggests that a resource redistribution principle is inappropriate in the international realm because the argument in its favour misdiagnoses the causes of national wealth. Rawls argues that the source of a nation's wealth derives not from its holdings of natural resources but from its domestic institutions and cultural traditions.[28] Second, he rejects a global difference principle because such a principle might require continual wealth transfers between rich and poor societies. This would be inappropriate, Rawls believes, because it does not take into account the collective responsibility that a society should bear for decisions it makes about whether and how to develop its economy. In place of either of these options, Rawls proposes a 'duty of assistance' that has as its 'target' and 'cut-off point' the establishment of well-ordered institutions in hitherto burdened societies. Rawls, thus, reaches a similar conclusion to Barry, in that he rejects Beitz's cosmopolitan reading of his theory.

The legacy: a cosmopolitan political theory?

These critical reflections on Beitz's attempt to 'globalize' Rawls continue to frame debates about the prospects for cosmopolitan justice. The afterword included in the revised edition of *PTIR* constitutes a continuation of these debates and includes a reformulation of the case for globalized principles of justice in light of some of the criticisms raised against the arguments in the original text. It is perhaps a testament to the status of *PTIR* that these revisions have provoked almost as much discussion as the original text. In drawing this discussion to a close, it is appropriate to summarize these modifications as a prelude to evaluating the legacy of *PTIR* as an effort to lay the groundwork for a cosmopolitan political theory.

The reformulated defence of global justice alluded to in the new afterword continues to work within a broadly Rawlsian framework. Beitz remains committed to a cosmopolitan interpretation of that framework, in part because he finds Rawls's reasons for preferring a statist alternative to be unpersuasive. He criticizes Rawls for overlooking the extent to which national wealth can be traced to a complex combination of factors, including natural resource endowments, public political culture, and their relative bargaining power in global economic arrangements. He also suggests that Rawls's appeal to national responsibility rests on a faulty analogy between individual and collective responsibility, as it is unlikely that all members of a society are in a position to impact on the pattern of decisions that determine its collective wealth over time.[29] The criticism that is most troubling for Beitz relates to the role of social cooperation in his original argument for a global difference principle. Beitz had argued that because there is social cooperation at the global level, this realm should be regulated according to Rawls's principles of social justice. This position, as we have seen, is vulnerable to Barry's objection that what we see at the global level is not social cooperation, or at least not the sort of cooperation that triggers the application of Rawlsian justice. Although Beitz does not accept Barry's interpretation of the Rawlsian idea of social cooperation, he apparently does want to avoid resting his case for global justice on the empirical claim that global interconnectivity amounts to social cooperation (pp. 200–03). He now proposes that we take *some* kind of global basic structure as 'required and inevitable', given the facts about the extent and character of social and economic relations, and work towards principles that the structure should satisfy if it is to be acceptable to individuals conceived, in Rawls's phrase, as 'free and equal' (p. 203).[30] This approach recommends the inclusion of all global persons in a hypothetical contract to select principles to regulate the global basic structure, irrespective of whether or not all persons are in fact participating in forms of interaction at the global level that could be characterized as social cooperation (p. 204). The empirical observation that there is significant global interconnectivity in our world remains relevant, though, in that it demonstrates the feasibility and 'practical relevance' of a conception of global justice (pp. 204–05).

This reformulation may appear to be interesting only for those of us who fret over the finer details of Rawlsian justice, but such a reaction misses the larger point of these apparently arcane discussions. An important theme of *PTIR* is the structure, or 'form', of a cosmopolitan political theory. This theme is important because, as has already been discussed, Beitz believes that an alternative normative framework is needed to address flaws in the dominant realist and statist paradigms. Although cosmopolitanism is a recurring motif of political philosophy since the Greek Stoics, it has, until recently, seldom been developed into a clear and coherent position. The aim of *PTIR* is, in part, to fix ideas about what distinguishes cosmopolitanism from its rivals. The afterword returns to this theme by refining the brief characterization of 'cosmopolitan liberalism' found in the original text:

It does not take societies as fundamental and aims to identify principles which are acceptable from a point of view in which each person's prospects, rather than the prospects of each society or people, are equally represented. Because it accords no privilege to domestic societies or to national (or multinational or non-national) states, cosmopolitan liberalism extends to the world the criteria of distributive justice that apply within a single society (p. 215).

This characterization brings to the fore the underlying motive behind the reformulation of the argument noted above. In refining his account of global interconnectivity, Beitz hopes to achieve a closer fit between his theory and the cosmopolitan intuition that the interests of *all* persons, conceptualized as free and equal, must be taken into account in a global social contract. This move, he hopes, will lend further support to his contention that the principles of justice selected for the global realm should be treated as an extension of the corresponding principles selected for domestic contexts. This commitment to the *form* of a cosmopolitan theory is, as he makes clear in the afterword, a more fundamental concern for Beitz than his suggestions about the specific *content* of these principles (p. 199).

The principal legacy of *PTIR*, to my mind, is its contribution to debates about what a cosmopolitan view in international political thought should look like. This is reflected in the number of authors who follow Beitz in conceptualizing cosmopolitanism as an attempt to globalize conceptions of justice hitherto treated as limited in their scope to domestic contexts.[31] Cosmopolitanism has thus become an umbrella term for a family of views in international political theory, which share a commitment to globalizing principles of justice but often differ in their specific recommendations about the content of those principles.[32] The likelihood is that debates in international political theory will continue to revolve around interpretations and criticisms of cosmopolitanism as defined by Beitz. In terms of critical reflection on this legacy, at least two observations should be made. The first relates to its focus on the *moral* contours of cosmopolitan theory at the expense of its *institutional* implications. The value of this move is that it encourages scholars to reflect with greater care on the underlying normative principles of international relations. The concern – which Beitz has since acknowledged – is that it risks pushing to the margins the equally pressing issue of the policies and practices that must be established in order to realize cosmopolitan principles.[33] The second relates to the adequacy of Beitz's definition of cosmopolitanism as a doctrine that calls for domestic and global contexts to be governed according to the same principles of justice. The value of this move, as noted, is that it establishes 'clear blue water' between cosmopolitan and non-cosmopolitan interpretations of liberalism. The price, though, is that we are left with quite a narrow and, indeed, exclusionary definition, which appears to cast out from the cosmopolitan liberal family those theories that aim to reconcile equal concern for all persons with contrasting principles of domestic and global justice.[34] These concerns, however, do not detract from the achievements of *PTIR* as a work that has more or less set the agenda for theorizing about global justice for the past 30 years. This achievement lends meaning to the suggestion, explicit in the title of an essay by Chris Brown, that current theoretical debate is, to a great extent, a 'house that Chuck built'.[35]

Notes

1 I am extremely grateful to Charles Beitz for comments on earlier versions of this chapter.

2 Nicholas Rengger, 'Reading Charles Beitz: Twenty-Five Years of *Political Theory and International Relations*', *Review of International Studies*, 2005, vol. 31, 361–69, at p. 361.
3 Chris Brown, *International Relations Theory: New Normative Approaches*, New York: Harvester Wheatsheaf, 1992, p. 3. The introduction of Brown's book discusses the relationship between international political theory and International Relations.
4 John Rawls, *A Theory of Justice: Revised Edition*, Oxford: Oxford University Press, 1999. The first edition was published in 1971.
5 Brown, *International Relations Theory*, pp. 8–11.
6 Charles R. Beitz, *Political Theory and International Relations: Revised and with a New Afterword by the Author*, Princeton, NJ: Princeton University Press, 1999. Page numbers placed in parentheses in the text refer to this edition.
7 Beitz returned to Princeton in 2001 to take the position of Edwards S. Sanford Professor of Politics.
8 Chris Brown, 'The House that Chuck Built: Twenty-Five Years of Reading Charles Beitz', *Review of International Studies*, 2005, vol. 31, 371–79, at p. 371.
9 The designation of *PTIR* as a 'landmark' text is from Kok-Chor Tan, *Justice Without Borders: Cosmopolitanism, Nationalism and Patriotism*, Cambridge: Cambridge University Press, 2004, p. 57.
10 Rawls, *A Theory of Justice*, pp. 266–67. An accessible summary of Rawls's theory is in Will Kymlicka, *Contemporary Political Theory: An Introduction*, 2nd edn, Oxford: Oxford University Press, 2001, Chapter 2.
11 Rawls, *A Theory of Justice*, pp. 331–33. This aspect of Rawls's argument is discussed in Chris Brown, *Sovereignty, Rights and Justice: International Political Theory*, Cambridge: Polity, 2002, pp.163–67.
12 Henry Shue, 'The Geography of Justice: Beitz's Critique of Scepticism and Statism', *Ethics*, 1982, vol. 92, 710–19.
13 Rengger, 'Reading Charles Beitz', p. 362.
14 Shue, 'The Geography of Justice', p. 712–13.
15 Brown, 'The House that Chuck Built', pp. 374–75.
16 Brown, 'The House that Chuck Built', p. 375.
17 Brown, 'The House that Chuck Built', p. 376.
18 For Beitz's response to concerns about his characterization of realism, see Charles R. Beitz, 'Reflections', *Review of International Studies*, 2005, vol. 31, 409–23, at 410–11.
19 Beitz, 'Reflections', p. 412.
20 Michael Walzer, 'The Moral Standing of States', *Philosophy & Public Affairs*, 1980, vol. 9, 209–29; Terry Nardin, *Law, Morality and the Relations of States*, Princeton, NJ: Princeton University Press, 1983; and Robert Jackson, *The Global Covenant*, Oxford: Oxford University Press, 2000.
21 David Miller, 'Defending Political Autonomy: A Discussion of Charles Beitz', *Review of International Studies*, 2005, vol. 31, 381–88.
22 Miller, 'Defending Political Autonomy', p. 385.
23 Brown, 'The House that Chuck Built', pp. 376–77.
24 Brown, *Sovereignty, Rights and Justice*, p. 171.
25 Tan, *Justice Beyond Borders*, Chapter 3.
26 Brian Barry, 'Humanity and Justice in Global Perspective', in J. Roland Pennock and John W. Chapman (eds), *Ethics, Economics and the Law of Property*, Nomos 24, New York: New York University Press, 1982, pp. 219–52. For counter-criticism of Barry, see Thomas Pogge, *Realizing Rawls*, Ithaca, NY: Cornell University Press, 1989, pp. 263–65.
27 John Rawls, *The Law of Peoples: With 'The Idea of Public Reason Revisited'*, Cambridge, MA: Harvard University Press, 1999, pp. 115–19.
28 It should be noted that Beitz's argument does not rest on the view that natural resources are the principal source of national wealth (p. 141). Rawls none the less appears to think that the appeal of a resource redistribution principle is diminished if we accept the primacy of institutions and culture as sources of national wealth (Rawls, *The Law of Peoples*, p. 117).
29 Charles R. Beitz, 'Rawls's Law of Peoples', *Ethics*, 2000, vol. 110, 669–96, at pp. 690–92.
30 The shift is influenced by David A. J. Richards 'International Distributive Justice', in J. Roland Pennock and John W. Chapman (eds), *Ethics, Economics and the Law of Property*,

pp. 275–99, at pp. 287–93. See Charles R. Beitz, 'Cosmopolitan Ideals and National Sentiment', *Journal of Philosophy*, 1983, vol. 80, 591–600, at p. 595.

31 Simon Caney, *Justice Beyond Borders: A Global Political Theory*, Oxford: Oxford University Press, 2005; Pogge, *Realizing Rawls*; and Tan, *Justice Without Borders*.

32 Not all cosmopolitans follow Beitz in identifying global justice with Rawls's principles of justice (see e.g. Caney, *Justice Beyond Borders*). On this issue, see Charles R. Beitz, 'Cosmopolitanism and Global Justice', *Journal of Ethics*, 2005, vol. 9, 11–27.

33 Beitz, 'Reflections', p. 423.

34 Erin Kelly, 'Human Rights as Foreign Policy Imperatives', in Deen K. Chatterjee (ed.), *The Ethics of Assistance: Morality and the Distant Needy*, Cambridge: Cambridge University Press, 2004, pp. 177–92.

35 Brown, 'The House that Chuck Built', pp. 371ff. The phrase, as Brown makes clear, draws a parallel with Rawls's influence on contemporary political theory, by reformulating the title of A. S. Laden, 'The House that Jack Built: Thirty Years of Reading Rawls', *Ethics*, 2003, vol. 113, 367–90.

18 Obligations beyond the state: Andrew Linklater's *Men and Citizens in the Theory of International Relations*

Richard Devetak and Juliette Gout[1]

The early 1980s saw the emergence of critical theories of international relations. A small but significant number of scholars published work that challenged fundamental premises of orthodox theories by reflecting on the relationship between knowledge and values and championing the ideals of change and emancipation. Among the seminal contributions to the development of critical theories of international relations are Cox's 1981 *Millennium* article, Ashley's 1981 *International Studies Quarterly* article, Walker's 1981 *Alternatives* article, and Linklater's 1982 *Men and Citizens in the Theory of International Relations* (hereafter referred to as *Men and Citizens*).[2] In addition to using the term 'critical theory', these contributions sought to transform the discipline of International Relations (IR) by setting out ambitious normative theory programmes capable of challenging the intellectual hegemony of realism and liberalism and their disavowal of normative political philosophy and philosophical history in favour of more empirical and functional forms of 'problem-solving' theory.[3]

That, at least, is the conventional story told from the vantage point of the twenty-first century.[4] A similar story could be told of the way that *Men and Citizens* marked the first instalment of a trilogy of books by the man who would become the Woodrow Wilson Professor of Politics at Aberystwyth and the discipline's leading proponent of critical theory. While these narratives make sense as *post facto* reconstructions, they neglect the actual intentions and motives behind these seminal contributions. In an effort to understand and interpret the text's meaning, this chapter begins by elucidating the intentions and motives that led Linklater to write *Men and Citizens*. This will require outlining the intellectual context to which *Men and Citizens* responded. The chapter then provides a close reading of the book, highlighting its originality in formulating a normative theory of international relations tailored to the recovery of universal ethical reasoning. In the third and final part, the chapter reflects on the reception of *Men and Citizens* before trying to capture what makes the book a contemporary classic of IR.

Men and Citizens in context

Men and Citizens began its life as a doctoral thesis at the London School of Economics under the supervision of Michael Donelan. It was submitted in 1978 with the title *Obligations beyond the State: The Individual, the State and Humanity in International Theory*. Two years after its submission as a thesis, in September 1980, the book manuscript was dispatched to the publishers, Macmillan, from Hobart, Australia. Forced by a flat UK job market at the time, Linklater had secured a post at the University of

Tasmania in 1976, staying five years before making the short journey across Bass Strait to Monash University, Melbourne, in 1982. It was during his time at the antipodean city of Hobart that he revised the manuscript for publication.

Linklater self-consciously located his book in what he perceived as a 'resurgence of international political theory in Britain' (p. ix). This resurgence supplied the themes on which *Men and Citizens* sought to 'build a general theory of relations between political communities' (ibid.). Within this resurgence, it is important to make three observations to further ground the intellectual context in which *Men and Citizens* was formed. First, to the extent that Linklater adopts an approach derived from philosophy, history and natural jurisprudence, as opposed to a 'scientific' approach intended to emulate the physical sciences, *Men and Citizens* takes up a position which, despite differences, stands on the same side of the battle-line drawn by Hedley Bull in his case for a 'classical approach' to IR. *Men and Citizens* is certainly bereft of the anxiety, more prevalent in the USA than Australia or the UK, to place the study of politics or international relations on a scientific footing by embracing empiricist or quantitative methods of analysis. A further affinity with the so-called classical approach is the close engagement with natural law theories for their 'vital historical role', as Bull puts it, 'in the emergence of the European states-system'.[5] Second, though consistent with the 'classical' approach, Linklater's *Men and Citizens* marked an innovative departure by making a moral question central to his study. To this end, Linklater took seriously the philosophical writings of Kant, Hegel and Marx and engaged with historical materialism and the Frankfurt School of social philosophy.[6] While Linklater's engagement with the Frankfurt School and Habermas in particular would become more extensive in subsequent works, *Men and Citizens* shares with the early Habermas the classical doctrine of politics as the continuation of ethics.[7] Third, Linklater situates his argument in relation to the growing body of literature describing transformations in the international system. Drawing on the functionalist and neo-functionalist theories of David Mitrany and Ernst Haas as well as the interdependence theories of Robert O. Keohane and Joseph S. Nye, Linklater (pp. 5–7) accepts that changing patterns of social and economic relations compel reconsideration of the categories on which conventional theories of international relations are developed. However, for Linklater, such theories require orientation by normative political theory, informed by reconstructed traditions of political philosophy and natural law. Ultimately, Linklater shows, it is not the challenge of interdependence that the international theorist must face, but the tension between competing concepts of moral and political obligation: those based on either citizenship or humanity.

Reading *Men and Citizens*: towards a normative political theory of international relations

Men and Citizens is an exploration of the way in which various ethical, political and jurisprudential theories have handled the 'bifurcated nature of modern moral and political experience' (p. 39), especially the dichotomized ethical obligations that extend from the distinction between men and citizens. In other words, it explores how the problematic and tensile relationship between men and citizens – which structures international politics by allocating ethical obligations on the basis of a humanity divided into territorial sovereign states – is treated in the history of international thought. The book's purpose is not to provide the kind of explanatory or 'mechanistic' theory of international relations already supplied by varieties of realism and liberalism, but to propose an alternative international theory – informed by ethical, political and jurisprudential philosophy and philosophical history – with two aims: first, to analyse critically this bifurcated experience of 'men' as citizens and as members of the human community; and second, to articulate alternative philosophical and political principles for overcoming this bifurcation. By taking the conflicting ethical obligations held by men and citizens as his point of departure, Linklater subjects the fundamental legitimacy of the states-system to normative philosophical questioning (p. 62). However, if Linklater's contemporaries used the rise of complex interdependence as a reason to reflect on the states-system's moral legitimacy, Linklater finds those reasons in the history of international thought itself.

Looking backwards in time to an array of theoretical interventions made during the formation of the early modern states-system, and forwards to a future global political system liberated from the dualism of men and citizens, Linklater's approach adheres to the view propounded by Donelan that '[t]he study of international relations is the study of international thought'.[8] Recovering and reconstructing past thought becomes integral to an understanding of present thinking either through highlighting what is distinctive about the present, and contrasts with the past or by tracing the descent and reception of ideas (pp. 4–5).

Men and Citizens may be fairly described as an intellectual act of recovery and reconstruction. It revisits and reconstructs major theoretical interventions in early modern political thought with two aims in mind: first, to identify the emergence of dominant conceptions of moral and political obligation; second, to identify and salvage conceptual resources for an international theory capable of moving beyond the antinomy between men and citizens. It elegantly pursues these aims through a reconstruction of classical rationalism – embodied in the natural law theories of Pufendorf and Vattel – and the historicist critique it provoked – embodied in Hegel – before a Kantian framework is rescued from these attacks by reconciling it with Marxist social theory to produce a philosophical history. This Kantian- and Marxist-inspired philosophical history allows Linklater to set forth principles for a 'critical theory of international relations' oriented towards humanity's advancement and the realization of universal justice, freedom and autonomy.

External and internal conceptions of ethical obligations are first reconstructed through the 'rationalist' writings, as Linklater calls them, of Pufendorf and Vattel.[9] Internal conceptions of obligations – that is, obligations imposed by and limited to the territorial jurisdiction of the state – are privileged, and the rights and duties of citizens are contractarian obligations stemming from an overriding interest in security and a normalized identification with a limited political community. Broader moral obligations to the rest of humanity, beyond the borders of the state, are rendered secondary and discretionary or, in the language of the time, 'imperfect'. Pufendorf, embracing the Hobbesian premises of the state of nature, accepts the territorial limitation of moral obligations as a pay-off against the security afforded by the sovereign state's creation of civil society (p. 65). While the law's of nature may recommend duties to humanity, they cannot be enforced under the political conditions of a states-system, and sovereigns remain unaccountable for their actions, either to their subject-citizens or to other states. In this way, Linklater finds Pufendorf's theory deficient for 'its failure to construct a philosophy of world political organization which seeks to give institutional expression to man's horizontal ties' (p. 77).

Vattel advances beyond Pufendorf, according to Linklater, by developing a fuller conception of the society of states and the obligations states owe to each other within such a society. Given the 'natural liberty' of sovereign states, no limitation may be imposed upon sovereigns; but that does not mean that the state's exercise of sovereignty remains without limit. Conduct is constrained by an awareness and acceptance of moral obligations designed to maintain the structure of international society itself, that is, the balance of power, by protecting the natural liberty and independence of states against aggressive encroachment (p. 83).[10] For Linklater, Vattel's notion of the society of states provides a weak moral framework since it leaves to individual states themselves the judgement of whether and to whom an obligation may be owed (p. 84). Linklater is critical of Vattel for adhering to a subjectivist account of natural law and ethics which relegates duties to humanity to voluntary or 'imperfect' duties (pp. 87–88).

Linklater shows that for Kant, both Vattel's and Pufendorf's accounts, and indeed the natural law tradition generally, inadequately capture the obligation to recognize universal moral claims, or the imperatives which ought to drive a theory of the states-system. Kant's progressive theoretical move was to introduce a philosophy of history, which envisioned states progressing towards a kingdom of ends, and an ethical theory of international politics built around perfect duties to humanity. Kant prescribed an uncompromising universal ethical reasoning where justice and perpetual peace were categorical ends which humankind was rationally driven to pursue in striving to realize the full human potential of freedom. This universalist conception of rational ethics leads Kant to a theory of international relations not grounded in contractarian obligations to the state, but in abstract moral obligations to humanity. Kant's cosmopolitan political theory also culminates in the location of security not within sovereign states – which, by their particularistic nature, are vulnerable to interstate war and conflict – but within a cosmopolitan system geared towards universal justice and freedom. In so doing, it also challenges the distinction between domestic and international politics. Linklater thus characterizes Kant's theory of IR as the culmination of a philosophical history able to overcome the limitations inherent to earlier rationalists (p. 120).

However, Kant and other rationalists were vulnerable to historicism's attack, which disputed the rational essence of humanity and transcendent, universal values (Chapter 7). Historicists rejected the idea of a universal human community about which shared moral claims could be made. Instead, as Linklater explains, in opposition to natural law thinkers, historicists placed greater emphasis on cultural difference revealing the values and claims of rationalist natural law theory to be instead social and historical products rather than transcendental truths. In Linklater's narrative, ethical universalism threatened to descend down the rabbit hole of cultural relativism unless or until both concepts were sublimated by Hegelian and then Marxist philosophical histories. These philosophical histories would claim to go beyond Kant by reconciling reason and freedom, individualism and universalism, in history (Chapter 8). Linklater embraces these philosophical histories by reading the history of international thought as an ongoing dialectical movement from rationalism, through the moral philosophy of Kant, to the historicist philosophies of Hegel and Marx. It is a story where the strengths of each thinker's ethical theory are retained, and weaknesses jettisoned, in the progressive philosophical realization of a free (self-determining and fully self-conscious) humanity.

Here, Linklater makes his boldest move, inscribing Marxist insights onto a Kantian moral vision of international politics. In historicist fashion, Marx grounded normative principles in changing political and social structures, most fundamentally in the changing relations of production (p. 159). Loosening the bonds of particularistic categories of political association, which had been reified through historically different forms such as tribal society and the national state, was considered key to humanity achieving its capacity for being self-determining and free. This recovery of Kantian principles within a philosophical theory of history, arrived at through Marx's social-theoretical insights, allowed Linklater to build his 'general theory of relations between political communities' (p. ix) upon foundations of ethical universalism. Such a theory would embody a philosophical 'scale of forms', derived from R. G. Collingwood, whereby international systems are placed on a hierarchical scale and judged according to their adequacy or deficiency in realizing universal freedom or overcoming estrangement and necessity in relations between societies.

The introduction of this philosophical device allows Linklater not just to mark a dialectical ascension beyond rationalism and historicism, but also to map a loose empirical progression from tribal societies through to the modern state. The actual historical progress of the modern states-system can then be measured against the idealized political forms given expression in the ascending scale of political and international theories. It is the discrepancy between the empirical actuality of the international system and the intellectual idea of the Kantian 'universal kingdom of ends' that drives forward Linklater's programme for a critical theory of IR; one that 'challenges the rationale for a state-centred international relations' and articulates a 'more humanised international relations' by recovering the ideal of a morally and politically unified humanity (p. 203).

The reception, extension and critique of *Men and Citizens*

As already noted, Linklater's *Men and Citizens* was not alone in alluding to a critical theory of international relations in the early 1980s. The writings of Ashley, Cox, Maclean and Walker were equally concerned with challenging the conventional theoretical frameworks available for the study of international relations and invoked the motif of 'critical theory' in doing so.[11] However, there was little shared understanding of the methods and values that should guide any critical theory of international relations. Cox, for example, was influenced as much by Vico and modern historicists and realists as he was by Marx and Gramsci, resulting in a far less normative philosophy than Linklater.[12] The point is that while *Men and Citizens* may retrospectively be identified with the origins of a critical theory of international relations, its primary intention at the time was to affirm the case for a philosophically informed and ethically motivated political theory of international relations (see Preface and p. 3).

Linklater was not alone in advocating a more philosophical form of international political theory.[13] Such a case was also cogently argued by Walker, whose theory programme closely aligned with Linklater's.[14] Like Linklater, Walker engaged closely with the canonical thinkers of Western political thought and focused on the way that IR theory was organized around sharp dichotomies: from the rival approaches of realism and idealism to the binary oppositions of universalism and pluralism, domestic and international, order and justice, inside and outside.[15] Linklater and Walker shared the view that, far from being 'timeless truths', these dichotomies had histories and were the products of intellectual activity that required recovery and reconstruction before they could be subjected to philosophical problematization and ethical critique. Moreover, they shared the view that these dichotomies were sustained by a problematic assumption that political theory and international theory represented divergent traditions of thought occupied with radically different realms of political experience. Walker denied that the distinction between domestic and international politics demanded 'a cleavage at the level of methodology'; Linklater argued that '[n]o special method' distinguished political from international theory (p. 3).[16] This, of course, contrasted with the prevailing trend within IR which was to argue that the study of relations among states demanded its own theoretical concepts and methods. Such arguments were strongly expressed by leading IR scholars in the late 1970s, including Wight, Bull and Waltz, all of whom agreed that concepts such as progress, justice, freedom and the 'good life' had little if any application beyond the borders of the state. To believe that they did, was to fall prey to what Bull called 'the domestic analogy'.[17]

Linklater's *Men and Citizens* thus participates in a broader intellectual movement to rethink the fundamental division between political theory as a theory of the 'good life' and international theory as a theory of 'survival', to use Wight's terms.[18] This would cultivate the ground for later attempts to examine and problematize the distinction between inside and outside, not least Walker's seminal contribution (see Chapter 21 of this volume).[19] If Walker was primarily concerned to expose the limits of political imagination when evidence of global transformation ran up against the dichotomy of inside/outside, Linklater was primarily concerned to highlight the ethical limits of a political imagination constrained by the distinction between internal and external obligations. After all, the distinction between men and citizens is a particular instance of the more general distinction between inside and outside.[20]

Linklater would pursue this normative philosophical enquiry further in later works, which reaffirmed and extended the critique of the states-system and expansion of moral and political community first outlined in *Men and Citizens*, and gave substance to a more refined and comprehensive 'critical theory of international relations'.[21] In fact, Linklater's trilogy of books, *Men and Citizens*, *Beyond Realism and Marxism* and *Transformation of Political Community*, form a powerful statement of the case for a critical theory of international relations; one that presents international theory as political theory, that defends Enlightenment ethical universalism and that grafts a Marxist-informed historical sociology onto a Kantian-inspired philosophical history. These elements of critical international theory, which were present *in nuce* in *Men and Citizens*, inspired a number of subsequent interventions in IR, especially in what can be called 'normative international theory'.[22] Although they did not necessarily accept all the arguments and conclusions of *Men and Citizens*, these normative international theorists accepted Linklater's case for a political theory of international relations and took seriously his challenge to rethink the foundations of IR such that obligations to humanity could be extended and human freedom enhanced. Linklater's *Men and Citizens* thus played a vital role in making normative international theory intellectually legitimate within the bounds of IR.

Yet, the more notable legacy of *Men and Citizens* has been its harnessing to the development of a critical international theory – the purpose of which is to criticize and transform world politics with a view to realizing universal human emancipation. Both Linklater himself and others would find in *Men and Citizens* the prolegomena to a more comprehensive critical theory of international relations. If *Men and Citizens* provided the normative philosophical critique of the modern states-system, Linklater's later writings would add an important sociological dimension to his concerted efforts at developing a critical theory programme by focusing on the range of empirical historical forces shaping the boundaries of moral and political community.[23] In

Linklater's favoured formulation, the point was to develop a critical sociology of the moral norms governing international relations.[24] Appealing to Habermas's notion of an 'empirical philosophy of history with a critical intent', Linklater proposed to buttress the philosophical and normative dimensions of critical theory with a sociological investigation of the historical logics of inclusion and exclusion in international relations.[25] Arguably this placed his work in close proximity to feminist and poststructuralist theories of international relations which also emphasized the moral deficits inherent in the modern states-system's patterns of domination and exclusion, even if some prominent exponents of these theories have voiced doubts about Linklater's credentials in this regard.[26] It also allowed some constructivist theorists to locate their research within 'a broadly defined critical theory of international relations' by offering a more complex sociological account of the changing patterns of inclusion and exclusion in global politics.[27] If nothing else, these subsequent engagements with Linklater help to confirm the notion that *Men and Citizens* was, or at least is seen as, an important progenitor of critical theories of international relations.

This is not to say that *Men and Citizens* has been without its critics. From the very outset, some scholars raised doubts about Linklater's method of philosophical history. Moorhead Wright, for example, found it to be 'curiously dismissive of history itself', bearing little more than 'rough correspondence with actual historical forms', as Linklater readily concedes (p. 167).[28] Some years later Beate Jahn made a similar, if more damning, argument, finding *Men and Citizens* bereft of empirical history and complicit with theoretical justifications for the dispossession of indigenous peoples.[29] Jahn also criticized Linklater for employing a 'scale of forms' to produce a stadial history which, she contends, simply reflects the self-image of Western modernity as the highest stage of civilization or the end of history. There are good reasons to be suspicious of the scale of forms. Placing societies in a hierarchy according to their level of ethical advancement runs counter to our late modern sensibilities, and invites allegations of insensitivity, or worse, cultural imperialism and arrogance. This perhaps accounts for Linklater's abandonment of the device in later work, though Jahn still discerns in those later writings the residue of a Eurocentric scale of forms that fails to represent the universal values to which it aspires, merely converting the scale of forms from a temporal to a spatial dimension with Europe as the highest form.[30] This aspect of *Men and Citizens* is unlikely to find support from theorists sensitive to postcolonial critiques of Western modernity and its accompanying conception of history.

Nor will it appeal to realists such as Schweller who are liable to perceive *Men and Citizens* as 'fantasy theory', preoccupied with philosophical musings at the expense of engagement with the harsh realities of political life.[31] For Schweller, such theorizing is a 'luxury' that genuine practitioners of political theory cannot afford, weighed down as they are with 'real-world' concerns of foreign policy. Wright objected to *Men and Citizens* on similar grounds, finding its failure to point to clear political and ethical obligations stark given its focus on such obligations. The suspicion that re-imaginings of political communities are mere folly, or that they ought to be valued only insofar as they conform to realist expectations about practical application, illustrates the dominance (and limitations) of the problem-solving theories that Linklater and his critical contemporaries sought to challenge in devising their normative theories of international relations.

Conclusion

Men and Citizens represents a continuing challenge to the dominant realist and liberal conceptions of international relations three decades after it was first published. Its recovery and reconstruction of IR as political and ethical theory remains as powerful and persuasive today as it did in the early 1980s when it affirmed the method of philosophical history and made the moral distinction between men and citizens central to the study of IR. Linklater showed how Kantian obligations to humanity represented as 'perfect' obligations beyond state borders could be improved by a reconciliation with Marxist historicism to create a critical theory of IR. This reinsertion of Enlightenment political philosophy into IR theory remains a singular contribution to the discipline.

What is remarkable about Linklater's endeavours is the unintentional legacy of *Men and Citizens* as a foundational work, both for critical international theory generally, and for Linklater personally, who would later build on *Men and Citizens* in such a way that it would become the first in a trilogy of books pursuing a critical theory programme. The placement of *Men and Citizens* in the broader context of burgeoning critical international theory ensures that it is a stablemate to the articles written in 1981 by Cox, Ashley and Walker. What sets it apart from these works is Linklater's interrogation of the political system through the ethically motivated tradition of Kantian philosophical reasoning.

The persistence of realist hegemony in IR has not eliminated enduring concerns regarding external and internal concepts of obligation. The moral disquiet that is evoked by suffering across international borders – poverty, famine, forced displacement, human rights violations, war, crimes against humanity and so forth – raises anew questions of moral obligation that the modern states-system has never sufficiently addressed: how to reconcile duties to humanity with the fact of a humanity divided into sovereign territorial states. Linklater's *Men and Citizens*, thus, retains moral and political relevance in a contemporary theoretical landscape as much dominated by realist conceptions of IR as that in which the book emerged. It is the enduring ability of *Men and Citizens* to provide theoretical insight into the normative foundations of international relations that makes it a modern classic in the field of IR.

Notes

1 The authors would like to express their thanks to Andrew Linklater for his benevolent and helpful comments on this chapter.
2 R. W. Cox, 'Social Forces, States and World Orders: Beyond International Relations Theory', *Millennium: Journal of International Studies*, 1981, vol. 19, 126–55; Richard K. Ashley, 'Political Realism and Human Interests', *International Studies Quarterly*, 1981, vol. 25, 204–36; R. B. J. Walker, 'World Politics and Western Reason: Universalism, Pluralism, Hegemony', *Alternatives*, 1981, vol. 7, 195–227; and Andrew Linklater, *Men and Citizens in the Theory of International Relations*, London: Macmillan, 1982. Page numbers placed in parentheses in the text refer to this edition.
3 See Cox, 'Social Forces, States and World Orders'.
4 See Nicholas Rengger and Ben Thirkell-White, 'Editors' Introduction', special issue: Critical International Relations Theory after 25 Years, *Review of International Studies*, 2007, vol. 33, 3–24, at p. 4; and Shannon Brincat, Laura Lima and João Nunes, 'Introduction: The Life of Critique', in Shannon Brincat, Laura Lima and João Nunes (eds), *Critical Theory in International Relations and Security Studies*, London: Routledge, 2011, pp. 1–11, at p. 5.
5 Hedley Bull, 'Natural Law and International Relations', *British Journal of International Studies*, 1979, vol. 5, 171–81, at p. 171.

6 In the 'Notes and References' of *Men and Citizens*, see Chapter 2, footnote 44, p. 210 on Marcuse; and Chapter 8, footnote 1, p. 218 on Habermas. Martin Jay's *The Dialectical Imagination: A History of the Frankfurt School and the Institute of Social Research, 1923–1950* (Boston, MA: Little Brown, 1973) remains the best account of the Frankfurt School.

7 Jürgen Habermas, *Theory and Practice*, trans. John Viertel, London: Heinemann, 1974, p. 42. See Andrew Linklater, *Beyond Realism and Marxism: Critical Theory and International Relations*, London: Macmillan, 1990; and Andrew Linklater, *The Transformation of Political Community: Ethical Foundations of the Post-Westphalian Era*, Cambridge: Polity Press, 1998 for Linklater's extended engagements with Frankfurt School Critical Theory and Habermas.

8 Michael Donelan, 'Introduction', in Michael Donelan (ed.), *The Reason of States: A Study in International Political Theory*, London: George Allen and Unwin, 1978, p. 11.

9 Whether the writings of Pufendorf and Vattel are best classified as rationalist is not an issue that need detain us here. Suffice to say that this is common to Kantian philosophical histories which portray Kant's philosophy as the culminating transcendence of the dialectic between rationalism and empiricism. See Ian Hunter, *Rival Enlightenments: Civil and Metaphysical Philosophy in Early Modern Germany,* Cambridge: Cambridge University Press, 2001.

10 On Vattel's treatment of the balance of power, see Richard Devetak, 'Law of Nations as Reason of State: Diplomacy and the Balance of Power in Vattel's *Law of Nations*', *Parergon*, 2011, vol. 28, 105–28.

11 Richard K. Ashley, 'Political Realism and Human Interest'; Cox, 'Social Forces, States and World Orders'; and John Maclean, 'Political Theory, International Theory, and Problems of Ideology', *Millennium: Journal of International Studies*, 1981, vol. 10, 102–25.

12 For an account of the competing critical theory programs offered by Linklater and Cox, see Richard Devetak, 'Vico contra Kant: The Competing Critical Theories of Cox and Linklater', in Brincat, Lima and Nunes, *Critical Theory*, pp. 115–26.

13 See also W. B. Gallie, 'Wanted: A Philosophy of International Relations', *Political Studies*, 1979, vol. 27, 484–92; and the chapter by William Smith in this volume.

14 More recently Walker has been at pains to distance himself from Linklater's normative philosophical history approach and its perceived universalism and hierarchicalism. See Walker, 'The Hierarchicalization of Political Community', *Review of International Studies*, 1999, vol. 25, 151–56; and the more obscure, R. B. J. Walker, *After the Globe, Before the World*, London: Routledge, 2010, Chapter 3.

15 See R. B. J. Walker, *Political Theory and the Transformation of World Politics*, World Order Studies Program, Occasional Paper No. 8, Center of International Studies, Princeton University, 1980, and 'World Politics and Western Reason'.

16 Walker, *Political Theory*, p. 17.

17 Hedley Bull, *The Anarchical Society: A Study of Order in World Politics*, London: Macmillan, 1977, p. 46.

18 Martin Wight, 'Why Is There No International Theory?', in Butterfield and Wight (eds), *Diplomatic Investigations: Essays in the Theory of International Politics*, London: George Allen and Unwin, 1966, p. 33.

19 R. B. J. Walker, *Inside/Outside: International Relations as Political Theory,* Cambridge: Cambridge University Press, 1993.

20 A point noted by Hidemi Suganami, 'Reflections on the Domestic Analogy: The Case of Bull, Beitz and Linklater', *Review of International Studies*, 1986, vol. 12, 145–58, at p. 152.

21 Andrew Linklater, *Beyond Realism and Marxism: Critical Theory and International Relations*, London: Macmillan, 1990; Andrew Linklater, 'The Problem of Community in International Relations', *Alternatives*, 1990, vol. 15, 135–53; and Andrew Linklater, *The Transformation of Political Community: Ethical Foundations of the Post-Westphalian Era*, Cambridge: Polity Press, 1998.

22 For a sample of the best interventions see Chris Brown, *International Relations Theory: New Normative* Approaches, London: Harvester Wheatsheaf, 1992; Kimberly Hutchings, *International Political Theory: Rethinking Ethics in a Global Era*, London: Sage, 1999; Richard Shapcott, *Justice, Community, and Dialogue in International Relations*, Cambridge: Cambridge University Press, 2001; and Toni Erskine, *Embedded Cosmopolitanism: Duties to Strangers and Enemies in a World of 'Dislocated Communities'*, Oxford: Oxford University Press, 2008.

23 See Andrew Linklater, 'Realism, Marxism and Critical International Theory', *Review of International Studies*, 1986, vol. 12, 301–12; Linklater, *Beyond Realism and Marxism*; and Andrew Linklater, 'The Question of the Next Stage in International Relations Theory: A Critical Theoretical Point of View', *Millennium: Journal of International Studies*, 1992, vol. 21, 77–98; and Linklater, *Transformation of Political Community.*

24 This is how he puts it in a postscript to the second edition of *Men and Citizens*, London: Macmillan, 1990, p. 209.

25 Linklater, *Beyond Realism and Marxism*, p. 164.

26 See Jim George, *Discourses of Global Politics: A Critical (Re)Introduction to International Relations*, Boulder, CO: Lynne Rienner, 1994; Brooke Ackerly, 'Uncritical Theory', in Brincat, Lima and Nunes, *Critical Theory*, pp. 140–49; and Jacqui True, 'What Is Critical about Critical Theory Revisited? The Case of Four International Relations Scholars and Gender', in Brincat, Lima and Nunes, *Critical Theory*, pp. 150–58

27 Christian Reus-Smit, *The Moral Purpose of the State: Culture, Social Identity, and Institutional Rationality in International Relations*, Princeton, NJ: Princeton University Press, 1999, pp. 168–69.

28 Moorhead Wright, 'Central but Ambiguous: States and International Theory', *Review of International Studies*, 1984, vol. 10, 233–37, at p. 235.

29 Beate Jahn, 'One Step Forward, Two Steps Back: Critical Theory as the Latest Edition of Liberal Idealism', *Millennium: Journal of International Studies*, 1998, vol. 27, 613–41.

30 Jahn, 'One Step Forward, Two Steps Back', pp. 632–33. For a more sophisticated theoretical critique of philosophical history, see Barry Hindess, 'The Past Is Another Country', *International Political Sociology*, 2007, vol. 1, 325–38.

31 Although Randall Schweller uses this phrase to describe *Transformation of Political Community*, there is no reason to believe that he would not also use it to describe *Men and Citizens*. See 'Fantasy Theory', *Review of International Studies*, 1999, vol. 25, 147–50.

19 The making of IR/IPE: Robert W. Cox's *Production, Power and World Order*

Randall Germain[1]

The work of Robert W. Cox is indelibly associated with the fields of critical International Relations (IR) theory and International Political Economy (IPE). He was the first to use the term neorealism in 1981, in an article that yielded two other phrases now synonymous with his writings: 'theory is always *for* someone and *for* some purpose'; and the distinction between critical theory and problem-solving theory.[2] A subsequent article published in the same journal two years later introduced an entire generation of scholars to the work of the Italian Marxist theoretician Antonio Gramsci, providing a rich set of concepts for the study of IPE, including a reworked understanding of the term 'hegemony' along with the ideas of 'passive revolution' and 'historic bloc'.[3] The framework of historical structures, elaborated most completely in his landmark publication *Production, Power and World Order* (*PPWO*), has similarly inspired scholars to range widely over the changing anatomy of world order.[4] These seminal contributions persuaded Benjamin Cohen to include Cox as one of the 'Magnificent Seven' group of scholars who helped to usher in the modern rebirth of IPE.[5]

The principal animating force behind Cox's scholarship is an abiding concern to understand the changing modalities of global or world order. From his earliest writings on executive leadership in international organizations through to his mid-career interest in the material and ideational underpinnings of US hegemony to his late career fascination with intersubjective and civilizational *mentalitiés*,[6] the question of how to understand world order and its elements or layers forms the bedrock of his investigations.[7] It is the problematic of world order that runs as a singular unifying theme through his work, with each successive phase adding a new but interrelated aspect to his investigations. Indeed, one can see in this problematic an enduring coherence that simply uses different vantage points for its exploration. Within this context, *PPWO* occupies what is perhaps a unique Archimedean point, both looking back to his formal international organization phase while at the same time also suggestively pointing towards his later interest in civilizations.

While *PPWO* is considered to be a classic text within the field of IPE, its status as a classic text within IR might be viewed more ambiguously. After all, it does not rest its methodological foundations on IR scholarship, preferring instead a modified and in some ways extended Weberian formulation.[8] Its ontological foundation is distinctly historical materialist in its embrace of production and especially class as the key units of organization and investigation. And its epistemological cues come from the tradition of historicism as a mode of learning rather than from the standard tropes normally associated with the social sciences as they have developed in the Western academy (namely rationalism, positivism and recently philosophical realism).

Nevertheless, the argument for including *PPWO* as a classic of IR is persuasive for two reasons. First, its publication occurred at a seminal moment in the historiography of IR, during the nexus of debates over the status of neorealism as a key approach to IR theory and more empirically oriented questions about the continuation of US dominance or hegemony. It should, thus, be included as one of a handful of texts which defined a critical inflection point in the development of IR and IPE theory.[9] Furthermore, unusually among this small number of texts, *PPWO* moves easily across disciplinary boundaries, providing students and scholars with a model of how scholarship can usefully engage with multiple debates.

Second, and more importantly, *PPWO* stands as a testament to how historical materialism as an approach to IR and IPE can usefully contribute to broader disciplinary debates. As a statement of this approach to IR and IPE, its coherence and systematic completeness is unsurpassed, although not uncontested. It offers a suggestive and sophisticated way to conceive of world order that encapsulates both the domestic and global balance of social forces in political and economic terms. At the same time, it recognizes that the impetus for these forces derives from fundamental social dynamics associated with the way that power is generated and exercised through existing institutional relationships, whether national or global. It also provides a useful way to think about future possible trajectories of development. Indeed, its conclusions stand up remarkably well even today. As I shall suggest below, its classic status thus rests on the way that it innovates in the formulation of theory and how it integrates diverse traditions of thought into its analysis.

Background and themes

PPWO is the culmination of nearly two decades of reflection by Cox on the changing structure of world order. In one sense, he had been involved personally and professionally with the issues that dominate the book since he joined the International Labour Organization (ILO) just after World War II, fresh from completing a Master's degree in history at McGill University in Canada. His work at the ILO brought him into contact not only with the idea of labour as a force in society and the world's political economy, but also with the myriad of direct and indirect ways that international relations are instantiated both 'above' the level of the state in international organizations, and 'below' the level of the state in the domestic organization of production and its attendant social relations. His work as an international civil servant might have placed him at one of the more obscure interstices of power in the postwar global system, but it was nevertheless a place where an astute observer could see at first-hand how power actually worked in the world of international politics. On a purely personal level, then, *PPWO* can be regarded as a statement about the interconnections that bind world politics into a cohesive and structured whole, informed by an intimate involvement with an international organization concerned with how work is organized.

However, *PPWO* was also published at a uniquely significant point in time. By 1987 the global position of the USA had been under sustained pressure for at least a decade, prompting a significant debate among IR theorists about the possibility of US decline. This debate in turn coincided with the discipline's recent debate about the philosophy of science, which was a deeply theoretical debate about how to study the subject matter of world politics.[10] *PPWO* engaged with both sets of debates in a manner that was synoptic as well as systematic. It was synoptic in the sense that Cox's scholarship reached out to a diverse body of knowledge for insights into how social relations should be understood and studied. This is a critical and innovative aspect of *PPWO*. However, it was also systematic in that Cox provides a framework for considering the structure of world order that integrates key elements used separately by other leading scholars. In this sense his work stands as a kind of juncture where both sets of debates could intersect and speak to each other. This is a rare example of a critical interlocutor at work in IR and IPE.

As a text, *PPWO* is divided into three principal sections: 1) an elaboration of his method and a description of the ideal type arrangements into which one can categorize the social relations of production; 2) a historical enquiry into the origins and evolution of such social relations on a world scale; and 3) an attempt to sketch future possible scenarios for the social relations of production, based upon insights generated by the preceding historical investigation. The first section is the most descriptive part of the book in the sense that it presents a variety of ideal type arrangements by which we can understand and portray the social relations of production. Cox identifies 12 of these arrangements, which he labels as 'modes of social relations', and they range from simple subsistence and peasant-lord modes through to more complex modes such as tripartism and central planning. The methodology employed to consider these modes is derived from Max Weber's use of ideal types to grasp the fixed properties of particular sets of social relationships; it is a way of freezing history in order to identify and unpack its complex, moving parts. For Cox, trying to portray these social relationships anatomically, that is, in terms of their structural patterns of interaction, allows for an initial assessment as to which relations are significant and longer term, and which are simply derivative and more contingent. The result of this initial cut, however, is not simply a static taxonomy of modes of social relations. He introduces motion, or diachrony, into these modes by considering the way in which each mode develops a reciprocity or fit between the objective, subjective and institutional relations within them. In particular, the manner in which objective or material forms of social power (as determined by levels of production, access to military resources or pools of capital, the reach of particular institutions, etc.) interact with more subjective forms of consciousness (intersubjective images, forms of ethical reasoning, established common sense ideological traditions, etc.) provides a key barometer for the possibility of effecting change within a mode, and especially within its institutional infrastructure. This is how the social relations of production become instantiated *within* the structure of world order even as they become a terrain of engagement *with* that structure.

The historical trajectories associated with the particular ways that this instantiation proceeds are the subject of the second part of *PPWO*. Here Cox examines the history of these modes of social relations of production as they intersect with and are entwined within an evolving structure of world order. He begins with the emergence and consolidation of the liberal order (the *Pax Britannica*), then traces the erosion and collapse of this period into what he calls the era of rival imperialisms before charting the reconstruction of a new form of liberalism under the *Pax Americana*. He identifies this era as *neoliberal*, to distinguish it from the earlier liberal order. These three chapters form the analytical heart of *PPWO*, in that here Cox brings the rich conceptual tradition of historical materialism to bear on the 'making' of history. During this process he identifies a number of analytical propositions relevant to understanding transformation in forms of state and world order structures. At the centre of his analysis is the development of historic blocs as a product of class struggle. Each of the time periods he examines is driven by a different constellation of class forces in relation to the organization of production, the development of national political institutions, and the world historical balance of interstate power. The liberal order, the era of rival imperialisms and the *Pax Americana* each reflect their own particular fit between the objective and subjective factors that constitute for Cox a particular structure of world order. Here Cox's own unique contribution is to elaborate a number of analytical propositions to guide us in our understanding of how this 'fit' operates. For example, his sixth proposition suggests that 'a world hegemonic order can be founded only by a country in which social hegemony has been or is being achieved' (p. 149). The UK in the mid-nineteenth century and the USA and Russia in the mid-twentieth century had gone through complete social revolutions; Germany and Japan during these periods had not. Thus, it was that as British economic and political leadership eroded during the first decade of the twentieth century, none of its erstwhile challengers could replace its leadership with their own. Their social transformations were not yet complete. The era of rival imperialisms was the result.

Cox's use of the concepts of class and historic bloc deserves some comment here, as he does not consider them in a manner consistent with orthodox Marxist theory. Class, for example, is not considered as an objectively determined social force generated through the operation of the mode of production, but rather as a historically conditioned form of agency whose authority and capability to act rests as much upon its collective consciousness and intersubjective understanding about its own possibility as upon its apparently objective relationship to the mode of production.[11] In this he follows a form of historical reasoning that bridges the philosophy of historical idealism associated with the Oxford philosopher R. G. Collingwood with the historicist interpretation of historical materialism advanced by the radical English historian E. P. Thompson.[12] In this innovative fusion, a concept such as class acquires a certain analytical elasticity that permits us to follow how its inner ideational dynamic shapes its actual historical impact. In Collingwood's formulation, the utility of concepts lies precisely in their ability to reveal the inside of events, the self-awareness of actors that organically connects their activities to the larger structures within which they find themselves.[13]

Cox's use of the idea of 'historic bloc' to understand the trajectory of world order further reflects this deeply historicist epistemology. He took the idea of historic bloc from Antonio Gramsci, who used it principally to understand the course of Italian history from the period of the *Risorgimento* through to the consolidation of the fascist state under Mussolini. What was useful in this concept for Cox was its ability not only to illustrate how a cohesive social formation could be formed, but also to point to how such a social formation might extend the basis of its power from a national to an international or global configuration. His unique contribution to IR and IPE was to take what was effectively a concept previously applied at the national level and construe it on a global basis.[14] This analytical move added a social dimension to the explanation of US hegemony, which up until that point had been considered primarily in narrow political and economic terms. And as with the concept of class, Cox stressed the intersubjective dimension of a historic bloc as the critical element to understand and unpack. Cox historicized both concepts by emphasizing the *inside* of their formulation, their ideational and ideological contours, as the key to understanding how the 'fit' between the subjective and objective elements of world order could be generated. Mapping the changing contours of historic blocs thus provides the analytical means by which to understand the 'making' of history.

The third section of *PPWO* turns from an analysis of the making of history to a consideration of the historical future. Using the analytical tools developed in the second section, Cox sketches the conditions out of which different possible future scenarios for world order might unfold. He first charts the onset of economic crisis in the world economy throughout the 1970s, paying close attention to how this crisis was affecting the historic bloc associated with the dominant form of state during this period, the neoliberal state (what we would today perhaps call the corporate-liberal state, to distinguish it from both its nineteenth-century liberal predecessor and its post-1989 genuinely neoliberal successor, what Cox himself calls the *hyper-liberal* state). He then turns his attention to the changes that this crisis is imposing upon the processes of accumulation within modern capitalist forms of production. For Cox, the erosion of the neoliberal historic bloc and state form together with ongoing mutations in the regime of accumulation herald the possibility of significant transformations in the structure of world order. Detailing these possibilities in relation to existing class relations occupies the final chapter of *PPWO*.

Twenty-five years after these final chapters were written, Cox's reflections hold up quite well to the actual historical record. The power of the two key dominant groups that he identifies – a transnational managerial class and a national bourgeois class – have in fact been played out over two key social terrains: 1) a contest over the levers of state power; and 2) a contest over intensifying competition in the global organization of production chains. In *PPWO* Cox highlights how these two sets of class forces are becoming associated with the hyper-liberal and neo-mercantalist forms of state, respectively, and considers how they might forge alliances with various combinations of subordinate class forces, all of whom face severe constraints on the extent of their own political agency. While he refrains from making explicit predictions, his delineation of the power dynamics at play is accurate. We can see from his analysis not only how the two decades between 1987 and 2007 reflect the gathering strength of the transnationally oriented managerial class, but also how, since the onset of the global financial crisis, the clash between a hyper-liberal and neo-mercantalist state form has re-emerged as a key battleground of global capitalism.[15] In fact, it might come as a surprise to some that in concluding *PPWO*, Cox considers the state to be the vital and necessary key to understanding the unfolding structure of world order: 'Although production was the point of departure, the crucial role, it turns out, is played by the state' (p. 399). The levers of state power are both critically important for shaping the conditions of production and absolutely categorical for establishing the mechanisms and apparatuses of world order. For a social structure of accumulation to exist at the global level, sufficient class forces need to forge a historic bloc organized around adequate access to state power. An historic bloc without state power cannot shape or manage the pressures of world order; one might even go so far as to say that an historic bloc without the state is a logical impossibility. The state as an organized form of political power is the indispensable agent through which production and world order are fused concretely under a hegemonic structure. Absent adequate state power, a global structure of production (and world order) is not possible.

When considered alongside Cox's broader canvas of work, we can see that the intellectual agenda encapsulated by *PPWO* has inspired two generations of scholars, working mostly but not exclusively within the traditions of critical IR theory and historical materialism. His work was picked up first by a clutch of scholars identified by some as the 'new Gramscians' or 'neo-Gramscians', who used the very suggestive formulation of historical structures and intersubjectivity he advanced to investigate the changing contours of hegemony at the global level.[16] Much of this work was published from the late 1980s through to the mid-1990s, and it constitutes the first integrative attempt to conceptualize world order on a basis distinct from liberal, neorealist and classical realist analyses. A second generation of scholarship, however, has taken up some of the debates sparked by the first generation, both to return to Gramsci's work and to carry forward the attempt to examine the changing parameters of world order on the so-called periphery of the world political economy. Many of these scholars are now using Cox's categories of analysis to consider the very fluid formulation of hegemony and passive revolution among emerging market economies.[17] In this way *PPWO* – and Cox's work more broadly – can be considered to be a classic mode of analysis in IR and IPE precisely because it has been picked up and refined by a distinctive scholarly community.

Cox and the 'making' of IR/IPE: innovator extraordinaire

The scholarly reception of and engagement with Cox's work, including *PPWO*, has been well documented elsewhere.[18] The most enduring lines of critical engagement cluster around his theoretical eclecticism, his understanding of the state, and the particular manner in which he negotiates the ideational/material divide in theoretical terms. In each of these areas his critics worry about the extent to which his innovative use of different tools of analysis compromise or contaminate the purity of long-standing and perhaps more pristine avenues of enquiry. As Michael Schechter carefully documents, Cox is often accused of straying from the purity of orthodox Marxism and its Gramscian offshoot.[19] Yet, as Benjamin Cohen correctly emphasizes, one of Cox's chief contributions to IR and IPE is to resolutely ask 'big picture' questions that place an emphasis upon thinking holistically about the world's political economy.[20] This way of thinking about global politics and political economy has several advantages. It allows Cox to consider class in a multidimensional framework which is resistant to most forms of reductionism. It questions the place of positivism and actor-centric orientations in the social sciences on the basis that the epistemological and ontological claims associated with these theoretical stances are predicated upon dividing up what is in effect a seamless reality. As Cox suggests in one of his most well-received publications, 'Hegemony at the international level is thus not merely an order among states ... [it] can be described as a social structure, an economic structure, and a political structure; and it cannot be simply one of these things but must be all three'.[21]

In the context of IPE (as well as IR), this holistic approach stands in contrast to much mainstream theorizing. The 'American School' of IPE, for example, which Benjamin Cohen counter-poses to the 'British School', has persistently narrowed its intellectual focus and confined its methodological principles and epistemological claims over time. Cox, on the other hand, offers a vision of IPE that extends its remit and harvests diverse intellectual traditions in the pursuit of knowledge, in a manner reminiscent of Susan Strange's dictum of the early 1980s to preserve IPE's unfenced habitat.[22] The conceptual framework of *PPWO* draws on scholarship ranging across world history, IR and political economy, while his subsequent scholarship also reaches out to embrace cultural and civilizational studies. His work, in other words, challenges us to identify and understand the broad structures of world order, which for him is the principal context within which world politics and political economy unfold. When set within the increasingly constricted theoretical debates in IR and IPE, this amounts to an innovation of the first order, one which is not perhaps unique to Cox, but which he nevertheless carries off with singular analytical clarity and coherence. However, perhaps the most powerful single element of Cox's innovation is his historicism, or what I have elsewhere called his *historical idealism*.[23] Historicism of course has a long history as an avenue of enquiry in IR and IPE, but the particular twist that Cox gives to it is to privilege that strand of historicism associated with political economy, and to strengthen it with an appreciation of the way that collective frameworks of thought – intersubjectivity, to use the term he prefers – evolve and direct collective purposive human action. He develops this dimension of his work by drawing on the tradition of historical reflection primarily associated with Giambattista Vico and Collingwood, and supported by the work of Georges Sorel and Fernand Braudel.[24] The hallmark of this tradition, exemplified most acutely in the writings of Vico and Collingwood, is that the enterprise of the social sciences needs to be centred on understanding the modification of human consciousness. A central aspect of this is the recognition that historical knowledge about human self-development is the principal means through which we can frame an understanding of the wellsprings of history, while a further key element lies in Collingwood's injunction to always look to the *inside* of events for their actual historical meaning (rather than to the *outside* of events, or to their phenomenology). Together with the more structural vantage point offered by the work of Sorel and Braudel, this historical idealist philosophy allows Cox to pinpoint with some accuracy changes to the deeply historicized ethos of successive structures of world order.[25]

This historicism is also visible in the innovative way that Cox deals with the idea of the state in *PPWO*. Most importantly, he refuses to grant the state an autonomy that it does not and cannot possess. Instead, throughout *PPWO* he considers the state in terms of a state-society complex, where the general power of the state emerges out of the particular relationship it has to the broader arrangement of social forces. It is only once social forces acquire a certain dynamic agency that he labels them as classes, in order to demonstrate historically and concretely how they can become integrated into larger institutional configurations: the agency of class as a political force only becomes possible once a 'class' achieves a cohesion within the institutions of the state. For Cox, class has appeared too often in historical materialist scholarship as an independent force, endowed not by any form of contested and collective social consciousness, but rather brought into being through a set of objective processes that *act* on class rather than *give life* to class. In *PPWO* Cox confronts this challenge and provides a way of understanding how class is *made* as a social force through the historical interconnections between three primary social configurations: production, the state and structures of world order. Each of these both act on and constrain class configurations even as they also *make* class configurations, and indeed by the end of the book we see how class is as much a 'product' of history as it is a 'producer' of history. Here once again we see how the innovative aspect of Cox's work sets him apart from mainstream IR and IPE.[26]

Conclusion

In an essay written to commemorate an award given to Susan Strange, a long-time friend and colleague, Cox wrote about how theorizing in academia tends to be organized around a 'groupie' model where gatekeepers act to ensure the sanctity of theoretical

developments and the acceptability of professionalization practices.[27] By contrast the
'loner' model – which by implication he associated with Strange's career – involved
neither the cultivation of groupies nor the stunted recounting of sacred debates, but
rather a proclivity to range widely over diverse material and a personal commitment to
intellectual integrity. Loners might influence one another and inadvertently on occasion
have groups form around them, but their vocation drives them to maintain their unique
vantage point through which to view the world. In some ways we might consider Cox
to be an exemplar of a 'loner', but one who nevertheless attracted considerable attention and who – inadvertently in some ways – found himself at the centre of several key
debates in a discipline into which he was neither trained nor professionalized.

   PPWO is a classic text that lies at the centre of Cox's intellectual status within the
disciplines of IR and IPE. By asking big picture questions about world order, and by
ranging widely in pursuit of historically relevant questions focused on change and
transformation, it provides us with a model of scholarship that focuses on enduring and
critical sets of complex social relationships. These relationships, the most important of
which are relations of class, state forms, interstate politics, intersubjectivity and production, generate the basic parameters of our evolving social consciousness, which in
turn informs how we are able to respond collectively to the problems facing our communities. Ultimately, for Cox as for the rest of us, responding to the pressures which the
global economy and its attendant structure of world order throw at us is among the
most important responsibilities facing scholars and citizens alike. The world may be a
seamless web of real, social relations, but for that very reason we need to range intellectually as widely as we can in pursuit of the best kind of knowledge for this task. The
theoretical eclecticism and reliance on a historical mode of thought that lies at the
heart of *PPWO* provides a model through which we can pursue this knowledge, and for
this reason it deserves its status as a classic text of IR that will inspire future generations
of IR and IPE scholars.

Notes

1 I would like to thank Eric Helleiner for helpful comments on a previous draft.
2 Robert W. Cox, 'Social Forces, States and World Orders: Beyond International Relations
  Theory', *Millennium: Journal of International Studies*, 1981, vol. 10, 126–55.
3 Robert W. Cox, 'Gramsci, Hegemony, and International Relations: An Essay in Method',
  1983, *Millennium: Journal of International Studies*, 1983, vol. 12, 162–75.
4 Robert W. Cox, *Production, Power and World Order: Social Forces in the Making of History*,
  New York: Columbia University Press, 1987. Page numbers placed in parentheses in the text
  refer to this edition. This framework of historical structures was developed in close collaboration with Harold Jacobson, a lifelong collaborator and friend, and Jeffrey Harrod, Cox's first
  graduate student. See Robert W. Cox and Harold K. Jacobson, *Anatomy of Influence*, New
  Haven, CT: Yale University Press, 1972; Jeffrey Harrod, *Power, Production, and the Unprotected
  Worker*, New York: Columbia University Press, 1987. The latter was written as a companion
  volume to *PPWO*.
5 Benjamin J. Cohen, *International Political Economy: An Intellectual History*, Princeton, NJ:
  Princeton University Press, 2008.
6 Cox took the term *mentalité* from the 'Annales' school of French historians, who understood
  it as the long-term and general mental frameworks which inform how people understand their
  position in the world. See Fernand Braudel, 'History and the Social Sciences: The *Longue
  Durée*', in Braudel, *On History*, trans. S. Matthews, London: Weidenfeld & Nicolson, 1980.
7 In addition to *Anatomy of Influence* and *PPWO*, see Cox, *The Political Economy of a Plural
  World: Critical Reflections on Power, Morals and Civilization*, London: Routledge, 2002.

8 See James H. Mittelman, 'Coxian Historicism as an Alternative Perspective in International Studies', *Alternatives*, 1998, vol. 23, 63–92.

9 See also Kenneth Waltz, *Theory of International Politics*, Reading, MA: Addison-Wesley, 1979; Robert Keohane, *After Hegemony*, Princeton, NJ: Princeton University Press, 1984; Robert Gilpin, *The Political Economy of International Relations*, Princeton, NJ: Princeton University Press, 1987; Susan Strange, *States and Markets*, London: Pinter, 1988.

10 See for example Brian Schmidt, *The Political Discourse of Anarchy: A Disciplinary History of International Relations*, Albany, NY: State University of New York Press, 1998.

11 For an example of Cox's historical approach to key concepts, see 'Civil Society at the Turn of the Millennium: Prospects for an Alternative World Order', *Review of International Studies*, 1999, vol. 25, 3–28.

12 R. G. Collingwood, *The Idea of History*, Oxford: Clarendon Press, 1946; E.P. Thompson, *The Poverty of Theory and Other Essays*, London: Monthly Review Press, 1978. Cox also develops his form of historical reasoning through a close reading of the work of the seventeenth-century philologist Giambattista Vico. See Giambattista Vico, *The New Science of Giambattista Vico*, trans. T. G. Bergin and M. H. Fisch, Ithaca, NY: Cornell University Press, [1946] 1984. His discussion of Vico can be found in *Political Economy of a Plural World*, Chapter 4.

13 Collingwood, *Idea of History*, p. 214.

14 Gramsci's ideas had begun to be applied to understanding the neo-liberal turn in Western Europe in the late 1970s and early 1980s, but almost exclusively in connection with individual countries. For an overview see Michael Kenny, *The First New Left: British Intellectuals after Stalin*, London: Lawrence & Wishart, 1995.

15 For an analysis of how this clash has developed, see Eric Helleiner and Stefano Pagliari, 'Between the Storms: Patterns in Global Financial Governance', in Geoffrey R. D. Underhill, Jasper Blom and Daniel Mügge (eds), *Global Financial Integration Thirty Years On: From Reform to Crisis*, Cambridge: Cambridge University Press, 2010, pp. 42–57; Randall Germain, *Global Politics and Financial Governance*, Basingstoke: Palgrave Macmillan, 2010.

16 Much of this work is the subject of Randall Germain and Michael Kenny, 'Engaging Gramsci: International Relations Theory and the "New" Gramscians', *Review of International Studies*, 1998, vol. 24, 3–21.

17 See for example Randolph B. Persaud, *Counter-Hegemony and Foreign Policy: The Dialectic of Marginalized and Global Forces in Jamaica*, Albany, NY: State University of New York Press, 2001; William I. Robinson, *A Theory of Global Capitalism: Production, Class and State in a Transnational World*, Baltimore, MD: Johns Hopkins University Press, 2004; Adam D. Morton, *Unraveling Gramsci: Hegemony and Passive Revolution in the Global Political Economy*, London: Pluto Press, 2007.

18 See Timothy J. Sinclair, 'Beyond International Relations Theory: Robert W. Cox and Approaches to World Order,' in Robert W. Cox with Timothy J. Sinclair, *Approaches to World Order*, Cambridge: Cambridge University Press, 1996, pp. 3–18; Stephen R. Gill and James H. Mittelman (eds), *Innovation and Transformation in International Studies*, Cambridge: Cambridge University Press, 1997; Mittelman, 'Coxian Historicism'; Michael G. Schechter, 'Critiques of Coxian Theory: Background to a Conversation,' in Cox, *Political Economy of a Plural World*, pp. 1–25.

19 Schechter, 'Critiques of Coxian Theory', pp. 3–7.

20 Cohen, *International Political Economy*, pp. 84–87.

21 Cox, 'Gramsci, Hegemony and International Relations', pp. 171–72.

22 Susan Strange, 'Preface', in Susan Strange (ed.), *Pathways to International Political Economy*, London: George, Allen & Unwin, 1984, p. ix.

23 Randall Germain, 'Critical Political Economy, Historical Materialism and Adam Morton,' *Politics*, 2007, vol. 27, 127–31, at p. 128.

24 Collingwood, *Idea of History*; Vico, *New Science*; Georges Sorel, *Reflections on Violence*, trans. T. E. Hulme, New York: Peter Smith, [1906] 1941; Fernand Braudel, *Civilization and Capitalism, 15th to 18th Centuries, Volume 3: The Perspective of the World*, trans., Sian Reynolds, London: Collins/Fontana, [1979] 1984.

25 The specificity of such an ethos is illustrated in an earlier publication that examines how a seemingly minor internal conflict over labour control and organization within states actually marked a significant structural shift in world order. Robert W. Cox, 'Labor and Hegemony', *International Organization*, 1977, vol. 31, 385–424.

26 For another example see Robert W. Cox, 'Towards a Post-Hegemonic Conception of World Order: Reflections on the Relevancy of Ibn Khaldun,' in James N. Rosenau and Ernst-Otto Czempiel (eds), *Governance Without Government: Order and Change in World Politics*, Cambridge: Cambridge University Press, 1992, pp. 132–59.
27 Robert W. Cox, 'Take Six Eggs: Theory, Finance and the Real Economy in the Work of Susan Strange,' in Cox, *Approaches to World Order*, 1996, pp. 174–88.

20 Gendering geopolitics, gendering IR: Cynthia Enloe's *Bananas, Beaches and Bases*

Alexandra Hyde and Marsha Henry[1]

Bananas, Beaches and Bases[2] was first published in 1989, towards the end of the Cold War and the beginning of feminism's engagement with International Relations (IR). The book has gained iconic status and, with subsequent works on related themes,[3] Enloe has achieved broad recognition as a key contributor to both feminism and IR scholarship. A critical appraisal of *Bananas, Beaches and Bases* therefore has to deal with its ambiguous position in and between the discipline of IR and the field of Gender or Women's Studies. Arguably any work that seeks to expose gaps in 'traditional' disciplines risks a very partial kind of success – appreciated somewhat selectively, as an intriguing curiosity perhaps, but rarely absorbed into the established 'canon'. It is encouraging then that *Bananas, Beaches and Bases* has made it through to this collection of classics in IR. Like other outliers such as Virginia Woolf's *Three Guineas*[4] and Stanley Kubrick's *Dr. Strangelove*,[5] *Bananas, Beaches and Bases* intervenes in IR by means of a different form and field of representation. More than 20 years after publication it is still original and unruly enough not to be ignored, while Enloe herself remains a scholar who persistently uses a non-academic arsenal to challenge IR scholarship from within. What is striking from the start is the breadth of the book's register, its accessibility of tone and above all the wit with which Enloe sets out her argument and in so doing, the stealth by which she intercepts and plays upon our preconceptions and expectations – of IR, of feminism, and of the world around us. In such ways, *Bananas, Beaches and Bases* is not simply about showing an alternative view of international relations. Drawing from feminist theory and practice, Enloe's work requires its readers not only to see but to *think* in new ways: with the situatedness of their knowledge rather than the illusion of objectivity; with a reflexive sense of familiarity that throws what is unfamiliar, because hidden, into relief; or to think at the intersection of multiple, analytical categories such as gender, race and sexuality rather than taking a single, linear approach. As such, *Bananas, Beaches and Bases* is a kind of collage that cuts up the neatly delineated, ethnocentric fabric of IR and brings these monotone pieces together with fragments from political and cultural reality as it is lived and experienced, embodied or enacted by different people around the world. Assembled together in this way, Enloe is able to reveal new and surprising angles from which international relations might be understood and conceptualized.

Enloe's demonstrative combination of the everyday and the international is key to the impact and originality of *Bananas, Beaches and Bases*. Yet the same juxtaposition of macro-level geopolitics and micro-level gender relations is also what renders it susceptible to being discounted as 'proper' IR. It is true that *Bananas, Beaches and Bases* does not engage explicitly on an epistemological level with much of the classic theoretical work featured in this volume, for example. Critics have agreed that *Bananas, Beaches and Bases* and other works in Enloe's inimitable style might challenge an academic audience to take them seriously.[6] As such, Enloe's recalibration of international relations to take account of what is personal as well as political (to use an old-fashioned phrase more current at the time when *Bananas, Beaches and Bases* was published than it is now) comes with the occupational hazard of being 'easy to trivialize'.[7] However, what Enloe qualifies as the '*desire* to trivialize'[8] her work within the discipline of IR, is still an important factor in assessing whether or not the book will endure as a classic. Enloe announces her intervention into IR by asking 'Where are the women?' (pp. 7, 200). It is a simple question, and one to which Enloe has more or less adhered in many of her subsequent monographs.[9] However, surely the fact that this question still needs to be asked shows that gender as a mode of analysis has not been fully absorbed as a common denominator across IR research? How far has feminist IR come in its adaptation of Enloe's question into a suitably sharp and nuanced tool that can be incorporated into the analytical machinery of IR as a whole? If the same question *is* still being asked, then perhaps Enloe's ultimate aim in *Bananas, Beaches and Bases* might be argued to have failed. Nevertheless, feminist IR has developed at a steady rate over the past 30 years, at the same time adopting a more reflexive assessment of its own status within IR.[10] As will be discussed in the second half of this chapter, an appraisal of *Bananas, Beaches and Bases* as an IR classic must not only consider how far feminist IR has come, but how far it still has to go. First, however, this chapter aims to provide some textual insights into Enloe's approach in *Bananas, Beaches and Bases*, considering both its critical reception, and some of the ways in which it opened the door for a deeper investigation of the central tenets of IR. We then consider some of the ways in which feminist IR has measured its own impact in terms of integrating gender analysis alongside other 'turns' in critical theory, before considering the contemporary relevance of *Bananas, Beaches and Bases* and its potential to endure as a classic of both gender studies and IR.

The sliding scale of international relations

The correct order of alliterative B-words in the title *Bananas, Beaches and Bases* can be difficult to remember. The key is to start small, with something entirely mundane: the humble *banana*, enduringly quirky both as an object and as a topic of debate (p. 127). From the export of goods from subtropical climes, to global brands promoting consumer loyalty around a generic fruit (p. 129), Enloe takes stock of the 'International Politics of the Banana' (p. 124) as a series of strategic manoeuvres that are far from banal or benign. Long before globalization produced social movements based on the fairness of trade or the fashionable lifestyle choice of 'buying local', Enloe was questioning the racial division of labour in banana plantations and the sexual division of labour in small-scale subsistence farming (pp. 134–37). So it is, she argues, that everyday items such as the banana, harvested by hand in one place or bought by Japanese housewives in another (p. 132), fuel a set of relationships that 'we once imagined were private or merely social', but are 'in fact infused with power, usually unequal' (p. 195). Next, the title of the book expands beyond the 'humdrum' (p. 14) of everyday life to the place where many people go to escape it: *beaches*, to the very edge of national territory or the outer fringes of another. The beaches in *Bananas, Beaches and Bases* are internationalized sites of leisure and pleasure, where a developing country's lack of infrastructure, health care, good roads or education can be rebranded as 'unspoilt' (p. 31).

With this, Enloe posits an alternative reading of travel brochure blurb, revealing the political economy of government policies that promote tourism as a developing country's principal vehicle for growth. For Enloe, the international politics of tourism can be plotted on a sliding scale that, like the International Monetary Fund (IMF) chief and the hotel chambermaid, connects macroeconomic relationships of debt, investment and foreign exchange to the unreliable wages of seasonal labour and the feminization of an 'unskilled' service industry. If however, 'tourism is not discussed as seriously by conventional political commentators as oil or weaponry' (p. 40), then Enloe's concession to conventional IR comes with the inclusion of *bases* in her title. With state security, *Bananas, Beaches and Bases* is on solid ground. At the same time, however, Enloe advocates for a much broader conceptualization of militarized power than that which the discipline generally takes into account. This includes the soft power camouflage of cultural assimilation that renders a US military base politically invisible in the UK (p. 67), or the visibility of a base town as it is embodied by female sex workers in South Korea (p. 87). Such examples comprise an alternative set of 'international relations' involved in the extension of state power beyond national borders, but they also highlight the methods through which these relations are culturally and politically constructed on both an international and a local scale. Although Enloe is concerned with the ways in which local and global power relations can be co-constructed via social, cultural and discursive means, the materiality of the subjects she chooses – the banana, the beaches, the military base – emphasize the tangible cause and effect of what might otherwise be dismissed as 'merely' ideological or theoretical.

Looking closely or indeed, stepping back to take in something of its breadth and scope, it is possible to see that *Bananas, Beaches and Bases* is made up of a series of microcosms, from plantations, factories and hotels to social movements, armies and diplomatic corps. These are the 'self-contained worlds' (p. 140) that represent the sharp end of gender relations, comprised of their own social, political and cultural orders at the same time as they are linked to macro-level power relations through trade, labour, production, consumption, security or statecraft. The sliding scale that Enloe uses to accommodate bananas, beaches and bases together in her irreverent book title also acts as an analytic tool through which what is apparently personal, familiar, or pedestrian is shown by gradual degrees of connection to be far more than its apparent triviality suggests. According to such criteria, the package tour, the clothing brand, the colonial administrator, the peace activist, the Hollywood star, the diplomat's wife and the plantation worker all take their place in an immense web of relations that are international and suffused with power. It is not that the Japanese multinational, the Egyptian nationalist movement, the US Department of Defense, the British diplomatic service or the IMF do not count. It is just that Enloe sets out to read power both 'backwards and forwards' (p. 196). In other words, by plotting both the 'everyday' and the 'international' on the same axis – by starting with the banana and ending with the military base or vice versa – Enloe reveals an immense volume and variety of power that can be said to play its part, no matter how small, in global politics. Moreover, Enloe argues, it is *gender* that accounts for the vastness and variability of such power and most significantly, its unequal distribution.

'Gendering' geopolitics within IR

The main instrument of *Bananas, Beaches and Bases* – the lens that permits Enloe to focus so vividly on a range of different scales – is gender. For Enloe, feminist analysis is about revealing the gendered dimensions of power on an everyday level and linking them to the operation of the international political system, with a view to demonstrating that gender relations are always in play and moreover, that they *matter*. Enloe implicitly challenges the categories of sex and gender by making visible what is taken for granted as 'natural' or 'common sense' (such as the sexual division of labour), and exploring the systems and structures that have been put in place to construct and control this 'reality' (such as ideas about masculinity and femininity). When it was first published, *Bananas, Beaches and Bases* went further than most IR scholarship to demonstrate how all kinds of power relations are socially constructed and contribute to women's particular experiences globally. When Enloe emphasizes not only that the personal is political but that '*the international is personal*' (p. 196), her aim is to show how geopolitics plays a part in how we can understand – and change – gender power. This is the starting point from which she launches her critique:

> As one learns to look at the world through feminist eyes, one learns to ask whether anything that passes for inevitable, inherent, 'traditional' or biological has in fact been *made*. One begins to ask how all sorts of things have been made – a treeless landscape, a rifle-wielding police force, the 'Irishman joke', an all-woman typing pool. Asking how something has been made implies that it has been made by someone. Suddenly there are clues to trace; there is also blame, credit and responsibility to apportion, not just at the start but at each point along the way (p. 3).

In other words, the different symbolic and social values that are attached to particular identities, relations and experiences, play a direct role in determining the material and economic conditions of people's lives. Enloe calls attention to what she argues is the expressly *political* power of factors traditionally beyond the scope of IR. These are slippery concepts that are not only hard to define, but constantly conceal their own effects: 'Ignoring women on the landscape of international politics perpetuates the notion that certain power relations are merely a matter of taste and culture' (p. 3).

Bananas, Beaches and Bases sets out to demonstrate that suffused throughout international relations are a host of 'cultural' ideas pertaining to men and women that give meaning, order and expression to the experience of social reality. Taking the example of the tourist industry, Enloe draws attention to the ways in which flight attendants and chambermaids provide sexualized services that are propagated by ideas about femininity. 'Femininity' can be sexualized when uniformed in an obligatory skirt or more prosaically, housekeeping can be feminized as 'natural' and therefore unskilled labour for women, which allows multinational hotel firms to pay their local female workforce less (p. 34). Somewhere along this continuum of ideas about gender, labour and tourism, Enloe plots the migration of workers from rural areas to coastal towns or cities (p. 86) where over time, particular jobs and roles become associated with different ethnic identities. Next, she introduces the use of some of these same towns for 'R&R' by US soldiers on leave (p. 36). By this point, the growth of sex tourism appears anything but anomalous and the social, economic and cultural assumptions that go with it are revealed as simply another 'strand of the gendered tourism industry' (ibid.). The flipside of 'culture' then is that this seemingly benign, catchall concept can be used to whitewash the role of gender in international politics by turning it into something that is just natural, like the apparent libido of US marines or the apparent sexual availability of Thai women, for example. Further linking tourism, masculinity and femininity to the construction of national identity, Enloe argues that '[i]f a state is a vertical creature of authority, a nation is a horizontal creature of identity' (p. 46). But which nationalist movement appropriates the oppressed chambermaid as its political symbol? None, it turns out. Enloe wagers that the figure of the chambermaid is far less compelling as a symbol of the corrosion of national identity than for example, the men at the core of Caribbean nationalist movements who have been emasculated and transformed into a 'nation of busboys' working in white resorts (p. 34). There has been no gendered reduction of power, no 'unnatural' reversal of roles in the transformation of thousands of women into housekeepers: 'after all, a woman who has traded work as an unpaid agricultural worker for work as a hotel cleaner hasn't lost any of her femininity' (p. 36). Only when idealized forms of femininity are compromised, however, do women finally make it through as agents of national identity, and only then to be rescued like the figure of the female sex worker, or protected like the figure of the veiled Muslim woman (p. 42).

Rather than focusing on nation states as unitary actors within the international political system, *Bananas, Beaches and Bases* is comprised of a vast range of empirical snapshots, interconnected in ways that confound or decentre the analytic and geographical boundaries of IR. Enloe's internationalist methodology draws on feminist standpoint theory in its accommodation of a range of different – and global – perspectives from which social reality might be understood and experienced.[11] Feminist standpoint theory[12] recognizes that knowledge (and therefore power) is situated in the particular context of its production, be that a question or combination of academic disciplines, free market economics, social relations, geographical locations or political representation. Enloe's contribution is to point out that conceptualizing international relations as a vertical set of top-down transactions obscures the kinds of knowledge and power that are negotiated at the margins. In other words, that it is often at the opposite end of the scale to macro-level forms of knowledge and power that international relations reach their material apotheosis. In *Bananas, Beaches and Bases*, the global economic market for consumer goods such as designer jeans (p. 151) is examined in terms of local conditions of production in factories in South Korea (p. 168) or Mexico (p. 169). More recently, feminist scholars such as V. Spike Peterson and Penny Griffin have provided valuable schemata for the relationship between gender and international political economy.[13] At the time that *Bananas, Beaches and Bases* was published (and in her earlier work with Wendy Chapkis[14]), Enloe and other feminist scholars were primarily concerned with making visible the role of women's labour in 'the new industrial map of the world'.[15] By focusing on the empirical effects of macroeconomics on a micro scale, Enloe opened the door for IR to take seriously a much broader range of power relations with respect to shifts in the international division of labour and the 'feminization' (p. 176) of particular kinds of employment. Importantly, Enloe's formulation of such power relations includes women's organizing both locally (p. 170) and transnationally (p. 173), providing a more nuanced view of women's role in a country's development and their empowerment through wage labour and political consciousness (p. 175). At the same time, Enloe's attention to the material and experiential margins of IR goes much deeper than the positivist/rationalist[16] proposition of simply 'adding' women to the economic equation. If in *Bananas, Beaches and Bases*, Enloe chooses to focus as much on the role of symbolic and cultural capital in shaping material and social reality, it is because her constructivist critique of IR is concerned not only with the ways in which women's labour is exploited, but also the social and cultural conditions by which women's labour comes to be exploit*able*. As such, her focus on the effects of macroeconomics yields considerable insight into their micro-level causes. Incidentally, this includes the tendency of feminist scholars in the West to 'collapse all women in Third World countries into a single homogenous category' (p. 175), or the contradictory case of the 'feminist domestic employer' (p. 179). What Enloe is at pains to point out by writing against or outside traditional ideas about productive labour, is precisely what more conventional IR perspectives obscure: namely the gendered, racialized or class-based structures of knowledge and power that underpin international divisions of labour and the value attached to them. However, while alert to the multiple political economies arising from and within the formal structure of nation states, Enloe pays less attention to the shadow economies that operate to disrupt the existence – and the conceptualization – of a single international political system. Here *Bananas, Beaches and Bases* is out-paced by more recent work on phenomena such as 'global care chains',[17] which accounts for gender within processes of globalization by highlighting the counter-systems that are generated by informal or illegal markets such as human trafficking, for example. Enloe is interested in patriarchy as a structure of oppression and does much to illustrate its cooperation with global and local patterns of class and ethnicity (p. 186). At the same time, however, her emphasis on the social, cultural and collective dynamics of international relations leaves the role of individual agency unexplored. It is not as if *Bananas, Beaches and Bases* is not vividly populated by real-life politics. Rather, to fully deconstruct the superstructure of the international system requires insight into how these relations are renegotiated or resisted on an individual or subjective level. *Bananas, Beaches and Bases* was not ahead of its time in all respects perhaps, but as we explore below no book can be all things to all people in relation to feminism and IR.

Although Enloe's ideas about gender, power and culture can be traced back to feminist standpoint and postmodern constructivism,[18] she does not offer a comprehensive account of the mechanics of these ideas, nor their epistemological foundations. Consequently the parameters of gender power – as either distinct from or mutually constituted by other forms of power – can appear undefined, lending gender a singularity and centricity that is sometimes at odds with the intersectional nature of oppression that Enloe is keen to emphasize in other parts of the book. One might argue that without unpicking the epistemological foundations of IR as a discipline, it is not possible to incorporate the threads of gender analysis in the comprehensive way that Enloe claims is necessary. At the same time, the question as to whether or not a work of IR scholarship must be founded upon or produce broad cross-cutting theories as a precondition of its relevance and applicability to a broad, cross-cutting discipline is perhaps the very point in question. Animated as it is by something of the activist's zeal as opposed to the academic's constant qualification, *Bananas, Beaches and Bases* challenges disciplinary boundaries in form as well as content. In this sense, it remains a breakthrough work: forthright, occasionally blunt and heavy-handed, but as its inclusion in this volume attests, undoubtedly effective in clearing a space so that other questions – more systematic and nuanced perhaps – can begin to be asked. Enloe herself has acknowledged that following the question 'Where are the women?' (pp. 7, 200), come others such as 'why are they there, who got them there, and what happens to your understanding of the people you have already painted in once you see them there?'[19] Feminist IR is rooted at least partially in a critical tradition that views IR as constructed from a Western, masculinist perspective, its production of knowledge a historical instrument of domination and control over global political and economic systems.[20] Enloe does not disavow the need for 'explanatory generalization that is above the particular',[21] but insists that theory is inevitably tested in reality: 'My kind of theorizing constantly goes back and forth between general and particular because I want to actually test my theories on the page with the reader'.[22] There can be no doubt that the accessibility of *Bananas, Beaches and Bases* has helped it to reach a great many readers, with the book a common fixture of reading lists at both undergraduate and graduate level, published in its second edition with a new preface by the author in 2000. The paradox of *Bananas, Beaches and Bases* and its potential stumbling block within the 'serious' discipline of IR, however, is that both its content and its accessible style are rooted in another core principle of feminist research – the importance of considering 'the everyday'. In other words, at the same time as *Bananas, Beaches and Bases* challenges what counts as international relations, it also challenges what might count as IR epistemology.

(Inter)disciplinary tensions

To the extent that any 'classic' gains its status as a placeholder for a particular school of thought or approach, it is necessary to go beyond the individual factors that make *Bananas, Beaches and Bases* relevant to both feminism and IR, and consider more carefully some of the disciplinary tensions it provokes. *Bananas, Beaches and Bases* takes its place alongside Jean Bethke Elshtain's *Women and War*[23] and J. Ann Tickner's *Gender in International Relations* to form a kind of holy trinity, canonized by ensuing scholarship[24] as the first wave of feminist IR. Enloe, Tickner, Elshtain and others[25] take up individual and sometimes overlapping positions from across a range of theoretical and disciplinary approaches, from standpoint theory to discourse analysis and peace studies. Since then, and perhaps inevitably for a theoretical tradition that promotes a reflexive assessment of its own production of knowledge, feminist IR has also turned its attention inwards, assessing its own origins and complicity with the Western historical and intellectual traditions that were the very same foundations for disciplines such as IR. Gender studies and its purpose or impact with regards to IR continues to be debated by scholars.[26] Even the necessity for anything called 'feminist IR' has been argued to expose the failure of gender theory to reach its potential as a common analytical category across the field as a whole.[27] However, the interdisciplinary world of feminist scholarship is itself far from coherent, marked as Kimberley Hutchings has put it, by the 'contrast and continuity' that results from multiple approaches combined under one banner.[28] More recently, Marysia Zalewski has questioned the helpfulness of tidying up feminism to take on such institutional behemoths as IR.[29] She presents a scenario where in order to 'undo' IR, feminism is forced to deny the productive tensions that result from its interdisciplinarity, tying up its loose ends to take on the solid mass of IR as a coherent discipline.[30] It is significant then that Enloe refused the temptation to streamline her investigations in order to produce a generalizable pattern or theory through which gender as a category of analysis might achieve 'universal' applicability – and *Bananas, Beaches and Bases* a kind of universal acceptance.

  The push for disciplinary coherence within feminist IR also derives from a feminist politics that seeks a social, transformative role for the knowledge it produces.[31] Indeed, if *Bananas, Beaches and Bases* is a 'classic' feminist text in any sense, it would qualify solely on the basis of the explicit link that Enloe draws between feminist theory and praxis, analysis and activism, and social change. Enloe is interested in the differences *between* and *among* women, for example the differences in race, class and sexuality between women serving in, married to or protesting against military institutions (p. 65). Her ultimate aim is to demonstrate how the relations between women are structured according to social orders of distinction that are co-opted in the interests of military effectiveness, for example (p. 92) and to the detriment of women's collective (and transnational) political potential:

> If women active in anti-bases movements see developing contacts with women in alternative countries as integral to their work, there is a better chance of the removal of a military base producing a fundamental reassessment of global strategy, not simply a transfer of equipment and personnel. If military wives and women soldiers begin to explore the ways that prostitution pollutes not only their on-base lives but the life of the country off which they are living, the respect they seek for themselves is likely to have deeper roots. Such an exploration might also prompt them to broaden their political horizons, to focus less exclusively on benefits and ask more questions about the consequences of militarisation. (p. 92)

Enloe's considerable ambitions for feminist activism might not be best suited to the field of IR, where Adam Jones has argued that[32] 'the recognition of the importance and politicized nature of the domestic realm does not automatically lead to a particular set of prescriptions for conducting politics within or among states'[33] Neo-feminist scholars also highlight the failure of feminism to provide a gender analysis that is broad enough to accommodate the relative oppressions not just between different women, but between different women and different men. According to this viewpoint, the classical feminist canon is outdated in only taking women's lives as its starting point: 'Attention to the large mass of ordinary men in international society is not absent in Enloe's work (as it is in most feminist writing); but it seems disconcertingly permeated by the male-as-power-broker stereotype.'[34] An increasing attention to men and masculinities has emerged in gender studies in recent years, with the work of theorists such as R. W. Connell[35] informing debates on the role of gender within military institutions, for example.[36] Jones' own solution, however, is to devote his analysis to 'concrete' matters and 'real-world issues', rather than a 'more abstract investigation into the *construction* of gender, the *continuum* of gender *identities*, and so on' (emphasis added).[37] He calls for more examples, statistics and comparisons by 'strictly quantitative measure' that will 'outweigh the female-grounded examples'[38] given by scholars such as Enloe. However, stereotypes are not defeated simply by being outnumbered, they must first be recognized for what they are: cultural constructions, produced and perpetuated, Enloe would argue, by a strategic politics of representation (and yes, perhaps on occasion, by feminist politics of representation). Counter-examples alone cannot negate the persistence of particular stereotypes. This is only half the battle, and only a fraction of what Enloe does in *Bananas, Beaches and Bases*. The achievement of Enloe's approach is not only to show what social, cultural and political forms gender takes, but also to show how those constructions are *made* and how they are *used*. Contrary to Jones' criticism, Enloe's point is that the construction of gender *is* a concrete matter and that gender ideology contributes to the sharp end of social reality.

Conclusion

Enloe's question: 'Where are the women?' (pp. 7, 200) has perhaps become an unfashionable proposition during the transition in scholarship from feminist or women's studies to a range of disciplines with the prefix 'Gender and ... '. But *Bananas, Beaches and Bases* is not only about the impact of international relations upon women, or the impact of women upon international relations. Enloe takes feminism's deep-rooted concern with the production of knowledge and questions the very process by which IR as a discipline draws the boundaries of what counts as IR. She does this not only by revealing the places where gender *matter*s, but also by critiquing the gendered ways in which our knowledge about international relations is produced.[39] Enloe's focus on the constructedness of things, the way things are made and indeed, made to *appear*, would seem to limit her analysis to a solely descriptive rather than a prescriptive role, neglecting a 'radical redefinition of what actually constitutes "power"'.[40] However, in reassessing the scripts, codes, modes and boundaries of this power, *Bananas, Beaches and Bases* sets a clear and unequivocal mandate for a reconfiguration of IR and its methodology. Enloe reveals that the mechanics of IR work together in a precise way, the direction of one part being dependent on the reversal of another, so that on the face of it the world keeps turning as before. What Enloe brings to the classical canon of IR is the question of what international power is, if it is not constituted by its *application*. One way of responding to this question is to seek to understand the profoundly gendered and material ways in which power is exercised and experienced.

Notes

1 We are grateful to Cynthia Enloe for generous feedback on several key aspects of this chapter.
2 Cynthia Enloe, *Bananas, Beaches and Bases: Making Feminist Sense of International Politics*, London: Pandora, 2000. Page numbers placed in parentheses in the text refer to this edition.
3 Including: Enloe, *Maneuvers: The International Politics of Militarizing Women's Lives*, Berkeley, CA: University of California Press, 2000; *The Morning After: Sexual Politics at the End of the Cold War*, Berkeley, CA: University of California Press, 1993.
4 Virginia Woolf, *Three Guineas*, London: Hogarth Press, 1938.
5 *Dr. Strangelove or: How I Learned to Stop Worrying and Love the Bomb*, directed by Stanley Kubrick, 95 min., Columbia Pictures and Hawk Films, 1964.
6 Cristine Sylvester, *Feminist International Relations: An Unfinished Journey*, Cambridge: Cambridge University Press, 2001, p. 32; Judith Stiehm, 'Book Review: Cynthia Enloe, Maneuvers', *Millennium: Journal of International Studies*, 2000, vol. 29, 489–92.
7 Cynthia Enloe and Marysia Zalewski, 'Feminist Theorizing from Bananas to Maneuvers' *International Feminist Journal of Politics*, 2001, vol. 1, 138–47, at p. 139.
8 Enloe and Zalewski, 'Feminist Theorizing from Bananas to Maneuvers', p. 139.
9 Other selected works include Enloe, *Nimo's War, Emma's War: Making Feminist Sense of the Iraq War*, Berkley, CA: University of California Press, 2010; Enloe, *Globalization and Militarism: Feminists Make the Link*, Lanham, MD: Rowman & Littlefield, 2007; Enloe, *The Curious Feminist: Searching for Women in The New Age of Empire*, Berkeley, CA and London: University of California Press, 2004.
10 Kimberley Hutchings, '1988 and 1998: Contrast and Continuity in Feminist International Relations', *Millennium: Journal of International Studies*, 2008, vol. 37, 97–106.
11 Kimberley Hutchings, 'The Personal is International: Feminist Epistemology and the Case of International Relations', in Kathleen Lennon & Margaret Whitford (eds), *Knowing the Difference: Feminist Perspectives in Epistemology*, London: Routledge, 1994, p. 155.
12 Key contributions to feminist standpoint theory include Sandra Harding, *Whose Science/ Whose Knowledge?*, Milton Keynes: Open University Press, 1991; Sandra Harding, 'Rethinking Standpoint Epistemology: What is Strong Objectivity?', in Linda Alcoff and

Elizabeth Potter (eds), *Feminist Epistemologies*, New York and London: Routledge, 1993; Sandra Harding (ed.), *The Feminist Standpoint Theory Reader*, New York and London: Routledge, 2004; Donna Haraway, 'Situated Knowledges', in Harding, *Feminist Standpoint Theory Reader*, pp. 81–102; Nancy Hartsock, 'The Feminist Standpoint: Developing the Ground for a Specifically Feminist Historical Materialism', in Harding, *Feminist Standpoint Theory Reader*, pp. 35–54; Patricia Hill Collins, *Black Feminist Thought: Knowledge, Consciousness and the Politics of Empowerment*, New York and London: Routledge, 1990; Patricia Hill Collins, 'Learning from the Outsider Within: The Sociological Significance of Black Feminist Thought', in Harding, *Feminist Standpoint Theory Reader*, pp. 103–26; Dorothy Smith, 'Women's Perspective as a Radical Critique of Sociology', in Harding, *Feminist Standpoint Theory Reader*, pp. 21–34.

13 V. Spike Peterson, 'How (the Meaning of) Gender Matters in Political Economy', *New Political Economy*, 2005, vol. 10, 499–521; Penny Griffin, 'Refashioning IPE: What and How Gender Analysis Teaches International (Global) Political Economy', in *Review of International Political Economy*, 2007, vol. 14, 719–36.

14 Wendy Chapkis and Cynthia Enloe, *Of Common Cloth: Women in the Global Textile Industry*, Washington, DC: Transnational Institute, 1983.

15 Ruth Pearson, 'Nimble Fingers Revisited: Reflections on Women and Third World Industrialisation in the Late Twentieth Century', in Cecile Jackson and Ruth Pearson (eds), *Feminist Visions of Development, Gender Analysis and Policy*, Oxford and New York: Routledge, 1998, pp. 171–88, at p. 171.

16 For a comprehensive discussion of these and other epistemological approaches within IPE see Peterson, 'How (the Meaning of) Gender Matters', p. 502.

17 Rhacel Parrenas, *Servants of Globalization: Women, Migration, and Domestic Work*, Stanford, CA: Stanford University Press, 2001.

18 Sylvester, *Feminist International Relations*, p. 8.

19 Enloe and Zalewski, 'Feminist Theorizing', p. 138.

20 J. Ann Tickner, *Gender in International Relations: Feminist Perspectives on Achieving Global Security*, New York: Columbia University Press, 1992, p. ix.

21 Enloe and Zalewski, 'Feminist Theorizing', p. 141.

22 Enloe and Zalewski, 'Feminist Theorizing', p. 6.

23 Jean Bethke Elshtain, *Women and War*, Brighton: Harvester Press, 1987.

24 Sylvester, *Feminist International Relations*, p. 18.

25 See, for example, Carol Cohn, 'Sex and Death in the Rational World of Defense Intellectuals', *Signs*, 1987, vol. 12, 687–718; Sarah Ruddick, *Maternal Thinking: Towards A Politics of Peace*, Boston: Beacon Press, 1989; Jan Jindy Pettman, *Worlding Women: A Feminist International Politics*, Sydney: Allen & Unwin, 1996.

26 Selected examples include Robert O. Keohane, 'International Relations Theory: Contributions of a Feminist Standpoint', in Rebecca Grant and Kathleen Newland (eds), *Gender and International Relations*, Milton Keynes: Open University Press, 1991, pp. 41–51; J. Ann Tickner, 'You Just Don't Understand: Troubled Engagements between Feminists and IR Theorists', *International Studies Quarterly*, 1997, vol. 41, 611–32; and Gillian Youngs, 'Feminist International Relations: A Contradiction in Terms? Or: Why Women and Gender Are Essential to Understanding the World "We" Live In', *International Affairs*, 2004, vol. 80, 75–87.

27 Youngs, 'Feminist International Relations', p. 76.

28 Hutchings, '1988 and 1998', p. 97.

29 Marysia Zalewski, 'Do We Understand Each Other Yet? Troubling Feminist Encounters With(in) International Relations', *The British Journal of Politics and International Relations*, 2007, vol. 9, 302–12.

30 Zalewski, 'Do We Understand Each Other Yet?', p. 305.

31 Zalewski, 'Do We Understand Each Other Yet?', p. 305.

32 Adam Jones, 'Does "Gender" Make the World Go Round? Feminist Critiques of International Relations', *Review of International Studies*, 1996, vol. 22, 405–29.

33 Jones, 'Does "Gender" Make the World Go Round?', p. 412.

34 Jones, 'Does "Gender" Make the World Go Round?', p. 421.

35 R. W. Connell, *Masculinities*, Cambridge: Polity Press, 1995.

36 Paul Higate (ed.), *Military Masculinities: Identity and the State*, Westport, CT: Praeger, 2003.
37 Jones, 'Does "Gender" Make the World Go Round?', p. 424.
38 Jones, 'Does "Gender" Make the World Go Round?', p. 424.
39 Tickner, *Gender in International Relations*, p. 129.
40 Jones, 'Does "Gender" Make the World Go Round?', p. 414.

21 The limits of international relations: R. B. J. Walker's *Inside/outside: International Relations as Political Theory*

Tom Lundborg and Nick Vaughan-Williams[1]

While R. B. J. Walker's *Inside/outside: International Relations as Political Theory* (*Inside/outside*) is in many ways a classic, there are several difficulties – and indeed ironies – in referring to it as a classic *of* International Relations (IR).[2] Here, we are not dealing with a work that seeks to improve on contemporary theories of IR, either by providing better and more accurate explanations of 'international relations', or by offering new visions of 'world politics'. Such criteria might usually be employed to judge whether a particular contribution to IR is worthy of the accolade of being a 'classic', but they do not apply in Walker's case. Rather, his is a collection of essays that engage critically with some of the underlying assumptions upon which the very notion of IR as a separate 'discipline' relies. Perhaps most of all, it is a text that questions the constitutive limits of IR – understood as a discipline that concerns itself with what is said to happen 'outside' rather than 'inside' the sovereign territorial state, in the realm of 'international' as opposed to 'domestic' politics. Through the establishment and maintenance of these limits Walker argues that IR is (re)produced as a separate field of study and is distinct from Political Theory.

By refusing to take the distinctions between inside and outside, International Relations and Political Theory for granted, *Inside/outside* is not so much a classic *of* IR – indeed Walker is highly sceptical of the practice of canonizing in scholarship – but rather a particular (and political) intervention that opened up new ways of thinking about the very (im)possibility of IR as a *separate discipline*: a move that, ultimately, can either be read as a victory for Walker or the discipline depending on whether one accepts the former's bold critique of the latter. It encourages scholars and students alike to challenge the limits that the notion of a separate discipline relies upon, not least by examining the underlying assumptions upon which theories of IR either claim to speak the 'truth' of the eternal realities and structural necessities of the international system of sovereign states, or construct visions of how the world should be organized differently. Understood in this light, *Inside/outside* stands as one of the most important – and certainly most subversive – contributions ever made to the theoretical body of literature produced by the 'discipline' of IR.

One of the greatest contributions of *Inside/outside* lies in its refusal to rely on one master narrative, particular explanation or specific starting point for questioning the disciplinary boundaries of IR. While the text is sometimes associated with the positivism/post-positivism debate in IR theory, any attempt to categorize it using terms like reflectivism, post-modernism, post-structuralism or post-positivism is highly problematic – not least because Walker himself staunchly rejects these labels. Indeed, none of these terms – nor any other 'ism' – offers an adequate reflection of Walker's critique, which does not stem from *one* particular approach. Instead, Walker draws from a rich tapestry of philosophical traditions, including the history of ideas, ideology critique, immanent critique, as well as a more general literature on alterity, running from G. W. F. Hegel through to Michel Foucault, Edward Said and Tzvetan Todorov, among others.[3]

Furthermore, Walker's critique is not directed *against* one particular strand of IR theory. Instead, it highlights many of the logical impossibilities and conceptual conundrums upon which the very notion of IR as a separate discipline is maintained and reproduced by different theoretical approaches. *Inside/outside* should, thus, not be viewed as an attempt to add a new or better theory to already existing theories. The problem is that to add in this context would be to valorize the foundational starting points of IR that Walker aims to call into question: the modern logic of inside/outside predicated on a sharp distinction between the presence of political life inside the modern state and the absence thereof outside.

In this chapter we cannot pretend to do justice to the complexity of *Inside/outside.* Instead, we draw out what we consider to be some of the main themes of the book as it has influenced us in our own research and engagement with the discipline. These themes relate specifically to the problem of sovereignty (dealt with in Chapters 3 and 8 of the text); questions about time, historicity and origins (Chapters 1, 2, 4 and 5); and space, territory and borders (Chapters 1, 6 and 7). Having discussed these central themes we then look at the reception of *Inside/outside* and consider some of the critiques levelled against it before offering some of our own concluding remarks.

The modern logic of inside/outside

Instead of accepting the distinctions between inside and outside, domestic and international, International Relations and Political Theory, as pre-given and natural starting points for thinking about politics, *Inside/outside* questions how these binary oppositions are produced and what work they do in shaping the modern political imagination. In this context, theories of IR become particularly interesting to examine as examples of how certain distinctions are inscribed and produced, and how this production both reflects and affirms the limits of thinking about politics in the late modern world. Here, the key move Walker makes is to treat theoretical works produced by IR as constitutive of rather than somehow divorced from the aspects of contemporary political life they purport merely to describe. Once this move is made, the notion, discipline and practice of IR, defined by the *presence* of sovereign states and the *absence* of sovereign authority, can be recast as constitutive of that which it seeks to explain (p. 171). In the Preface, Walker explains that his book offers a 'reading of modern theories of IR as a discourse that systematically reifies an historically specific spatial ontology, a sharp delineation of here and there, a discourse that both expresses and constantly affirms the presence and absence of political life inside and outside the modern state as the only ground on which structural necessities can be understood and new realms of freedom and history can be revealed' (p. ix).

While highlighting a historically specific spatial ontology of the sovereign state, the distinction between inside and outside can also be seen as constitutive of certain *limits* of thinking about politics. These limits are illustrated both by the neorealist commitment to explaining the structural necessities of the interstate system, but also by other (apparently contrasting) approaches, such as neoliberalism and cosmopolitanism, in trying to think of politics otherwise.

To think of politics 'otherwise' has become a key concern not least against the background of widespread claims that the modern world is undergoing profound changes, as illustrated by the increasing significance of non-territorial global flows of people, money and information. In the context of such claims, realist approaches may seem increasingly outdated, offering anachronistic images of the world based on clear lines and distinctions. At the same time, it is also possible to argue that realist approaches have proved to be extremely resilient in terms of their ability to reaffirm the spatial ontology of states and the distinction of life within and between sovereign states. This distinction, Walker notes, offers an elegant yet complex resolution of the puzzles of modern political thought, perhaps the most important of which relates to the problem of negotiating the relationship between the 'universal' and the 'particular'. Following the modern solution to this problem, the distinction between inside and outside allows for ideas about the universally good – i.e. notions of progress, justice, ethics and so on – to be aspired to *within* the limits of the particular sovereign state. Hence, it also allows for a distinction to be made between the possibility of progress inside the sovereign state and mere repetition and timelessness outside the state.

On the basis of the modern logic of inside/outside, IR is commonly reduced to a choice of either/or – a choice between the eternal game of relations between sovereign states or the possibility of finding some kind of universal community beyond the state. This choice, which is often framed as a choice between realism and idealism, both reflects and affirms the limits of the modern logic of inside/outside. Specifically, it reflects and affirms the spatial ontology of the sovereign territorial state as an indisputable starting point for thinking about politics. While answers to questions about 'where we should go from here' may vary, it is nevertheless this particular starting point, informed by specific assumptions of 'where we are now', that defines the limits of the questions and, consequently, the limits of the answers provided by theories of IR.

The problem of sovereignty

While there may be increasing evidence that processes of globalization can no longer be contained within the borders of the state, the principle of state sovereignty continues to provide the main horizons for thinking about politics in the late modern world. According to Walker, sovereignty seems to be 'quite uninteresting, the preserve of legal scholars and constitutional experts rather than the subject of heated exchanges among social and political theorists' (p. 62). However, one of the core thematics of *Inside/outside* is an emphasis on how this concept is far from straightforward and indeed should be treated precisely as a *problem* rather than a static principle or 'thing'.

In part, sovereignty relates to practices that attempt to create something out of nothing: for example, the attempt to secure a clear 'presence' of the state in the 'absence' of any foundations thereof. Precisely because there are no secure or ultimate foundations upon which the sovereign state can rest, the very notion of a 'ground', 'origin' or 'foundation' must be *produced*. Rather than relying on an ahistorical understanding of state sovereignty as a simple given, Walker emphasizes that we need to analyse it in its historical context as 'an historically specific account of ethical possibility in the form of an answer to questions about the nature and location of political community' (p. 62). Moreover, in order to explain the persistence of this principle it is necessary to think of sovereignty not in relation to some kind of pre-established 'essence' or 'meaning', but rather as a discursive practice that continuously reproduces 'it' as an organizing principle of modern political life. It is precisely on the basis of such practices that IR in a rather paradoxical sense can be understood *both* as an outdated discipline *and* a powerful reaffirmation of the spatial ontology of the sovereign state. As Walker summarizes one of the main arguments of his book:

> Theories of international relations, I will argue, are interesting less for the substantive explanations they offer about political conditions in the modern world than as expressions of the limits of the contemporary political imagination when confronted with persistent claims about and evidence of fundamental historical and structural transformation (p. 5).

Despite seemingly endless evidence that major historical and structural transformations are under way, it is still in relation to the distinction between inside and outside that claims regarding the political significance of such transformations gain legitimacy. They become 'legitimate' in the sense of not being automatically ruled out as naïve, utopian or unable to accept some of the so-called eternal wisdoms that realist IR is said to offer. In this sense it also becomes extremely difficult to offer any alternative solutions to the puzzle of universalism and particularism – solutions based for example on ideas about a 'world politics', a 'universalist ethics' or a 'common humanity'. If such ideas are to be taken seriously they must first recognize the inside/outside distinction as a 'natural' starting point upon which their ideas are formulated. Hence, they must also come to terms with the limits of their own possibility to move beyond the spatial order of sovereign states.

Beginnings and endings

A key theme of *Inside/outside*, which relates to the notion of legitimate 'starting points', is that ideas about what constitute legitimate 'beginnings' have an enormous impact on our ability to think about the possibility of alternative 'endings'. Walker offers a sophisticated analysis of how IR seems to be caught up in a cycle of reproducing certain limits concerning the possibility of the latter by constantly failing to address the problems of relying on specific articulations of the former. In discourses of IR, beginnings often translate into claims about the origins of the modern sovereign state. The spatial distinction between inside and outside is consequently linked to a temporal separation between life 'before' and 'after' international relations. As Walker notes: 'By identifying when interstate relations began and providing a sharp contrast with what came before', stories about the origins of international relations 'offer a powerful account of what interstate politics must be given what it has always been since the presumed beginning' (p. 89).

Stories about origins have important consequences for how the sovereign state and the relations between states tend to be thought of as *either* present *or* absent. In this respect '1648' is often invoked as an origin of the state and the states-system as if both were brought into being overnight by the Treaty of Westphalia rather than through decades of conflict in Europe. For Walker, this kind of temporal distinction constitutes an integral part of the necessary *myths* that theories of IR must rely on in order to reproduce the spatial ontology of the state as a given starting point. These myths are 'necessary' in that they prevent difficult questions concerning the choice between different possible points of origin; questions about whether one can speak of clear breaks in history in the first place; questions related to the difficulties of examining cause and effect, and so on. In this sense, while the notion of IR as a separate discipline may rely on a history of origins and beginnings, it can also be seen as vulnerable to debates on historicity. It is especially vulnerable to any claims that might question the origins of the sovereign state as a natural and indisputable starting point for thinking about politics.

It is important to point out that Walker takes into account variations between different realist traditions and their respective views of history, some of which are more sensitive to history than others. While, for example, he notes that 'classical realists' such as E. H. Carr and Hans J. Morgenthau arguably demonstrate a more nuanced approach to history, at least in some of their work, Kenneth Waltz's version of neorealism reduces history to universal laws and eternal structures. Hence, while both classical realist and neorealist approaches are pessimistic about the possibilities of historical and structural transformations, the former can be said to leave the door open to change, so to speak, which also makes its opposition to political 'idealism' less straightforward.

Walker argues that the reduction of history to structure is also evident when considering how early modern thinkers such as Niccolò Machiavelli, Thomas Hobbes and Jean-Jacques Rousseau have been appropriated by realist approaches, especially neorealism. The latter, he argues, relies on an ignorance of the historical contexts in which the early-modern thinkers articulated the problems with which they struggled. This ignorance becomes especially clear when considering how the struggles of the early modern thinkers have been translated into eternal wisdoms and structural laws explaining how things *really are*. As Walker notes:

> The history of political thought turns into an ahistorical repetition in which the struggles of these thinkers to make sense of the historical transformations in which they were caught are erased in favour of assertions about how they all articulate essential truths about the same unchanging and usually tragic reality: the eternal game of relations between states (p. 92).

In order to counter the realist tendency to reduce international politics to structural factors, Walker discusses various attempts to bring history back to IR. However, in trying to contest the ahistorical character that dominates realist approaches, he identifies a host of other problems, not least concerning the very possibility of rational historical interpretation, based on simplistic logics of cause and effect, in the Rankean tradition.[4]

There are similar problems faced by scholars trying to transcend the spatial distinction between inside and outside of the sovereign state in favour of some kind of universal identity such as a cosmopolitan order or a world state. These problems are once again born out of the persistence of claims to the sovereignty of the modern state and states-system as a 'natural' starting point for thinking about the place and meaning of modern political life. As long as such claims hold their grip over our understanding of politics it becomes difficult to speak of the political significance of rupture, contingency and events, in a way that challenges the myths of origins and structural necessities of an international system of sovereign states.[5] In this way, the upshot of Walker's critical engagement with history and structure in IR is not a call to produce 'better' knowledge of the former, but rather to question the very framing of history as a mere 'complement' to the neorealist emphasis on the latter.

Problematizing the border of the state

Running through *Inside/outside* is a deep concern with the borders that constitute the modern geopolitical imagination, particularly the concept of the border of the state.[6] Walker contends that this concept, in much the same way as sovereignty, is often taken by theoretical works produced in IR as a straightforward and apolitical demarcation located at the outer edge of the modern territorial state. It is taken to be an epistemological and ontological ground upon which sovereign states are already assumed to be distinct from each other and whose relations under anarchical conditions may then be plotted and predicted. By contrast, Walker's diagnosis of the modern logic of inside/outside problematizes the border of the state as a site of authority, violence and struggle. He stresses that this concept must be placed within the historical context of developments in geometric thinking that made it possible to think in terms of points, lines and planes. In post-Renaissance Europe this thinking became fused with the principle of state sovereignty, which in turn gave rise to a politically significant 'sense of inviolable and sharply delimited space' (p. 129).

According to Walker, as an historical construct, the concept of the border of the state must not be treated as mere 'background noise' (p. 131). Rather, it should be problematized as 'Cartesian coordinates that have allowed us to situate and naturalise a comfortable home for power and authority' (p. 178). Crucially, such problematization calls into question the *politics* of space. Instead of seeing borders between states as peaceful 'fences between neighbours' they are re-conceptualized as memorials of violent conflict. Historically, Walker reminds us, the transition from a system of overlapping loyalties and allegiances in favour of sharp borders between supposedly sovereign units did not happen peacefully.

In this context, however, it is possible to identify something of a tension in Walker's diagnoses. On the one hand, the logic of inside/outside underpinning IR theory is arguably treated as a sort of 'iron cage', within which the modern geopolitical imagination is presented as being trapped. On the other hand, Walker also appeals to empirical observation to suggest that this logic is no longer apposite to contemporary conditions. Thus, for example, in the opening paragraphs it is claimed that 'ours is an age of speed and temporal accelerations', and throughout the text it is implied that something is happening to the concept of the border of the state and the edifice built upon it (see pp. 20, 159, 161). Yet, while Walker acknowledges that: 'Better explanations – of contemporary political life – are no doubt called for', such explanations are ultimately not offered in *Inside/outside* and he argues that 'they are unlikely to emerge without a more sustained reconsideration of fundamental theoretical and philosophical assumptions than can be found in most of the literature on international relations theory' (p. 159). In this regard the text at once poses but in the end leaves hanging the tantalizing question of whether it is possible – or indeed politically desirable – to think beyond inside/outside. The extent to which Walker remains reliant on and constrained by the logics of IR that he seeks to problematize is a theme picked up by several of Walker's critics, as we shall see in the following section.

The reception of *Inside/outside*

Following Walker's insistence on the importance of the historical specificity of the period in which the 'classics' of political theory were written, *Inside/outside* must itself be read in the context of a disciplinary landscape that was in many respects far removed from today's. Although the text was published in 1993, its scholarly origins span the period from the height of Cold War tensions to the aftermath of the dissolution of the Soviet Union and revolutions across Eastern Europe. This tumultuous period in global history was reflected in seismic shifts in the disciplinary culture of IR, which saw a growing dissatisfaction with *both* realism as the hegemonic explanatory framework for explaining international politics *and* alternatives such as neoliberalism as the horizon for articulating alternative visions of what the future should look like. A new wave of scholarship – often associated with labels such as the 'Reflectivist Turn' – sought to problematize the realism/liberalism dichotomy itself as a product of Western power/knowledge relations.[7] It is in this specific context that, along with post-structuralist, postcolonial, and feminist works of the period – some recognized as classics (and included in this volume), others marginalized (and left out) – *Inside/outside* is often emplaced and understood as a specific intervention.

Yet, what is curious about Walker's 'classic' is that its contemporary reception and latter-day legacy remain somewhat ambiguous. On the one hand, the book's status as a highly cited piece of scholarship, not only in IR but across the humanities and social sciences, is hard to deny. On the other hand, however, the frequency with which Walker's text is cited belies the depth of engagement with his core arguments. Indeed, what is so striking about the reception of this classic is that sympathetic and unsympathetic scholars alike seem more willing to merely refer to it than to embrace its radical implications in any substantive sense.[8] This tendency is typified by the recent remarks of one (sympathetic) commentator who, reflecting on Walker's work as a whole, said: 'On the one hand, I have long enjoyed the insights that Rob Walker brings to IR theory … On the other hand … I am not directly concerned with the central aporia of inside/outside … Instead, I have rather come to "use" him, quite instrumentally, as a clearly identifiable reference point, a quote when seeking to express how certain debates are just missing the point'.[9] It is apparent that a footnote to *Inside/outside* is often 'used' to feign an awareness not only of that particular text, but also of a range of otherwise heterogeneous interventions – some more obviously 'represented' by Walker's book than others – including 'post-structuralism', 'post-modernism', 'critical' approaches to the state, sovereignty and borders, and so on. This is problematic not least because Walker himself eschews labels such as 'post-structuralism', and anyone who has read *Inside/outside* in its entirety will recognize that the essays when taken as a whole defy straightforward classification.

The relatively small number of serious engagements with *Inside/outside* can also surely be explained by its radical nature. While IR is made up of many different perspectives and theoretical approaches, what arguably brings most of these together is their obsession with solutions, as well as their unwillingness to engage with the difficulties and aporetic dimensions of the problems they seek to address. In this light it is hardly surprising that Walker's strategy of questioning the very assumptions upon which the search for solutions relies has been met with a lack of enthusiasm, and in some cases, as review essays by Fred Halliday and R. E. Jones illustrate, outright hostility.[10] Nevertheless, two notable exceptions to the tendency identified above are the critical commentaries offered by Jens Bartelson and Justin Rosenberg.

While in large parts sympathetic to Walker's work, Bartelson argues that Walker ends up reaffirming the necessity of the sovereign state without offering a way out. According to Bartelson, this reaffirmation can be linked to Walker's deconstructive critique, which reproduces the same conceptual distinctions that it sets out to criticize as well as eradicate: 'we find ourselves imprisoned within the same state which decon-struction promised to dissolve'.[11] From Bartelson's point of view, by problematizing the notion of a coherent 'inside' of the sovereign state in relation to an external 'outside', Walker's critique highlights a sense of circularity as well as closure, and is ultimately unable to open up to something that might lie beyond the state and the logic of inside/outside. Although Bartelson points to an interesting tension in Walker's work as noted previously, he nevertheless misses a core point of *Inside/outside*. On our reading at least, Walker's critique does not seek to 'dissolve' the state *per se*. Rather, the aim is to investigate the *politics* of inscribing borders, foundations and origins, not to show how the latter can be dissolved and ultimately overcome. Moreover, while this form of immanent critique relies upon the assumption that there is indeed something that lies 'beyond' the presence of the state, the point is not to show how this 'beyond' can be grasped or reached as such. The aim is rather to show how that 'beyond' participates in the ongoing reproduction of the state and the modern logic of inside/outside as a 'constitutive outside' of the state/interstate system.[12]

Justin Rosenberg offers a more sustained interrogation of *Inside/outside* from a clas-sical Marxist perspective.[13] His critique focuses upon what he considers to be at once the two main distinctive features of and yet the central weaknesses in Walker's overall logic. First, Rosenberg contends that Walker's account privileges the concept of space and the role that spatial logics play in underpinning modern politics without offering sufficient intellectual or empirical justification for this assertion. While Rosenberg claims that space is no doubt of importance in the cultural expressions of modernity, he argues, drawing on Benedict Anderson's work among others, that equal if not more weight could be given to *time* in characterizing the period. Moreover, Rosenberg argues that other factors, such as the effects of the emergence of capitalist society, would surely have disrupted the continuation between modern expressions of politics and their early modern ante-cedents and yet Walker does not account for these. Second, Rosenberg takes Walker to task for his treatment of the modern international as a specific historical construction. According to Rosenberg other historical worlds reveal that the international is not a specific product of the spatial categories of early modern Europe. To explain the emergence of the state/states-system as a projection of the influence of Euclidean geo-metry is to reduce the international to a particular account of the *modern* international. Rather, the category of 'the international' has a longer-term trans-historical presence shaped by material factors than Walker's narrower spatially oriented account allows.

Rosenberg's critique, while serious and based on largely careful if unsympathetic readings of Walker's text, is nevertheless highly contentious. His claim about the privi-leging of space in *Inside/outside* is perilously close to the same sort of rhetorical mis-characterization of which he accuses Walker. Indeed, one of the insistences of Walker's approach is precisely the inseparability of spatial and temporal assumptions in the Cartesian logic of inside/outside and the forms of politics it gives rise to. In addition, the issue of the international is one on which Rosenberg and Walker are clearly destined to disagree, although it must be pointed out that the former's commitment to trans-historicity is precisely that which the latter warns against.

Conclusion

In many ways the subtitle *International Relations as Political Theory* holds the key to understanding the main thesis of *Inside/outside*. 'International Relations', Walker argues, *cannot* be understood as a separate discipline, which is somehow divorced from 'Political Theory'. Rather, IR is inextricably linked to Political Theory, in ways that make them inseparable from the same political imaginary of modernity. Following this imaginary there can be no 'International Relations' without 'Political Theory' and vice versa; each 'discipline' relies upon something that lies outside its own disciplinary boundaries, something that supposedly 'belongs' to the 'other' discipline.

On the one hand, as a discipline that is supposed to be concerned with what happens *outside* the sovereign state, IR relies upon a set of assumptions regarding the purpose and meaning of political community *inside* the state. Modern theories of IR are expressions of an *idealized* understanding of the sovereign state, in which ethics and ideas about the universally good can be aspired towards only within the borders of the state. On the other hand, as a discipline that is supposed to be concerned with questions about what goes on *inside* the limits of political community, Political Theory must nevertheless rely on a set of assumptions regarding what lies *outside* the state: a world of IR characterized by the *lack* of political community and authority. Ideas about a legitimate political order and good government *within* states are, thus, defined *against* the dangers, violence and lack of order *beyond* states. In this respect, an alternative subtitle to *Inside/outside* would be *Political Theory as International Relations*.

While demonstrating how inside and outside, Political Theory and International Relations, the domestic and the international are interdependent and co-constitutive, *Inside/outside* is nevertheless limited to a critical engagement with the relationship between the inside and the outside of the *state*. In subsequent publications, however, Walker has developed his critique further, taking into account several co-existing layers of borders, boundaries and limits. With the publication of *After the Globe, Before the World* (2010), Walker has shown how, in order to engage critically with the limits of the modern political imagination, it is necessary to expand the analysis beyond a narrow focus on the modern logic of inside/outside of the sovereign state.[15] Taking into account not only the constitutive outside of the sovereign state but the double constitutive outside of the state and international *system* of states, Walker demonstrates the difficulty of rethinking modern assumptions about the place and meaning of political life in the so co-called late modern era. In doing so, Walker takes his accomplishments in *Inside/outside* to a new level and sets the bar even higher for students and scholars of IR who are trying to come to terms with the profound challenges of thinking about politics in the contemporary world.

Notes

1 We would like to thank Rob Walker for his comments on an earlier draft and support of our work more generally.
2 R. B. J. Walker, *Inside/outside: International Relations as Political Theory*, Cambridge: Cambridge University Press, 1993. Page numbers placed in parentheses in the text refer to this edition.
3 Email correspondence between the authors and R. B. J. Walker, August 2011.
4 For a discussion of the politics of historicity in IR, influenced by Walker's approach among others', see Nick Vaughan-Williams, 'International Relations and the "Problem of History"', *Millennium: Journal of International Studies*, 2005, vol. 34, 115–36.
5 For a further engagement with this difficulty, see Tom Lundborg, *Politics of the Event: Time, Movement, Becoming*, London: Routledge, 2012.
6 For a fuller discussion of the concept of the border in Walker's work see Nick Vaughan-Williams, *Border Politics: The Limits of Sovereign Power*, Edinburgh: Edinburgh University Press, 2009.

 7 See Yosef Lapid, 'The Third Debate: On the Prospects of International Theory in a Post-Positivist Era', *International Studies Quarterly*, 1989, vol. 33, 235–54.
 8 Two important exceptions to the lack of more substantial engagements with the core arguments of *Inside/outside* are Lene Hansen, 'R. B. J. Walker and International Relations: Deconstructing a Discipline', in Iver B. Neumann and Ole Wæver (eds), *The Future of International Relations: Masters in the Making*, London: Routledge, 1997, pp. 316–36, and Colin Hoadley, 'Machiavelli, A Man of "His" Time: R. B. J. Walker and The Prince', *Millennium: Journal of International Studies*, 2003, vol. 30, 1–18.
 9 James Brassett, 'After Walker', *Contemporary Political Theory*, 2010, vol. 10, 291–93.
10 Fred Halliday, 'Book Review: R. B. J. Walker, "Inside/outside: International Relations as Political Theory"', *Millennium: Journal of International Studies*, 1993, vol. 22, 362–65 and R. E. Jones, 'The Responsibility to Educate', *Review of International Studies*, 1994, vol. 20, 299–311.
11 Jens Bartelson, *The Critique of the State*, Cambridge: Cambridge University Press, 2001, p. 167.
12 We have elaborated on this theme in our own respective work. See Vaughan-Williams, *Border Politics* and Tom Lundborg, 'What Lies Beyond Lies Within: Global Information Flows and the Politics of the State/Inter-State System', *Alternatives*, 2011, vol. 36, 103–17.
13 Justin Rosenberg, *The Follies of Globalisation Theory*, London: Verso, 2000.
14 R. B. J. Walker, *After the Globe, Before the World*, London: Routledge, 2010.

22 The state has a mind: Alexander Wendt's *Social Theory of International Politics*

Alan Chong

If international relations can be reduced to the question of imagining enemies and partners within a policy-making game, Alexander Wendt would invite its students to ponder how and why these frames of thought were created. Social theory is essentially the study of how society shapes one's experiences and lifelong psychic repositories a priori. By borrowing heavily from this field of sociology, Wendt's theory of constructivism hews more broadly to the generic ideas of theorizing about both personal motivations and the obscured structures that underpin the trajectories of thinking that precede personal action. One of Wendt's own doctoral students has described his mentor's work as being akin to a social scientist struggling with history, a history, that is, of modern man perpetually trying to represent the material world surrounding him in politically intelligible terms.[1] To this one can agree, considering that Wendtian constructivism aims to explain international politics in terms of the inquiry into the *social* setting of political behaviour. People generate action in politics; material forces do not do so of their own accord.

Not surprisingly, Wendt's ideas seek to improve upon 'structural' theories of international relations that take as given a deterministic power-driven account of human decision-making at the level of a system of states. Kenneth Waltz's theory of neorealism serves as the foil for Wendtian constructivism. The book *Social Theory of International Politics* (hereafter *Social Theory*)[2] is intended as a corrective to Waltzian neorealism as implied by its prefix to Waltz's classic *Theory of International Politics*.[3]

Social Theory aims to show that behaviour in international relations is driven by shared ideas more than material forces such as biology, technology or the environment. In order to do this, Wendt demands that readers permit his indulgence in explaining structures and agents as the builders of knowledge that enable international politics to be conducted. He also expects his audience to embrace his assumption that international relations will continue to remain the exclusive realm of politics among nation states. This 'politics among nation states' is first explored in terms of the possibilities of four sociologies of the structure: individualist; holist; materialist; and ideational (which Wendt labels as 'idealist'). As Wendt explains, these sociologies emerge naturally as thought experiments derived from the awkward coexistence of sovereign nation states in a tenuous 'society' when they interact with one another. A nation state might act towards its rivals on the basis of 'individual' self-interest, relabelled as 'national interest'. Other nation states might behave in 'holist' ways through rigorous adherence to international law and other norms (p. 2). Some other nation states may assume that all relationships are driven by 'materialist' motivations such as natural resources, geography, economic forces and military forces under the direction of an immutable human nature

(p. 23). Yet other nation states may be driven by ideas ensconced in international regimes, norms and the like – hence they are '*idea*-list' in Wendtian terminology (p. 24). These four sociologies explain how far ideas alone drive international behaviour, or whether they act in tandem with material forces and to what extent. Wendt frames his readers into a social scientific journey that explains the ontology, or worldview, underlying international behaviour in contrast to what the observer of politics can perceive in terms of direct causation. He argues that mostly assigning causation of events to the sheer force of ideas offers a penetrating exposition of how states behave logically even when they need to rattle the sabre up to the brink of war. After elaborating the social theory framework, he then delves into the interpretation of international relations through the 'corporate agency' of the state, the varying cultures of anarchy (Hobbesian, Lockean and Kantian) that can be constructed from state agencies and, finally, the possibilities for changes to the structure of international politics. The Hobbesian label refers to the self-help culture of state behaviour exemplified by the realism derived from a crude reading of Thomas Hobbes, E. H. Carr and Hans J. Morgenthau. The Lockean culture refers to that set of libertarian beliefs embodied by John Locke and extrapolated into international thought by John Gerard Ruggie and Friedrich Kratochwil. The Kantian culture is a label that describes a culture of state behaviour broadly derived from Immanuel Kant's *Perpetual Peace* and his interpreters Karl Deutsch, Emanuel Adler, Michael Barnett and Robert Keohane, all of whom advocate friendship between nation states on the normative and rational basis of settling disputes without war and adhering to collective security schemes (pp. 298–99). Wendt's point is to argue that since ideas can be infectious and socialize state behaviour through learning, including the experience of collective pain from military collisions, states in anarchical society learn to discard Hobbesian culture, become acclimatized to Lockean culture and ultimately may embrace a more peaceable Kantian culture. At the very least, states that are socialized into the avoidance of armed solutions should not regress towards Hobbesian culture (pp. 250–51, Chapter 6).

The notion of ideas as the prime explanatory path inevitably triggers ripostes from discerning scholars as to how rigorous his claim to scientism will ever be. Moreover, when ideas are formed through hard-hitting encounters with the realities already 'out there', one wonders how much manoeuvrable space there is for the identity of the encountering party, or agent, to change in response to the realities embedded in the environment, or structure.[4] This is not unlike what physicists understand as nuclear fission: when a neutron strikes the uranium atom, the latter splits into two, releasing more neutrons which strike other uranium atoms, thus producing a chain reaction with unpredictable pathways. Therefore ideas, in the form of identities, must be accounted for in terms of their possibilities for undergoing chameleon-like transformations that may be more than skin-deep. Conversely, one might ask about the equal possibility of autonomous identity transformations on the side of the structure, or of the 'other agents' that inhabit the environment of the encountering agent. The familiar 'chicken and egg' and 'horse and cart' analogies in social science argument come to haunt Wendt's project.[5] Finally, another powerful critique is posed by those who ponder whether Wendt's version of constructivism wilfully neglects the philosophical question of whether it can be more than a method. Some critics venture to ask if Wendtian constructivism addresses normative questions in world politics while noting that his erstwhile intellectual targets, such as neorealism and neoliberalism, do so either by omission or addition.[6]

Nonetheless, in order to elucidate this chapter's subject more simply, *Social Theory* first aims to establish International Relations (IR) as a field of knowledge inquiry: how can one know about every political consideration that is visible, or invisible, such as the impact of ideas on foreign policy conduct? Second, it strives to establish constructivism as an IR enterprise that expects its scholars to practise storytelling and genealogy in order to explain why states behave the way they do. This chapter will analyse Wendt's densely layered arguments through the subheadings of language and construction, agent and structure; materialism versus idealism; the intrinsic method of storytelling in applying constructivism; and finally, the importance of taking IR ontology and epistemology seriously as a route towards democratizing the discipline. Constructivist IR democratizes in the sense that unlike realism and liberalism, it carries negligible cultural traits that may hinder objective analyses of the international politics of the non-Western world.

Language and construction, agent and structure

Constructivism poses a challenge for the scholar more attuned to the standard debates between realism and liberalism, or between behaviouralism and qualitative method, principally because it calls attention to the role of context and its creation of meaning. Wendt's work draws from the intellectual well of scientific realism, linguistic theory and symbolic interactionism[7] to illuminate these dimensions of international politics while attempting to retain the scientific status of constructivist research. By invoking scientific realism, Wendt is referring to that branch of the philosophy of science that is premised on the belief that there are objects and beliefs that exist independently of our minds.[8] This is distinct from the standard realism as a school of IR, premised on reading politics pragmatically with power considerations uppermost in policy-making considerations. In his Preface to the middle section of *Social Theory*, Wendt argues that if one discusses for instance the Soviet threat during the Cold War, or the Aztec leader Montezuma's response to the Spanish *Conquistadores* in 1519, the lack of access to the 'external worlds' that regulated their empirical perceptions of their 'opponents' contributed to decisions that set them on a collision course with the Other. To Wendt, 'what is needed is a theory of reference that takes account of the contribution of mind and language yet is anchored to external reality'. In other words 'mind and language help to determine meaning, but meaning is also regulated by a mind-independent, extra-linguistic world' (p. 57). In his book, Wendt references John Searle and Ferdinand de Saussure in relation to linguistics. Essentially, linguistic theory contends that language is more than a conveyance of factual information – that is, symbols that specifically confirm 'truth' or 'falsehood' – and it is increasingly also about wider meanings implied in the use of language.[9] Namely, any word carries with it a generative grammar of meanings, rules of intentions, and so forth. To John Searle, a speech act is 'rule-governed in ways quite similar to those in which getting a base hit in baseball or moving a knight in chess are rule-governed forms of acts'.[10]

Where speech acts illuminate the possibilities that multiple universes exist behind language, the invocation of scientific realism by Wendt offers further grounding for constructivism through three propositions: (i) the world is independent of the mind and language of individual observers; (ii) mature scientific theories typically refer to this world; and (iii) even when it is not directly observable (p. 51).

Invoking these propositions make it 'possible to conceive of states and states systems as real and knowable, but it does not tell us that they exist, what they are made of, or how they behave. That is a job for social scientists, not philosophers' (p. 51). One scientific realist answer would be to derive the existence of states from observable reality: their collective organization of human labour; the physical existence of human beings in their habitats governed by visible authorities; literally, stamping collective identity through the issue of identification cards and passports; and the physical attributes of military force such as guns, tanks and aircraft with common insignia. However, these material, naturally observable kinds can in turn generate 'social kinds' – what Wendt refers to as 'the materially grounded tendency of *homo sapiens* to designate things as "this" or "that"'. Hence, 'a theory of social kinds must refer to natural kinds, including human bodies and their physical behaviour, which are amenable to a causal theory of reference. Constructivism without nature goes too far' (p. 72). In this way, Wendt claims that scientific realism offers constructivism a bridge, a *via media* between positivist epistemology (the state of knowledge) and post-positivist ontology (the worldview or the nature of being). Scientific IR research can therefore embrace causation by building upon the actions of visible and known entities involved in politics, and it can also probe causation that stems from the unobservable such as ideas.

Following this trajectory of reasoning, one can understand the introduction of structuration theory that lies at the heart of Wendtian constructivism. Structuration contends that identities and interests of actors in a social setting are literally constructed by shared ideas rather than being assigned by nature. The actor, or agent, produces an impact, for example in politics, only by virtue of co-constituting its identity together with its perceived reality/structure. The work of sociologist Anthony Giddens has inspired Wendt's thinking.[11] According to Giddens, the actor, or agent, is an entity capable of exercising power 'to "make a difference" to a pre-existing state of affairs or course of events'.[12] Structure is in turn 'regarded as rules and resources recursively implicated in social reproduction; institutionalized features of social systems have structural properties in the sense that relationships are stabilized across time and space'.[13] How then does society, or any social context, come into being and persist across time and space? According to Giddens:

> The constitution of agents and structures are not two independently given sets of phenomena, a dualism, but represent a duality. According to the notion of the duality of structure, the structural properties of social systems are both medium and outcome of the practices they recursively organise ... Structure is not to be equated with constraint but is always both constraining and enabling ... Structure has no existence independent of the knowledge that agents have about what they do in their day-to-day activity.[14]

Wendt attempts to reproduce this logic in his elaboration of why structure and agency come together to explain why and how 'culture', broadly interpreted as values, ideas and intentions, matter in international politics. Culture as a form of structure can bring about a meeting of minds and bodies on the basis that each self-regarding agent has acted simply on the basis of predicting the other's moves based on common knowledge derived from prior socialization in the pre-encounter period. Culture can also be constitutive in the sense that mental states are derived from pre-existing 'brain states' that paint a picture which directs the agent to believe, or imagine, a reality that accommodates a role destined for the agent (p. 173). If the individual human agent can be likened to the corporate agency of an entire nation state, then one can imagine how the

US hegemon may sometimes perceive itself to be acting benignly to thwart 'rogue state actions' threatening itself and the general peace, while the rest of the international community condemns the USA for reckless unilateral behaviour on the basis of alternative shared identities. Compare, for instance, the Group of 20's communiqués relating to world order with the stance taken by Washington. If one considers the possibility that common knowledge might be widely disseminated, and hence shared, by both the USA and the international community prior to policing 'rogue states' such as Iran and North Korea, the USA's behaviour might not incur any opprobrium at all among the international community (pp. 176–77).

Materialism versus idealism

In the middle of the book, Wendt begins to shape his social theory of international politics by posing the question 'ideas all the way down?' in the title of Chapter 3 and then adding the suffix 'on the constitution of power and interest'. Political realism, which is generally regarded as that school of thought enjoying the status of primogeniture in the field, is set up as a target for its emphasis upon explaining events with reference to 'material' factors that are often reduced to power and interest. In fact, human appetites for domination, the lust for relative gain, technology itself and the physical environment are symptomatic of materialist explanations, as Wendt suggests. Human steering is limited to the spaces marked out by fixed constraints. Liberal thought is similarly criticized for treating ideas as intervening variables that sit alongside the material ones that may eventually trump ideational explanations. Marxism comes under withering attack for its dishonest attribution of causation in politics to the forces of production, when actually Marxists often have to provide a thick account of the relationship of production to labour as a foundation for their advocacy of revolution across national frontiers. Therefore, Marxists ought to concede right from the start that capitalism is a cultural form. An idea-based account, or 'idealism' in Wendtian parlance, is necessary to complete the explanations presented by these other schools of IR.

For Wendt, these traditional IR approaches conflate material factors with their existence as objectively existing realities (p. 95). Realities do not arise of their own accord; they are constituted by human thought, hence the increasing turn towards embracing idealism in the study of international politics under monikers such as identity, culture, discourse and ideology. Wendt's mission is to ensure that the traditional schools acknowledge the importance of their 'suppressed constructivist assumptions about the content and distribution of ideas' (p. 96). Waltzian neorealism comes under the microscope of the materialist versus idealist debate, as Wendt argues that Waltz's obsession with treating states as being analogous to profit-maximizing firms in a market, his faith in the automaticity of balancing power and states' concern with relative gains over absolute ones, ignore assumptions about motivation. The much-touted logic of anarchy among the system of states is not inevitable. For Wendt, states may treat respect for the norms of participating in a society more seriously than operating in a system of total predictability of power balancing, submission and war. Moreover, there is the problem of the availability of information to enable states to make their calculations on how to behave within a neorealist 'system': states as social actors need to be able to read their rivals' minds accurately, make assumptions and hopefully correct these assumptions when their rivals' mentalities are revealed to have been different or have changed over time. Wendt does concede that while a 'rump materialism' may affect states' calculations towards one another, 'ultimately it is our ambitions, fears, and hopes – the things we want material forces *for* – that drive social evolution, not material forces as such' (p. 113).

Wendt directs his criticism next at the version of rational choice theory popular in IR. Rational choice theory appears on the surface to favour idealism since its core assumption is that desire plus belief equals action, but it also 'treats desire (or preference or interest) and belief (or expectations or ideas) as distinct variables, which suggests that desires do not depend on beliefs and are therefore material' (p. 115). Moreover, rationalists often lack curiosity as to where interests come from: are states inevitably selfish, or are they occasionally capable of exercising a collective interest? The content of desires and beliefs require deep scrutiny if any explanation is to be thorough. There is after all a strong deliberative basis to desire, and Wendt illustrates this by arguing that wholly structural explanations for the collapse of the USSR would never stand up on their own: 'Soviet behaviour changed because they redefined their existing desires and beliefs self-critically' (p. 129). Wendt resorts to his familiar device of arguing that another version of 'rump materialism' is needed to properly appraise the role of ideas: rational choice frameworks need to be placed alongside physical security objectives, those of ontological security ('relatively stable expectations about the natural and especially social world around them' (p. 131)), social contact, self-esteem and transcendence ('human beings need to grow, develop, and improve their life condition' (p. 132)). Wendt restates the advantages of embracing his 'idealist approach' to the study of interests in international relations as follows. First, there can be a programme for the systematic study of 'real world state interests'. Second, cognition and culture can be linked and explained in terms of their impact on statesmen's actions on the international stage. Third, an idealist approach opens up possibilities for explaining 'foreign policy and systemic change' (p. 134). Through these arguments one perceives the contours of Wendt's suggestion that a constructivist analysis of international politics needs to begin with the concept that any state's agency and the structure of international relations are co-constituted, and the attendant explanations must offer thick accounts of how this has come to pass.

None the less, some trenchant criticisms focus on Wendt's imprecision in delineating the balance between his idealism and his 'rump materialism'. Robert O. Keohane challenged him to specify this relationship more clearly in what is likely to become a standard 'alternative text' in IR,[15] while Stephen Krasner warned that the explanatory and motivational aspects of idealism alone could be as metaphorically dangerous as attributing wars, hotel fires and plane crashes to acts of social construction.[16] Lives could be lost through fevered imaginings or erroneous assumptions being put into practice. Steve Smith also criticizes Wendt in much the same vein but cautions that the greatest weakness in Wendt's book is his intrinsically unstated ambivalence towards causal (positivist) and constitutive theorizing. Causal theory has been slammed by Wendt as being too mechanistic and hence runs into a unidimensional materialistic groove. His favoured constitutive explanations ironically ride upon the same social scientific biases as the causal factor – ideas need to be supported in tandem with materialism.[17] Roxanne Lynn Doty on the other hand celebrates Wendt's efforts to decentre IR as a discipline, but criticizes him for not acknowledging that it is desire that drives causation. Constructivism, in her view, is a close relative of postmodern international thought, and Wendt is simply being disingenuous in trying to retain elements of positivist methodology in justifying an idea-driven analysis of politics.[18] Debating the explanatory power of ideas in social context remains infinitely vulnerable to the searching question of whether events can be explained autonomously. It is telling that in Wendt's response to these critics, he avoids responding to them on the loaded question of whether militarized nuclear technology has caused fundamental change in the way states view those who have it as friends or enemies. Instead, he argues that constructivist explanations enjoy their greatest merit in explaining the triumph at the dawn of the twenty-first century of global capitalism and the spread of democracy, which 'are at base cultural, involving the spread of new and very deep ways of thinking about ourselves, each other, and our relationship to nature. ... For students of international politics, philosophy should be the servant, not the master'.[19]

Storytelling as application of constructivism

Since the agencies and their corresponding structures exist across time and space in international politics, and are described as possessing 'lives' of their own, action in the international arena presupposes human qualities in the key actor – the state. In support of his belief that the humane orientation of philosophy should render it the servant of inquiry for students of international politics,[20] Wendt frequently pointed to the human aspiration towards possessing viewpoints, engaging in reflection or correcting existing situations. These exercises can only be carried out if the state had a past, against which present and future courses of action could be compared. Wendt himself argued that the application of constructivism to analysis required that the state be treated as a person armed with a 'homeostatic'[21] understanding of these five characteristics: '(1) an institutional-legal order, (2) an organization claiming a monopoly on the legitimate use of organized violence, (3) an organization with sovereignty, (4) a society, and (5) territory' (p. 202). Whether one still adopts realist, liberal, or Marxist views of the state, these five characteristics will imply a collective effort to produce them, and consequently maintain them: states have to develop their own bureaucrats, establish their police forces and train military personnel to man their defences against violations of sovereignty. Since the functioning state *acts collectively*, it is therefore understandable that Wendt obstinately defends the need to treat states as persons (pp. 8–10). This is a point that Wendt has reiterated in order to counter the criticism that this assumption ignores the possibility that individuals within the state might feel oppressed under the very discipline of that collective institution.[22]

None the less, the everyday operational assumption in governments everywhere is that ministries and their subordinate bodies strive to act in unison to fulfil the objectives of policy-implementing efficiency as well as constitutionality. Both elected and unelected governments work in the same way (pp. 195–202). Media reporting will also impute human characteristics to policy actions, for example when states are described as 'reacting in horror' to human rights violations 'committed' by another state.

All of these constructivist speech acts involve narrating a record of compliance or disobedience prior to the act concerned. Moreover, moral censure is also a product of human psychology derived in turn from some aspects of extended socialization. In this regard, one might venture that virtually the entire sub-field of Foreign Policy Analysis is constructivist at its core.[23] Foreign policies are formulated through a mixture of idiosyncratic human factors, standard operating procedures in bureaucracies and the cumulative strictures of domestic and international laws. When policies are announced and implemented, the justification for them nearly always employs the terms 'we', 'them', 'I' and 'you' in order to help both world and domestic publics to

understand the reason for these policies (pp. 21–22). Methodologically, this personification of states as unitary actors requires students of constructivism to act as 'good
storytellers' in the sense that they should trace processes of decision-making down
to the evolution of biases, the maintenance of grudges, the inclination to rely on stereotypes to size up one's opponents, the moral grounds for attacking the Other, and
simply the 'history' of behaviours by this and that state actor with a view to incrimi-
nating or befriending the Other. This is evident in Wendt's suggestive exposition of 'the
national interest' as a constantly kaleidoscopic policy concept (pp. 233–38).
Explaining agencies and structures will require an exacting interpretation of the
'history' of both equally in tandem. It is only after these have been narrated that the
observer can detect the co-constitution of agents and structures in any international
political event. In this regard, Wendt ought not to have associated himself too closely
with the positivist method of delineating 'independent' and 'dependent' variables in
analysis (p. 11). Constructivists should instead declare that agents and structures are
equally dependent.

The mind of the state: the politics of reality, social memory and area studies in IR

How then might one assess such an enormously complex book? In a very ironic way,
some of the salient criticisms of Wendt's work pay *Social Theory* its highest compli-
ments. The book is an enduring contribution to IR because it lends itself to debating
the seemingly intangible assumptions that underpin the construction of reality. Maja
Zehfuss's interpretation of constructivism opens up the 'politics of reality' that constructivists of three different stripes, Wendt, Kratochwil and Onuf, introduce but
stumble over in their explanatory angles: 'although constructivism is about construction,
it takes reality as in many ways given. In other words, constructivism purports to
explain construction whilst still taking account of "reality"'.[24] Utilizing an extended case
study of the intense framing debates over German military commitments to humanitarian missions in Bosnia-Herzegovina and Somalia in the early 1990s, Zehfuss takes
aim at Wendt's silence on the realities of how policy actors frame 'the necessary multiplicity of origins referred to in telling identity'.[25] The Federal Republic of Germany
was partly construable by some political quarters as the morally purified successor to
the Nazi regime that initiated World War Two, and there was also space for rival
politicians to assert that the Federal Republic was a NATO member with significant
overseas responsibilities in burden sharing. Moreover, post-1945 'war guilt' could also be
debated by parliamentarians across the political spectrum through the frame of its consistency, or lack thereof, with the Federal Republic's *Grundgesetz* (Basic Law). It is
therefore uncertain which parts of structure, or agency, should a 'Wendtian' analysis
have chosen to explain a constructed German military action abroad.

Taking Wendtian constructivism to a more sophisticated level is perhaps the work of
Karin Fierke. In her book *Diplomatic Interventions: Conflict and Change in a Globalizing
World*, Fierke argues that constructivists can perform an invaluable service by drawing
attention to the fact that every cross-border physical intervention is constituted by a
range of prior interventions. To Fierke, 'intervention is a more general term that refers
to that which through its presence modifies an existing state of affairs'.[26] These are
'diplomatic interventions' to the extent that 'they may involve some form of communication to avoid or limit recourse to force, as well as to realize it'.[27] Interventions are
morally, psychologically and economically costly affairs – take, for example, those in

Bosnia, Afghanistan, Iraq, Libya and Syria – simply because statesmen, soldiers and non-governmental activists have had to make their case for participation, as well as to endure the censure of policies that have gone awry midway through the physical inter-ventions. Likewise, the nuclear security scholarship of Nina Tannenwald and Carol Atkinson has treated nuclear weapon 'non-use' in the similar vein of an ideational intervention that by itself acts as a potent instrument of latent power for manipulating agendas in world politics.[28] Witness, for instance, North Korean and Iranian behaviour from 2002 to 2012. An even more recent attempt at synthesizing realism, neoliberalism and constructivism under the grand label of 'cosmopolitan power' has also adapted a very basic understanding of constructivist 'intervention' to substantiate the argument that soft power is a major augmentation of pre-existing 'hard' achievements by nation states in economics, popular culture, political prestige and military power.[29]

In her other works Fierke introduces the constructivist concept of social memory and trauma as a conditioner of international politics. This extends Wendtian arguments about treating nation states as the primary and personified actors in world politics. Nation states systematically collect traces of memory through their hierarchies of functionaries as a guide towards future policy behaviour, and equally with a view towards avoiding the perceived mistakes of the past. In Karin Fierke's elaboration:

> social memory as a picture of past trauma, may, at one and the same time, take a narrative form and provide a script for re-enacting a cultural package inherited from the past. Both help to bind together the identity of the group. What is reproduced is less an identical set of practices than a relationship between victim and perpetrator, which in 'acting out' is reversed.[30]

In this way, Wendtian obsessions with language and agency, pondering the dialectics between material and ideational motivations, and constructivism's application through the storytelling technique, can all be brought to bear in a very elementary manner in accounting for the diplomatic burden of the Holocaust in Germany's foreign relations, the Vietnam Syndrome in US foreign policy, or the shadow of the Nanjing Massacre in Sino-Japanese relations.

Area studies also stand to benefit from constructivist approaches. Consider Asia for instance. First, this is a region that has practised the form and function of the modern nation state for less than a century. In fact, the nation state was an idea grafted artifi-cially onto Asian polities in the pursuit of decolonization. A great number of political ideas in Asia exist therefore on an experimental stage, implemented piecemeal, amounting to curious outcomes such as the Association of Southeast Asian Nations (ASEAN), which observes Westphalian principles with informal 'face saving' procedures for avoiding open confrontation between member states. Asians seem to be proficient in synthesizing mainstream diplomatic norms, such as those practised at the UN, and local preferences, to match complex local reality. This is captured in the scholarship of Amitav Acharya who claims that Asian regionalism has contributed the constructivist-derived lexicon of 'constitutive localization' of norms governing pacific state behaviour. In Acharya's words, constitutive localization 'may start with the reinterpretation and re-representation of the external norm, but may also extend into more complex pro-cesses of reconstitution to make an external norm congruent with an existing local normative order'.[31] Second, Asia, like so many political regions of the world, is still in pursuit of equilibrium between Western-originated ideas of modern development and the rediscovery of pre-modern indigenous ideals. Constructivism is normatively liberating as a method of analysing the emerging Asian cultures of international relations insofar as, unlike its rivals, it does not carry preconceived ideological baggage such as realism, liberalism, Marxism and neo-Marxism. Asian nation states are still struggling to stabilize domestic governance, and in the process will generate changes in their national outlooks on foreign relations. In this context, the Wendtian framework of 'ideas most of the way down' can illuminate Asian perspectives in their treatment of materialistic considerations in either forging peace or waging war.[32] Acharya and many others believe that Asian ideas that have become operational on the international stage are not likely to constitute a clash on the scale predicted by Samuel Huntington's famous thesis.[33] There could instead be a constitutive dialogue of civilizations underway in the present century where norms are shared through local filters. Constructivism is therefore potentially less of a formal 'IR theory' as Wendt confesses (p. 7), and closer to a value-free method of comprehending the non-Western world. One can be reasonably certain that African and Latin American scholars will also agree that this is probably the greatest contribution of *Social Theory*, apart from co-constituting agency and structure.

A complex world with multiple stories

Wendtian constructivism has turned out to be a methodological school of IR theorizing. As its 'Rosetta stone', *Social Theory* challenges its readers to implement analysis according to the framework of the co-constitution of agency and structure. Although the criticisms are valid about Wendt's imprecision concerning the relative explanatory weight of materialist and idealist factors, they should not obscure the possibilities that a sharper focus on the empowering and disempowering roles of ideas in international politics might bring. In this regard, one might do better to sympathize with the potential of constructivism to supply a frame for the discursive deconstruction of, or appreciation for, ideas that predetermine the shape of non-Western international relationships. Roxanne Doty's preference for reading Wendt as a closet postmodern international theorist focused on explaining 'desire' as the motivation for international action is conducive to this angle of reading constructivism as an approach that liberates the complex make-up of, for instance, non-Western regional order and its attitudes towards international institutions. In one of his most extensive responses to his critics, Wendt has demonstrated a generous humility in acknowledging the bulk of their criticisms but argues none the less that ideas have a way of sorting themselves out into an operational coherence. He resorts to the familiar claim made by scholars of sovereignty and foreign policy studies: 'states are structured, self-organizing systems … All that is necessary for the assumption of state personhood to be justified at the system level is that domestic contestation be sufficiently structured that it produces unitary collective intentions toward other states at any given moment'.[34] He has controversially suggested that state personhood, in struggling for its self-recognition, might also find in the twenty-first century constructive possibilities for joining some federated version of a world state insofar as such a 'global constitution' can secure sovereignty under the terms of law rather than war.[35] Such is the flexibility of Wendtian methodology that folds realism into liberalism without ideological obstacles. *Social Theory* therefore earns its status as a classic of IR scholarship because it sheds light on the dynamics of how states communicate, debate and crystallize their identities.

Notes

1 Erik Ringmar, 'Alexander Wendt: A Social Scientist Struggling with History', in Iver B. Neumann and Ole Wæver (eds), *The Future of International Relations: Masters in the Making?*, London: Routledge, 1997, pp. 269–89.
2 Alexander Wendt, *Social Theory of International Politics*, Cambridge: Cambridge University Press, 1999, p. xiii. Page numbers placed in parentheses in the text refer to this edition.
3 Cf. Anders Wivel's chapter on Waltz's *Theory of International Politics* in this volume.
4 Friedrich Kratochwil, 'Constructing a New Orthodoxy? Wendt's *Social Theory of International Politics* and the Constructivist Challenge', in Stefano Guzzini and Anna Leander (eds), *Constructivism and International Relations: Alexander Wendt and His Critics*, Abingdon: Routledge, 2006, pp. 28–38.
5 Hidemi Suganami, 'Wendt, IR, and Philosophy: A Critique', in Guzzini and Leander (eds), *Constructivism and International Relations*, pp. 57–72.
6 Andreas Behnke, 'Grand Theory in the Age of its Impossibility: Contemplations on Alexander Wendt', in Guzzini and Leander (eds), *Constructivism and International Relations*, p. 55.
7 Cf. the writings of George Herbert Mead.
8 See, for instance, Anjan Chakravartty, 'Scientific Realism', in Edward N. Zalta (ed.), *The Stanford Encyclopedia of Philosophy* (Summer 2011 Edition), Stanford, CA: Stanford University, 2011. Available at: http://plato.stanford.edu/archives/sum2011/entries/scientific-realism/ (accessed 29 February 2012).
9 John R. Searle, 'Introduction', in John R. Searle (ed.), *The Philosophy of Language*, Oxford: Oxford University Press, 1971, pp. 1–12.
10 John R. Searle, 'What Is a Speech Act?', in Searle (ed.), *The Philosophy of Language*, pp. 39–53, at p. 40.
11 See also Alexander Wendt, 'Anarchy Is What States Make of It: The Social Construction of Power Politics', *International Organization*, 1992, vol. 46, 391–425.
12 Anthony Giddens, *The Constitution of Society: Outline of the Theory of Structuration*, 2nd edn, Oxford: Polity Press, 1986, p. 14.
13 Giddens, *The Constitution of Society*, p. xxxi.
14 Giddens, *The Constitution of Society*, pp. 25–26.
15 Robert O. Keohane, 'Ideas Part-Way Down', *Review of International Studies*, 2000, vol. 26, 125–30.
16 Stephen D. Krasner, 'Wars, Hotel Fires and Plane Crashes', *Review of International Studies*, 2000, vol. 26, 131–36.
17 Steve Smith, 'Wendt's World', *Review of International Studies*, 2000, vol. 26, 156–58.
18 Roxanne Lynn Doty, 'Desire All the Way Down', *Review of International Studies*, 2000, vol. 26, 137–39.
19 Alexander Wendt, 'On the Via Media: A Response to the Critics', *Review of International Studies*, 2000, vol. 26, 178–80.
20 Wendt, 'On the Via Media: A Response to the Critics'.
21 A biological reference to the ability to heal oneself or adjust to changes in the physical environment.
22 Peter Lomas, 'Anthropomorphism, Personification and Ethics: A Reply to Alexander Wendt', *Review of International Studies*, 2005, vol. 31, 349–56; and see Wendt's response in the same volume: 'How Not to Argue against State Personhood: A Reply to Lomas', *Review of International Studies*, 2005, vol. 31, 357–60.
23 See, for example, Steve Smith's chapter entitled 'Foreign Policy Is What States Make of It: Social Construction and International Relations Theory', in Vendulka Kubalkova (ed.), *Foreign Policy in a Constructed World*, Armonk, NY: M.E. Sharpe, 2001, pp. 38–55. The remainder of the volume explores this intriguing question about whether Foreign Policy Analysis is mostly partial towards constructivist frameworks.
24 Maja Zehfuss, *Constructivism in International Relations: The Politics of Reality*, Cambridge: Cambridge University Press, 2002, p. 35.
25 Zehfuss, *Constructivism in International Relations*, p. 87.
26 Karin M. Fierke, *Diplomatic Interventions: Conflict and Change in a Globalizing World*, Basingstoke: Palgrave Macmillan, 2005, p. viii.

27 Fierke, *Diplomatic Interventions*, p. viii.
28 Nina Tannenwald, *The Nuclear Taboo: The US and the Non-Use of Nuclear Weapons since 1945*, Cambridge: Cambridge University Press, 2007; and Carol Atkinson, 'Using Nuclear Weapons', *Review of International Studies*, 2010, vol. 36, 839–51.
29 Giulio M. Gallarotti, *Cosmopolitan Power in International Relations: A Synthesis of Realism, Neoliberalism, and Constructivism*, Cambridge: Cambridge University Press, 2010.
30 Karin M. Fierke, 'Bewitched by the Past: Social Memory, Trauma and International Relations', in Duncan Bell (ed.), *Memory, Trauma and World Politics: Reflections on the Relationship between Past and Present*, Basingstoke: Palgrave Macmillan, 2006, p. 133.
31 Amitav Acharya, *Whose Ideas Matter? Agency and Power in Asian Regionalism*, Singapore and Ithaca, NY: ISEAS and Cornell University Press, 2010, p. 14.
32 In this regard I disagree with Hayward Alker's concern that Wendt's imprecision in explaining the relative proportionality of ideational and materialistic explanations may retard constructivism's theoretical appeal among Asian scholars of international politics. See Hayward R. Alker, 'On Learning from Wendt', *Review of International Studies*, 2000, vol. 26, 141–50.
33 Samuel P. Huntington, *The Clash of Civilizations and the Remaking of World Order*, New York: Simon and Schuster, 1996.
34 Alexander Wendt, 'Social Theory as Cartesian Science: An Auto-Critique from a Quantum Perspective', in Guzzini and Leander (eds), *Constructivism and International Relations: Alexander Wendt and His Critics*, Abingdon: Routledge, 2006, pp. 205–06.
35 Alexander Wendt, 'Why a World State Is Inevitable', *European Journal of International Relations*, 2003, vol. 9, 491–542.

23 A modest realist in a tragic world: John J. Mearsheimer's *The Tragedy of Great Power Politics*

Brian C. Schmidt

Designating a book that was only published ten years ago a classic of the field is always going to be contentious. This is especially the case when the book has generated an array of reactions ranging from outlandish praise to outright condemnation. Nevertheless, in this chapter I am going to argue that John J. Mearsheimer's *The Tragedy of Great Power Politics* (*TGPP*) will, in time, become a classic work of International Relations (IR).[1] In the process of reviewing the main arguments of Mearsheimer's book, I will provide three principal reasons that justify designating *TGPP* a classic in the making. First, the book makes an important contribution to the realist tradition, which continues to be the most influential tradition of IR. Second, the theory that Mearsheimer develops – offensive realism – has not only become an important new branch of realist theory, but it has precipitated a number of debates within realism, including a key debate with Kenneth Waltz's version of structural realism. Offensive realism is deliberately meant to provide a different account of international politics than that provided by Waltz, and those designated as defensive realists. Most fundamentally, offensive realism argues that great powers are continuously seeking opportunities to increase their power relative to other states. Third, the arguments that Mearsheimer develops in his book have influenced some of the important post-Cold War US foreign policy debates. To his credit, Mearsheimer has not shied away from the public arena, and he has used his theory to make a number of controversial predictions and policy recommendations.[2] When all three of these reasons are considered together, there is ample justification for my claim that *TGPP* will be recognized as a classic text of IR.

Offensive realism and the realist tradition

It is not overly controversial to declare that realism is the principal tradition in the field of IR.[3] While there are plenty of analytical accounts of the realist tradition that trace its origins to classical philosophers such as Thucydides or Machiavelli, the historical tradition that I am referring to is the deliberate attempt, by succeeding generations of IR scholars, to develop a realist theory of international politics.[4] In the USA, the origins of this tradition are most often associated with the work of Hans J. Morgenthau, a German émigré, who wrote his classic text, *Politics Among Nations: The Struggle for Power and Peace*, in 1948, and was largely responsible for establishing realism as one of the leading theories in the field.[5] As criticisms of Morgenthau's version of realism intensified during the 1960s and 1970s, and liberalism ascended, Waltz wrote his enormously influential book, *Theory of International Politics* (1979), which resulted in a new structural version of realism – neorealism – replacing what is now commonly referred to as classical, or human nature, realism.[6] Despite the differences between Morgenthau and Waltz's theory, it is now generally recognized that they both belong to the same realist tradition.

Mearsheimer explicitly situates his book in the realist tradition. His theoretical explanation for why great powers seek to maximize their relative power is based on five basic assumptions that he makes about the international system: one, it is anarchic in that it lacks a central authority above states; two, all great powers possess some offensive military capability that might be used to hurt or destroy other states; three, states can never be certain about the intentions of other states; four, survival is the primary goal of states; and five, states are rational actors (pp. 30–31). On the basis of these five assumptions, Mearsheimer derives three general patterns of behaviour. The first is fear: great powers, he argues, have good reasons to fear each other. The basis of this fear is threefold: (i) all great powers possess the means to inflict violence; (ii) there is no mechanism to prevent the use of violence; and (iii) there is no institution to turn to for help once a state has been victimized. The second general pattern of behaviour is self-help. In the absence of a central authority, states must rely on themselves to ensure their own survival. The third pattern, which the theory of offensive realism accentuates, is power maximization. According to Mearsheimer, 'apprehensive about the ultimate intentions of other states, and aware that they operate in a self-help system, states quickly understand that the best way to ensure their survival is to be the most powerful state in the system' (p. 33). Great powers, according to Mearsheimer, are continually searching for opportunities to gain power at the expense of other states.

Like other members of the realist tradition, Mearsheimer seeks to convey the notion that power is the main currency of international politics. He writes, 'for all realists, calculations about power lie at the heart of how states think about the world around them' (p. 12). The end of the Cold War, for Mearsheimer, did not signify the dawn of perpetual peace as many liberals expected. Instead, he argues that the familiar patterns of interstate violence and power competition that characterized much of the nineteenth and twentieth century would be replicated in the post-Cold War international system. The aim of his book is to explain why these patterns of behaviour are enduring features of international politics. In order to provide such an explanation, Mearsheimer recognizes that he has to home in on the elusive concept of power. The book itself is organized around six questions dealing with power (pp. 12–13).[7]

By attempting to provide a definition of power and a way to measure it, Mearsheimer enters the fray over the best way to conceptualize the concept of power. Political scientists have found power to be an elusive concept, and this is true for realists, despite the fact that they are considered to be the theorists of power politics.[8] While it is true that those in the realist tradition base their analysis of international politics on the role of power, realists do hold different ideas about the causes of the power impulse. Mearsheimer discerns two distinct schools within realism that offer competing answers to the question of why states pursue power: human nature realism and defensive realism. With respect to human nature realism, what Arnold Wolfers termed the 'evil school', the pursuit of power is attributed to deep-rooted propensities found in the nature of human beings.[9] Instead of explaining the ubiquitous quest for power on the basis of human nature, structural realists substitute, in Wolfers' terms, 'tragedy' for 'evil'. As the title suggests, *TGPP* is firmly situated in the tradition of tragedy where the condition of anarchy and the relative distribution of power are held responsible for the perpetual security competition that has characterized the great powers of the past and today.

Mearsheimer argues that the structure of the international system, not regime type, ideology, internal socio-political structure, or the personalities of statesmen, largely determines the power seeking behaviour of states. While Mearsheimer agrees with Waltz that it is the structure of the international system that compels states to take self-help measures, especially the accumulation of power, to safeguard their own security, they reach a fundamentally different conclusion on the question of how much power states desire.

Before turning to the disagreement between Mearsheimer and Waltz over the question of whether it is wise for states to maximize power, it is instructive to review how Mearsheimer understands the concept of power. Mearsheimer, like Waltz, endorses an elements-of-national-power approach, which equates power with the possession of material resources. He rejects the relational approach that equates power with the ability to influence another actor. For Mearsheimer, the problem of equating power with outcomes is that there are plenty of historical examples in which the side with seemingly more material power did not prevail. He argues that the essence of a state's effective power is its military power, based largely on the size and strength of the army, as it compares to the military forces of other states. Mearsheimer explains that he defines 'power largely in military terms because offensive realism emphasizes that force is the *ultima ratio* of international politics' (p. 56). According to Mearsheimer, land power is the dominant form of military power, and he concludes that a state with the most formidable army is the most powerful state. The bias that Mearsheimer displays towards land power has important implications for his understanding of why great power politics is ultimately tragic. Although he claims that the goal of every great power is to be the hegemon of the international system, Mearsheimer argues that what he terms 'the stopping power of water' prevents even the strongest army from conquering and holding distant territories. Yet, tragically, the alleged stopping power of water has not prevented any number of states throughout history from attempting to achieve the esteemed position of global hegemon. Whether or not Mearsheimer's stopping power of water thesis is correct, his willingness to theorize geography is a significant contribution to the realist tradition.

Based on his understanding of power, along with the five assumptions that he makes about the international system, especially the assumption that states can never be certain about the intentions of others states, Mearsheimer concludes that there are no status quo powers. All great powers have revisionist aims with the supreme goal being hegemony. Given the environment that states inhabit, they quickly recognize that security is largely a function of military power, and the more power a state has, the more secure it will be. Yet, while all states desire security, Mearsheimer's theory recognizes that states are also motivated by non-security concerns. International politics, according to Mearsheimer, is one of perpetual competition with the great powers struggling against each other to achieve a dominant position. It is a realm of activity where conquest frequently does pay, and where states, consequently, are primed for offence. Unless a state is able to attain the unachievable position of global hegemon, they remain unsatisfied with their position in the international system. Whenever the opportunity arises, a great power will seek to alter the existing distribution of power in its favour by amassing more power.

Offensive-defensive realism debate

While the field of IR is frequently portrayed as a contested terrain where competing paradigms, or 'isms', battle for supremacy, it is, nevertheless, possible to discern a number of key debates taking place within a particular research tradition. This has, since the end of the Cold War, certainly been the case with realism. The growing consensus appears to be that intra-paradigm debates hold out a greater prospect of theoretical progress than inter-paradigm debates.[10] In this regard, the theoretical debate that offensive realism has precipitated with defensive realism represents another enduring contribution of *TGPP*. The importance of the intra-realist debate that Mearsheimer helped to launch should not be underestimated. In addition to the theoretical insights that have been gained by a careful examination of the auxiliary assumptions of each theory, the debate has important foreign policy implications. The essence of the debate between offensive realism and defensive realism involves a fundamental disagreement about the type of behaviour that should be expected of the great powers in the anarchical international system.[11] The key question of a structural theory of international politics is what is the impact of the international system on state behaviour? Essentially, offensive realism argues that the international system provides strong incentives for states to maximize their share of power, while defensive realism maintains that states should only seek an appropriate amount of power necessary to ensure their own survival. In a significant passage, Waltz writes that 'the ultimate concern of states is not for power but for security', implying that they will sometimes forego acquiring more power if this is seen as jeopardizing their security.[12] Rather than the anarchical international system being hostile and predatory, as Mearsheimer describes it, Waltz's account is rather benign as he argues that conflict can often be avoided, and that war hardly ever makes strategic sense.

How can Mearsheimer and Waltz depict such different patterns of behaviour when they share so many of the same assumptions and belong to the same tragedy school? A number of ideas, including differences about state preferences, the implications of anarchy, assumptions about state motivation and the effectiveness of the balance of power mechanism, have been put forth to explain the theoretical divergence between offensive and defensive realism.[13] Here I want to suggest that the principal differences between offensive and defensive realism rest on two assumptions that are present in Mearsheimer's theory, but absent in Waltz's: uncertainty about state intentions and the rational actor assumption. Mearsheimer believes that both assumptions are vital in that they accurately reflect the real world, and thus need to be included in the theory. According to Mearsheimer, a good theory – one that provides maximum explanatory power – should be based on assumptions that conform to reality. Waltz does not include these assumptions; neither does he believe that theory must include assumptions that mimic reality.

There is no doubt that Mearsheimer's assumption that states are never able to decipher clearly the intentions of other states does a lot of work in helping to support his claim that the international system compels states to maximize their share of relative power. A strong case can be made that the uncertainty assumption underlies all three of the general patterns of behaviour that Mearsheimer argues characterizes great power politics: fear, self-help and power maximization. Starting from the baseline assumption that the international system is anarchic, Mearsheimer writes, 'apprehensive about the ultimate intentions of other states, and aware that they operate in a self-help system, states quickly understand that the best way to ensure their survival is to be the most powerful state in the system' (p. 33). While he perceptively recognizes that fear is a relative concept that is intimately linked to the capabilities that a state possesses relative to other states, as well as to whether the distribution of power in the international system is characterized by bipolarity, balanced multipolarity, or unbalanced multipolarity,

Mearsheimer argues that it is the ubiquitousness of fear that propels states to accumulate more power in the belief that it is the surest of way of guaranteeing their own survival. Tragically, states sometimes fight wars with the aim of accumulating power to reduce their fear of an uncertain future. Yet, the uncertainty about the present and future intentions of other states never goes away, and thus Mearsheimer depicts his theory as providing a timeless, albeit tragic, account of great power politics.

Defensive realists do not include uncertainty as a basic assumption of their theory. In fact, they argue that states often are able to signal their intentions, thus reducing the uncertainty that exists among the great powers. This means that for defensive realists, the security dilemma, which is a central dynamic of the international system, can be mitigated. In other words, contrary to Mearsheimer's claim that 'little can be done to ameliorate the security dilemma as long as states operate in anarchy' (p. 36), defensive realists such as Glaser argue that information and material variables can significantly reduce the insecurity and competition that fuels the security dilemma.[14] One of the key concepts of defensive realism is the offence-defensive balance, which attempts to assess the relative ease or difficulty of conquest.[15] Proponents of the offence-defence balance include a number of intervening variables, or what Taliaferro terms 'structural modifiers', such as geography, technology and, most importantly, military doctrine, to make their case that conquest rarely pays and that security can be readily achieved under anarchy. Mearsheimer does not believe that the concept of the offence-defence balance is pertinent in the real world as history provides plenty of examples where it has been impossible to distinguish between offensive and defensive capabilities. He concludes that it would be unwise for any state to forego the opportunity to acquire more power in the naïve belief that a state signalling that it has status quo intentions today will also have them in the future.

Waltz and defensive realists argue that the quest for more power to alleviate the fear of being conquered is unwise because of the prevalent tendency for states to engage in balance of power politics. Aggressive and expansionist behaviour often, according to Waltz, proves to be counterproductive because it automatically triggers a counterbalancing coalition. As a result of Waltz's belief that states are strongly inclined to balance against aggressive powers, they are, in Grieco's terms, 'defensive positionalists' and 'will only seek the minimum level of power that is needed to attain and to maintain their security and survival'.[16] Mearsheimer, conversely, does not believe that balancing is as automatic and prevalent as Waltz maintains. Mearsheimer introduces the innovative concept of buck-passing, whereby a threatened state attempts to get another state to expend its resources to deal with a pending threat while it remains on the sidelines. The aim of buck-passing is to defend the balance of power against an aggressor, but unlike balancing, the threatened state tries to get someone else to do the heavy lifting.

The second significant difference between Waltz and Mearsheimer is that the latter explicitly adopts the rational actor assumption whereas the former does not.[17] While many incorrectly assume that all realists embrace the rational actor assumption, it is quite clear that this is not the case. By omitting the assumption of rationality, Waltz admits that his theory cannot explain the specific foreign policy choices that a state makes at a particular point in history. Waltz has insisted that his version of structural realism is strictly a theory of international politics and, as such, can only explain international outcomes. Mearsheimer disapproves of the distinction that Waltz and others have made between a theory of international politics on the one hand and a theory of foreign policy on the other. By including the rational actor assumption, Mearsheimer's theory is intended to explain both international outcomes and foreign policy behaviour. He expects that, most of the time, states will act according to the logic of offensive realism. Furthermore, because Mearsheimer assumes that states are rational, he anticipates that his theory should be able to account for a good deal of the behaviour that has characterized the history of great power politics.

The debate between and offensive and defensive realism is not going to be settled by determining who has the better assumptions, but rather by the historical record – whose theory best explains the history of international politics. Yet, by foregoing the rational actor assumption, Waltz's theory, when applied to the historical record, is difficult to disprove. When a state does act in a manner contrary to what defensive realism would expect, the behaviour can be deemed 'foolish' or 'reckless', but this does not in itself discredit the theory as Waltz limits himself to explaining international outcomes, not state behaviour. This is not the case with offensive realism. Mearsheimer writes, 'the ultimate test of any theory is how well it explains events in the real world' (p. 6). The second major task of his book is to demonstrate that the theory of offensive realism 'tells us a lot about the history of international politics' (p. 6). As one might expect, Mearsheimer finds that much of the history of great power politics, from the French Revolutionary and Napoleonic Wars in 1792 to the present time, is consistent with his theory of offensive realism. Critics, on the other hand, have pointed to a number of anomalies that Mearsheimer's theory cannot account for without seriously distorting the historical record.[18] In particular, critics have noted that there are historical inconsistencies with respect to his interpretation of the behaviour of insular powers such as Great Britain, Imperial Japan and the USA.

The case of the USA, which Mearsheimer claims is the only state in history to have successfully achieved the esteemed position of regional hegemony, has proved to be especially puzzling. There are at least two puzzles that arise from Mearsheimer's historical account of the USA, both of which have implications for his US foreign policy recommendations. The first puzzle stems from Mearsheimer's interpretation of the USA as a regional hegemon. In the aftermath of the Cold War, he argues that the international system is characterized by the presence of three great powers: the USA, China and Russia. This characterization, which is entirely consistent with how he defines a great power, contradicts the prevailing view that the post-Cold War international system is unipolar with the USA being the global hegemon.[19] For many, it is simply a fact that the USA is currently a global hegemon. This leads to a second puzzle. Mearsheimer's theory predicts that insular, regional hegemons should adopt an offshore balancing grand strategy whereby they seek to maintain their power either through a buck-passing or balancing strategy in order to forestall the emergence of a hegemon in another region of the world. In spite of the supposed stopping power of water, Mearsheimer argues that regional hegemons prefer not to have peer competitors. Consequently, they work hard to prevent such a scenario from arising. Critics have questioned the logic of this argument asking why, if water prevents any state from achieving global hegemony, should a regional hegemon be worried about the activities of other states in distant regions.[20] Mearsheimer's response is that another regional hegemon would be free to roam in the Western Hemisphere and possibly form an alliance with an adversary of the USA. An alternative answer to this question is that, as evidenced by the foreign policy of the USA, water is not a formidable obstacle to a state with great power projection capabilities. Indeed, the very logic of offensive realism can lead to the conclusion that an insular regional hegemon should seek the capabilities to project power over great distances – air, land and water – and impose global hegemony. For many, this describes the contemporary history of the USA perfectly.[21] However, Mearsheimer insists that the USA, after ruthlessly achieving regional hegemony at the end of the nineteenth century, has, like Great Britain during the nineteenth century, exercised a classic offshore balancing grand strategy. The USA, according to Mearsheimer, has only projected its power to Asia and Europe when the threat of a hegemon arising in these regions was imminent.

Conclusion: offensive realism, the future and US foreign policy

In the concluding chapter, Mearsheimer uses his theory of offensive realism to make a number of predictions about great power politics in the twenty-first century. Despite the hazards that are involved in making predictions, the third major task of his book is to peer into the future to see how well offensive realism can anticipate the events associated with great power politics. Although the book was published shortly after the 9/11 terrorist attacks, his basic outlook on international politics was not, in any way, undermined by the events of that dreadful day. Indeed, Mearsheimer stood somewhat alone in the crowd by refusing to concede that 9/11 changed everything about international politics. Courageously, he attempted to thwart the Bush Administration's rush to war in Afghanistan and Iraq by arguing that the USA should concentrate its attention on the central dynamics of great power politics that were outlined in his book. Spending treasure on an imperial crusade to rid the world of terrorism is fundamentally inconsistent with the theory of offensive realism. Prophetically, Mearsheimer predicted that China, a state that he does believe poses a significant future threat to the USA, would be the beneficiary of the Bush Administration's decision to fight unnecessary wars against weak opponents in the guise of the global war on terror.

Many of the predictions that Mearsheimer makes are based on his view that the USA will continue to pursue an offshore balancing grand strategy, which is how offensive realism expects regional hegemons to behave. One of his bolder predictions is that with the fall of the Soviet Union, the USA would begin to bring its troops home from Europe, which would, in turn, intensify security competition in Europe. While Mearsheimer acknowledges that the presence of US troops in Europe has, since the end of World War Two, helped to keep the peace, he maintains that the only reason why the USA committed troops in the first place was to prevent the Soviet Union from becoming a rival hegemon. Now that this is an unlikely scenario, Mearsheimer foresees the removal of US troops from Europe. In the absence of the US pacifier, he predicts a return of great power rivalry in an unbalanced multipolar European system. The situation in North-East Asia is even more troubling as Mearsheimer predicts that a rising China will eventually clash with the USA's interest in preventing a peer competitor in Asia. Owing to the real possibility of China becoming a hegemon in North-East Asia, he predicts that the USA will abandon its accommodating policies and increasingly move towards containing the Chinese threat.

Ten years after *TGPP* was published, it is fairly obvious that some of Mearsheimer's predictions have not come true. Even more problematic is the fact that the USA has not behaved in a manner consistent with the dictates of offensive realism. A big factor that might account for the disjuncture between the predictions of offensive realism on the one hand and the post-Cold War practice of international politics on the other is that Mearsheimer has misinterpreted US grand strategy. Many argue that the USA has not pursued an offshore balancing grand strategy, but rather primacy.[22] If one accepts that the USA has pursued global hegemony since World War II, then the behaviour of the USA in ceaselessly pursuing more and more power, including the capabilities to overcome the alleged constraints of large bodies of water, is actually consistent with offensive realism. Although he makes a sharp distinction between normative and explanatory theory, it is possible to suggest that Mearsheimer wishes that the USA would act like an offshore balancer. He certainly has not hesitated to critique many of the USA's post-Cold War foreign policies, including its policies in Bosnia, China, Afghanistan and Iraq, on the grounds that not only are they inconsistent with an off-shore balancing grand strategy, but antithetical to the US national interest.[23] Yet the fact that Mearsheimer has had to intervene repeatedly in policy debates in order to prescribe how the USA should behave appears, for some, to undermine the claim that offensive realism accurately describes the real world.[24]

Not only have critics noted the discrepancy between Mearsheimer's predictive theory and his persistent policy interventions, but they have pointed out that he has drawn on non-structural factors, such as the role of domestic lobbies, to explain the episodes where US foreign policy has deviated from how offensive realism would have expected the USA to behave.[25] Mearsheimer's admission of unit level factors has confirmed, for many, the limits of a purely structural theory to explain the actual foreign policy choices of a country such as the USA. In an otherwise sympathetic review in the *New Left Review*, Peter Gowan remarks that Mearsheimer's refusal to concede the importance of the internal socio-political structures of states limits the ability of his theory to shed sufficient light on both the past and the present.[26] Although there is no denying that Mearsheimer makes a number of bold claims in his classic text, he is actually a modest realist. He openly admits that there are limits to offensive realism's explanatory power. He acknowledges that the theory cannot answer every question that arises in world politics (pp. 10–11). He allows, much like Waltz, for the possibility that states will, from time to time, behave foolishly. However, as the historical record demonstrates, there often is a steep price to pay for acting in way that contravenes the timeless principles of realism. Like his realist predecessors, this is one of the main messages that Mearsheimer's classic text attempts to convey to the reader. Mearsheimer, in recasting the principles of realism in a theoretically vigorous manner in order to explain great power politics, has provided an invaluable service to the field of IR and to the general public. As with other classic works in the realist tradition, *TGPP* will no doubt withstand the test of time. It is impossible to deny that realist theory captures many of the central dynamics of international politics. Mearsheimer's classic text provides a compelling explanation of the timeless quality of international politics and will therefore continue to be read by those seeking to understand the tragic nature of great power politics.

Notes

1 John J. Mearsheimer, *The Tragedy of Great Power Politics*, New York: W. W. Norton, 2001. Page numbers placed in parentheses in the text refer to this edition.

2 For an interesting interview, see 'Conversations in International Relations – Interviews with John J. Mearsheimer (Part I)', *International Relations*, 2006, vol. 20, 105–24 and 'Conversations in International Relations – Interviews with John J. Mearsheimer (Part II)', *International Relations*, 2006, vol. 20, 231–43. For an interesting recent reappraisal, see Robert D.

Kaplan, 'Why John J. Mearsheimer Is Right (About Some Things)', *The Atlantic*, January/ February 2012.

3 See e.g. Robert O. Keohane, 'Theory of World Politics: Structural Realism and Beyond', in Ada W. Finifter (ed.), *Political Science: The State of the Discipline*, Washington, DC: American Political Science Association, 1983, pp. 503–40; Stefano Guzzini, *Realism in International Relations and International Political Economy: The Continuing Story of a Death Foretold*, London: Routledge, 1998; and Stephen M. Walt, 'The Enduring Relevance of the Realist Tradition', in Ira Katznelson and Helen V. Milner (eds), *Political Science: The State of the Discipline*, New York: W. W. Norton, 2002, pp. 199–230.

4 On the difference between a historical and an analytical tradition, see Brian C. Schmidt, *The Political Discourse of Anarchy: A Disciplinary History of International Relations*, Albany, NY: SUNY Press, 1998.

5 See Nicolas Guilhot (ed.), *The Invention of International Relations Theory: Realism, the Rockefeller Foundation, and the 1954 Conference on Theory*, New York: Columbia University Press, 2011 and his chapter on this book in this volume.

6 See Anders Wivel's chapter on this book in this volume.

7 The six questions are: (i) why do great powers want power?; (ii) how much power do states want?; (iii) what is power?; (iv) what strategies do states pursue to gain power?; (v) what are the causes of war?; and (vi) when do threatened great powers balance against a dangerous adversary and why do they attempt to pass the buck to another threatened state?

8 See Brian C. Schmidt, 'Competing Realist Conceptions of Power', *Millennium: Journal of International Studies*, 2005, vol. 33, 523–49.

9 On the 'evil school', see Arnold Wolfers, *Discord and Collaboration: Essays on International Politics*, Baltimore, MD: Johns Hopkins University Press, 1962.

10 There are a number of scholars who concur with this assessment. See e.g. Walt, 'The Enduring Relevance of the Realist Tradition'; Jeffrey W. Taliaferro, 'Security Seeking Under Anarchy: Defensive Realism Revisited', *International Security*, 2000/2001, vol. 25, 128–61; and Robert Jervis, 'Realism and the Study of World Politics', *International Organization*, 1998, vol. 52, 971–91.

11 For more on the offensive realism-defensive realism debate, see Charles Glaser, *Rational Theory of International Politics: The Logic of Competition and Cooperation*, Princeton, NJ: Princeton University Press, 2010.

12 Kenneth N. Waltz, 'The Origins of War in Neorealist Theory', in Robert I. Rotberg and Theodore K. Rabb (eds), *The Origin and Prevention of Major Wars*, Cambridge: Cambridge University Press, 1989, pp. 39–52, at p. 40.

13 See Jeffrey D. Berejikian, 'The Rationality of Sanctions Reconsidered: Offensive or Defensive Realism?', paper presented at the annual meeting of the Southern Political Science Association, New Orleans, January 6–9, 2004; Taliaferro, 'Security Seeking under Anarchy'; Brian C. Schmidt, 'Realism as Tragedy', *Review of International Studies*, 2004, vol. 30, 427–41; and Peter Toft, 'John J. Mearsheimer: An Offensive Realist between Geopolitics and Power', *Journal of International Relations and Development*, 2005, vol. 8, 381–408.

14 See also Glaser, *Rational Theory of International Politics*.

15 On the offence-defence balance, see Robert Jervis, 'Cooperation under the Security Dilemma', *World Politics*, 1978, vol. 30, 167–214; and Sean M. Lynn-Jones, 'Offense-Defense Theory and its Critics', *Security Studies*, 1995, vol. 4, 660–91.

16 Joseph M. Grieco, 'Realist International Theory and the Study of World Politics', in Michael W. Doyle and G. John Ikenberry (eds), *New Thinking in International Relations Theory*, Boulder, CO: Westview Press, 1997, pp. 163–201, at p. 167.

17 See John J. Mearsheimer, 'Reckless States and Realism', *International Relations*, 2009, vol. 23, 241–56.

18 See e.g. Barry R. Posen, 'The Best Defense', *The National Interest*, 2002, vol. 67, 119–26; Peter Gowan, 'A Calculus of Power', *New Left Review*, vol. 16, 47–67; Shiping Tang, 'Social Evolution of International Politics', *European Journal of International Relations*, 2010, vol. 16, 31–55; and Toft, 'John J. Mearsheimer: An Offensive Realist between Geopolitics and Power'.

19 See Stephen G. Brooks and William C. Wohlforth, *World Out of Balance: International Relations and the Challenge of American Primacy*, Princeton, NJ: Princeton University Press, 2008.

20 Christopher Layne, 'The "Poster Child for Offensive Realism": America as a Global Hegemon', *Security Studies*, 2002/2003, vol. 12, 120–64.
21 See Barry R. Posen, 'Command of the Commons: The Military Foundation of U.S. Hegemony', *International Security*, 2003, vol. 28, 5–46.
22 Mearsheimer now concedes that from Clinton on the US has pursued global dominance. See 'Imperial By Design', *The National Interest*, 2010, vol. 111, 16–34.
23 See e.g. the following articles by John J. Mearsheimer: 'The Only Exit from Bosnia', *New York Times*, 7 October 1997; 'The Gathering Storm: China's Challenge to US Power in Asia', *The Chinese Journal of International Politics*, 2010, vol. 3, 381–96; 'Guns Won't Win the Afghan War', *New York Times*, 4 November 2001; and, with Stephen M. Walt, 'An Unnecessary War', *Foreign Policy*, 2003, vol. 134, 50–59; and 'Keeping Saddam in a Box', *New York Times*, 2 February 2003.
24 See Ido Oren, 'The Unrealism of Contemporary Realism: The Tension between Realist Theory and Realists' Practice', *Perspectives on Politics*, 2009, vol. 7, 283–301.
25 On the role of domestic lobbies, see John J. Mearsheimer and Stephen M. Walt, *The Israel Lobby and U.S. Foreign Policy*, New York: Farrar, Straus and Giroux, 2007. Also see John J. Mearsheimer, *Why Leaders Lie*, Oxford: Oxford University Press, 2011.
26 Gowan, 'A Calculus of Power'.

24 Interrogating the subject: Errol Morris's *The Fog of War*

Casper Sylvest[1]

An imaginative and thought-provoking feature-length film, *The Fog of War* (*FOW*) is also highly controversial.[2] Apart from the fact that it premiered in 2003, the year of the contentious US-led war on Iraq, it reignited controversies over the policies and legacy of its subject, Robert Strange McNamara (1916–2009). A partaker in mid-twentieth-century US wars, hot and cold, McNamara was and remains one of the most divisive figures in US public life. The immediate reception of the film reflected not only historical disagreements over the Cold War and Vietnam but also admiration for the film's ability to speak to both contemporary and perhaps even universal questions. Director Errol Morris (b. 1948) was accused of being too lenient on McNamara, of uncritically allowing his interviewee to present a self-serving, historically inaccurate and hand-wringing narrative.[3] On the other hand, the film won an Academy Award for best documentary and has been praised as 'a stunning historical work' in the pages of *The American Historical Review*.[4]

The film quickly became a teaching tool in colleges and universities in the USA and abroad. As anyone who has watched *FOW* will know, it deals with a host of gruelling problems in politics, ethics and contemporary history. The *Official Teacher's Guide for the Fog of War*[5] draws out these themes in an effort to facilitate learning through student-based discussion. The film is also one of few documentaries to have attracted serious interest from scholars of International Relations (IR). Some of these contributions deal more with McNamara than with *FOW* (to the extent that the two are now separable), while others interpret the film's message by focusing on its narrative and the film-making techniques deployed by Morris.[6]

In this chapter, I shall argue that *FOW*, despite its form and genre, should be seen as an alternative classic of IR. The film raises a number of specific issues of interest to IR scholars. These include the place of morality in political decisions concerning the use of military force, the importance of communication, perception and signalling in social relations between (adversarial) actors in international politics and the nature and burdens of statesmanship. These issues are clearly relevant to the Just War tradition and a broad spectrum of IR theories, including constructivism, the English School, liberalism and classical realism.

Moreover, for IR scholars *FOW* was (and is) a current affairs movie in a double sense. First, it echoes the reflective mood within the discipline that followed in the wake of 9/11 and the Iraq War. In particular, the film highlighted an increasingly popular analogy between Iraq and the US failure in Vietnam. Errol Morris has since explained his own view of the analogy by pointing out that '[e]very historical situation is different ... there is only one thing that remains the same in history, and that's human idiocy'.[7] Second, *FOW* also examines philosophical issues of direct relevance to current theory debates within IR. Read through the prism of the discipline's more or less continuously ongoing *Methodenstreit* that has culminated in the so-called fourth debate, *FOW* contributes to the revolt against rationalism. McNamara, the *Wunderkind* of managerialism and rationalism, appears in front of the camera as a bewildered 'post-war technocratic hubristic fable'.[8] In the same vein, the film's emphasis on empathy has been used to bolster a defence of (political and theoretical) pluralism as an ethos of the discipline.[9]

These are all sound reasons for appraising the film. Yet, reading the film as an argument on par with conventionally transmitted (i.e. written) arguments within IR, I shall argue that it deserves its classic status not for providing a theory of international politics, but for presenting us with a familiar but paradoxical landscape of (theoretical) assumptions and (normative) commitments – made up of 'Eleven Lessons from the Life of Robert S. McNamara' – while simultaneously interrogating the strengths, emphases, and blind spots of the individual objects and features of this landscape. Through a combination of historical study, interviews and cinematic technique, I argue, *FOW* becomes a deeply ironic metaphorical essay on international politics. Out of deference to this argument, I put much emphasis on the intellectual and technical aspects of Morris's film-making.

I proceed in three steps. First, I discuss the politics of documentary film-making and Morris's production. I then briefly sketch the narrative of the film in a way that also serves as an introduction to the biography of McNamara. The third section then moves on to discuss *FOW* as a critical intervention in a discourse about conflict and social life that is jarringly stimulating for students of IR.

The politics of documentary film-making

> 'Filmmakers like Errol Morris are the reason the definition of "documentary" is so contentious.'[10]

While the relationship between politics and film-making or photography has long been of interest to the human sciences, there has been a tendency to ignore or downplay the role of documentaries in such analyses, perhaps because the once-dusty genre has either been seen to unproblematically reflect reality or to embody fiction in sheep's clothing. Both positions are unsatisfactory. *Bowling for Columbine* (2002), *Supersize Me* (2004), *An Inconvenient Truth* (2006) and numerous other films, including recent releases like *The Cove* (2009) or *Restrepo* (2010), have accorded documentaries a new prominence. In conjunction with technological developments and a wider proliferation of film-making equipment, more films portraying, or pretending to portray, reality are available. Since the 1990s film studies has increasingly delved into the history and nature of 'docs'.[11] Political studies have so far not followed suit despite the recent explosion in politically relevant documentaries. While recent decades have witnessed the emergence of a literature on film and IR which reflects a broader interest in various forms of visual representation, the nexus between politics, culture and documentary film-making remains curiously understudied.[12]

Defining documentary is no easy feat. A watertight definition is 'effectively impossible', one scholar maintains.[13] Even negative criteria that appear as obvious minimum requirements – like not using a script or not using actors – are challenged by films that are commonly accepted to be part of the genre. Indeed, documentary film has been likened to a 'pluripotent stem cell' that produces a variety of sub-genres (from rockumentaries to *cinema vérité*).[14] While these films are supposed to deal with 'real people' or 'real phenomena', accuracy is an unproductive yardstick.[15] Relying on common sense ('we know a documentary when we see one!') is a seductively appealing but intellectually unsatisfactory option. Conversely, we could acknowledge that there *is* a difference between fiction feature films and documentaries – not least with respect to the ways in which the latter lay claim to (parts of the) truth or reality – yet otherwise concentrate on the most obvious similarity between them: they are both edited!

From this perspective, since documentaries deal with themes, figures or phenomena that are, directly or indirectly, of public interest they are inherently *political*. Non-fiction (as well as fiction) films can serve a host of purposes, but they are perhaps best seen as narrative structures that (like other narratives making use of other mediums) claim, show, argue, posit, assume and criticize.[16] Together with other forms of communication they share a challenge of ensuring that an intended meaning, even if it is equivocal, is received and accepted by the audience. Clearly, the editing process is paramount in this context. It is an intensely political practice, which virtually all directors recognize as such. This is no less true of Morris, who fittingly considers documentaries to offer 'almost unlimited possibilities of self-expression'. The narrative structures and force of Morris's films emerge through a 'process of discovery' in the editing room, during which a massive condensation and elimination of material takes place.[17]

Apart from *FOW*, his best-known production, Morris's output includes the portraits of the USA *Gates of Heaven* (1978) and *Vernon, Florida* (1981), the 'detective-documentary' *The Thin Blue Line* (1988) that solved the murder of a Dallas policeman and led to the overturning of the conviction of an innocent man (who later sued Morris for the rights to his life story), the portrait of Stephen Hawking in *A Brief History of Time* (1991), and *Mr Death* (1999), a harrowing portrait of the 40-cups-of-coffee and 120-cigarettes-per-day engineer Fred Leuchter, whose libertarianism and professional career as a designer of execution equipment for US penitentiaries led Leuchter to conduct an amateurish 'investigation' of Auschwitz that was later exploited by Holocaust deniers. His latest films include *Tabloid* (2010) and *Standard Operating Procedure* (2008). The latter revolves around the Abu Ghraib prison scandal in Iraq and is simultaneously an investigation into the nature of photography and an attempt to question the superficial public condemnation of Lynndie England and other members of the 372nd Military Police Company. Morris looks beyond and behind the photographs and (indirectly) questions the political and military establishment and their role in creating a culture in which torture and degradation was anything but untoward.[18]

In most of Morris's work, simple existential or epistemological questions are pursued in a manner that evokes philosophical debate more than ideological crusade. This is unsurprising given Morris's academic background. He studied history at the University of Wisconsin, before unsuccessfully pursuing graduate studies in the history and philosophy of science at the Universities of Princeton and Berkeley. As well as struggling with writer's block and other difficulties, Morris also fell out with his supervisor, Thomas Kuhn, who 'physically assaulted me and shortly after that threw me out of Princeton'.[19]

Truth, self-deception, the achievement of justice, guilt, evil (or the capacity to do evil), the metaphysics of killing and overcoming or dealing with human suffering are recurring themes in films by Morris. Clearly, a miscarriage of justice, the naivety and hubris of a little-known engineer and the political career of McNamara are only superficially related; yet, they all expose the marvels and mysteries of human self-creation.

> I've always been fascinated by how people see themselves as virtually anything. It's like our capacity for credulity, our capability of believ[ing] utter nonsense, to imagine things that are utterly ridiculous and clearly untrue. Our abilities are unfettered in that direction.[20]

The eccentric, delusional and often controversial subjects of Morris's films are used, then, to illuminate something important and familiar about the human condition. However, their lives or deeds and their own understanding of these are always central concerns. 'My films don't document news stories or external events, they're more excursions into people's personal dreamscapes.'[21] Through a mixture of wit, authenticity and an engagement with deeply ethical and metaphysical questions, Morris manages to humanize and expose his subjects (or victims as some critics would have it).

Morris achieves these qualities in his film-making through a cynical interview style and cinematic techniques that have become trademarks of his first-person film-making. His notorious interview machine, the 'Interrotron', etymologically derived from 'interview' and 'terror', works by projecting Morris's image onto a two-way mirror placed directly in front of a camera through which the interview is recorded. The device allows Morris to conduct interviews that create directness, eye contact, authenticity *and* create a distance between Morris and the interviewee, which in turn makes the interviewee talk.[22] Yet, talk is intensely interesting since, 'the thing that makes civilization possible', according to Morris, 'is that people lie to one another routinely'.[23] And to themselves one might add.

In the technologically mediated intimacy created by the 'Interrotron' focus is (after a while) shifted *away* from the interview process which in turn facilitates an exploitation of uncomfortable silences. Enter Morris's three-minute rule: 'My rule of thumb is to leave people alone, let them talk, and in two or three minutes they'll show you how crazy they really are.'[24] Experience has taught Morris that combining silence with the appearance of an attentive listener is a successful strategy. This well-staged 'let-'em-talk-until-they-spill-the-beans' procedure reveals that for Morris, ironically, a good interview is almost a monologue.

Morris's films often have a deft comic quality to them despite dealing with themes such as evil, death and wrongdoing. Although the interview is mediated and constructed, Morris's editing adds a further layer. The documentary, a term with which Morris is distinctly uncomfortable due to its *cinéma verité* connotations, is clearly *not* pure film-making.[25] Often using modernist music, re-enactments (a term Morris is not keen on) and an aggressive editing style, the subjects at the centre of Morris's films *appear* to speak for themselves – but clearly not under circumstances of their own choosing.

The silhouette of McNamara in *The Fog of War*

> 'You can have more war and you can have more appeasement. And we don't want more of either.'[26]

FOW is an intense movie. Apart from Morris's voice which can be heard shouting between eight and ten times during the film, the only contemporary figure that the viewer meets is McNamara. The film is based on more than 20 hours of filmed inter-views begun in May 2001. Mixed with historical audio and audiovisual clips, McNamara is the central narrating voice on a journey that has three key diachronic reference points: the allied strategic bombing of Japanese cities during the Second World War, the legendary 13 days of October 1962 during which the Cuban Missile Crisis unfolded and US troop and conflict escalation during the Vietnam War. These are not only some of the most excruciating events of the World War II and the Cold War; they are also milestones in the personal life of McNamara: he shaped and was shaped by US strat-egy and policy. The film does not directly deal with McNamara's public life after he left government in the late 1960s. During this latter part of McNamara's life he was President of the World Bank (1968–81) and later an outspoken critic of US nuclear policy, one among many former US government officials that are collectively known as 'the eliminators'.[27] Yet, many other dimensions of McNamara's life – from childhood, university education (Berkeley) and professional life (from Harvard Business School to Ford Motor Company) – are woven into a selective political and cultural history of the USA during the middle quarters of the twentieth century.[28]

The film begins with a poised, professional and slick-looking McNamara who is about to begin a Pentagon press briefing during the Vietnam War. Utterly at ease in the situation, McNamara pronounces the first words of the film: 'Is this chart a reasonable height for you?' This is perhaps the dominant image of McNamara: the brightest of the bright, the whizz-kid par excellence. One hour and forty-five minutes later, the film closes with a determined McNamara refusing to engage in further discussion about Vietnam ('I would rather be damned if I don't'), set to footage of this aged, bleak-looking man driving his Ford around Washington, DC. In between this front and back cover of the movie, Morris takes us through the Cuban Missile Crisis, the First World War, the Depression, the World War II, the Tonkin Gulf Affair and the heated debates about Vietnam inside and outside the White House.

What makes the narrative riveting and intense are not only Morris's skills as a director, but also the fact that McNamara since retirement has tried to come to grips with his involvement in and decisions during some of these controversial events.[29] Visually this self-reflexive exercise conducted in McNamara's gripping voice is accom-panied by historical documents, footage, re-enactments and texted audio clips against a background of the legendary rolling tape recorder. Unsurprisingly, a great deal of the debate surrounding *FOW* has been about Cuba and Vietnam, *the* symbolic pointers of Cold War history and politics. Morris has received the harshest criticism in relation to McNamara's role in and recollection of the Cuban Missile Crisis and his responsibility for and his (failed) attempt to avert the Vietnam tragedy.[30] The gist of this critique is that Morris is too soft on McNamara, that Morris fails to bring out what Hendrickson has called the 'deep and rigid and almost schizoid but in any case deceitful code of opposites' in McNamara's character.[31]

At first sight, Morris might look guilty as charged. 'I'm never in an adversarial position with the people that I film', he has argued.[32] This is also true of McNamara: the pair promoted the film together, a desolate McNamara dominates the commercial packaging of the film, and Morris has relayed how he grew to like McNamara and his (in Morris's opinion) sincere attempt to come to grips with his political deeds and misdeeds. Clearly, Morris's treatment of the most controversial aspects of the Cuban Missile Crisis and Vietnam – was the second letter from Khrushchev 'dictated by a bunch of hard-liners' as McNamara argued, was McNamara trying to help Kennedy to 'keep us out of the war' and was McNamara responsible for the escalation of the Vietnam War or did he try to prevent it? – glosses over significant historical complexities and controversies. The debates among historians about these issues, essentially political debates about the legacies of statesmen and policies, are endlessly interesting. Film is, however, an unpromising media in which to conduct such discussions, even if it can be persuasively argued that Morris succeeds in unsettling ingrained prejudices. Yet, what redeems the film is the effect that Morris seeks and achieves with his audience: critical reflection.

The Fog of War as a classic of IR

'Hope is the final pestilence.'[33]

FOW is a powerful reminder that in international politics what you believe governs what you do and that action, while often irreversible, provides stimulus for reflection and, possibly, learning. Yet, a case can be made for seeing the film as an allegory on international politics more broadly. Morris has described the film as 'part history, part self-analysis, part mystery, part self-justification',[34] but even this is unnecessarily restrictive. Indeed, the composition of *FOW* and Morris's editing and film-making style turns the film into an unresolved, tension-ridden and challenging essay on fundamental issues in international relations, including communication, learning, weapons and war. At this point, it is worth returning to the aforementioned 11 lessons, which both serve as the subtitle and main organising device of the film (these lessons are recapitulated in Box 24.1). It is in the matrix – or maze, rather – constructed by these 'lessons' and through his subject McNamara that Morris's near-nihilism and ceaseless, poignant questioning of central themes in the conduct and study of international politics emerge: 'I often think that if my movies are any good it's because they are full of unresolved questions you can keep thinking about.'[35] Using this yardstick, I argue, *FOW* is indeed a successful movie.

Box 24.1 Eleven lessons from the life of Robert S. McNamara

Lesson #1: Empathize with your enemy
Lesson #2: Rationality will not save us
Lesson #3: There's something beyond one's self
Lesson #4: Maximize efficiency
Lesson #5: Proportionality should be a guideline in war
Lesson #6: Get the data
Lesson #7: Belief and seeing are both often wrong
Lesson #8: Be prepared to re-examine your reasoning
Lesson #9: In order to do good, you may have to engage in evil
Lesson #10: Never say never
Lesson #11: You can't change human nature

While the lessons are extrapolated from McNamara's life and recollections, they can, by the same token, be read as an ironic and deeply pessimistic philosophy of international politics: 'I don't think that the lessons in any way summarize the film. They have, if anything, an ironic absurdist quality that leads you from one step to the other.'[36] Part of this thought-provoking quality has to do with the alluring nature of the lessons *and* their obviously strained interrelations. While every lesson is, on its own, trivially reasonable, as a collective the lessons groan loudly against each other. For example, while the second lesson teaches that 'rationality will not save us', the fourth lesson (presented to the audience a mere ten minutes later) pays homage to undiluted means-end rationality by urging us to 'maximize efficiency'. As Morris puts it, 'McNamara is a control freak, yet he explains to us that the world is, essentially, out of control'.[37] Similarly, the sixth lesson teaches us to 'get the data', while the seventh lesson invalidates our sensory experiences by proclaiming that 'belief and seeing are both often wrong'. Indeed, it has persuasively been argued that:

> [T]he lesson of the lessons is that they are without lesson: they do not summarize a formalizable knowledge that can be transmitted … [T]he lesson of McNamara's lessons is that he has intuited something about the nature of knowing, especially in times of crisis when unprecedented events unfold in unprecedented ways such that one must reckon with what exceeds present categories of comprehension, decision, action, and anticipatable consequence, putting one in the position of having to invent on the spot new means of responding to the danger at hand.[38]

This is a precise description of the incongruity that Morris lays bare and the challenges he presents for IR scholars. It is a position that has some affinities with classical realism and its understanding of politics as tragedy,[39] yet it is also, ultimately, more misanthropic in its resignation to the tragicomic nemesis of human folly. Indeed, while the film could be taken merely as a sign of the confusion which McNamara's soul-searching has landed him in, there is more at play. This is most obvious towards the end of the film when any illusions about intellectual and moral progress in politics made through the first 10 lessons are punctured in a moment of supreme irony: the final, eleventh lesson bluntly states that 'you can't change human nature'.

The intention, I submit, is to stimulate reflection, and in *FOW*, Morris deploys cinematic technique to achieve this objective. Despite the fact that Morris only interviews one person and that success is defined as the breakdown of dialogue, the film is *a double interrogation*. On the one hand, McNamara's near-monologues are clearly provoked by Morris's pointed questions and the intimidating interview context. On the other hand, *FOW* is a bombardment of the senses in which a juggernaut of music and editing virtually assault, enhance or question anything McNamara has to say during the film. Set to Philip Glass' vexing scores, aggressive editing techniques – historical footage, close-up photos of print media and the interviewee, the de-centring of McNamara in the frame, and re-enactments – accompany McNamara's spoken word while simultaneously structuring and pacing the narrative.

While these techniques can be read as legitimating what McNamara portrays as necessary evils,[40] this is unduly confined. Sometimes the editing supports or illustrates a point or a logic described, at other times it adds to the characterization of McNamara. At yet other junctures in the film, it works to expose McNamara and his worrying concept of empathy. In these passages, the music and editing do seem to be a strategy of suspicion that is used to visualize or question statements or assumptions made by McNamara that appear to be uncontroversial or trivial but which turn out to harbour deep moral, political and philosophical dilemmas. Perhaps the best example of this is the recurrence of objects dropping towards the ground: skulls, bombs, napalm, Agent Orange, dominos or a graphic manipulation of numbers from one of McNamara's World War II reports about bombing efficiency. The free fall transmits both a measure of serenity and eeriness but without putting across one equivocal point. Other iconic images of war – the bomber, the mounting of weapons on aircrafts, the strategy meetings of generals, and panorama images of large-scale destruction – while apparently creating distance between political decisions and actual suffering and violence are nevertheless paced and cut into the film in ways that produce dissonance, evoke doubt and facilitate reflection. One example of this is the way in which target destruction rates of Japanese cities during the World War II are illustrated (using accelerating cuts) by reference to US cities of equivalent size.

Why, one might well ask. Why does Morris seek to place his audience in this tangle of politics, hypocrisy, normative principles, apparently good intentions and mostly shocking consequences (in the McNamarian sense in which 'results are what we expect and consequences are what we get')? Well, '[l]anguage is the ultimate tool of concealment', Morris argues.[41] The same could be said of film, but in Morris's hands the documentary is above all critical by virtue of exposing the philosophical, political, and moral dilemmas and paradoxes that we too often keep under wraps in trying to make sense of international politics. This is why *FOW* is a classic of IR.

Notes

1 I thank Duncan Bell, Signe Blaabjerg Christoffersen, James Der Derian, Suzette Frovin, Rens van Munster, Nils Arne Sørensen and my students for stimulating discussions about Morris' film-making.
2 *The Fog of War*, directed by Errol Morris, 106 min., Sony Pictures Classics, 2003.
3 Fred Kaplan, 'The Evasions of Robert McNamara: What's True and What's a Lie in The Fog of War?', *Slate Magazine*, 19 December 2003. Available at: www.slate.com/id/2092916/ (accessed 19 January 2012). The film was also accompanied by the publication of a book: James G. Blight and Janet M. Lang, *The Fog of War: Lessons from the Life of Robert S. McNamara*, New York: Rowman & Littlefield, 2005.
4 Seth Fein, Review of *The Fog of War*, *American Historical Review*, 2004, vol. 109, 1260.
5 Choices Program and the Critical Oral History Project at the Watson Institute for International Studies, Brown University, *Official Teacher's Guide for the Fog of War* (2004). Available at: www.choices.edu/resources/supplemental_fogofwar.php (accessed 19 January 2012).
6 Michael J. Shapiro, 'The Fog of War', *Security Dialogue*, 2005, vol. 36, 233–46; Lloyd S. Etheredge (ed.), 'Symposium: McNamara's Lessons and *The Fog of War*', prepared for *Perspectives on Politics*. Available at: www.policyscience.net/mcnamara.pdf (accessed 19 January 2012). See also Richard New Lebow, 'Robert S. McNamara: Max Weber's Nightmare', *International Relations*, 2006, vol. 20, 211–24. In film studies, Morris' work is more widely appreciated. For recent, well-referenced studies, see Zoë Drucik, 'Documenting False History: Errol Morris and *Mr. Death*', *Studies in Documentary Film*, 2007, vol. 1, 207–19; William Rothman (ed.), *Three Documentary Filmmakers: Errol Morris, Ross McElwee, Jean Rouch*, New York: SUNY Press, 2009; Lucia Ricciardelli, 'Documentary Filmmaking in the Postmodern Age: Errol Morris & *The Fog of Truth*', *Studies in Documentary Film*, 2010, vol. 4, 35–50.
7 Errol Morris, 'The Anti-Postmodern Postmodernist', in Livia Bloom (ed.), *Errol Morris Interviews*, Jackson, MI: University Press of Mississippi, 2010, pp. 118–30, at p. 128. For the reflective mood, see e.g. John J. Mearsheimer, 'Hans Morgenthau and the Iraq War: Realism versus Neo-conservatism', *Open Democracy*, 18 May 2005. Available at: www.opendemocracy.net/democracy-americanpower/morgenthau_2522.jsp (accessed 19 January 2012).

 8 The phrase is from Paul Hendrickson, *The Living and the Dead: Robert McNamara and Five Lives of a Lost War*, London: Papermac, 1997, p. 356.
 9 Chris Brown with Kirstin Ainley, *Understanding International Relations*, 4th edn, Basingstoke: Palgrave Macmillan, 2009, p. 14.
10 Roy Grundmann and Cynthia Rockwell, 'Truth is Not Subjective', reprinted in Bloom (ed.), *Errol Morris Interviews*, pp. 86–101, at p. 86.
11 See particularly Patricia Aufderheide, *Documentary Film: A Very Short Introduction*, Oxford: Oxford University Press, 2007; Michael Chanan, *The Politics of Documentary*, London: British Film Institute, 2007; Jonathan Kahana, *The Politics of American Documentary*, New York: Columbia University Press, 2008.
12 Rens van Munster and Casper Sylvest, 'Documenting and International Relations: Documentary Film and the Creative Arrangment of Perceptibility', unpublished manuscript, March 2013. On film and IR see e.g. Cynthia Weber, *International Relations Theory: A Critical Introduction*, 3rd edn, London: Routledge, 2009; Michael J. Shapiro, *Cinematic Geopolitics*, London: Routledge, 2009. Conspicuously, prominent scholars in the field, like Cynthia Weber, Michael T. Klare and James Der Derian, have recently turned to (documentary) film-making.
13 Chanan, *The Politics of Documentary*, p. 5.
14 Marsha McCreadie, *Documentary Superstars: How Today's Filmmakers Are Reinventing the Form*, New York: Allworth Press, 2008, p. ix.
15 See e.g. Felicity Mellor, 'The Politics of Accuracy in Judging Global Warming Films', *Environmental Communication*, 2009, vol. 3, 134–50.
16 For a discussion of these characteristics of the genre attuned to the agenda of IR as well as a typology of subgenres, see Sylvest and van Munster, 'Documenting International Relations'.
17 This was also the case for *FOW*. See Paul Cronin, 'It Could All Be Wrong: An Unfinished Interview with Errol Morris', in Bloom (ed.), *Errol Morris Interviews*, pp. 144–209, at pp. 176, 187, 194.
18 The film was also accompanied by a book: Philip Gourevitch and Errol Morris, *Standard Operating Procedure: A War Story*, London: Picador, 2008.
19 Morris in Cronin, 'It Could All Be Wrong', p. 194.
20 Morris in Alice Arshalooys Kelikian, 'Film and Friendship: Werner and Errol', in Bloom (ed.), *Errol Morris Interviews*, pp. 210–29, at p. 216.
21 Cronin, 'It Could All Be Wrong', p. 184.
22 The Interrotron has since been superseded by the more technologically advanced Megatron. Morris has directed many commercials using the Interrotron, a phenomenon that has since exploded. Morris' production also includes commercials for the 2008 Obama campaign ('People in the Middle for Obama'. Available at: www.youtube.com/user/middleforobama/featured (accessed 19 January 2012)).
23 Morris quoted in Alan Chang, 'Planet of the Apes', reprinted in Bloom (ed.), *Errol Morris Interviews*, pp. 55–61, at p. 55.
24 Bloom (ed.), *Errol Morris Interviews*, back cover.
25 Morris pursues some of these concerns about the relationship between photography and truth on his *New York Times* blog. Available at: http://opinionator.blogs.nytimes.com/category/errol-morris/ (accessed 19 January 2012).
26 President Lyndon B. Johnson, 25 February, 1964 (in telephone conversation with McNamara), in *The Fog of War*. All references to the film are taken from the transcript available on Morris' website. Available at: www.errolmorris.com/film/fow_transcript.html (accessed 19 January 2012).
27 The eliminators (not to be confused with the professional wrestling tag team of the same name) are made up of former national security cabinet officials who seek to eliminate nuclear weapons. McNamara has characterized US nuclear policy as 'immoral, illegal, militarily unnecessary, and dreadfully dangerous'. (Robert S. McNamara, 'Apocalypse Soon', *Foreign Policy*, 2005, 148, p. 28.) See also Joseph Cirincione and Alexandra Bell, 'The Eliminators', *Center for American Progress*, 17 January 2008. Available at: www.americanprogress.org/issues/2008/01/the_eliminators.html (accessed 19 January 2012).
28 For a fuller sketch see Tim Weiner, 'Robert S. McNamara, Architect of a Futile War, Dies at 93', *New York Times*, 7 July 2009; and Hendrickson's excellent *The Living and the Dead*.

29 Robert S. McNamara, *Blundering into Disaster: Surviving the First Century of the Nuclear Age*, New York: Pantheon, 1986; Robert S. McNamara, *In Retrospect: The Tragedy and Lessons of Vietnam*, New York: Random House, 1995; Robert S. McNamara and James G. Blight, *Wilson's Ghost: Reducing the Risk of Conflict, Killing and Catastrophe in the 21st Century*, New York: Public Affairs, 2001.

30 See particularly Kaplan, 'The Evasions of Robert McNamara'. More heated versions of the same argument include Eric Alterman, 'The Century of the "Son of a Bitch"', *The Nation*, 26 November 2003 and the ensuing debate with Morris (7 January 2004); Alexander Cockburn, 'The Fog of Cop-Out', *The Nation*, 9 February 2004 (A longer version is available at: www.counterpunch.org/cockburn03012004.html (accessed 19 January 2012)).

31 Hendrickson, *The Living and the Dead*, p. 23.

32 McCreadie, *Documentary Superstars*, p. 92.

33 Errol Morris, 'Musings on the Universe', in Bloom (ed.), *Errol Morris Interviews*, pp. 251–56, at p. 251.

34 Morris quoted in Kenneth Turan, 'Movie Review: The Fog of War', *Los Angeles Times*, 19 December 2003. Available at: www.errolmorris.com/content/review/fog_turan.html (accessed 19 January 2012).

35 Morris in Cronin, 'It Could All Be Wrong', p. 204.

36 Livia Bloom, 'Clearing the Fog', in Bloom (ed.), *Errol Morris Interviews*, pp. 131–35, at p. 132.

37 Morris in Cronin, 'It Could All Be Wrong', p. 193. See also p. 206. It is worth noting that in the supplementary material on the *FOW* DVD, McNamara is given opportunity to introduce ten more complicated and consistent lessons that he himself prepared.

38 Timothy Donovan, A. Samuel Kimball and Jilian Smith, 'Fog of War: What Yet Remains', *Postmodern Culture*, 2005, vol. 16 (no pagination).

39 Cf. the chapters on Carr, Morgenthau and Herz in this volume. See also the discussion in Carl Platinga, 'The Philosophy of Errol Morris', in Rothman, *Three Documentary Film-makers*, pp. 43–62.

40 See Shapiro's contribution to Etheredge (ed.), 'Symposium' and Shapiro, 'The Fog of War', esp. pp. 241–45.

41 Morris in Cronin, 'It Could All Be Wrong', p. 200.

25 Restraint in the global polity, the remix: Daniel Deudney's *Bounding Power*

Brent J. Steele[1]

With all that has been written on international relations in the history of the field that bears its name, one would think that there is nothing else left to be said, theoretically anyway, that represents anything more than the clichéd 'putting old wine into new bottles'. Yet, to briefly extend that metaphor, sometimes scholars come along who say something creative by *blending* the wine in unique ways. They do so to such effect that we really couldn't care less how old, popular, or worn-out each 'component' wine is that went into the blend – because the outcome, its product and what it *does for us* is so crisp, sharp and useful, that we know we have consumed something so new that it surely will alter the field. Such achievements make it possible to *see* the world and the arrangements through which humans have confronted violence differently as *both* more dangerous and fragile, as well as more hopeful, stable and secure, than we previously considered.

Despite its charged shortcomings, Daniel Deudney's *Bounding Power* is such a book, and it is the way in which *Bounding Power* gets us to that point that makes it a 'classic-in-the-making' of International Relations (IR). Although it goes against the grain of much conventional analysis, Deudney's use of exegesis and reconstruction is a method actually deployed quite frequently, and especially by those in the emerging fields of international political theory.[2] It is simply one of the most exceptional examples of the best that this method can provide us. A combination of various philosophical and theoretical perspectives, exegesis and reconstruction is itself a *skill* that has for far too long been ignored as such. I liken this method's underrated status to the debates in the 1990s about 'sampling' in the US hip-hop scene. When it appeared with greater frequency in the early years of that decade, sampling was seen as a simple regurgitation of past music onto existing tracks. What critics failed to recognize was that hip-hop artists during that time had to figure out not only which parts of which songs belonged on a music track, but also how those parts worked together to create a particular product, a particular sound or beat, and a particular 'collage'.[3] Furthermore, not just anyone could 'sample' – one needed the skills to not only represent each individual 'track' or 'artist', but to know how they could fit together into a coherent flow. Yes, some of the thinkers (samples) Deudney engages with have been engaged with before – but not *in this way*, not *in this combination*, and certainly not in a time period where the world, and the USA itself, was trying to come to grips with the changing material and geopolitical contexts which bedevilled the 1990s and 2000s. What comes through in Deudney's exegesis and reconstruction is a product with insights that urgently focus our attention on the stakes of potential violence that republican security theory takes so seriously.

This chapter engages Deudney's text, summarizes the core arguments and propositions of *Bounding Power*, acknowledges its shortcomings, and assesses its status as a 'classic' text of IR. While it is difficult to maintain that *Bounding Power* is a classic text in the way that books treated in the previous chapters are, and while other practical aspects of the work should be commended, it is the methodological contribution of Deudney's work that especially deserves our attention – for it is this achievement that may prove to be *Bounding Power*'s lasting success.

Overview of main argument and contents of *Bounding Power*

Daniel H. Deudney received his BA from Yale University, USA in 1975 in the fields of political science and philosophy, an MPA in science, technology and public policy from George Washington University, and an MA and PhD in Political Science from Princeton University in 1989. He spent time as a senior researcher at the Worldwatch Institute in Washington, DC in the 1980s, and was a consultant for the US State and Defense Departments. He was an Assistant Professor at the University of Pennsylvania before moving to his current position (as at the time of writing) as an associate professor at Johns Hopkins University. In 2007 he published *Bounding Power,* a proposal for republican security theory. Taking basic assumptions of both realist and liberal traditions of thought, Deudney posits two important 'problematiques' in global politics. The first is the 'anarchy-interdependence' problematique, or the 'relationship between variations in material context, the scope of security-compatible anarchy, and the scope of authoritative government necessary for security' (p. 28). While contemporary realist international theory recognizes the importance of anarchy, it fails to account for differing levels of interdependence, especially the one variable that Deudney claims 'stands out first in importance: *violence interdependence*' (p. 29, emphasis in the original). According to Deudney, while realists focus on violence, and liberals focus on interdependence, violence interdependence – 'the capacity of actors to do violent harm to one another' (p. 35) – entails a much more nuanced understanding of material context. It focuses on factors such as technology and geography which make a security context more or less prone to violence over time. A 'second problematique' arises from the first – when variations in the size of government across territory become large, hierarchy develops, and the key concern is whether it can be restrained and liberty preserved – hence the 'hierarchy-restraint' problematique.

In this way, the book develops an understanding of republican security theory by existing above realist and liberal international theory, drawing elements and assumptions partially from each tradition but asserting some critical messages towards each as well. The wisdom of republican forms of organization is their ability to avoid two common political orders – anarchy and hierarchy, in favour of what Deudney calls negarchy, the 'simultaneous negation of both anarchy and hierarchy through the imposition of mutual restraints' (p. 4). While seemingly novel, Deudney demonstrates how republican security theory (and practice) has existed in various forms for millennia, and it is Deudney's aforementioned method of 'exegesis and reconstruction' that helps to demonstrate the different sets of 'theoretical arguments as they appear across many centuries and in several conceptual idioms'. These arguments exhibit the interplay between material context and political structures as 'reflections on the practical security problems of historically specific republican polities' (pp. 20–21). As one of Deudney's main insights is the fragility, and unique historical occurrence of republican arrangements, his temporal frame for possible exegesis is long – extending from the insights of the ancients through the modern writings of Montesquieu, Publius, Dewey and Wells, to contemporary treatments of republicanism as well as its modern-day 'descendants'.[4]

The purpose of the book is captured at the end of Chapter One, itself the major theoretical map of Deudney's argument, when he states that the book produces a:

> political science that is practical in character and more inspired by medicine than physics, economics and cybernetics ... Political science knowledge is sought to preserve the survival, health and well-being of the 'body politic'. Sound practical knowledge is that which is useful in protecting human animal corporeality from destruction in an indifferent and complex natural-material environment (p. 60).

The book advances this argument through three parts, beginning with Part One, which advances the main argument and views its 'relatives and descendants'. A second part, 'From the Polis to Federal Union', cross-examines republican security theory as explicated from various thinkers beginning in antiquity (Greek and Roman), extending through works on European republicanism, and ending in the founding of the USA. Part Three, 'Toward the Global Village', begins by examining the various insights on world government provided by Kant and Publius, Scottish Enlightenment thinkers, and early twentieth-century writers like H. G. Wells and John Dewey. The book concludes with two chapters examining world government in both a nuclear age and a 'global village' context.

Bounding Power: A classic of IR?

There is a reason for this being the penultimate chapter of a volume on *Classics of International Relations*, because Deudney's book is the most recently published to be included as a classic. This makes it difficult – but as I intimated in the introduction to this chapter, not impossible – to pinpoint how Deudney's work can be considered at least a 'classic-in-the-making'. The difficulty arises given the limited time period we have to assess its reception or influence on the field. For instance, a Google Scholar citations count, as at the time of writing, yields just over 125 sources citing Deudney's book.[5] Furthermore, the book has been favourably reviewed and generated a number of critical discussions since its publication just a few years ago.[6] This indicates that the book is getting noticed, rather quickly at that (considering the time it takes for a book to be read, written about, and then for that writing to go through peer review and, ultimately, appear in print). Yet, it is still too early to tell, based on this crude measure, how broadly read and regarded this book will be in the near to distant future.

That said, *Bounding Power* was one of three books to be awarded the International Studies Association's coveted 'book of the decade' for the 2000s, and it was the one most recently published of those three.[7] It was also awarded the Jervis-Schroeder Award for the Best Book on International Politics and History by the American Political Science Association. This was in no small part owing to the number of significant contributions provided by *Bounding Power*. Perhaps most importantly, in an era during which scholars are increasingly encouraged to specialize and market themselves as focusing on specific, precise, and technical issues, *Bounding Power* ambitiously asks and seeks to answer the big questions other 'Classics of IR' engage. It does this through a series of fusions of long-held traditions or binaries. Rather than simply assuming either anarchy (as neorealism might assume) or hierarchy (as preponderance or hegemonic stability theorists might), Deudney provides us with a dynamic spectrum where a global order is transformed here or there owing to levels of violence interdependence. Deudney's insights also provide us with a very helpful combination of the once formidable 'material-ideational' ontology binary that was quite influential in categorizing IR theory during the past two decades.[8] While there is an emphasis on bringing back a 'physiopolitics' ('variations in material context through time and space') throughout the book, Deudney states plainly the interplay between 'natural material contexts' and 'human agency', as a *mixed ontology*, where:

> human political security arrangements are practically constructed mediations between the unchanging natural need for security and the variable and changing constraints and opportunities of the material context ... Political practices and structures are not part of nature ... but *which* political arrangements and structures are security-viable in a particular context is not socially constructed (p. 59, emphasis in the original).

Thus, Deudney brings us back to the interplay between materials and ideas, between the physique of political violence and the minds which shape its use, purpose and context.

In addition to these necessary and creative combinations of seemingly opposing binaries, Deudney once again demonstrates what we have come to expect as his signature conceptual contribution to IR theory – the role of technology on security (and vice versa), a contribution that goes back to at least his seminal works from the 1990s.[9] Deudney casts technology as a material context just like geography – and, like different geographic formations, a development that is not socially constructed but 'discovered'. The role of technology in security arrangements comes through most vividly in Chapter 7, in the book's exegesis of H. G. Wells and John Dewey. It was not the former's predictions that prove useful for Deudney, but rather the emphasis by Wells on the transformations – good and bad – that technology was bringing (or would bring) about in global politics. Of Dewey, Deudney explicates the role in which technology (specifically the industrial revolution) was altering (in Dewey's time) notions of community and extending an 'industrial public', an alteration which governments and policymakers had yet to catch up to. However, even today, technology itself has not only pushed the boundaries of *material* frontiers, it has transformed our understanding *of* a frontier, where science and technology *are* that frontier, whereby 'the interaction between nature and politics is still open and subject to major change' (p. 243).

These contributions have been noted by others,[10] but the contribution identified in the Introduction to this chapter – as a stellar methodological example of exegesis and reconstruction, is the one I would suggest makes *Bounding Power* such a provocative but also meaningful work of IR. As Deudney states from the beginning, republican security theory is 'formulated in ways alien to contemporary academic social science', containing 'normative, scientific and design claims' (p. 21). Far from being a unique approach to politics, this is one which is based in, indeed depends upon, the 'traditions' of international theory, those which Deudney assertively characterizes as having persistence and value which 'constitute almost all of the quite limited set of major insights about security politics produced by Western political science' (p. 265). Yet Deudney develops the exegesis and reconstruction of texts as more than just a practice (one which he demonstrates splendidly throughout the book), via the 'metaphors of constellations and maps' in his conclusion (p. 265). The scholar uses this method to 'assemble' texts – as Deudney does in this book – into 'simple pictoral constellation(s)'.

In response to an 'anything goes' critique, Deudney informs us that different generations will pull together different points across these texts into 'different constellations'.[11] The constellation provided by *Bounding Power* is one which speaks to the present, with an eye on the future, by combining insights from texts and authors seemingly overlooked by contemporary international theorists. Deudney's is, thus, a unique recombination (or 'blend' to connect to my Introduction) of these thinkers, compared to previous revisitations of the 'classical' resources of each tradition. Michael Doyle, for instance, in his *Ways of War and Peace*, focused on 'typical' philosophical progenitors of realism – such as Machiavelli and Hobbes; and liberalism – such as Kant (especially), and Locke. Deudney's construction of these traditions via the ancients, as well as modern theorists such as Montesquieu, not only draws out a forceful and novel set of assertions regarding republican security theory – it renders the traditions of realism and liberalism richer and more complex. And, further, it *radically alters* our understanding of different security environments: what produces them, what they help to produce, and how robust – or fragile – they have been through time. As an example, Deudney points to the almost radically contingent – rather than inevitable – nature of 'republics'. In his Conclusion, and after having consulted a more diverse array of thinkers than liberal internationalists have consulted in their works, Deudney precisely captures the concluding function of this philosophical 'constellation':

> Enlightenment theorists posit a world where commerce is extensive and democratic republics are numerous enough to populate state systems and then make optimistic predictions about the potential to pacify interstate relations. In contrast, early republican security theorists begin at the beginning, with a much more realistic state-of-nature in which republican polities are rare, precarious, and subject to debilitating internal maladies, and then draw pessimistic prognoses for republics (p. 270).

Republican union, not only as a form of government but as a practical security framework, prevented the USA from suffering the same hierarchically implosive fate as other republics (such as the Roman), and, further, allowed 'republics to attain the size and thus security previously only available to despotic empires' while keeping intact notions of 'liberty' and popular sovereignty. The key was that a too-small republic risked its own survival (a result of anarchy); a too-large republic risked despotic rule (radical hierarchy). Instead, republics like the USA were both still around, and powerful enough, to 'protect smaller liberal democracies' during the conflicts of the twentieth century. As a result, 'security through federal union, not peace among democracies, *has been the most important security fact for free polities over the last two centuries*' (p. 270, emphasis added).

I might also expand on the insight, personally and intellectually, which I found to be the most provocative and useful contribution of *Bounding Power* – namely, its critique of the Kantian origins of liberal international theory and its pragmatic and useful provision of *restraint*. Several scholars of my generation have reacted to some of the more strident applications of 'Wilsonian' internationalist policies of the past decade by seeking refuge largely within what Deudney would call the post-WWII generation of classical realist writings, marshalling insights from those works to formulate particular critiques of the liberal-idealist policies of especially the USA and the UK. Inspired by reinterpretations of the works of Niebuhr, Morgenthau and Herz in particular,[12] I once entitled this movement 'reflexive realism,' which I defined as 'the attempt to restore classical realist principles ... to provide a practical-ethical view of international politics',[13] and in another co-authored study characterized it as consisting of 'a broad and pluralistic cadre of efforts to (re)convene discussions about realism's philosophical and humanistic roots and the practical issues that engrossed the progenitors of the field'.[14] The point in identifying this trend was not that it was the first occasion (nor the last) when scholars engaged and utilized insights from classical realists. Rather, the point was that there was something about the application of classical realist insights in the 2000s that seemed particularly pointed, focused, and even urgent. For myself, it was the realist focus on restraint as a form of prudence, whereby 'being prudent means to restrain from the use of force even on occasions when such force could easily be employed', which seemed a potentially useful (although, admittedly also *elusive*) tonic to the hyperreactive tendencies of a US polity seeking to grapple with the anxious 'global war on terror' environment following the 9/11 attacks.[15] The proposal here was on how the self of a polity could promote a practical principle of restraint, a principle made possible, however, through *self-discipline*. Cian O'Driscoll, commenting on similar assumptions pervading international society and *jus ad bellum* in the early twentieth century describes this as empowering 'states to gauge *for themselves* the rights and wrongs of any particular use of force that pertained to their interests. This was an approach ... that stressed the "self" in self-limitation, self-judgment, and self-help'.[16] Yet, O'Driscoll exposes in one line the drawback to any proposal – or ethos – which emphasizes self-restraint, it has been at times 'exposed as a catastrophe waiting to happen', during episodes such as World War I, or in the face of any modern crisis or adversity (such as transnational terrorism, for instance).[17]

It is here that Deudney's proposal for 'restraint' republicanism, the 'bounding' of power itself, is so useful. Deudney focuses our attention on the many ways in which negarchy might develop and expand its *political-structural* restraint, a restraint that is both material and political-strategic. Deudney's republicanism, thus, puts forth not just principles to be executed through republican practices, but *material facts* and *contexts* such as 'nature as it presents itself for human activity' which serves as both enabling and restraining factors of violence: 'Global technological interdependence has altered the scope of interaction and hence number of humans and human groups *among whom restraint of violence is necessary for security*' (p. 274, emphasis added). It should be noted that some of the most persuasive 'reflexive realist' works, especially towards the end of the 2000s were those which *also* drew out the republican themes of classical realism, and the restraint made possible by changes in material-technological contexts.[18]

Shortcomings

With a book so complex, rich, analytically rigorous but stylistically argued, it is hard to detect too many shortcomings, especially this soon after *Bounding Power's* publication. Time will tell how influential the proposals of the book will be, for both the study and practice of global politics. That said, others have identified some would-be problems in the text, ones which after the past decade of US foreign policy would seem to require urgent attention. William Scheuerman has a particularly vivid critique of Deudney's text – for all its merits, it may actually reproduce, in an 'America-first' fashion, a 'nationalistic' version of world government.[19] Scheuerman points out that Deudney's reading of the Philadelphian system is 'tendentious,' serving to cherry-pick the favourable attributes at the expense of the rather unfavourable, and even dark, history of the period. In one borderline incendiary charge, Scheuerman notes:

> Apparently, we can neatly separate the so-called Philadelphian republican security model from the horrors of slavery ... Interestingly, Deudney never offers a sustained defence of this position, in part perhaps because core aspects of the mutual restraint arrangement about which he waxes enthusiastic were directly linked to slavery, or at least to political and institutional compromises necessitated by it.[20]

The built-in restraint of this system rested on a form of 'states rights', and an individual lauded by Deudney for intellectually defending negarchical structures – John C. Calhoun – is rightfully noted by Scheuerman as one of 'the intellectually most impressive southern defender[s] of states' rights (and slavery)'.[21]

This particular criticism of Scheuerman's is correct, of course, but it also feels a bit strained. Deudney's proposal for negarchy is an attempt to take particular aspects of past republican security arrangements and suggest their use in restraining violent practices in contemporary global politics. If one were to think that such arrangements in a contemporary context would throw out the baby with the bathwater – that slavery would immediately return with a global version of the Philadelphian system – then this criticism would seem more persuasive. We might further note that the same system and individuals that Deudney lauds were also commended in the same way by some of the same realists that Scheuerman defends, like Morgenthau for example.[22] Finally, Scheuerman's criticism would also be persuasive if we failed to notice what Deudney himself discloses in his Preface, namely that 'as an American writing about a significantly American topic, I am animated by American anxieties (shared by many non-Americans) about America', and Deudney notes that these include the way in which the US Republican party 'expends its formidable energies in an at-times hysterical ... war against domestic public welfare government, but largely ignores (or even embraces) the far more ominous (at least from the founders' standpoint) national security state that necessity and opportunity led the Americans to construct over the last half-century' (p. xiii).

However, Deudney does not, admittedly, confront this 'anxiety' as directly as he might have throughout the text, and thus what Scheuerman's overall critique does open up are two of what I would call missed opportunities found in *Bounding Power*. These missed opportunities represent how the argument could have been extended to confront concerns like Scheuerman's. What Scheuerman is calling for is a more interrogative engagement, it seems, of the US polity's past. Thus, the book's propositions regarding the republican security practices – especially their role in restraining both radical extremes of anarchy and hierarchy – could have contributed a more chastened view of US history to ongoing debates over neoconservatism, a perspective celebrating the founding of the USA and its history as a republic.[23] On a few occasions, Deudney does make passing reference to neoconservatism as a strand of Wilsonianism – and points out, briefly, Wilsonians' inadequate grasping of the 'republican security logic behind the American Liberal internationalist project and the central role violence interdependence plays in it' (p. 186).

One of the core insights of republican security theory is that the answer to anarchy is not hierarchy, but negarchy, a more stable form of ordering because of its built-in mechanisms of mutual restraint. *This* is one missed opportunity of *Bounding Power,* as this argument is in some ways 180 degrees at odds with neoconservatism's view of the USA's leadership role in a world that hijacks US ambitions and confronts the gravest threats in 'slow motion'.[24] Indeed, when reading *Bounding Power,* one thinks of Michael Williams' closing remark in his seminal 2005 article on neoconservatism and IR theory, that 'IR possesses resources within its theoretical traditions that provide a basis for a direct and critical engagement with neoconservatism at its very foundations'.[25] Republican security theory, especially as it is rendered by Deudney, surely provides us a lot of fuel for just such a rigorously critical and *intellectual* engagement of neoconservatism. However, Deudney does not directly confront neoconservatism, and it leaves him open to the types of charges levelled by Scheuerman. While one cannot engage everything that is 'out there' in the field of international theory, engaging neoconservatism more directly would have demonstrated what I find to be a significant distinction between Deudney's proposal and one which fails, according to Scheuerman, to 'rais[e] the necessary critical questions about the deeply ambivalent and by no means consistently beneficial role of the United States in foreign affairs in the last century'.[26]

A similar lack of engagement with the English School represents another missed opportunity for extending *Bounding Power*'s arguments into other 'International Theory' perspectives. As with neoconservatism, Deudney does have a few direct and indirect assessments of English School theory (p. 159). Yet, considering Hedley Bull's proffering of an 'anarchical *society*', and that, furthermore, his assertion that the great powers were the 'custodians' of this international society and its rules,[27] there appears to be some overlap with Deudney's views of negarchy. For instance, it would have been interesting to consider how negarchy might be considered not only as a 'negation' of both anarchy and hierarchy but as an ordering arrangement set along the so-called international system-international society-world society 'triad' of the English School.[28] The debates in the English School over how societies form – the so-called *Gemeinschaft* versus *Gesellschaft* formation of international societies – and how they disintegrate can also be linked with Deudney's recognition of the fragility of global arrangements of mutual restraint. While the English School discusses how societies *form*, it might be aided by Deudney's thesis that changes in technology (such as the Industrial Revolution leading up to World War I) represent forms of violent interdependence that threaten to unravel those arrangements within a short period of time.

Alas, the engagement with either neoconservatism or the English School does not occur here, and so is left to others to take Deudney's argument and critically assess these two perspectives. In this way, both of the shortcomings represent heuristic opportunities for current and future IR theorists.

The contemporary relevance of *Bounding Power*

In such a sweeping and comprehensive treatment of ancient and modern thinkers and different historical epochs, one would think that *Bounding Power*'s contribution to contemporary relevance would be contemplative and suggestive, rather than one of direct application. Yet, Deudney effectively and even forcefully applies the insights of his work to contemporary settings, in several fashions. First, by engaging the notion of a 'global village' at the end of his book, Deudney is able to scale ancient and classical theories as modern, international (political) theories, but with a twist. In a global village, conflict between nation states is 'de facto civil' rather than 'international.' Thus, an interdependent global polity (even one linked by violence) still has a stake in seeking a secure and stable global order. Second, Deudney reconsiders the record of democratic peace and the variables truly responsible for a 'peace among democracies' as US power, or in the case of nineteenth-century Europe, 'restraining material foundations'. From this, Deudney reminds us that a mere expansion in the 'rim' of national republics, globally, may not necessarily arrive coupled with a continued robust peace between these regimes, and, in a related fashion, that republics themselves tend to be rare, themselves depending on 'fortuitous geographic restraints.' Policy-makers and budding international theorists alike would do well to heed these cautionary assertions regarding especially the 'fact' of a democratic peace.[29]

Third, *Bounding Power* can speak to a global distribution of power that is currently in flux. Some scholars see the world transitioning to a multipolar entity; others see US hegemony, based on material factors such as military spending, as a fact. Still others proffer that we are in a 'non-polar world,' one where polar 'centers' no longer exist.[30] *Bounding Power*'s legacy to this contemporary debate may well be heuristic – providing us with a 'middle pole' of the debate where scholars and policy-makers engage as to how closely the world is transforming not into another polarity within anarchy, nor remaining a unipolar hierarchy, but rather into a qualified global arrangement of negarchy. As Deudney suggests, however, such an arrangement would hardly be novel, rather it would be the product of 'a long familiar pattern' going back to antiquity (p. 275). Again, both political and geographic-physical factors have facilitated such arrangements, evidenced by a variety of historical examples including the Greek city-state republics, the polities of 'Venice and then Holland and Britain', the Swiss confederation, and the aforementioned 'Philadelphian system' of the first 75 years of the US polity (p. 57). Such a development is not only possible – it is most likely *happening before our very eyes* – and is more than likely to be met not with astonishment but a shrug of the shoulders.

Finally, and most stridently, Deudney's propositions bear upon the seemingly everlasting concern regarding nuclear proliferation. Applying his 'modified nuclear one worldism' approach (itself again derived from republican security theory) to the contemporary landscape,[31] Deudney suggests that now, more than ever before, is the time for global security arrangements to help control the transfer and proliferation of nuclear weapons. Our only alternative treatment of this problem is found in the increasing hierarchical concentration of surveillance capabilities by 'even the most Liberal governments' to 'progressively greater restrictions on individuals and groups'. This alternative has its drawbacks, as Deudney accurately notes:

> If global nuclear material controls are weak, states will be compelled to increasingly penetrate civil society with controls. If global nuclear material containment is strong, then Liberal states will be able to stay Liberal ... to an unprecedented extent, the preservation of domestic liberty comes to hinge upon the success in abridging international anarchy (p. 262).

In this passage, and throughout this impressive work, **Deudney** captures one of the final messages of *Bounding Power* – the value of republican security theory's promotion of restraint – not only in suppressing the 'evil urges' of others, but by constraining our own tendencies to overreact to the phantasms of those possible urges with ones of our own.

In the years and decades that follow its recent appearance on the scene of IR theory, scholars may debate Deudney's work with regard to a variety of the book's features – especially how he arrives at some of these conclusions via his particular readings on, and combinations of, theorists. While it is a safe bet that its resurrection of republican security theory will not only be regarded as an important historical and theoretical feat, it may also be considered a proposal that only suggests and intimates how contemporary and future generations might make the world more secure in the future. Yet, what I have suggested in this chapter is that the contribution of a text to IR rests not only (or solely) in its practical application to contemporary problems, but also in the exemplary demonstration of a method – in this case reconstruction and exegesis – which has for too long gone unappreciated and unvalued in IR. Thus, the immediate value of Daniel Deudney's *Bounding Power* lies in its testimony to the ability of a scholar who can take theory and thought, whether centuries-old or contemporary in their inception, and remix, reformulate and *craft* them so that they refocus our attention on global politics – its past and its present – in novel ways.

Notes

1 Daniel H. Deudney, *Bounding Power: Republican Security Theory from the Polis to the Global Village*, Princeton, NJ: Princeton University Press, 2007. Page numbers placed in parentheses in the text refer to this edition.

2 On how the engagement of texts can take on meanings outside of what was intended by the original author, see Richard Ned Lebow, *The Tragic Vision of Politics*, Cambridge: Cambridge University Press, 2003, Chapter 2.

3 The term 'collage' is Murray Forman and Mark Anthony Neal's, *That's the Joint! The Hip-Hop Studies Reader*, London: Routledge, 2004, p. 75.

4 Deudney only engages it on occasion, but Onuf's classic work on the topic is perhaps the best-known of these treatments: Nicholas Onuf, *The Republican Legacy in International Thought*, Cambridge: Cambridge University Press, 1998.

5 Available at: http://scholar.google.com/scholar?q=bounding+power+deudney&hl=en&btnG=Search&as_sdt=1%2C5&as_sdtp=on (accessed 17 April 2012). Alexander Wendt, *Social Theory of International Politics*, Cambridge: Cambridge University Press, 1999, by comparison (and published eight years earlier), has over 3,300 citation 'hits' on the same search engine.

6 Casper Sylvest, *Political Studies Review,* 2007, vol. 5, 440; Bryan Mabee, *Millennium*, 2008, vol. 36, 651–53; Chris Brown, *Political Theory*, 2008, vol. 36, 647–50.

7 The other two were Joshua S. Goldstein, *War and Gender: How Gender Shapes the War System and Vice-Versa*, Cambridge: Cambridge University Press, 2001, and Bruce Russett and John Oneal, *Triangulating Peace*, New York: W. W. Norton & Company, 2000.

8 The binary is presented in detail in Wendt's *Social Theory*, especially Figure 1 (p. 29), which is a take on Hollis and Smith's *Explanation and Understanding in International Relations*, Oxford: Clarendon Press, 1991.

9 See especially his 'Geopolitics and Change', in Michael Doyle and John G. Ikenberry (eds), *New Thinking in International Relations Theory*, Boulder, CO: Westview Press, 1997, pp. 91–127.

10 See especially Bryan Mabee's review noted above.

11 Kratochwil, in a seminal article which discusses the way in which we defend ourselves against the 'anything goes' charge, posits that '[i]nstead, warrants are provided or defeated by the inter-subjective defensibility of the assertions made in our arguments', Friedrich Kratochwil, 'History, Action and Identity: Revisiting the "Second" Great Debate and Assessing its Importance for Social Theory', *European Journal of International Relations*, 2006, vol. 12, 5–29, at p. 7.

12 Some examples include Michael C. Williams, *The Realist Tradition and the Limits of International Relations*, Cambridge: Cambridge University Press, 2004; Michael C. Williams (ed.), *Realism Reconsidered*, Oxford: Oxford University Press, 2007; Anthony F. Lang, *Agency and Ethics*, Albany, NY: SUNY Press, 2002; Lebow, *The Tragic Vision*; Vibeke Schou Tjalve,

Realist Strategies of Republican Peace: Neibuhr, Morgenthau and the Politics of Patriotic Dissent, New York: Palgrave Macmillan, 2008; Casper Sylvest, 'Realism and International Law: The challenge of John Herz', *International Theory*, 2010, vol. 2, 410–45.

13 Brent J. Steele, '"Eavesdropping on honored ghosts": From Classical to Reflexive Realism', *Journal of International Relations and Development*, 2007, vol. 10, 272–300, at p. 273.

14 Andrew R. Hom and Brent J. Steele, 'Open Horizons: The Temporal Visions of Reflexive Realism'*, International Studies Review*, 2010, vol. 12, 271–300, at p. 271.

15 Steele, 'Eavesdropping on honored ghosts', p. 278.

16 Cian O'Driscoll, 'Just War in the Twentieth Century', in E.A Heinze and B.J. Steele (eds), *Ethics, Authority, and War: Non-State Actors and the Just War Tradition*, New York: Palgrave Macmillan, 2009, emphasis added.

17 O'Driscoll, 'Just War in the Twentieth Century', 26.

18 In this vein, Tjalve and Sylvest's works, noted above, deserve special mention.

19 William E. Scheuerman, 'Deudney's Neorepublicanism: One-world or America first?', *International Politics*, 2010, vol. 47, 523–34.

20 Scheuerman, 'Deudney's Neorepublicanism', p. 531.

21 Scheuerman, 'Deudney's Neorepublicanism', p. 531.

22 See the opening paragraph to H.J. Morgenthau, 'The Mainsprings of American Foreign Policy', *American Political Science Review*, 1950, vol. 44, 833–54, specifically that the 'political wisdom' of the commonwealth of the USA was found in the 'first generation of Americans', many of whom, if we were taking Scheuerman's argument whole cloth, were slave-owners themselves.

23 This topic is finally getting a rigorous treatment by IR theorists: Michael C. Williams, 'What Is the National Interest? The Neoconservative Challenge in IR Theory', *European Journal of International Relations*, 2005, vol. 11, 307–37; and Brian C. Schmidt and Michael C. Williams, 'The Bush Doctrine and the Iraq War: Neoconservatives versus realists', *Security Studies*, 2008, vol. 17, 191–220.

24 These are John Bolton's words describing the problems with the 'multilateral diplomatic course' that the USA tried to utilize in confronting the 'seriousness' of the Iranian nuclear 'threat'. John Bolton, *Surrender Is Not an Option*, New York: Simon & Schuster, 2007, p. 314.

25 Williams, 'What Is the National Interest?' p. 327

26 Scheuerman, 'Deudney's Neorepublicanism', p. 532.

27 Hedley Bull, *The Anarchical Society*, New York: Columbia University Press, 1977, p. 17.

28 See Tim Dunne, 'The English School', in Tim Dunne, Milja Kurki, and Steve Smith (eds), *International Relations Theories: Discipline and Diversity*, 2nd edn, Oxford: Oxford University Press, 2010, pp. 148–49.

29 This is a play on the title of the first chapter of Bruce Russett, *Grasping the Democratic Peace*, Princeton, NJ: Princeton University Press, 1993.

30 Two unrelated examples can be seen in Thomas Friedman's *The World Is Flat*, New York: Farrar, Straus, and Giroux, 2005, and Richard N. Haas, 'The Age of Nonpolarity: What Will Follow U.S. Dominance?' *Foreign Affairs*, 2008, vol. 87, 44–56.

31 Deudney distinguishes this modified approach to 'classical one worldism' near the end of *Bounding Power*. Whereas classical one worldism 'assumed that nuclear weapons had shifted the scale of state formation processes' the 'modified diagnosis is that nuclear weapons, combined with the general increase and diffusion of violence capability [to non-state actors, for instance], have greatly reduced the problem of interstate aggression, while creating a new threat of general annihilation' (p. 258).

26 Conclusion

Henrik Bliddal, Casper Sylvest and Peter Wilson[1]

In closing, it is fitting to begin where the last classic presented in this volume left off. In the conclusion to *Bounding Power*, Deudney writes:

> Traditions are composed of distant luminaries, great intellectual figures of the past whose works are perennially burning lights that can be observed but never changed. Acts of reading and interpreting assemble illuminating texts into various constellations by 'connecting the dots' into a simple pictoral constellation.[2]

Surely Deudney wrote these words in a different context, but if we think of International Relations (IR) as a tradition, albeit today a highly diverse one, this volume has also sought to 'connect the dots'. As we see it, the works appraised here represent some of the brightest stars in the firmament of IR. Not everyone will agree with our particular mapping of it, and some scholars, including the authors of some of the classics covered, might reject the very notion of an IR firmament. We see our job, however, not in terms of the presentation of a definitive case but to further the debate about which works should be considered IR classics, and what this particular status means – for the work, the author and the discipline.

Mappings of the discipline are unavoidable. Some might find this regrettable, but we believe that this practice, if carefully undertaken, is essential to the health of the field.[3] As Deudney continues, '[w]e draw these pictures to make our world more intelligible and, like mariners at sea or shepherds in the wilderness, to help tell us where we are and how we might travel safely to where we want to be'.[4] Nevertheless, we need to be careful not to fix our constellations too firmly and to be prepared periodically to redraw our charts. After all, stars fade away or implode, and shooting stars burn out. We may have also misjudged the brightness of some and failed to spot others. In short, we intend this book to be the beginning of a new engagement with classics of the discipline, not the end. In this spirit we offer two sets of concluding observations. First, we reflect upon the characteristics of the classics we have uncovered in this book. What makes these works stand out in importance? No single pattern or 'recipe' can be detected, but there are some important commonalities. This leads to our second purpose: a brief discussion of the future of the classic work in IR and the social and intellectual factors likely to influence its fate.

Some observations about classics of IR

If the essentialist understanding of what makes a classic in literature (see Introduction) held sway well into the twentieth century, an essentialist understanding of what makes a classic of IR prevailed even longer. This may come as a surprise to those new to the field given the increasingly wide acknowledgement in social studies of the absence of a transhistorical and/or transcultural basis for making truth claims. However, works such as *The Twenty Years' Crisis*, *Politics Among Nations* and *Man, the State and War* were held by many to be classics well into the 1980s because they captured timeless truths about international life, lifting the veil of moralism, progressivism and liberal wishful thinking that shrouded the harsh realities of an anarchical international system.[5] Today, it is likely that all but a few would accept the sociological conception of the classic; in other words, a classic is a work widely considered to be a classic within any given social setting or community. An IR classic, certainly, is a work deemed to be seminal or exemplary in some way. It is a work that has exerted influence and in many cases continues to do so. It may be a work widely considered to be pivotal in some given movement of thought. Often, most simply and powerfully, it is a work deemed to be an intellectual landmark. All these notions are wrapped up in our understanding of a classic.

In his chapter about Waltz's *Theory of International Politics*, Wivel offers five tongue-in-cheek rules on how to write a classic. Of course, it is not that easy. No simple or even complex formula exists. Indeed, one could begin by pointing out the conditions that do not appear necessary. One does not need to be a gifted or imaginative writer pouring forth elegant prose and/or fine turns of phrase on every page – though clearly this quality has been no hindrance to the longevity of Woolf's *Three Guineas*, Carr's *The Twenty Years' Crisis* or Beitz's *Political Theory and International Relations*. One does not need to be widely read, either generally or in academia – just being thought of as a classic within a certain cultural or intellectual milieu might suffice, as is the case with Mitrany's *Working Peace System* or Aron's *Peace and War*. One does not have to be useful to policy-makers, although a work such as Jervis's *Perception and Misperception* certainly is useful. One does not need to share the humility of an Aron, Bull or Jervis, even though it would surely be beneficial to most people if they walked away from a book with 'a slightly deflated (or at least, a less inflated) ego', an effect Shiping Tang in his chapter attributes to *Perception and Misperception*. One does not need to produce a text that is popular in the classroom, though Bull's *Anarchical Society* and especially Morgenthau's *Politics Among Nations* became best-selling student texts almost immediately on publication, nor does one need to devise a great teaching aid, though Kubrick's *Dr. Strangelove* and Morris's *Fog of War* are often used in this way. One does not need to be as intellectually bold or adventurous as Waltz with *Theory of International Politics* or Walker with *Inside/outside*; circumspection can be an advantage too, as Aron's *Peace and War* and Keohane and Nye's *Power and Interdependence* illustrate. Some of these characteristics may be important, but none of them are necessary and certainly not sufficient for creating a classic of the field. So beyond the near-truism that an IR classic is a work deemed by the IR community to be in some way seminal, exemplary or pivotal, is it possible to identify any commonalities among the works discussed in this volume that make them stand out?

The centrality of the questions

One common denominator of the classics presented in this book is that they ask fundamental questions about international politics. In the Introduction, we identified a set of concerns and phenomena – war, peace, power, the state, international law, order, justice, diplomacy, anarchy and sovereignty – around which such questions have traditionally revolved. Of course, the specific nature of this questioning depends on the learning and intellectual imagination of the various authors, which has led to questions that we did not know we ought to ask before someone asked them. For example, in their chapter Hyde and Henry make a powerful case that Enloe's *Bananas, Beaches and Bases* has done exactly that. The same might be said of that other work of gender and the international featured in this volume, Woolf's *Three Guineas*, as argued in Wilson's chapter.

It is remarkable that the quality, and perhaps the staying power, of a classic work of IR is often determined not by the particular answers given but by the questions and the way they are asked, structured or presented. In Frost's chapter on *Peace and War* for example, Henry Kissinger is quoted to the effect that 'Mr. Aron does better than give us answers – he teaches us which questions are significant'. Answers to specific questions will change over time, as circumstances change and new factors emerge. Some key works of IR, however, have raised questions that have barely changed for decades. One example concerns the effect of formal and informal networks of interdependence on patterns of inter-state cooperation and conflict, as asked by Keohane and Nye. Another example is the way in which Waltz, in *Man, the State, and War*, organized and explored three levels at which the causes of war had been located in the history of political thought – at the level of the individual, the states or the system. Schmidt contends in his chapter that 'it is incredibly difficult to imagine how IR would have evolved if he had not written this book'. In short, the centrality of the questions to our quest to understand the human condition matter. This is also why some classics did not make their mark upon release and why some may have been forgotten but later rediscovered. Their questions and particular answers may not have seemed relevant to many at the time but they matter at the time of their rediscovery. Works such as *The European Anarchy* and *Three Guineas* fall into this camp; not, it should be added, because their answers command universal assent, far from it, but because the questions they asked and the way they framed them was ahead of their time.

The question of position

IR takes place within a social setting, and as with any other 'society' the position of agents within this social setting is crucial. At any given time – but particularly since the accelerating professionalization of the discipline from the 1950s, which issued in a higher degree of awareness of theory and a common theoretical canon[6] – a 'mainstream' of IR exists where most of the debates are taking place. It is rare for classic works to be positioned at the centre of this mainstream at the time of their publication. After all, most writers probably want to influence the field of IR and 'shift' or 'tilt' scholarship in a direction that suits their ideas and interests. Still, Claude's *Power and International Relations* and Bull's *The Anarchical Society* can be seen as archetypical classics in the sense that they typify the mainstream of the discipline. They quickly became regarded as *loci classici* of certain central concepts, the balance of power and collective security in the case of Claude, order and international society in the case of

Bull. More generally, they also came to be seen as representative of certain central schools of IR thought – realism with regard to Claude and the English School with regard to Bull. In a slightly different manner, Mearsheimer's theory of offensive realism as developed in *The Tragedy of Great Power Politics* is staunchly rooted in orthodox neorealism, arguably still at the very centre of the (predominantly US) IR mainstream. Even so, as Schmidt writes in his chapter on this work, 'in recasting the principles of realism in a theoretically vigorous manner in order to explain great power politics, [Mearsheimer] has provided an invaluable service to the field of IR and to the general public'.

A more prominent path taken, however, is to challenge the mainstream from its margins, or as Wivel puts it with regard to *Theory of International Politics*: 'Challenge the orthodoxy, politically and academically, but stay safely within the dominant discourse'. Sometimes staying within the dominant discourse is a matter of argumentative strategy. Walker suggests, for example, that in *Power and Interdependence* Keohane and Nye's 'decision to distance their ideas from liberal internationalism may have been strategic. Any direct assault on traditional *realpolitik* or the realist paradigm may have led to a quick dismissal of their ideas'. A number of classic works also aspire to bring together different mainstream approaches. For example, *Power and Independence* and Deudney's *Bounding Power* seek to overcome what they considered to be the sterile opposition between realism and liberalism, and Wendt's *Social Theory of International Politics* attempts something similar in seeking to position constructivism as a *via media* between rationalism and reflectivism. What might be called the practice of *via media*-ing is, indeed, a prominent feature of a number of texts that have acquired classic status. It is evident in Carr's attempt to find a *via media* between utopianism and realism. It is evident in Mitrany's attempt, as Ashworth argued, to cut a middle path between realism and federalism, humanitarian idealism and national self-interest, and political laissez-faire and constitutionalism. In both of these cases the *via media*-ing was done partly to make a set of radical ideas more palatable to a broader audience. While the target audiences may differ, there is nothing new in the practice of strategic positioning.

A third type of positioning follows from a direct and fundamental challenge to the mainstream from the outside. In their different ways, Linklater's *Men and Citizens in the Theory of International Relations*, Cox's *Production, Power and World Order* as well as Walker's *Inside/outside* are all poignant examples. One could also include Morris's *Fog of War* and Carr's *The Twenty Years' Crisis* in this group. Of course, it could be argued that by successfully challenging the mainstream, the challengers end up occupying a new mainstream, where they do not feel altogether at ease. The irony of including Walker's *Inside/outside* in this volume is pointed out in Lundborg and Vaughan Williams's chapter when they note that it 'is not so much a classic *of* IR – indeed Walker is highly sceptical of the practice of canonising in scholarship – but rather a particular (and political) intervention that opened up new ways of thinking about the very (im)possibility of IR as a *separate discipline*'. Often, challenging convention, either from within or without, involves laying the foundations of a new approach, school or sub-field, with which the work in time becomes heavily identified. This is sometimes not the author's intention, but for better or worse the social logic of academic disciplines leads to labels being produced to stick on people and their work.

Positioning often involves the injection of ideas from other fields of social science or the humanities. One scholar once jokingly observed that it was easy to have a 'hit' in IR: you simply get lost in some obscure hallway of a library, pick up a book and graft its ideas onto IR.[7] It would be safe to say that this ploy might not work on every occasion, but theoretical innovation and the establishment of fertile research fields are often the result of the importation of ideas or approaches from other fields, and the bringing together of disciplines that have hitherto existed in splendid isolation. Think functional sociology in Mitrany's *A Working Peace System*, psychology in Jervis' *Perception and Misperception*, micro-economic theory in *Theory of International Politics*, sociology in *Social Theory of International Relations*, and the bringing together of political and IR theory in many of the other books reappraised here.

The question of timing

Another crucial dimension of a classic is the timing of its release. Perhaps the majority of classics reappraised in this volume can claim to have been released 'at the right time'. This could be in relation to real world events. Indeed, all classics up until the 1950s are responses to major crises in world politics: great power war, the prospect of fascist/Nazi domination, the possibility of nuclear annihilation. Later, academic crises or stalemates and the need to resolve them emerged as the driving factors behind classic works: *Power and Independence* and the works of critical theory of the 1980s are cases in point. Again, the establishment of a more exclusively academic discipline in the post-war period appears to have been a decisive factor. Yet, even here real-world events exert their influence. Often, these works express dissatisfaction with conventional, predominantly realist, accounts and their inability to contend, analytically and normatively, with rising 'real-world' interdependence and globalization. In the case of *Power and Interdependence* the OPEC oil embargo, the collapse of the Bretton Woods system, and the US retreat from Vietnam were important 'real-world' factors – traditional military and security concerns were, it seemed, being increasingly shaped, even trumped, by economic concerns. Even the success of Waltz's *Theory of International Politics* – and with it the 'return' of realism – could be seen partly in the light of real-world events. The book was published at a time of heightened international tension, with Islamic revolution and the hostage crisis in Iran, the Soviet invasion of Afghanistan and the onset of the Second Cold War.

Some works treated in this volume may derive their status as much from their timing and impact at a particular historic juncture as their originality. Angell's arguments in *The Great Illusion*, for example, were hardly new, but came at an important inflection point and became a symbolic reference in public debate and (later) the emerging discipline. Mitrany's impact with *A Working Peace System* might be comparable. In contrast, imagination, originality and a host of other qualities did not help Woolf's *Three Guineas* to find its place in the IR firmament. Being ahead of its time can be just as fatal to a work's initial success as being *passé*. Herz's *International Politics in the Atomic Age*, while popular at the time of publication, faded into obscurity until the questions he asked found renewed resonance. One can imagine a work such as Aron's *Peace and War* experiencing the same fate.

The future of the classic

If these are some of the salient characteristics of classics of international relations during the preceding century, what prospects do the next century and the more immediate future hold for the IR classic?

Academic disciplines do not fall from the sky, nor are their subjects and objects naturally given.[8] Indeed, it is fairly normal for disciplines to engage in protracted and sometimes heated debates over what are (or should be) their core concerns, theories and methodologies. Such matters are conditioned by the social structure of academic disciplines: their organization in and across institutions of higher learning as well as their conventions for rewarding scholarly work through the granting of esteem and (symbolic or organizational) power. IR is somewhat peculiar in that it has a strong sense of disciplinarity, but also a series of rich disagreements about fundamental intellectual questions.[9] An explanation for this state of affairs is the well-known narrative of great debates propelling the discipline forwards. Whatever the historical accuracy of this narrative, it does appear true that IR has become a theory-anchored discipline with a shared, overarching vocabulary. This is particularly true of the last half-century, during which time the discipline created a more exclusively academic discourse with its attendant criteria for success. This professionalization also changed the identity of scholars. Gone are the days of activists, advisors or public intellectuals like Angell, Carr and Aron writing for a broad audience about the conundrums of international politics (while perhaps, but not necessarily, occupying a university chair). Instead, the full-time university professor, at least one step removed from practice and policy advice, has long since emerged as triumphant. The revolving door between the professional study of international relations and its practice still exists in some quarters, and the link between analysis and activism remains strong in some cases. However, for the most part the leading thinkers in the field are today full time researchers and teachers writing for and engaging with specialized audiences.

The division of the field into ever-more specialized sub-fields is perhaps the most obvious manifestation of its growing heterogeneity. Yet, despite this, the field as a whole continues to display a certain degree of coherence. Those tilling it certainly share a strong sense of identity. Of course, professional associations and their journals, along with the general division of academic labour into departments, play a big role here, but so do the classics. They represent landmarks not only of individual but of collective achievement. They signify the ability of the discipline to innovate and adapt. They become emblems of the influential and resilient approaches which they, intentionally or not, helped to define and/or inspire.[10] Yet, sometimes the intellectual diversity that many of our classics served to foster is stymied by IR's strong social structure. Recent scholarship on the discipline's history and sociology and worries about its fragmentation or 'the end of theory'[11] may serve, paradoxically, to strengthen the sense of identity of the discipline, and its social structure. Despite its intention to foster debate, *Classics of International Relations* might have similar effects. In particular, it would be fair to say that the book reflects the 'geo-cultural' origins, and the continued Anglo-US dominance, of what is now a global discipline.[12] A work such as this might have the unintended consequence of strengthening this dominance. This highlights the fact that while IR is a diverse and inclusive socio-intellectual space, it remains also a discipline, a hierarchical social structure shot through with power and privilege.

Within this broad context there are, however, some general developments in research policy and practice that will influence the future of the discipline and within it the 'classic' text. Foremost among these are publication patterns. Internally, the discipline seems steadily more oriented towards the publication of articles in high-profile journals. Despite the diversity of the discipline as a whole and the proliferation of outlets, flagship publications that are fairly homogenous in terms of the epistemological, geographical and (less markedly) thematic character of their contributions, continue to dominate.[13] Externally, institutions of higher learning have undergone a quiet managerial revolution during the last few decades that have also impacted on publication patterns and perhaps contributed to an already existing trend towards specialization. Whether described (despairingly) as a neoliberal 'audit culture', (depressingly) as the imposition of US business school and management consultancy models of product evaluation and process control[14] or (benignly) as the professionalization of university management that enhances effectiveness and accountability, both publicly and privately funded universities are increasingly concerned with monitoring the research activities of their faculty. This has led to a plethora of elaborate systems for measuring academic performance in terms of quality or quantity or both. Taken together, these internal and external pressures have issued, it appears, in higher productivity, shorter production time and a stronger orientation towards top journal articles. The British Research Information Network, an organization financed by three British higher education funding and research councils and three national libraries, notes that particularly in the humanities and social sciences 'the rise of journals is more closely associated with an environment where there is increasing emphasis on measuring, assessing, and evaluating research, its outputs and impact'.[15] Time constraints and the increased importance of the short format have implications for the kind of scholarly work that is considered (and downloaded or read). Articles are often more uniform and standardized, particularly in terms of style and structure, just as they are frequently (and naturally so) more modest than books in terms of their ambition and contribution. The rigorous peer review process of the top journals is partly responsible for this standardization of style and structure – though this is certainly an unintended consequence – and perhaps also a curtailment of ambition.[16]

Given some of the characteristics of classics outlined above, these trends do not appear favourable soil for the growth of future classics. It is true that some classics have been written over a short period of time, in a sudden burst of intellectual energy, but many classics have required a longer period of gestation, for example *The Twenty Years' Crisis* and *The Anarchical Society*.[17] In the modern academy, this time to reflect may well become a luxury offered to the few rather than the many. The days of successful academic careers built on protracted contemplation – resulting perhaps in one or two books and a modest tally of scholarly articles on the big questions of the field – appear to be over. Productivity increases, but the output is broken down into smaller contributions that satisfy the demands of university managers obsessed with research rankings and league tables, research councils needing to justify their call on tight public funds, and the readership, including an increasing number of scholars themselves, which is socialized into the new managerial order of academic production.

Lest this should be interpreted as nostalgia for a time gone by, a more encouraging view is also possible. The complexity and sheer size of the IR research community mean that trends governing scholarship are not universal, and the quantity of scholarly publications, including books, is steadily rising. So while it is probably true that the standing of the book is in decline and that the number of books of genuine significance in proportion to the number published is also diminishing, there is hope that gems are hidden in the steady stream of works currently making it into print. Second, it is possible that the format of the classic is changing. Focusing on the last half-century, it would certainly be possible to assemble a body of classic articles that could illuminate central developments in the discipline – think, to name but a few, of Bull's *International Theory: The Case for a Classical Approach* (1966), Jervis's *Cooperation under the Security Dilemma* (1978), Cox's *Social Forces, States, and World Orders* (1981), Doyle's *Kant, Liberal Legacies and Foreign Affairs* (1983), Keohane's *International*

Institutions: Two Approaches (1988), Putnam's *Diplomacy and Domestic Politics: The Logic of Two-Level Games* (1988), Booth's *Security in Anarchy: Utopian Realism in Theory and Practice* (1991), Wendt's *Anarchy Is What States Make of It* (1992), Buzan's *From International System to International Society: Structural Realism and Regime Theory Meet the English School* (1993), Finnemore and Sikkink's *International Norm Dynamics and Political Change* (1998), and Waltz's *Structural Realism after the End of the Cold War* (2000). Viewed in a positive light, such short-format classics might become the stakes marking out IR's socio-intellectual space in an era where the heavy book is more likely to be tombstone than milestone. The problem with this development, however, is already familiar:[18] there is a clear hierarchy of journals that appear to play a large role in determining the success of such work, and the disciplining involved in their operation does not appear hospitable to the kind of searching, contrarian and visionary qualities that are characteristic of many of the classics, particularly perhaps the earlier classics, covered in this book. Again, however, counter-trends such as an increased number of outlets and the digital revolution in publishing might lead to a higher degree of independence for scholars.

Finally, and less optimistically for some, fragmentation and specialization may get the better of the discipline. These trends are in evidence in political science/studies more generally, with some observers warning that the result is scholasticism and irrelevance.[19] Several themes run together in such debates. One concerns specialization and relates to the quality and relevance of knowledge. Debates about the advantages and disadvantages of compartmentalizing and limiting inquiry in order to reach a higher level of detailed understanding are not new. Clearly few – certainly few of the many liberal-educated authors of classics of previous generations – would encourage specialization without a broad grounding in IR and neighboring fields such as politics, law, philosophy and history, or without some view to broader theoretical or practical relevance.[20] Another theme concerns the identity, coherence and meaningfulness of IR as a discipline. According to one scholar, who is favorably disposed towards the narrative of IR's great debates owing to the disciplinary coherence it creates, 'no single great debate fram[es] the entire field today'.[21] This might cause concern for some, while others may be less anxious about the health of the discipline and more critical of the conventional narratives that dominate IR's intellectual structure, whether they are framed as great debates or seen through the prism (or prison) of 'isms'.

However, perhaps these alternatives are too starkly opposed? With its strong social structures and what appears to be a global trend of increasing demand, IR is expanding and demonstrating a strong and healthy interest in its own historical development and sociological foundations. In this state, there might be more room to explore alternative ways in which IR intellectually hangs together. If the languages of 'isms' and debates are to some extent unavoidable, they also often obstruct our view of what IR has been, already is and could be. Invoking a discipline or a socio-intellectual space unavoidably entails mapping and ordering. Yet the classic might just offer a refreshing way of doing so. Our hope is that we can reorient and improve the conversations about shared concerns if we focus on what works should be considered classic, and what this attribution tells us about the shape and nature of our field, its strengths and shortcomings, and where it might be heading.

Notes

1 We would like to thank Manuel Almeida, Peter Marcus Kristensen and Brian Schmidt for their comments on an earlier draft of this chapter.

2 Daniel H. Deudney, *Bounding Power: Republican Security Theory from the Polis to the Global Village*, Princeton, NJ: Princeton University Press, 2007, p. 265.

3 For a valuable recent exchange on the virtues of mapping the field in terms of 'isms' see David A. Lake, 'Why "isms" Are Evil: Theory, Epistemology, and Academic Sects as Impediments to Understanding and Progress', *International Studies Quarterly*, 2011, vol. 55, 465–80; and replies by Rudra Sil and Peter Katzenstein, and Henry Nau, in the same issue.

4 Deudney, *Bounding Power*, p. 266.

5 The irony here of course is that the first two of these works contain forceful expositions of the situatedness of historical and political knowledge, as Peter Wilson and Nicolas Guilhot demonstrate in their chapters, which cast doubt on the possibility of 'timeless' historical or political truths.

6 See Peter Wilson, 'Where Are We Now in the Debate about the First Great Debate?', in Brian Schmidt, *International Relations and the First Great Debate*, London: Routledge, 2012, pp. 133–51; and many of the chapters in Nicolas Guilhot (ed.), *The Invention of International Relations Theory*, New York: Columbia University Press, 2011.

7 Ole Wæver is the source of this observation (personal correspondence with Henrik Bliddal, August 2012).

8 See e.g. Robert Adcock, Mark Bevir and Shannon C. Stimson, 'A History of Political Science: How? What? Why?', in R. Adcock, M. Bevir and C. Stimson (eds), *Modern Political Science: Anglo-American Exchanges since 1880*, Princeton, NJ: Princeton University Press, 2007, pp. 1–17.

9 See Ole Wæver, 'Still a Discipline After All These Debates?', in T. Dunne, M. Kurki and S. Smith (eds), *International Relations Theories: Discipline and Diversity*, Oxford: Oxford University Press, pp. 297–318.

10 This is exemplified by the use of classics by countries new to IR to prime themselves on the nature and state of the game. For the use of IR classics for this purpose in China since 1979 see Qin Yaqing, 'Why Is there no Chinese International Relations Theory?', *International Relations of the Asia-Pacific*, 2007, vol. 7, 313–40.

11 Wæver, 'Still a Discipline', pp. 311, 314. The notion of 'The End of International Relations Theory' was a noticeable theme at the 2012 ISA Annual Convention (San Diego, 1–4 April) and the 2012 Joint BISA-ISA International Conference (Edinburgh, 20–22 June), where the editors of one the discipline's flagship journals – *The European Journal of International Relations* (*EJIR*) – ran several panels on this theme (see e.g. www.uk.sagepub.com/ejt2012.sp (accessed 17 December 2012)). The papers of the panelists, all prominent figures in the discipline, are likely to be published in *EJIR* during 2013. Cf. also Chris Brown, 'IR Theory in Britain: The New Black?' *Review of International Studies,* 2006, vol. 32, 677–87.

12 See Arlene B. Ticker and Ole Wæver (eds), *International Relations Scholarship Around the World*, London: Routledge, 2009, particularly the Introduction and Conclusion. See also Stanley Hoffmann, 'An American Social Science: International Relations', *Daedalus*, 1977, vol. 106, 41–60; Yaqing, 'Why Is there no Chinese International Relations Theory?' 315–26.

13 Ole Wæver, 'The Sociology of a not so International Discipline', *International Organization*, 1998, vol. 52, 687–727; Marijke Breuning, Joseph Bredehoft and Eugene Walton, 'Promise and Performance: An Evaluation of Journals in International Relations', *International Studies Perspectives*, 2005, vol. 6, 447–61; Tickner and Wæver, 'Introduction: Geocultural Epistemologies', in Tickner and Wæver, *International Relations Scholarship around the World*, London: Routledge, 2009, pp. 1–31.

14 See Simon Head, 'The Grim Threat to British Universities', *The New York Review of Books*, 13 January 2011.

15 Research Information Network, *Communicating Knowledge: How and Why UK Researchers Publish and Disseminate their Findings*, London: RIN, 2009, p. 5; see also Laura Brown, Rebecca Griffiths and Matthew Rascoff, *University Publishing in a Digital Age*, Ithaka, 2009. Available at: www.ithaka.org/ithaka-s-r/strategyold/Ithaka%20University%20Publishing%20Report.pdf. Again, this is not a universal pattern. See Tickner and Wæver, 'Conclusion: Worlding where the World once Was', in Tickner and Wæver, *International Relations Scholarship around the World*, London: Routledge, 2009, pp. 328–41.

16 Few submissions make it through to publication in these journals today without substantial revisions, and a standard format is developing: introduction to subject; review of literature;

identification of problem; method for solving problem; solution; suggestions for further research; extensive notes and/or references. Increasingly, daring, unconventional or adventurous works do not make it into print as they fall short of high standards of proof required by most referees.

17 In the case of Carr, the gestation period began with Versailles (see Peter Wilson, 'Carr and his Early Critics: Responses to *The Twenty Years' Crisis, 1939–46*', in Michael Cox (ed.), *E. H. Carr: A Critical Reappraisal*, London: Palgrave Macmillan, 2000, p. 185). In the case of Bull it began with his work on *The Control of the Arms Race* (London: Weidenfeld & Nicolson, 1961) and his involvement (also from 1961) in the British Committee on the Theory of International Politics (see Tim Dunne, *Inventing International Society: A History of the English School*, London, Macmillan, 1998, pp. 89–115).

18 See Wæver, 'Sociology of a Not so International Discipline'. Moreover, flagship journals of the discipline also tend to reflect epistemological and geographical divides in the discipline. See Richard Jordan, Daniel Maliniak, Amy Oakes, Susan Peterson, Michael J. Tierney, *One Discipline or Many? TRIP Survey of International Relations Faculty in Ten Countries*, Williamsburg, VA: College of William and Mary, 2009; Barry Buzan and Ole Wæver, 'After the Return to Theory: The Past, Present, and Future of Security Studies', in Alan Collins (ed.), *Contemporary Security Studies*, 2nd edn, Oxford: Oxford University Press, 2010, pp. 463–83.

19 See e.g. Stephen van Evera, 'Director's Statement: Trends in Political Science and the Future of Security Studies', *MIT Security Studies Program: Annual Report 2009–2010* (2010).

20 See e.g. the remarks on Aron in Bryan-Paul Frost's chapter in this volume, and John H. Herz, 'The Relevancies and Irrelevancies of International Relations', *Polity*, 1971, vol. 4, 25–47.

21 Wæver, 'Still a Discipline', p. 297.

Index